JOHN WILCOCKSON

John Wilcockson has been writing about cycling for four decades. He first encountered Lance Armstrong when he was a teenage triathlete, has witnessed all his triumphs, and has interviewed him regularly over the past twenty years. He has been the editor of five cycling magazines, was the first cycling correspondent for *The Times* and has won awards for his journalistic services. He has written more than a dozen books. A graduate of the University of London, Wilcockson now lives in Bolder Colorado.

ALSO BY JOHN WILCOCKSON

23 Days in July: Inside Lance Armstrong's Record-breaking Victory in the Tour Da France

John Wilcockson's World of Cycling

LANCE ARMSTRONG

THE WORLD'S GREATEST CHAMPION

JOHN WILCOCKSON

JOHN MURRAY

First published in Great Britain in 2009 by John Murray (Publishers)
An Hachette UK Company

First published in paperback in 2010

1

Design by Jane Raese

A CIP catalogue record for this title is available from the British Library

ISBN 978-1-84854-469-7

Printed and bound by Clays Ltd, St Ives plc

John Murray policy is to use papers that are natural, renewable and recyclable products and made from wood grown in sustainable forests. The logging and manufacturing processes are expected to conform to the environmental regulations of the country of origin.

John Murray (Publishers)
338 Euston Road
London NW1 3BH

www.johnmurray.co.uk

To Fabio, who died on his bike and lived with a smile

To Rene and Rita, for their spirit and inspiration

CONTENTS

PREFACE

"HEY, JOHN, I'M ON TWITTER to tell people that we're doing an interview. How many Tours have you covered?"

"Forty," I answer.

"That'll blow their minds," says the winner of seven of those Tours de France.

He's now part of the race's history, but Lance Armstrong always wants to learn more; I tell him a story about one of its legendary champions.

"When I first saw the Tour, in 1963, my most vivid memory is being a spectator at the finish in Chamonix. It was the last day in the mountains, and Jacques Anquetil won the stage and took the yellow jersey. He walked right by me on his way to the podium. It was pouring rain, and when he was maybe five feet from me he took a comb from his back pocket and ran it through his wet, blond hair. He was like a movie star."

Anquetil was the first man to win the Tour de France five times. In the next three decades, three more Europeans equaled that record before an outspoken American who had raw talent, no respect for traditions, and no limits came along. Lance, like Anquetil, has a deep chest and long, lean legs and races a bike like the wind. But that's where the similarities end. Lance didn't even know that professional cycling existed when he grew up in suburban Plano, Texas.

Today, everyone knows the heroic story of a cyclist who survived a deadly cancer and went on to win the world's toughest sporting event multiple times. It's a story that has inspired millions around the world and given rise to a cancer-awareness movement that is now becoming global. But few know how this once brash young Texan emerged from a modest childhood, grew up in a football culture, and worked his way to the top of a very un-American sport—even before he was diagnosed with cancer.

Lance, with immense fortitude, tackled cancer as he would later tackle the Tour: working with a team of friends, experts, and advisors to find the best solutions to the most challenging questions. That approach, combined with unparalleled dedication and discipline, enabled him to revolutionize a sport that has been dubbed the world's most beautiful as well as its most brutal. Ultimately, by winning an unprecedented seven Tours in seven years, Lance laid claim to being the world's greatest champion.

Who else can be considered for this supreme title? That's a question I've thought about since I was very young.

Growing up in an England recovering from wartime, when the populace found relief by watching sports, my brother and I became sports addicts. We constantly discussed who was the best this or the best that in every conceivable sport. We played street soccer and cricket, ran through the woods, climbed what we thought were mountains, and eventually rode our bikes to Europe and the Tour de France.

Our parents took us to London, where we saw many of the champions we talked about. We watched the England cricket team play the national teams from Australia, South Africa, and the West Indies. We saw and learned about that sport's legendary Don Bradman, and we wondered how he compared with American baseball greats Babe Ruth and Ty Cobb. We went to watch our country's mythic miler Roger Bannister and Australia's tennis star Ken Rosewall. Before television, our crackling radio brought us live commentaries of the World Championship bouts of Joe Louis and Rocky Marciano, and Formula 1 motor races starring Argentina's Juan Manuel Fangio. We were ardent fans of our local soccer team and were awed by the skills of the immortal Pelé.

Could any of these men claim the title world's greatest champion?

Today, the most frequently touted candidates are the ballplayers. Michael Jordan electrified a nation with his competitive fire and sheer athleticism; Pelé commanded a soccer field with unique on-the-ball skills, acceleration, and power to score goals that amazed; Tiger Woods can drive, chip, and putt a golf ball more spectacularly and consistently than anyone in history; Ruth dominated his era in baseball; and cricket's Bradman, like Ruth, used his bat in the most punishing manner his sport has ever seen. Other contenders include Muhammad Ali, who transcended his sport with a combination of flashy showmanship, footwork, and counterpunching; runner Haile Gebrselassie, who, incredibly, set world records at every distance from five thousand meters to the marathon; and Formula One driver Michael Schumacher, who won a record seven world championships.

All of these athletes performed feats that dazzled the mind, but few conquered their sport's leading event more than a handful of times and none faced an event as daunting as the Tour de France—which is so physically, mentally, and emotionally demanding it has even been called sadistic. In twenty-three days, the racers subject themselves to an Olympian test of endurance, completing twenty-one hundred miles of racing at blinding speed, battling fierce crosswinds across the plains, climbing like eagles over dozens of mountain passes, and racing downhill at the limit of human possibility. Their bodies must adapt to chilling rain and broiling heat, and one quarter of the starters succumb to crashes, injuries, and sickness before the finish.

Professional cycling is one of the few sports that's contested by teams and yet results in an individual winner. A pure athlete can win the Tour, but to keep on winning, year after year, demands a different kind of sporting perfection. Lance displayed all the expected gifts and competence of a champion athlete; used technology, physical therapy, and innovative training to the maximum; and acquired a layer of executive skills that enabled him to assemble, prepare, and command the strongest team the Tour had seen in a hundred years. Those accomplishments, along with the utter confidence he displayed to overcome whatever stood in his way, resulted in Lance being a greater, more assertive champion than any of the Tour's five-time winners, going all the way back to cycling's first blond superstar, Jacques Anquetil, in the early sixties.

Lance's story is interspersed with the people who influenced the course of his journey and allowed him to acquire the skills, the knowledge, and the assurance he has displayed throughout his athletic career and iconic life. Each of them, perhaps by design, entered his life when he needed them most and helped him grow, reach his potential, and finally become the world's greatest champion.

LANCE ARMSTRONG

PROLOGUE: JUST AN IDEA

AUGUST 12, 2008. It was two weeks after the Tour de France ended. I was eating lunch at my laptop when an e-mail message from "Lance Armstrong" popped up on the screen. The subject line was "Chat." Curious, I clicked it open to read: "John, You got a second to chat with bill and I? Thanks, L." Bill would be Bill Stapleton, his business partner and friend. I had no idea what they wanted to talk about and was intrigued. I hadn't heard from Lance since before the Tour. That was in late June, when in response to one of my questions about this book, he replied: "Sorry for the delay. I am in santa barbara with my kids for the summer (escaping the heat!) and just relaxing. . . ."

Relaxing on the beach was exactly what he said he'd be doing when he retired from bike racing three years earlier. After winning the 2005 Tour's final time trial the day before the finish in Paris—where he planned to end his professional cycling career with a record seventh

Tour victory—Lance talked to the media for an hour at the race winner's traditional press conference. Sitting at a table on a high stage in a cavernous hall, he asked for one more question. A French reporter took the microphone and asked, "What will you be doing in July next year when the Tour is on?" Lance smiled. He seemed to relish the thought. "I'll be sitting on a beach with my kids," he said, "relaxing with a cold beer."

No one doubted him. Nor did anyone question his sincerity when he spoke the next day in Paris. Wearing the Tour winner's yellow jersey for what everyone believed was the final time, Lance grabbed the race announcer's mic to address the thousands of spectators lining the world's grandest boulevard, the Champs-Élysées. No Tour winner had ever spoken to the crowds in Paris before, not even Lance. But this was his last chance.

Few, if any, knew what he wanted to say, though most knew this would be no sentimental farewell. Lance, just as he was throughout his fourteen years as a pro cyclist, was assured and defiant. At first, like an Academy Award winner, he praised his competitors and thanked his friends, family, and colleagues who helped him in his career. Then, showing the hard edge he has had ever since he was a teenager racing against professional triathletes in the mid-1980s, Lance used the Tour podium as his bully pulpit to address the "cynics and skeptics," specifically the journalists who, ever since he came back from life-threatening cancer to win the Tour in 1999, tried to paint him as a doper.

"I am sorry for you. I am sorry you can't dream," he said on that last Sunday of July 2005. "I'm sorry you don't believe in miracles. But this is one helluva race, and there are no secrets. This is a hard sport, and it is hard work [that] wins it."

That was it. He was quitting the sport at thirty-three—a year older than the retirement age of the Tour's three previous dominant champions: Miguel Induráin of Spain (who last raced in 1996), Bernard Hinault of France (1986), and Eddy Merckx of Belgium (1978).

It's said the Tour is so grueling that every time you ride it you cut a year from your life. Lance had raced the Tour eleven times; he didn't want to cut any more years from *his* life. He told reporters he was mentally burned out. And there were other things he wanted to do.

Most importantly, he wanted to be a good father to his son, Luke, then five, and his twin daughters, Grace and Isabelle, then three. They stood next to their dad on the 2005 Tour podium, the girls wearing identical yellow sundresses to match their dad's yellow jersey. He handed the winner's yellow cellophane-covered bouquet to one of the girls and a stuffed yellow lion from race sponsor Crédit Lyonnais to the other. Luke waited patiently until his dad passed him the winner's trophy, a gold-rimmed Sèvres porcelain fruit bowl. Their mother, Kristin, whom Lance divorced in 2003, watched from the sidelines.

Stepping down from the stage and from his career in cycling, Lance didn't expect to become any less busy. Besides spending more time with his kids and enjoying his then two-year relationship with singer Sheryl Crow, he planned to expand his workload with his eponymous cancer-awareness foundation, build the associated Live-Strong brand with various business ventures, and continue to fulfill multimillion-dollar endorsement contracts.

But less than a month after the 2005 Tour, Lance's world was suddenly threatened. On August 23, the front-page headline of the powerful French sports newspaper, *L'Équipe*, was stark and accusing: *Le Mensonge Armstrong* ("Armstrong's Lie"). Inside was an exclusive story written by the paper's doping expert, investigative journalist Damien Ressiot. The sensational piece claimed that six of Lance's urine samples from the 1999 Tour, retested as part of an experimental program, showed traces of the banned blood-boosting drug recombinant erythropoietin (EPO). A test to identify this drug in urine wasn't approved by the World Anti-Doping Agency (WADA) until August 2000, so the agency allowed a French testing facility to look at old samples to increase scientific knowledge about the EPO test.

Lance denied the accusations, and an independent investigation by the former head of the Netherlands' anti-doping agency, lawyer Emile Vrijman, exonerated the Texan in a report to cycling's governing body, the International Cycling Union, which is known by its French acronym, the UCI. But soon after the story in *L'Équipe* appeared, Lance half-joked that he was going to come back just "to show the French" that he was a clean athlete. Some took him seriously, so he held a conference call with journalists to clarify his position. "I'm sick of this," he said. "Sitting here today, dealing with all this stuff again, knowing if I were to come back, there's no way I could get a fair shake—on the roadside, in doping control, or the labs. I'm happy with the way my career went and ended, and I'm not coming back."

Those words seemed to definitively end Lance's Tour career. He now turned his attention to the high-profile life he led as an icon in the cancer community and as an A-list celebrity. For the next three years, Lance focused on promoting cancer awareness: He spoke at fundraisers; participated in charity bike rides and marathons; visited with cancer patients; and even courted presidential candidates to advocate for more research dollars for cancer. By the time the 2008 Tour came around, the Lance Armstrong Foundation had raised more than $250 million.

One of Lance's biggest non-cycling challenges came in the fall of 2007, when he campaigned in Texas to help pass a statewide proposition that would raise $3 billion over ten years to fund cancer research. To promote the passage of such a historic bill, Lance worked his native state like a politician, advocating the proposition with an emotional speech in the Texas Senate and making a whistle-stop tour on a campaign bus, giving stump speeches in towns and cities around the state. Despite its high price tag, the measure passed by a surprisingly clear margin.

The expansion of his foundation's LiveStrong brand—which started with its ubiquitous yellow wristbands—continued with such major projects as an annual cancer-awareness summit, a "healthy living" Web site, and a planned global initiative to combat cancer. And just in case Lance needed more to do to expend his unlimited energy, he opened a boutique-style bike store, Mellow Johnny's (Texas speak for *maillot jaune*, French for "yellow jersey"). The store in Austin, his hometown of two decades, displays some of the offbeat artwork he loves buying at auctions for the Spanish-style mansion he owns there, the home he was buying in Aspen, Colorado, and a beach house in the Caribbean.

Lance flies much of the time in a chartered jet, and contacts on his BlackBerry include everyone from fellow activist Bono to President Barack Obama. In the years since his farewell Tour, the private life of the multimillionaire Texan—born in the backstreets of south Dallas—had turned not so private. The tabloid press loved his engagement (and subsequent split) with Sheryl, closely watched his long-distance relationship with fashion designer Tory Burch, and furiously photographed his two-month fling with movie star Kate Hudson.

Lance and Kate parted ways the same weekend that Spanish cyclist Carlos Sastre won the 2008 Tour de France. Less than two weeks later, Lance entered—for fun—a rugged 100-mile mountain-bike race through the Rockies, and he shocked everyone when he came in second to famed Colorado mountain biker Dave Wiens. It was four days after that race that Lance sent me his "Chat" e-mail. After receiving my affirmative response, he wrote back late that evening: "Thanks, John. We just want to run an idea by you." I went to bed curious about his idea. Perhaps it was another project like his Austin bike shop, but why include Stapleton in the conversation? And why run it by a writer?

His call came the next evening. "Sorry I didn't call before," he began, sounding a little hesitant, which is unusual for Lance. "I was traveling. I was in Aspen for a week of riding. Now I'm back in Santa Barbara. I wanted to talk because I think my idea will affect the book you're writing."

By now I was even more intrigued. Maybe it was something personal.

Then he said, "I'm thinking of riding the Tour de France next year. What do you think?"

As I dealt with the shock from his words, Lance continued, "I'll be thirty-seven next year, but I don't think I'm too old." I agreed and noted that Italian cyclist Davide Rebellin at age thirty-seven had just won the silver medal in the Olympic road race at Beijing.

"And," he continued, "there's all this publicity right now for swimmer Dara Torres winning medals. She's forty-one, so there should be a lot of interest in my idea." I told him that if he came back to race the Tour, there would be *huge* interest. The media would be stunned, I said.

Lance told me that he had discussed the idea with very few people—basically, his inner circle of Austin friends along with his long-time personal coach Chris Carmichael, his team director Johan Bruyneel, and his ex-wife Kristin Armstrong, who gave him her enthusiastic approval. "She's my number one fan," he said. "If she hadn't said yes, I wouldn't be doing this. Our kids are too important."

Lance now began to warm to the idea of riding the 2009 Tour. "I'll kick their asses," he said, sounding like the old Lance, the one who relished a fight and a challenge. "The Tour was a bit of a joke this year. I've got nothing against Sastre . . . or Christian Vande Velde. Christian's a nice guy, but finishing fifth in the Tour de France? Come on!"

"I haven't decided 100 percent yet," he added, "but, to be sure, I've already signed up with the UCI, WADA, and USADA [the U.S. Anti-Doping Agency], and I'm already on their testing programs."

Lance then turned to the sport's reputation and the bad image he felt was being perpetuated by Versus, the American TV cable station that owns the North American broadcast rights to the Tour.

"Did you see the Versus coverage?" he asked about their 2008 Tour de France programming. "They had this 'Take Back the Tour' campaign, as if the past Tours were all won by dopers. And I was pissed they had all these references to Triki Beltran and Tyler Hamilton and Roberto Heras and Floyd Landis—all these guys who were once on my team [and have since served doping suspensions]. Versus doesn't want to take back the Tour; they want to take back the ratings they had in '04 and '05!"

The more Lance talked, the more it seemed he was convincing himself that he *could* come back to bike racing at an elite level, he *could* ride the Tour again—and he could win. But, I asked him, why did he want to? When he revealed that he was thinking of posting all his anti-doping results on the Web, being totally transparent with the media, and creating an out-of-competition testing program overseen by an independent anti-doping expert, I realized that he'd be racing to clear his name, to prove to all those skeptics he addressed from the podium in 2005 that he could win the Tour indisputably clean.

But what was the real reason?

Lance went quiet for a moment. Then, clearly from his heart, he said, "I'm doing this for my kids. With news so accessible these days on the Web, they'll be able to read any story they want. And I don't want them growing up and reading all these things about me and doping."

It's just an idea, he'd said.

Sure, I thought, knowing that whenever Lance has an idea—from breaking every Tour record to creating a worldwide cancer foundation—he immediately rolls into action.

"What are you doing tomorrow?" I asked.

"Going for a four-hour training ride."

In the following weeks, Lance and his foundation CEO Doug Ulman recognized the opportunity his comeback could offer to take his cancer project to a global level. That's what he later told the media was the prime reason for his return to racing. And, he pointed out, it didn't matter if he won or lost; either way, cancer awareness would be raised.

This was all true, but it didn't negate the deeper, simpler truth he had confided on the phone. To be a good father and role model means everything to Lance. It's something he felt he never had. In a way, that's where it all began.

CHAPTER 1

ORIGINS

She instilled in me a sense of hard work and sacrifice,
and with the hard work comes toughness.
And she would say every day, "Go git 'em!"
—LANCE ARMSTRONG

LANCE'S MOM IS SMART and spunky, just like her son, and they have the same long face. But while Lance impresses with his athletic physique, Linda Armstrong Kelly has a petiteness that belies her fierce spirit. And she seems almost tiny sitting at a long breakfast bar beneath the lofty ceiling of her north Dallas home.

She has prepared a light lunch for us to eat as she talks about her life and her only child. In her mid-fifties, Linda has a soft lilt to her Texas drawl and an unexpectedly hearty laugh.

She says that her husband, Ed Kelly, is "a super guy, the man of my dreams." Linda married the Irish-American Kelly, a retired IBM executive, in 2002. It's her fourth marriage. And the best one, she says, adding that she has never been as happy. Their modern brick house backs onto a golf course, and when the phone rings, it plays "When Irish Eyes Are Smiling."

Their home in the suburb of Plano is less than an hour's drive, but a lifetime away, from where Linda grew up in south Dallas, on the wrong side of the Trinity River. She lived there with two younger siblings, Debbie and Alan, and their single mother, Elizabeth. When they were growing up, their father, Paul Mooneyham, was just back from the Vietnam War. His subsequent alcoholism and abusive behavior led to an early divorce.

"The drinking was an unfortunate, big part of our lives," says Linda's sister, Debbie Glanville.

Debbie is taller, louder, and more Texan than her sister. Her mouth is wider, her blonde-streaked hair less coiffed, and her lipstick's a brighter red. Married to a Baptist minister, and the mother of three girls, Debbie has worked as a high-school teacher in suburban Maryland for three decades.

After picking me up in her sporty sedan from Baltimore's Penn Station, Debbie seems uneasy driving through an inner-city neighborhood. Perhaps it reminds her of the hardscrabble Oak Cliff area where the Mooneyham children grew up in the sixties and early seventies, when crime and gang activity were rampant following school desegregation and white flight to the suburbs. "South Dallas is kind of old, just a very poor area," she says. "There's a lot of different ethnic groups. We were in the minority."

"We lived in apartments, always in rentals," Debbie adds, cradling a cup of coffee at a neighborhood café. "My mother moved so many times—I'm sure it was finances. My father sometimes sent child support; most of the time he did not. The last move we made was the lowest. It was probably all she could afford."

Debbie then leans in toward me, lowers her voice in deference to two black women chatting at the next table, and whispers, "But being the racial climate the way it was there. . . . It was a different scene—if you know what I mean—and I could remember getting off the bus at a different stop and walking, so people didn't know that's where I lived. Embarrassing."

Embarrassed or not, the dirt-poor Mooneyham sisters were still typical teenagers. Linda was on the drill team at Adamson High. "She was very popular in high school," Debbie says. "That's where we got our acclamation, from other students. And then, suddenly, Linda was pregnant. She just said, 'I got caught.' Because all the girls were having sex, all her friends. Of course, my mother didn't have talks about going on the pill; that was not the conversation they had back then.

"Linda told my mother first, then she told me. She was sixteen, I was fifteen. It was a very big shock. One of her really good friends had recently gotten pregnant and had to fly to Mexico for an abortion—because that was the day, you know, '70, '71."

Debbie says there were mixed feelings in the family about what to do. Their mother was upset that Linda had gotten herself "into trouble," but in the end they decided that Linda would have the baby. "I remember very clearly," Debbie says, "my vote was, two wrongs will not make a right. I was adamant that abortion was not an option."

And so it was agreed there would be a baby. A future champion was on his way.

"The biggest shock was Lance's father," Debbie says. "Eddie Gunderson was not the most desirable young man. They met at the high school. He was on the edge; he wasn't the cool guy; he was kind of a bad boy. But even at that age, a very young Linda was pragmatic: 'You know, it is what it is.' And I remember my dad—he lived nearby—saying to Linda, 'You're gonna get married.' So real quick we put a little wedding together, and I was like maid of honor."

They married on Linda's seventeenth birthday, February 12, 1971. "Linda wore one of her friend's prom dresses, and they had a fabulous church wedding," Debbie recalls. "The place was packed. All the high-school kids came." But the excitement didn't last for long.

"A lot of Linda's good friends abandoned her when she was pregnant," Debbie says. "Our little family tried to work together and make the best of it. She wore my dresses for maternity as I was always bigger than Linda, a lot bigger. My mother was never able to help financially, and Linda couldn't afford to buy anything. She left school and started work as a cashier for a grocery store, little jobs like that. Eddie threw newspapers. So she and this husband were able to get an apartment, a little rental duplex over there in Oak Cliff, and have the baby."

Born on September 18 that year, the baby boy was hefty, just under ten pounds. It was a difficult birth for a young woman as small as Linda. They named him Lance, after famed Dallas Cowboys wide receiver Lance Rentzel, and Edward, the middle name of Linda's father. (Ironically, the Cowboys let go of Rentzel that year, following an arrest for indecent exposure.)

"Lance brought such joy and happiness and stability to my life," Linda says, "because I just didn't ever have that. But it was a struggle. . . ."

She never told her son about her struggles growing up in south Dallas, nor about his difficult entry into the world, or the hardships during his early years. He found out when he read her book, *No Mountain High Enough*, in 2005. "I was like 'Oh. My. God,'" Lance tells me. "That's poor, that's desperate, that's tough, that's a struggle, that's no hope. Her book blew me away, really rocked my world. So when I read that—man, I never knew we had it bad. I was always provided for."

At first, there was a "let's make this work" attitude among the Mooneyham and Gunderson clans. Linda's dad bought the teenage parents a washer/dryer for their apartment, "and Eddie's mother, Willene—we called her Mamie—was pretty helpful," Debbie says. "She was very poor, but she would help with babysitting, and I would too. Their apartment was just up from us. They were such kids.

"I used to go over there and help Mamie get baby Lance to the nurse when I was a senior in high school. . . . You know, Eddie wasn't into sports, and Linda was never really athletic. So I've often wondered: Where did Lance get all that athleticism from? Eddie liked to ride bikes, but just for recreation. I played some sports, and my brother played some sports, but never at the same level as Lance did. And my parents? Nothing at all."

Eddie's family, though, came from hardy stock. His great-grandparents, Martin and Marie Gunderson, were born in Oslo, Norway, in the mid-nineteenth century, and they immigrated to a colony of Norwegians in tiny Prairieville, Texas. Prairieville is an isolated farming community fifty miles southeast of Dallas. It had a population of only two hundred at the turn of the twentieth century and just fifty people when the elderly Gundersons died there during the Great Depression.

Both of Lance's parents came from low-income families, but Eddie was less mature than Linda and much wilder. "When he offered me a ride to work at Dunkin Donuts," Debbie says, "I walked. You prayed if you drove with Eddie. He drove eighty miles an hour. He was very young and messed up."

Marriage and fatherhood at age seventeen didn't sit well with Eddie Gunderson. He felt deprived of his teenage freedom, and he took out his frustration on his young bride. "I admit that I wasn't an angel, and I've done a few things in my life that I'm not proud of, but I never beat Linda as she has suggested. I only remember slapping her once," Eddie said in 2005. "What I did was crazy. I'm sure Linda's told Lance a lot of things about me, and I'm sure most of the things are true."

Anger and altercations didn't provide the best environment for a marriage or for raising a baby. "Linda left Eddie once and moved in with my dad in a little one-bedroom apartment," Debbie says. "When she went back to Eddie, Dad told her, 'You can move one more time and that's it.' She knew he meant it. But then it all fell apart again, so she calls my dad, 'I need help. I gotta get out of here.'

"It was traumatic when Linda left Eddie the second time. I was always the big person, I was the muscle, so I went to help Dad move them. We had to go over and get the washer/dryer—along with Linda and Lance. And carrying the baby out, that was that.

"Eddie was just hurt. He wasn't physical, but he used vulgar language, the most vulgar language you can imagine, calling my father all this vulgar stuff to a point that *I* cried. My father didn't say anything to him, and Linda was like, 'I don't wanna talk to you.' And I think he knew that this was it. That was the end of Eddie. That was it."

The marriage had lasted less than two years. In the divorce settlement, it was agreed that Lance would live with Linda and stay with the Gundersons every other weekend. Eddie would pay $20 a week in child support.

Debbie, then a high-school senior, recalls, "Our father made Linda save money—you're earning this, you save this—and she got a little apartment. I've gotta commend him for that."

Eddie's child-support checks didn't always arrive, so Linda soon began thinking like a single mom. "Even though I was young and didn't know any better, I thought, 'I'm the barracuda mom and nobody is gonna mess with me,'" she says, displaying the feisty attitude she would pass on to her son.

Besides bravado, Linda relied on her faith to get through what was the toughest period in her life with Lance. It helped that her little boy was especially loved by Eddie's mother and Linda's family. "Lance was a blessing," says Debbie, "and regardless of what's going on, a baby is a blessing. For ten years, he was the only grandchild."

It also helped that Lance was strong, healthy, and precocious. He was walking by nine months, and he soon showed he was a quick learner. "When Lance was two years old he was going to a Christian daycare, and they had a Christmas play. I'd gotten him a little suit outfit from Sears," Linda remembers. "He got up on the stage, and he was so smart he quoted a whole Bible verse. And he was younger than all the other kids. That was a big deal."

By this time, Debbie says, Linda was slowly getting her life together. "She worked her way up to receptionist at a car dealership. And she did get her GED certificate later on."

She was concerned, though, about Lance growing up without a live-in father, something her faith and core values made her feel was essential. She had that in mind when she met Terry Armstrong, the adopted son of Raymond Armstrong, a First Christian Church minister in Paris, Texas. Terry had taken a job right out of college working for a company that sold corn dogs and barbecue beef. He was the kind of man, Linda thought, who'd be a good role model for her son.

Their meeting wasn't an accident, Terry tells me. "A friend of mine said, 'I'd like to introduce you to this girl I know.' We went to the car dealership where she worked and I thought, yeah. . . . And so later I went over to her apartment and knocked on the door. She said to wait a minute—she had a babysitter—and I walked in and saw this kid in a crib, and it was so, so phenomenal because it was a boy and I was a young man," he says, explaining that he was then looking for stability in his life. "It was such a flash because Linda was real cute, but it was a *family*—and the attraction I had to Linda was more the fact that she had a son than just her."

Terry Armstrong is speaking to me in the conference room of a modern office building in Plano, where he runs a regional sales office for Monterey Mushrooms. An avuncular figure in his late fifties, he has thinning gray hair and is wearing black wingtip leather shoes, neatly pressed gray pants, and a starched white shirt. Until now, he's avoided talking publicly about Lance. He speaks with a rich Texas twang.

"When I started dating Linda, she was still involved with Eddie," Terry says, since Linda's ex-husband was taking Lance to his mother's home every other weekend. "There were lots of times where Eddie didn't bring him back on time, and Linda was just in chaos. By then I knew that Eddie had a, uh, police background, so I was worried about this. In fact, I remember Linda telling me that when they were married, Eddie once threw a screwdriver at her, and it lodged in her leg.

"I saw all this and I was thinking about this little family: 'They live in a one-bedroom apartment in Oak Cliff, she doesn't make a lot of money, she has this problem with this kind of wacky ex-husband, and she doesn't get child support.' I could see the pain."

Seeing that pain and knowing that he was making a good living as a traveling salesman, Terry proposed marriage to Linda, and she accepted. "I still remember asking Paul [Mooneyham] for Linda's hand," Terry says. "We were in her apartment, Lance was in a crib, and I said, 'I'll protect your daughter.' Paul said, 'I know.'"

They married in 1974. Terry's father officiated at the young couple's wedding. Terry was twenty-two, Linda, twenty, Lance, two.

Despite having a new husband, Linda was not happy that her son's name was still Gunderson. It was a constant reminder of a man she did not want to remember. Adoption was the solution, but Eddie would first have to sign away his parental rights to Lance.

"One weekend, Eddie decided not to bring him back," Terry remembers. They called around frantically and got the police involved. "I kind of went ballistic. He had not paid child support for a long time, and I met him in the parking lot. After I took Lance, he and I had a confrontation.

"To me, he could have been nine feet tall and it wouldn't have bothered me. Because when you're dealing with a baby, which is now under your roof, and you're in love with his mother, I don't care how big he was. He was not going to do that to her. . . .

"So I said, 'Sign up, sign these papers, you're off the hook, you don't have to pay anymore.' And I told him, 'Don't *ever* come around again.'" Lance was just three years old; Eddie was twenty. They have not seen each other since that day.

After Eddie signed the papers, there was no holdup in the adoption process, which came to a simple conclusion. "The day that Terry adopted Lance, I went with Linda and Lance to the office," Debbie says. "No one else was there. It was just like a gathering. Change Lance's last name to Armstrong. And Eddie just went on his merry way. His mother tried to stay in contact, but Linda was like a light switch: 'Okay, done.'"

Two decades later, Eddie's mom, Willene, said this about Lance: "I've cried so many times and prayed so many tears. I don't want anything except to see him, put my arms around him, and tell him that I love him. He's my grandson. Even if you have others, you don't ever quit missing one."

Lance would remain an only child. "Not too long after Linda and I got married," Terry says, "we were at a friend's house, and Linda was saying, 'Let's have kids! Let's get pregnant!' And I said, 'No, I have a son. I have a responsibility, and I'm fairly young and I don't think we need another kid.' I guess it was almost like a selfishness, you know. I had my son—and he had my name.

"In my very young mind, I thought if I have no other children then Lance can get all of it . . . all the birthday presents, all the college education . . . everything. So why have another child? It made perfect sense. And I knew that Linda had gone through a childbirth that wasn't good. Why put her through another pain? For ego?"

So young Lance remained the center of attention, especially at holiday times. "Being the only child and only grandchild, they spoiled him to death," Linda says. She recalls one Christmas spent with her sister and brother, who had moved in with their father, just up the street in Oak Cliff. "Christmas was a fun event, and Lance completely loved Santa. My brother's friend dressed up as Santa and came knocking on the door. He was really believable. And that was the year my dad gave Lance his first bike that he learned to ride without training wheels."

Debbie remembers that time as well. "My dad had stopped drinking, and he worked at the post office," she says. "Once he stopped drinking, he started to get us back together and tried to help the kids in any way he could."

Debbie also remembers that Lance was real cute, which led to his first photo-op. "There was this big poster of Lance eating a corn dog, he could have only been three, promoting one of the items that Terry sold."

"The biggest place for us to sell that product was the schools," Terry explains, "because they have corn dogs on the menus in every school in the state. So I got a photo shop to get Lance holding this corn dog, and every show we went to we had a picture of Lance."

During those years, one of Lance's rare trips outside Texas was to visit Aunt Debbie in Maryland. "He came here with his mom and dad and spent a week," she says. "He had never seen a basement before. He was like, 'What's this?' They don't have basements in Texas. And he opened the door and fell down the stairs. Down he went!

"We were living with my husband's father at the time. He was an older guy, retired, very fit, wore a gardening hat—and Lance just took to him. Followed him around in the garden. We'd say, let's go to the amusement park, let's do this or that, but he was content just hanging out with my father-in-law. One day, my father-in-law started gardening and had his bathing suit on, and Lance comes up to me and goes, 'Aunt Debbie, how come Grandpop's got his underwear on?' He just called him that; I didn't ask him to."

Lance doesn't remember these incidents. In fact, he recalls hardly anything from his early childhood. One of the few memories he retains is an unpleasant one. "I was about four," he tells me. "I fell off this little Tonka toy truck and fell on my elbow, and I had to go to the hospital. I remember all that because the hospital was so scary, and I needed stitches."

Like his mother, Lance would later break off all contact with Terry Armstrong. But Terry's memories of his adopted son are warm ones: "After going on the road to sell my product, I'll never forget coming home and seeing him run across the grass, grab my jacket, and saying 'Daddy's home.' I remember what a joy it was to see his eyes light up when I'd buy him things, toys and stuff."

"He made pretty good money as a salesman," Debbie remembers, "and my mother often says, 'Terry really helped with money.'" With that help and with Linda working and making more each year, they were eventually able to fulfill Linda's longtime dream of leaving the run-down Oak Cliff neighborhood. The young family moved across the Trinity River to northeast Dallas, to the fast-expanding suburb of Richardson with its strip malls, country clubs, and neat subdivisions.

"I believe that when Linda moved," says her sister, "she made a conscious choice to move to the Richardson area, and that really began a chain of events. You could see it upped the level there—the higher degree of what people did and the things they achieved. It was a whole new ball game, and they got involved in all that. A nice home . . . and Lance eventually got in with this group of kids—they all had everything, the designer clothes, the society. . . . I think rubbing shoulders with all those people, Lance rose up to that rather than like, 'No, I can't handle this.'

"I think if they had stayed on in south Dallas," Debbie says, "it might have been a different story."

CHAPTER 2

RAISING LANCE

> Linda said Lance needed a mentor. Not a coaching mentor, but an adult mentor, someone to keep him out of trouble.
>
> —SCOTT EDER

JIM HOYT IS A WELL-KNOWN FIGURE in the bicycling world of Dallas. He has created one of the largest, most successful bike stores in the country. And, like many bike-shop owners, he encourages and helps support young, talented racers. Lance was one of them.

Hoyt grew up in the fifties in small-town Indiana. As a boy, he was always industrious and loved riding his bike; he worked at a bike shop from age ten. Instead of college, Hoyt moved to Chicago to work as a floor sweeper for Schwinn, then the country's largest bicycle manufacturer. But he was soon drafted to Vietnam, where he was badly injured.

"I was just blitzed in the leg, the chest, and the back," he says matter-of-factly, as we walk across the vast, empty parking lot in front of his store, Richardson Bike Mart. "After the war, I went back to Schwinn as a road rep. I was twenty-one, the youngest rep they ever had. My helmet from Vietnam had 'Texas' on the front, I don't know why, so when I got offered Denver or Dallas by Schwinn, I chose Dallas. The day I moved here in December 1970, it was weather like this," he says, gesturing to the soft sunshine slowly clearing a morning haze.

Hoyt shows me around his supermarket-sized store with its impressive array of new bicycles—everything from a kid's starter bike to the $8,000 Treks that are ridden in the Tour de France—before we sit down in his roomy, windowless office that's stuffed with metal filing cabinets and mismatched wooden desks and chairs. "I've always had the same desk," he says with pride.

Now in his sixties, Hoyt has a square face and steel-gray hair, and his rimless glasses emphasize twinkling eyes. He says he stays young by riding the bike thousands of miles a year with his wife, Rhonda. He never thought he'd leave Schwinn, until he got the chance to buy one of five Dallas Bike Mart stores in the early eighties. "I still work six days a week," he says. "Good service is the key."

His original store was two miles south of the present one. It happened to be "right across the street" from the apartment that the Armstrong family moved into on leaving Oak Cliff. The first time Hoyt saw Lance was when the first grader came into the store with his mother to buy a kid's BMX bike. "It was a Schwinn Mag Scrambler, chestnut brown with yellow wheels, and they got a little bit off the price," Hoyt remembers. "At that age, six years old, he was just another good kid. But as we progress along, he becomes a spirited young rascal."

Hoyt then points to the aging chair I'm sitting on. It has fraying upholstery and tilts to one side. Needs fixing, I suggest. "Yeah, it's starting to give up," he agrees, "but it's had twenty-eight seasons since

I've owned this store. There's a lot of history in that chair, and a lot of famous people have sat in it. It's the chair Lance used to sit in and tell me his dreams."

Lance often dreamed about being a successful athlete, Hoyt says, and having some of "the finer things in life." But it wouldn't be until Lance was in his mid-teens that he would talk about being a bike racer. Growing up on the home turf of the Dallas Cowboys, he was more exposed to football, and then Little League baseball and soccer. But team sports never really clicked with Lance, even though his new dad, Terry Armstrong, did what he could to encourage him by getting involved in coaching or buying him the best equipment.

"One of Terry's redeeming qualities was that he was a provider," says Lance's aunt, Debbie. "But he and Lance never really connected as father and son."

Maybe not, but in some ways, Terry gave it his best try. "When Lance first wanted to play baseball he wanted to be a catcher," Terry tells me. "I asked, 'Why would you want to be a catcher?' And he said, 'Because I figured out the catcher is in on every play.' So I bought him the best catcher's glove. I wanted to give him every chance I could."

Later, when the family moved to a house in nearby Garland and Lance joined the YMCA to play football and soccer, Terry got involved in coaching the football team. Linda says this was the one time she remembers Lance and Terry being close, and Lance agrees.

In wanting to help his son with sports, Terry was like most middle-class dads. "I was always worried about coaches, because you hear these war stories," Terry says. "So I felt like the easiest way for me to make sure that Lance had the right coaches was to be on the coaching staff. I started as an assistant, and the next year, when the head coach left, I took over the team.

"We were called the Oilers, so I got the decals from the real Oilers, from Houston, and bought the same type so we could stripe the helmets. I got Oilers' caps for the coaches, and I said we may not win anything, but we're sure gonna look good when we take the field. And we went undefeated. I gave every one of the players a plaque with their name on it and the scores. I still run into some of those guys, and they still call me Coach and say they never played on another undefeated team.

"Lance was a good football player, and when he went to baseball he was *really* good—as a catcher, he could almost hit second base. Then, in the middle of the season, he decided to be a pitcher. He says, 'These guys can't pitch, I can give it a better shot.' So he'd be the pitcher, and I'd be the catcher, and we'd throw for hours in the backyard.

"He ended up the season being voted to the all-star team as a pitcher. He loved being on the mound. I always wondered if that was the first start-up of his wanting to be a star. If you're on the mound as a little kid, you've got everyone's attention, and he thrived on that."

By fourth grade, Lance was losing interest in baseball and football. "Even though he seemed to excel in team sports," Terry says, "he didn't like to have to rely on somebody else. He hated it when a guy missed a block; he hated it when a guy dropped a fly ball."

At that time, one of the few individual sports open to a nine-year-old was BMX—bicycle motocross—racing small-wheel bicycles on a roller-coaster-style dirt course. "They had a little track over in south Richardson, and he kept on saying he wanted to go," Terry says. "So I went over to Jim Hoyt and said, 'Whatever bike Lance needs, I'll get it.'"

Terry pulls out a photo from a pile of fading prints he has stacked on the table at his office. It's Lance, already barrel-chested, astride a brand-new BMX racer. There's a big smile on the young boy's face. But neither BMX nor growing up proved easy for him.

"One time, he went to a race and fell off his bike, and he just slid on the dirt," Terry continues. "I went over to him and saw he was crying. I picked him up and said, 'We're finished.' And he goes, 'What do you mean?' 'If you're gonna cry, we're finished,' I said. 'I just got finished paying all this money. We're done. If you're gonna come out here and quit and cry, we're done.' And he goes, 'No, no, no.' And I said, 'No. We're *done*. I'm not gonna have a quitter.'

"I was gonna put the bike in the car and go back and give it to Jim; but there was one more race. 'I'll help you do it,' I offered. He did the race and ended up going every Saturday. That was 1981."

Like Lance, Terry was an only son. He had a good relationship with his adoptive parents, Raymond and Nel Armstrong, who lived one hundred miles northeast of Dallas in Paris. Nel played the organ at the church where her husband was the minister.

"We'd go to Paris on major holidays," Terry says. "Some Christmases we'd have Linda's mother in, other Christmases we'd have her dad, Paul. And in the summertime, Lance would go up and spend a week or two and run around with Dad. In fact, in the Paris Country Club, they always talk about little Lance driving dad's golf cart. And a lady there taught Lance to swim in her backyard pool. Then they'd have the grill, and he'd eat hamburgers and ice cream. Everybody in Paris, Texas, knew Lance . . . and they still remember him today."

Terry was very fond of his own father. "Dad loved working, and he loved people," he says. "He'd call me every day and ask me three questions: 'What are you doing for others? What are you doing for the church? And what are you doing for your kid?'"

Aunt Debbie also liked Terry's dad. "Yeah, he was a nice man," she says. "But I didn't really care for Terry's mother. I remember Lance spent a week with her and I went up there with Linda to get him, and he came out crying; he was probably eight or nine at that time. 'Just take me home.' This was Lance. And I looked across at Linda and said, 'Don't you ever take him here again. Don't ever let him stay here.'"

Incidents like these would contribute to Lance's souring relationship with his adoptive father and grandparents. He much preferred visiting with Papa Paul, who had moved to the Cedar Creek Lake area, fifty miles southeast of Dallas.

"My grandfather was military, got a good pension, didn't have to work much," Lance says. "At one point he was mayor of Seven Points, Texas. He's very religious. I would go there in the summer because of the lake, and we would go fishing. They had a fishing report in the Dallas paper. We would do well, and once I got my name in the paper for catching some big fish. That was cool."

Back at home, though, there was growing conflict between Terry and Linda. "We had a diabolical difference in raising Lance," Terry admits. "I always said, 'We need to make our decisions with Lance together.' But it was always a deal where I'd tell Lance no and she'd tell Lance yes. And she'd always refer back to the fact 'Well, he's my son.' That was always the take.

"But that would have probably worked out . . . and if I really had to pinpoint the demise of us as a family it's when Linda pulled out of the church. I was the youngest deacon in Northway Christian Church, in Dallas. We were very involved in church. Lance was in Sunday school, and we were going to church every Sunday. And then Linda said, 'I don't want to go to that church anymore.' And we quit going to church."

Terry still regrets that part of his life. "When you quit going to church as a family, and you're young, then your moral standards just. . . ." He leaves the sentence hanging as he slices the air with his hand. "I take responsibility because I should have insisted that we continue to go to church, as the spiritual leader of the family. But I didn't. And I can almost go back and say, 'When did the glue start to come apart?' I feel like if we'd stayed in church, things would probably have worked out."

Instead, Lance began to turn away from Terry and became more independent and closed. Talking about her nephew, Debbie says, "He was shy. When he was ten or eleven, he came up to Maryland and stayed the week with us; but he really wanted to be home. I don't think it was a real fun trip for him. . . . Also, school really wasn't Lance's thing. The same thing with Linda. Probably that bothers him. . . ."

Lance agrees. "I was not a great student in that I didn't really apply myself," he says. "I didn't have a lot of passion for it. I'd love to do it over. I would sit in school and think about what I considered to be my job, which is sport. I got by, but back then I thought, 'What do I have to learn Spanish for?'"

Debbie has a further explanation for her nephew's attitude toward schoolwork. "It's probably the education system, which I can say is not that great. I'm in it, so I know.

"I remember when he was about twelve, I was there in Plano, and Lance had been given an F for this Spanish paper. So Linda says, 'Why don't you let Aunt Debbie help you with that?' since I teach Spanish. I looked at it, and it was like hieroglyphics; I could hardly read it. But when I really took the time to read it, the answers were right! I told Lance, 'Your answers are right, but your teacher probably can't read it. Maybe the next time you hand a paper in, make sure your penmanship is better, so she can really read it.'"

With little interest in or success at school, Lance put more energy into sports—especially the individual ones such as BMX. And he was fortunate that his parents were willing to help him achieve his athletic goals.

"Guys were always kidding me," Terry recalls. "'You don't hunt, you don't fish, you don't play golf, you don't gamble, so what do you do?' I said, 'I'm involved with my kid.' They're going out playing eighteen holes, and I'm taking Lance to the BMX track. So my focus was always around Lance. When I bought our first house, we built in a neighborhood where Lance could walk to school because I didn't want him riding the bus."

The Armstrong family's new brick bungalow was in a pleasant subdivision of tree-lined streets and manicured lawns, just a few blocks from Dooley Elementary School. The next schools Lance would attend—Armstrong Middle School, Williams High, and Plano East High—were within a three-mile radius. Lance soon made friends with Adam Wilk, also in fourth grade, who lived just across the street on Mesa Drive. "It's a kind of low-rank country-club community," Wilk says, describing their old neighborhood that backs onto Los Rios Golf Club and Bob Woodruff Park. It was in sharp contrast to the rough Oak Cliff neighborhood where Linda was raised and where Lance began his life.

Wilk still lives in the Los Rios area. He worked for more than fifteen years as a manager at Keys Fitness, a manufacturer of home fitness equipment and treadmills. I went to meet him at the company's huge warehouse, which fronts a modern industrial park in nearby Garland, overlooking farmland.

We sit down in his office, where the desktop PC pings out a new e-mail message every few minutes. Wilk has a lean, athletic build and a small patch of gray hair on his balding head. When he's not "just a grunt," as he puts it, he's a national-level triathlete and a former national track cycling champion in the one-kilometer time trial.

"My father was a collegiate runner for Rutgers," Wilk says. "We moved to Plano in '81, '82. That's when I met Lance. Chann McRae lived about a quarter-mile away from us. The three of us are the same age, all thin. And we'd all go on to win national championships in cycling."

Another friend Lance made back then was John Boggan, who lived five doors down. "My house was the one where everyone came to hang out," Boggan says. "We had a lot of space, with a basketball hoop, and it backed up to the park. . . . My parents were real good about saying, 'Bring everyone over.' We all wanted to be with each other all the time, just messing around, trying to get in trouble. I was a swimmer, absolutely loved it. I didn't follow the traditional sports."

"John and I were the better athletes; we did tennis, basketball, everything," Wilk recalls. "Chann and I had joined the swim team at Los Rios, but Lance wasn't a member; he was on the football team at Armstrong Middle School. And I was running already."

His friends' interests in alternative sports had a strong influence on Lance, whether it was running with Wilk ("Lance, of course, wins the first running race he ever does") or swimming with Boggan. But the pivotal point, according to stepfather Terry, came when Lance was about thirteen years old. "I came home one day and he was watching the Ironman Triathlon on TV. And he said, 'I'm gonna do that. I'm gonna do the Ironman. I want to be a triathlete.'"

Triathlon is the swim-bike-run sport that encompasses everything from mini-events lasting less than an hour up to the world championship Hawaii Ironman that takes the winners more than eight hours to complete. Lance had good enough biking skills from BMX racing, and he had taken part in some 10K runs. "Mom did them too," he recalls. "I won the age-group prize in the first one. But I didn't run that serious . . . just ran to run."

Swimming, though, was a problem. Lance knew how to swim, but he didn't swim well. So he decided to take lessons with his mates, Adam, Chann, and John.

"We were all in eighth grade when we went and joined COPS (City of Plano Swimmers) and did swim tryouts," Wilk says. "Chann,

John, and I get put with the eighteen-year-olds, the senior development team, and Lance was put with the lower level. He swam like a ten-year-old kid."

Upset by his poor rating, Lance asked COPS coach Chris MacCurdy what it would take to get moved up. "I remember him standing at the metal bars that separate the public from the pool," MacCurdy tells me, "and he was watching his buddies train, and you could just see it in his eyes, trying to figure out how he's gonna get himself over with them. Sure enough, within a month, he was able to do it. It was probably a combination of his desire and his ability."

Within eighteen months, Lance not only qualified for the state swimming championships but also finished as one of the top five in the one-mile freestyle. To reach that level so quickly "is almost unheard of," MacCurdy says.

"Chris was a very good coach, though at the time I thought this guy could not be meaner," Lance recalls. "He was tough, probably good for me then. The workouts were meticulous. When we'd come in, the schedule was all on the chalkboard. We'd swim 5:30 to 6:45 in the morning, then go to school, and come back in the evening. Peak training was fifteen thousand meters a day—five thousand in the morning, ten thousand at night—and you were happy to do the morning one. If you missed practice or were late, he was a militant guy. He'd just get mad . . . although he did kick some guys off the team." But Lance stuck with it.

With his swimming proficiency now complementing his nascent running and biking skills, Lance felt he was ready to tackle his first triathlon. He told his parents he wanted to enter the local round of Ironkids, a national competition for young teenagers, which had regional qualifiers. But first he'd need a proper racing bike.

"There was a lot of money in that family for Lance," Wilk remembers, "to buy him drums, a kick-butt BMX bike, and then when we all got road bikes. His dad would definitely spend money on his son, especially when Lance went through a period of not talking to him."

Wilk says he's surprised that Lance rarely talks about Terry in interviews and seems to view him "almost like a cut-off, imaginary part of his life that never happened." But, Wilk points out, "there was some support there. Granted, it was maybe not emotional, but for sure there was financial support."

Lance clearly remembers the first racing bike his parents bought him so he could do Ironkids. It was a middle-range French ten-speed, a Mercier, "and it had toe clips, thin plastic handlebar tape, Campy [Campagnolo derailleur gears], big looping brake cables, and downtube shifters," he says. "Chann and I would ride all over. We even rode to downtown Dallas just to say we did it. And we didn't wear helmets—nobody did.

"I thought it was cool just to be out. When you're a kid and leave the house, and you get around the corner and there's nobody there, and you're alone, and you're private, and you're free. . . . That's true for little kids, but it was also true for me when I was thirteen and got on a road bike and you just go."

Debbie saw right away what the bike meant to Lance. "That bicycle was freedom for him. He would just get on there and go. He was a free spirit." She also saw another side of her nephew developing, a softness.

"I can remember him coming back from a ride when my kids were little, three and one-and-a-half, and he always wanted the baby. He wanted to play with the baby. So he had that real gentle side, too, which I've seen him show throughout the years with other children. He has a real tender heart."

But, as a teen, he also had a hard, out-of-control side that sometimes worried his mother. "It was the time of the difficult teenage years," Linda says. "He was not an angel. He was not perfect. Of all my friends, I thought I was the only one with a difficult teenager. Chris MacCurdy would be like, 'Oh, Lance got into trouble again today.' And to compound that, even people I worked with said, 'Oh, he's cocky.' But I knew that's what gave him the confidence to win. I'd rather look at things from a positive aspect than looking at that kind of attitude."

Terry didn't always see things so positively and was more likely to discipline their son—as he did when Lance cried after falling on the BMX track. Terry admits that he used his wooden fraternity paddle to spank Lance "now and again," but he adds that Linda was not ignorant of what was going on. "Oh, she knew about it," he says. "I never disciplined Lance with a paddle unless she was there."

"Yeah, that's true," Lance tells me. "I don't want to be unfair to him, as it was much more acceptable back then. I don't spank my children. There are days where I wish I did, damn it. And there are smart people that will say this is the best way to discipline your children. But do you do it with your fraternity paddle? Probably not. And it was big and thick and had a taped handle. They used that shit at school, too. If you fucked up, you got a paddle, and I got paddled a time or two; but I got paddled more by him.

"The only time I distinctly remember, and it was not as if this scarred me for life, was when I was about my son Luke's age, nine, ten. He said, 'Don't ever leave your drawers open.' And one time I left them open where shit's hanging out—socks, clothes, everything. And sure enough, he fucking comes at me with that paddle. It didn't hurt just physically, but also emotionally."

Perhaps, Linda suggests, it was the disciplining that spurred her son to excel in sports. Lance admits that he was often fueled by anger.

"The old wounds," he wrote, "become the stuff of competitive energy."

He was also spurred on by any hard challenge. "Most kids when they get a bike, they go up a couple of hills, and they're like, 'Holy shit, this is hard.' I just assumed that was part of it," Lance says. "I enjoyed that . . . I still do. Whatever it was that I had or acquired and started to like then, it's the same now. It doesn't bother me to go out and put it on the limit. I still run and ride and do extreme stuff."

That extreme stuff began with his first triathlon. Lance often acknowledges his mother's involvement in his early athletic endeavors and how she taught him, "Son, you never quit"; but Terry remembers the part he played too. "When Lance did the first Ironkids deal in Dallas, and being the proud dad, I knew that Lance was gonna kill everybody," Terry says. "He actually won the race, but they messed up all the timing, and they said, 'Well, we're just gonna pick three guys and they'll get to go to the championship.' The championship was in Orlando at Disney World. I said, 'No, we ain't playing that game.' I made such a stink they flew us to Houston, because that was the next one, and I picked up the hotel. And Lance won.

"In Orlando, sitting at a Disney World hotel, a guy came up and was bragging that his son would win. So I bet him five hundred bucks that my son would beat him—and Lance did, and finished second in the race. The guy handed me the five hundred bucks. And I didn't *have* five hundred bucks at that time. But I knew Lance would smoke him."

All Lance remembers, though, was that he didn't win the national title. "I was pretty bummed out to get beaten," he says.

"After Ironkids, it just went from there," Wilk says, referring to his friend's growing confidence in any competition he tackled. Lance soon began training for the following spring's major local event, the President's Triathlon, which would take place at Lake Lavon, not far from the Armstrongs' house. But two weeks before the race, the U.S. triathlon federation told organizer Jim Woodman that, because of a new ruling, he couldn't allow anyone under fifteen to participate or his indemnity insurance would be voided.

"There were about 20 kids among the 2,200 participants that fit the bill," Woodman says, "and we had to call their parents to let them know. Lance was one of those kids, and his parents were the only ones that wouldn't accept the news. They insisted that Lance race or he'd be devastated. 'How 'bout I bring you a birth certificate that shows he's really fifteen?' asked Terry Armstrong. Tired of all this hassle, I readily agreed, and later that evening Terry presented me with an obviously doctored birth certificate. 'Looks good to me,' I said. 'He's in the race.'"

Lance didn't do as well as he hoped that day, which wasn't surprising, given the event's unusually long distances: a 1.2-mile swim, 50-mile bike, and 10-mile run. "And I got a time penalty for drafting," he recalls. (On the bike leg of a triathlon, to take pace or draft in the slipstream of another competitor is forbidden.) But soon after that race, his emerging talent was confirmed in a duathlon at an upscale health club in the Dallas Galleria. It was called the Splash and Dash, a twelve-lap swim in a twenty-five-meter outdoor pool, followed by a four-lap run on a half-mile Astroturf track on the mall roof. Both Lance and his mom took part.

Though he was only fourteen, Lance was the overall male winner and earned a $100 certificate for a pair of Avia running shoes. The shoes were mailed to him, but they didn't fit well. Avia's local rep, Scott Eder, was asked to do a make-good, so he arranged to see the Armstrongs at their house in Plano.

Linda was working full time then, and with Terry often on the road doing sales, she worried about Lance being so much on his own.

When she found out that Eder, then in his late twenties, was an amateur athlete who had plenty of contacts in the sports industry, she had an idea.

"When we started talking," Eder tells me, "Linda said Lance needed a mentor. Not a coaching mentor, but an adult mentor, someone to keep him out of trouble and more focused. That's how our relationship began.

"I became kind of a friend with Linda, and she didn't ask a lot of questions. Lance and I would go run, or go to a workout, or go to the gym, and then we'd go out and eat and hang out before I dropped him off at home. We went out to lunch or dinner three days a week for a couple of years. Linda asked me to get him into races, get entry fees paid, get him equipment, take him to races, and get him back safely."

Lance's friends, who were also now entering triathlons, welcomed Eder into their world. "Once Scott started, we were on cloud nine," Wilk says. "We were just a bunch of kids, and Scott was kind of our big brother. He'd do whatever we wanted—like, 'Mom, you don't have to go. Scott's taking us.' Yes, he *was* kind of Lance's manager and looked after us, but he was also our friend. Before that, my mom was the only stay-at-home mom, and she would drive us everywhere."

One important task Eder performed was getting Lance back on good terms with bike-shop owner Jim Hoyt. "When I met Lance he was not welcome at the shop," Eder says. "I'd heard he'd been thrown out of Jim's shop a few times—at eleven years old, came back at thirteen, and was not welcome again. So my first move was to reunite them, vouch to Jim that he's a good kid now. That was the first sponsor-mending thing I did, got him back in with the Richardson Bike Mart. Jim ended up giving him a bike and four hundred dollars a month to use for training, travel, and racing."

A stipend of $400 a month was a huge boost at that time for a young athlete seeking success, especially in a sport rarely noticed by the American media. It was a risky investment for the Vietnam vet who was still trying to make a success of his bike store. But it was also a gesture that helped a kid get closer to the dreams he had shared with Hoyt while sitting on that rickety chair in his office many years before.

CHAPTER 3

BREAKING OUT

People would ask if I coached Lance,
and I'd say, "No. Nobody coaches Lance."
Lance did what he wanted. He was a natural.
—SCOTT EDER

MOST PEOPLE ARE AMAZED by how much Lance packs into a single day. "I learned that from Linda," he says. "She taught me by osmosis, or whatever you call that. She worked very hard and didn't complain about it, and she gave me a real sense of schedule. She would always say, every day, 'Today's the first day of the rest of your life.' It's kind of hokey, like something you see on a doctor's office wall. But now I schedule everything and drive some people crazy."

Filling every day has been the norm for Lance since he was fourteen and began winning triathlons. To be successful at his new sport, he had to train in swimming, running, and cycling, while keeping up at school. And he still found time to hang out with his buddies and live the life of a Texas teen in the eighties: girls, parties, pranks; drinking, rock music, and fast cars.

Other than the schoolwork, Lance enjoyed most of what he did. Still, he had to develop an extreme self-discipline to achieve his athletic goals—especially since Terry was frequently on the road as a salesman and his mother commuted to a full-time job. Linda felt bad that her son would come home to an empty house. But, she says, "I always had food for him to eat after a ride, like pasta. Things he could easily make."

What worried Linda most was that even though she had found a mentor for her son in Scott Eder, Lance looked ready for trouble. "I was the first to admit, 'Gee, he really *is* a difficult teenager.' And the difficulties were the smart mouth and the things that teenagers do," she says. "But why didn't the other moms say, 'Oh, mine does that, too.' I felt like I was the only one going through this. So much so, I was calling Tough Luck—a hotline where you could talk to somebody about things—because I was so worried. Other moms at swim meets and triathlons would say, 'Oh, my son does nothing like that!' Oh, God."

While Linda worried and reached out for help, her husband Terry was more reactive to their teenage son. "I didn't know Terry Armstrong then," Lance says, "and I certainly don't know him now. Once I was old enough, I figured out pretty quickly that he was full of shit, and I understood how to call someone on their bullshit."

That attitude led to what Terry describes as their "one really big disagreement," when Lance took a swing at him. "He was fifteen or so," Terry tells me. "When he took a swing at me, we had a kind of toss-and-turn-around on the living room floor. I guess being from the old school I learned, 'Don't take a swing at your dad; it may be your last swing.' Maybe that was the way I was brought up, when they always said, 'Don't mess with Dad.'

"So I threw him out of the house and said, 'Unfortunately, these are my rules, and if you're gonna take a swing at me, you're not gonna live in this house.' And with that, he came apart, he was crying, and I said, 'Sorry, this is the rule.' I remember him coming back and knocking on the door, and I said. 'Are you gonna play by my rules?' And he said, 'Yeah, that's okay.'"

But it wasn't okay. On a trip to a swim meet, waiting in the Dallas airport, Lance saw Terry make several attempts at writing a note before balling up the paper and tossing it into the trash. When his stepfather went to the restroom, Lance picked out the balls of paper and hid them in his bag. Later, he discovered that the notes were love letters—and not written to his mom. He didn't tell anyone, not even Linda. He didn't want to hurt her.

Lance felt shock, betrayal, and rage. But he kept all these feelings inside and used his anger to drive him in sports. Totally focused on winning, the young triathlete sought out anyone who could help him, whether it was his mentor, Eder, bike-shop owner Jim Hoyt, swim coach Chris MacCurdy, or any of his close friends: Adam Wilk, Chann McRae, John Boggan, or newcomer Steve Lewis.

"Lance was probably my best friend growing up," says Boggan, who now has an executive job with SCi telecommunications. "We were together from sunup to sundown and trained every day together, especially in the summers. Our days consisted of waking up, riding our bikes to swim practice, swimming for two hours, riding our bikes home, resting for a little while, then doing a run in the heat of the day or taking a ride at night. On days where we didn't swim, we'd focus on a longer ride.

"Our regular ride was straight down the frontage road on I-75. Lance would go to the longer turnaround than me, which would add four miles; the total ride was thirty-five miles. My goal was to take the shorter turnaround and not get caught. In the four years we did that ride, I made it home without getting caught by him only once. I wasn't a bad cyclist, but there was a vast difference between us, and I knew I needed to go to college, get an education, and get a job. I'd be a very poor pro triathlete."

Wilk, who did become a pro triathlete, remembers that, except for MacCurdy's swim coaching, none of their training was that scientific. "We would read books or just go run," he says. "We would do stupid things—like eat dinner before running and see who wouldn't throw up. We would eat steak and then run hard for seven, eight miles. We never went by the long-slow-distance training methods. When you're a kid, everything is done hard."

Boggan confirms how basic their training was. "We just ate what we wanted, rode bikes, ran, and swam," he says. "We just wanted to get better. Lance was very disciplined and driven, much more than me. He would drag me around when I would want to take the day off."

For the new triathlon season, Lance got a new bike, a top-end Raleigh, which had the latest aerodynamic Roval wheels with razor-like spokes. "They were the hottest new thing," Linda says. "I had no sooner bought him that bike than I get a phone call at work. Lance was in the emergency room. He got hit by a car when he was riding from Plano to Richardson to meet up with a buddy.

"My boss drove me to the hospital. Lance had hit his head and it was bleeding pretty bad. No helmets back then. He went over the car and landed on his head on a curb, right at an intersection. It could have been worse, but his V-shaped body helped him have a softer landing. The muscles of his upper body were so strong because of his swimming. He had a few stitches in his head and some in his toe, because that's where he clipped the front of the car.

"The doctor said, 'This leg isn't broken, but it's pretty bad. You need to go to the orthopedic doctor, but in the meantime, here's a brace.' It went from the waist all the way down. The doctor said, 'He's got to stay off of this leg, he can't ride, he can't run. . . .'

"And Lance had this big triathlon coming up in Lewisville the week after, and he said, 'Mom, I'm gonna do that race. That's it.' And I said, 'You can't run on that leg.' 'Oh, Mom, it's fine.' So he took his tennis shoes and cut a hole out of the toe. And I think my friend Sue took the stitches out of his head. Then he competed in that race and did well. It was a real cold, rainy day.

"To get people to write about Lance in the newspaper, I made calls to make sure they knew. And the orthopedic doctor later wrote us a letter saying, I would've never in a million years thought that he could have competed. Lance was like a cat with nine lives."

Lance was planning to do the President's Triathlon again, and as a build-up he did two of the region's top events, the Hillcrest-Tulsa and Waco triathlons; he won both in course-record times.

"When Lance won the race in Waco," Terry says, "I remember sitting on the sidelines with him and congratulating him, when this guy came across the line. He was like twenty-three, twenty-four. He was huffing and puffing and just jumping for joy, shouting, 'I won! I won!' And the race official said, 'No, you came in second; that kid over there won.' And the guy came over, and he looked at Lance and says, 'You know, I never saw you. I kept looking ahead, and there wasn't anybody in front of me, you were so far out.'"

Another competitor astounded by Lance's victory was a twenty-year-old from Austin, Bart Knaggs, doing his first triathlon. "I'd just started the run when the speaker announced that a fifteen-year-old kid named Lance Armstrong was about to finish," Knaggs says. "I couldn't believe it. I did the whole run trying to figure out how he could get thirty minutes ahead of me on just the swim and bike legs."

Lance was so far ahead that when he spotted his neighbor John Boggan in a group running toward him on the out-and-back run course, Lance crossed to the other side of the road and gave Boggan a high-five. "That was so cool. That's the sort of friend he was," Boggan says. "He just wanted to encourage me."

"He was a phenom, a freak," Knaggs adds. "I heard later that Lance didn't even drink water during the race. He would tape three bars of wrapped-up chewing gum to the bike's top tube and chew gum instead of drinking water."

For Lance, his emphatic Waco victory was just the confirmation he needed to switch categories and become a pro triathlete—so he could earn cash rather than amateur prizes. But since turning pro could endanger his potential status as an Olympic athlete in swimming or track and field, he applied to the state's University Interscholastic League for a ruling.

"Coach MacCurdy thought Lance had a shot at being an Olympic swimmer, so he didn't want him turning pro," Terry explains. "The UIL said that since triathlon was then a non-Olympic sport, he could make money at it and not upset his amateur status. But, as it happened, he and Chris got into knock-down drag-outs because Lance wanted to do triathlons, and Chris wanted him to be a swimmer."

Lance won. As others were starting to notice, once Lance made up his mind about something, he went straight for it, always charging ahead.

Eder says that what impressed him most about Lance the young triathlete was his "unbelievable killer instinct. Not so much discipline, but once the race started, just an incredible desire to crush people—not to win, but to crush people. I have a tape from when he was fourteen, and the interviewer asked him what's your goal, and Lance said, 'I want to be the best in the world within five years—by far, nobody close to me. No doubt about it.'"

Few athletes make such a bold proclamation at such a young age. One who did, though more privately, was Greg LeMond—who became the first American winner of the Tour de France the summer before Lance did his first race as a pro triathlete. But LeMond didn't broadcast his ambitions to the media. He was sixteen when he listed his private goals on a notepad, predicting (correctly) that he would win the world championships and the Tour before he was twenty-five.

Both Lance and LeMond have what the experts call "a big engine," one element of which is a genetically high capacity to utilize oxygen during exercise. Known as maximal oxygen uptake, or VO_2max, this parameter is measured in milliliters of oxygen per kilogram of bodyweight per minute. VO_2max is considered the best indicator of cardiovascular fitness and aerobic power. The number for an average amateur athlete is between 40 and 50 ml/kg/min. LeMond is said to have once recorded 92.5, just below the highest known VO_2max of 94, which was recorded by Norwegian cross-country skier Bjørn Daehlie, who won a record eight gold medals in the winter Olympics in the nineties.

At age fifteen, Lance discovered almost by accident just how high his own VO_2max was. Eder tells me the story: "A guy at the Cooper Clinic in Dallas, then called the Aerobic Center, invented a gadget he called the Cool Collar. It was like a necklace containing frozen coolant that was supposed to cool your core temperature. For the controlled study, I was asked to bring five runners who'd be paid to run for an hour while wearing the collar. I was one, and I took Lance along. He'd never run for a whole hour before, so I said, 'This guy is borderline, but he can probably do it.' Part of the payoff was a full physical workup, including an electrocardiogram and a VO_2max test."

In the fifteen-minute VO_2max test, the athlete runs on a treadmill that's tilted upward while the speed is gradually increased until the athlete is at the point of exhaustion; the athlete is constantly breathing into an airtight mask that's hooked up to a meter that measures the proportion of oxygen in his expired air and reveals the maximal uptake—which is reached when oxygen consumption remains at a steady state despite an increase in workload.

Eder continues, "Three days later the guy calls me up and says, 'Who's that kid you brought over here? He just scored the highest VO_2max we've ever had here, 79.5.' I said, 'That's interesting, because if you had tested him on a bike it would have been even higher.' We were all good athletes, but our numbers were all in the 60s. Oh, and that Cool Collar? It was never manufactured."

Now aware of his exceptional VO_2max, and with two big wins behind him, Lance headed to the President's Triathlon confident he could have a great race. His only uncertainty was competing against professionals for the first time. One of those pros would be Mark Allen, an American who had finished second in the previous year's Ironman Triathlon World Championship and was on the verge of becoming the sport's greatest champion.

"That year the race went down to the shorter international distance and moved over to Las Colinas Country Club, near the Dallas–Fort Worth airport. We swam in a small man-made lake, and I came out with the big boys," Lance recalls. "The Canadian, Andrew McNaughton, just blew us away on the bike. I stayed with Allen and came off the bike in second, then ran as hard as I could. It was so hot."

His mom came to watch the race with Eder, who says, "I was standing with Linda as they were coming into the transition area. When Lance came in ahead of Allen off the bike, we were like, 'Wow!' But that was his strategy, which was burn it up as fast as you can for as long as you can because he knew he could not run with those guys. And it was an incredibly hilly, incredibly steep run—all neighborhoods, residential streets. Brutal."

Lance astounded the pros with his eventual sixth-place finish. Allen passed him on the run and overhauled McNaughton to win the race; but Armstrong was the name on everyone's lips. "I was pumped after that," Lance says. "And Mark Allen? He was like surprised. . . ."

Allen still remembers that day: "He was just this young guy, and I was shocked when people told me his age. I wasn't ancient, probably twenty-five, but a ten-year difference at that age. . . . I thought back to what I was doing at age fifteen. I was a swimmer, and nowhere near world class.

"Athletically, development-wise, I just thought, man, here's this kid who's fifteen and keeping up with the best guys in the world . . . just this kid who's doing really well, who *told* people he was gonna do well."

"That was Lance's big breakthrough," Eder notes. "That was the springboard for the telephone calls, as I was kind of serving as his agent. People would ask if I coached Lance, and I'd say, 'No. Nobody coaches Lance.' Lance did what he wanted. He had innate talent. I never taught him to do anything. He was a natural."

That summer, Eder was able to get Lance into a few international triathlons. But the race that Eder handpicked for Lance was the U.S. National Sprint Championship, half the distance of the President's Triathlon, in Boca Pointe, Florida.

"I called the race director and said, 'I think Lance can win your race,'" Eder says. "The organizer was like, 'Yeah, right. Everyone's gonna be here. There's no way he can win.' So I said, 'I'll bet you when the run starts he's in the lead, and he's got a damn good chance to hang on and finish top five.' They were paying top seven. So I had the guy guarantee our trip against Lance's winnings. The hotel was gratis, the airfare was like two hundred fifty dollars each. If Lance didn't place, it was his loss; but if he did place, the five hundred dollars would go back to him.

"Mike Pigg was the winner, and Lance ended up fifth and won fifteen hundred dollars. So he came out with a thousand dollars. That was 1987. The following year, he'd surprise everyone and win it."

Despite Lance's growing reputation as a nationally rated triathlete, his fellow pros dubbed him "Junior," in deference to the fact that he was a fifteen-year-old muddling his way through high school. And while he had grown physically—already five-foot-ten and one hundred fifty pounds—he was still a mixed-up kid inside. That's how Mark Henricks, a Texas-based freelance writer, saw Lance when he interviewed the rising young star for *Sport* magazine in the fall of '87.

"The interview was with Lance, his mother, and Scott Eder," Henricks tells me over coffee on a blustery day in Austin. "Lance had just finished third in a triathlon and beaten a national champion, I believe. At fifteen, you're not supposed to be beating national champions. He was quite careful about what he said. He hadn't been interviewed many times, and he was really guarded. Quiet.

"I remember going away from it thinking, he doesn't have what it takes. He's just an ordinary kid with this incredible physical gift, but he doesn't have it here or here." Henricks points to his heart and head.

"Something compelled me to ask him about drug use," he adds. "His answer . . . again, it seemed like that of a very typical fifteen-year-old who'd probably been drinking beer, smoking pot, and didn't want to answer this question with his mom there. But he said, no, he'd never used drugs, with this kind of sidelong glance. And he was probably doing what every suburban Dallas kid does when they're fifteen . . . mixed in with a lot of training.

"The punch line is that I didn't think he was going anywhere. I'm not very good at picking winners, that's for sure."

A livelier, even raucous image of the fifteen-year-old Lance is offered by his old friend Wilk.

"We had tons of fights with a neighbor who was much older than us," Wilk says. "One time, Lance glued his mailbox shut. You can't do that; it's against the law. So they called the cops. When we hear them at the door, I go and hide in his mom's room, and he hides in his room. He had an 'Armstrong' street sign in his room that we'd taken off a pole. And of course it's illegal to steal street signs. The cops weren't happy.

"So was he a troublemaker? Sure."

Wilk then describes another caper, which Lance talked about in his memoir, *It's Not About the Bike.* "There were five or six guys over at his house to play fireball," says Wilk, adding that by then the Armstrongs had moved to a new single-story house, three miles away from their old Los Rios neighborhood. "Terry was rarely there, and his mom was working, so Lance's house was then the hang-out house. It was shaped like a C around a small courtyard. So we got this pail, poured gas in it, dipped the tennis ball in there, and then lit it.

"We were kind of hitting the ball against a wall, and the ball tends to hit the wood, and makes a little fire spot. If it would go up on a roof, we'd climb up and put it out, and then we'd throw it over the wall and run through the courtyard, through the garage, and put it out."

Getting more animated, Wilk continues, "Lance kind of mentions this in the book . . . but it hits the wall and that ball bounces, and bounces, and lands right in the bucket of gasoline. It shoots a flame and smoke like twenty stories high, and it's underneath the awning of the house. Everyone shouts, 'Kick it over! Kick it over!' We kick it over and his dad's brand-new bucket just melts into a big round piece of plastic.

"At this point, Lance and his dad were really getting into big arguments. We didn't want his dad to know we blew the bucket up, so we had to go and bury it in a field two streets over."

Wilk lists other pranks they played that rankled Lance's neighbors, things like lighting up fireworks before running off, throwing water balloons at cars, and garage hopping.

"We were good at that one," Wilk explains, "because you can grab beers from refrigerators in a garage, escape down the alleyways, and leave the garage open. They all had refrigerators in their garages. Lance called it garage hopping.

"And it was all based on running. We were such fast runners that if all hell broke loose and we had to get away, we'd always get away—whether it be fireworks, garage hopping, doing water balloons. We were just athletic kids being athletic. But then, once Lance got serious about triathlon, it all changed. He got good quickly."

One incident from his fifteenth year stayed in Lance's mind. "Lance told me a story from when he was a sophomore in high school," says Bob Mionske, one of the first Olympic cyclists whom Lance befriended when he was eighteen. "He was at a party that's mostly seniors, and he wanted to use the bathroom, and the door was locked. He got more and more impatient, and he started pounding on the door and then kicking the door. The seniors came out, and they knocked him down and got in a group, and they started kicking him and pounding him and beating him to a pulp. He was telling me the story because I could see it still affected him."

With Lance's sixteenth birthday coming up in September 1987, his parents were looking to buy him a car. "Because Linda and I were both working full time, and Lance had to get to an early swim class, we had already bought him a motor scooter. But I knew that he was gonna need a car," says Terry. "I was driving down the road one day, and I saw this red Fiat Spider convertible. So I went and bought the car for him—and sold the motorcycle."

Lance was eager to get his license and try out his new wheels. Soon, as Wilk tells it, "we were driving this little red convertible everywhere. Lance was a rock star already, driving to school himself at fifteen."

Just as the bike had meant freedom to Lance at thirteen, his secondhand Fiat gave him a new independence—to drive where he wanted, impress his schoolmates, and date the girls. And there were quite a few girls.

"There were many young women that I've felt for," Linda says. "Gina Di Luca was one. I loved that little girl. I can see her like yesterday."

"She was from Plano," adds Linda's sister, Debbie. "Italian. Green eyes. Dark hair. Beautiful girl."

"He likes his girls," Wilk confirms. "Gina Di Luca was the first one. That was seventh or eighth grade. One of his ex-girlfriends works at the gym where I work out today, see her all the time, Beth Seymour. That was back in the ninth, tenth grade. He would drive her around in that red convertible. We had a good group of girls around us."

"Lance is definitely a ladies' man," says Jim Hoyt. "He always wanted to be a rock star, that was no secret. Keeping him corralled was the problem."

CHAPTER 4

WANTING IT ALL

He would create this ripple wherever he went.
There was always so much energy around him.
—MARK ALLEN

LANCE WANTED TO BE THE COOLEST and the best—to drive the fastest car, date the prettiest girls, top each hill first on bike rides, and win every race he entered. And in his mid-teens, he says, it all seemed to come easy.

"I was pretty stoked that I had sponsorship and was able to see the world and win prize money. I also knew it was a big help to my mom because money was tight, and I was earning enough to pay for all my stuff—plus some. It's not as if I made sacrifices. In the off-season, in the winter, I'd mess around with the guys and have fun."

Scott Eder, the man Lance calls "a nice guy, a sort of coach meets agent meets big brother," traveled with him to two dozen triathlons, looking for deals and keeping Lance out of trouble. Two of those races were in the Caribbean, where Lance first competed at the international triathlon in St. Croix, one of the U.S. Virgin Islands. That's where Eder began to notice some of his young charge's traits.

"Lance was gregarious, very cocky, very crazy," says Eder, who's now in his early fifties and has a round face, short graying hair, and a high-pitched but rough voice. "He was sixteen, but he thought he was an adult, and he *was* competing with adults and mature for his age. He wanted to do the adult things, though, and if they were having a party, and there was alcohol, he wanted to get in the back door.

"After the race in St. Croix, he tried to sneak in the bar—it was like a fortress with an outdoor patio. All the triathletes were inside having a big victory party. I was hanging on the outside, keeping an eye on Lance.

"He would cruise around the side and try to get in, then cruise around the other side. Finally, he tried to climb a wall to get in the party. He was halfway up the wall when this bouncer came and put a big hand on his back and pulled him off. I had to talk the guy down from arresting Lance, saying, 'Leave him alone. He's here with a bunch of men, and he just wants to be a man.'"

It was the men, though, who won the rugged St. Croix Triathlon: Mark Allen and Mike Pigg, two of the sport's top stars, placed one-two. Lance finished far behind them in the longest race he had ever done.

"Lance was in over his head at St. Croix," Eder admits, "though he did well on the swim and bike legs." That he swam strongly on a two-mile ocean swim was not surprising since Lance had been swimming with his high-school coach, Chris MacCurdy, for more than two years, specializing in the one-mile freestyle. What did surprise his competitors was how well Lance performed on the almost sixty-mile cycling loop, which contained a hill so steep the athletes dubbed it "The Beast."

Everyone got an even better look at Lance in another offshore event, the Bermuda International Triathlon, which had a $100,000 prize list. Eder didn't go with him on that trip.

"No, Lance just called this guy in the hotel there and said he was coming for the race and he wanted a room," Eder explains. "And, my gosh, he got the deal! He had to put 'Bermuda Princess Hotel' on his shirt, and he did get them some good publicity. He was way up front on the swim and bike, riding with Mark Allen and Dave Scott. . . ."

By now, Allen knew that the kid from Texas was going to be strong on the bike, but he didn't know *how* strong. "It was just he and I and another guy," Allen recalls. "We get ourselves in the lead, and he pulled up to me on the bike, and he was saying, 'Are we doing good? Is this right? Is everything the way it should be here?' And I was redlined—I couldn't get enough oxygen—and I couldn't even get the guy to shut up. Lance didn't win the race . . . but that was the first time where I really saw how talented he was on the bike."

Allen, the star of the race—and the winner—was also seeing a star quality in Lance. "He was fairly brash," Allen says. "He just said what he was gonna do, and he did it—not like a lot of guys who say stuff but don't do it. He would create this ripple wherever he went. There was always so much energy around him."

Lance's high-school buddy Wilk sensed that energy, too. "He was driving cool cars, he was starting to make the TV stuff, and he was becoming a rock star real early."

His star quality was recognized by race organizers as well. When Eder and Lance returned to St. Croix the following spring, they were offered a big vacation home for their two-week stay. And this time, Lance *did* join the post-race party with some Dallas friends. They were due to leave the island the next morning, and it was Lance who had the biggest hangover.

"We had to get to the airport early," Eder recalls. "I've never drunk alcohol, but all the others were pretty drunk, and we were flying home together. Lance was out, like blacked out; there was no way to move him. He was probably 160 pounds by then, a pretty big guy. We were shaking him and shaking him, and in the end we literally carried him to the car and into the airport. He started to come to just before the flight. He was a very heavy sleeper, especially after he'd had a few drinks."

While Lance's efforts at growing up fast didn't always work, he was maturing quickly as an athlete. "He did four or five of the Bud Light U.S. Triathlon Series events when he was sixteen, in cities like Chicago and Tampa," says Eder. "He would usually be seventh, eighth, ninth. Took top-three once, and at Hilton Head, the national championships, he got seventh or eighth. Compared with the guys he was beating, he was probably training at only half their level—maybe 70 percent on the bike and 20 percent swimming and running. And he took the Rookie of the Year title."

It was at that national awards reception that I first saw Lance Armstrong. When he walked onto the stage with the country's leading triathletes, he seemed shy and a little uncomfortable as he faced an audience of a few hundred people. But he seemed very comfortable to be taking his place alongside the stars of his sport.

Lance was already competitive with triathlon superstars Allen, Pigg, and Dave Scott in swimming and cycling, but he needed to improve his overall stamina to capitalize on his innate running speed. The answer seemed to be training in cross-country, a more demanding discipline than track as it entails running longer distances over rough dirt trails and grass. So it wasn't long before Lance, along with his friends Wilk, Chann McRae, and John Boggan, made cross-country running part of their routine.

"Let me show you a funny picture after a cross-country in 1988," Lance says, as he goes to retrieve a photo from his den. "That's Chann on the left. He was a punk then." He smiles, looking at Chann's spiked hair. "And he's still a punk. That's me in the middle." He points to himself and laughs at the bushy hairstyle he then had. "And Adam Wilk, and John Boggan on the right. It was our senior year. The races were 5K, which was the longest we could run in high school."

"When we started cross-country," Wilk recalls, "our coach was James Mays, who was the rabbit, the pacesetter, for Steve Cram when he broke the world mile record in 1985. Mays would run with us, and he would run faster and faster and faster, so we would just get quick."

Mays made a big difference, Lance says. "He was a world-class 800-meter runner out of Texas Tech. Tall, light-skinned African-American, a frigging gazelle. We just thought he was the king. Drove a Porsche, made most of his money as a rabbit. We couldn't figure why he was a high-school cross-country coach. Yeah, he really got us motivated. He was cool."

Coach Mays's new students got a chance to do him proud in their senior year when they took part in—and won—the Dallas district cross-country team championships. It was the first time Plano East took the title. But Lance and his teammates didn't get the respect they'd expected, and they rebelled.

"Winning districts was the first time ever for our school, but in the school paper next day they didn't really say anything," Wilk says. "The football team lost by fifty points the night before—and they had a big write-up—but nothing about cross-country. So we decided to make a statement. That weekend, we were out late at night, and we spray-painted 'Plano East Cross-Country Kicking Ass' on a wall near the school. We didn't vandalize the school, and we intentionally had one of our other guys do the spray-painting, because if we'd have done it in our handwriting, we would've been caught. But sure enough, Monday morning comes and there's a call for 'Lance Armstrong and Chann McRae to the principal's office.' Those two got called in just because they were troublemakers."

They were also two of the school's best athletes but lacked recognition because they opted for alternative sports. Lance has written that in his high school, you only counted if you played football or were rich. He was neither skilled at football nor wealthy. Still, he had "two sets of friends, a circle of popular high-school kids . . . and then my athlete friends, the runners and triathletes." Nonetheless, the popular, moneyed, football-crazed crowd sometimes shunned him: "I was the guy who did weird sports and didn't wear the right labels."

But, as Wilk observes, "If Lance hadn't befriended me and Chann, who weren't into football and baseball and stuff, and he'd just been a guy that went to college, he'd never have known his potential. Lance was always part of the popular crowd, and the popular crowd picked football. If we hadn't been his friends, there's no *way* he'd have ever become a runner, or a cyclist, or a swimmer—not where *we* lived. It's Texas. It's Friday night lights. It's Texas football."

Lance arrived in triathlon just when the sport was taking off, and he knew that in order to advance, he would not only have to step up his training but also keep up with the latest technology. Triathletes compete on special bikes like those that Tour de France cyclists use only in time trials—individual races against the clock, in which the bike has to be as aerodynamically perfect as possible to help shave seconds from the rider's time.

As triathlon was exploding in the late eighties, there was strong competition to produce the most aero bikes and equipment. In 1987, three key innovations went into production: tri-bars, affordable disc wheels, and triathlon-specific bicycles.

American inventor Boone Lennon created the cumbersome-looking but effective Scott DH tri-bars that gave the cyclist a far-forward position (similar to downhill ski racers in an aerodynamic tuck) that enabled the torso to sit parallel to the road. Steve Hed mass-produced carbon-fiber disc wheels, which spin more smoothly through the air than the spokes of regular bicycle wheels, which cause more turbulence. And the Quintana Roo and Kestrel companies both pioneered bikes with steep-angle seat tubes that were needed to keep the rider in this extreme aero position. Road cyclists called them "funny" bikes because of their clunky appearance.

In 1988, Lance transitioned from his first tri' bike, an Italian-built Basso, to one of the first Kestrel carbon-fiber-frame bikes; he later raced on the highly aero Quintana Roo, which had twenty-six-inch wheels, one inch smaller than regular wheels.

As tri' bikes became radically different from regular road bikes, the athletes themselves split into different groups. There was even a feeling of animosity between the traditionalists and the tri' guys. "Lance would show up to our Sunday ride on his Basso funny bike," remembers Craig Staley, then a Dallas area bike racer, "until he eventually got a regular road bike. Okay, now you're normal. We were in the same club, called The High Wheeler—a little tiny shop, single owner—that had club rides. Lance was doing triathlons and just transitioning over to the road."

Lance was also doing the big group training rides that started from Jim Hoyt's Richardson Bike Mart, which sponsored the local Matrix race team. "When Lance first started riding with the team, with Bob Bird and Max Miley," Hoyt says, "they'd stay a hundred yards ahead of him and work his ass over. He'd pull up and say, 'So you don't like triathletes, huh?' But they became friends because he could ride with them. But if they decided, 'We're going to drop his ass,' they could do that because he was very young at the time."

Lance was impressed with the Bike Mart rides. "They were monstrous, tons of people," he says. "They included this group of very talented riders. I thought they were professionals. I didn't know they had real jobs. I said, 'These guys just ride bikes for a living. Imagine that.'"

Lance's friend and neighbor Wilk trained with him just to be able to do the group rides, some of which were as long as seventy miles. "We lived three miles from Southfork, the ranch made famous by *Dallas*, the TV series," he says. "Almost every training route we had went past Southfork. When summer came, we would ride around Lake Lavon, a sixty-five-mile ride. You just take two turns: ride twenty miles, turn, ride another twenty miles, turn, ride home. Most Texas roads are long and straight and flat like that. There's not a hill anywhere. And yet, Lance and Chann would eventually be among the better climbers in professional cycling.

"Our hills on the midweek Bike Mart ride were on a service road that goes up three little rises. They were our mountains. On a forty-five-mile ride, there was a quarter-mile of hills. And you got these two guys who'd end up being these stud climbers."

In 1988, Lance would get to climb some real mountains near San Diego, California. He and John Boggan were spending the summer there before their senior year. Eder helped facilitate the trip. "A friend of ours was going to medical school in San Diego," he says, "so they went out and stayed with this guy. They slept on couches in his apartment." "That was the first time he'd ever gone away, except for short trips," Linda says. "I sent my banana bread mix, which is my signature. And I was sending them puzzles and kites, thinking these guys needed to have some form of entertainment. I was very naïve."

Lance and Boggan soon became part of the San Diego triathlon community. Through that long summer, the two young Texans from Plano swam in the pool at Del Mar, biked the hills of Southern California, and ran along the Pacific coast with many of the top pro triathletes, including Mark Allen, Scott Molina, Dave Scott, and Scott Tinley, who were all in training for October's Hawaii Ironman world championship. "They were the gods," Lance states. "They were the idols, the big four."

"I was there for about eight weeks," Boggan says. "Lance was there the whole twelve weeks. We rode our bikes every day. We did the Wednesday one-hundred-mile ride out to Escondido and Palomar Mountain, which was our first exposure to climbing mountains.

"I did it three times in the eight weeks. I hated it. I thought it was the worst thing ever, climbing that thing. It was brutal. We would ride the twenty miles to the hill, and it was fourteen miles up. Lance would go, 'All right, I'll see you at the top.' He would beat me up those fourteen miles by thirty minutes. And that's when I was in great shape!"

According to Eder, the trip was another turning point for Lance, who was training with cyclists as well as triathletes and comparing the two sports. "I think Lance realized that triathlon was good, but cycling was maybe better as far as payoff," Eder says.

That was part of it, but Lance tells me the real reason he was considering a change in sports was the Olympics. The 1988 Summer Games in Seoul were in the news, and the first events took place on his seventeenth birthday. He'd be almost twenty-one when the next Olympics were held in Barcelona, and he wanted to be there. He just wasn't sure in which sport.

"Triathlon is the most logical Olympic sport," he says, "but there was all this conflict in the tri' world, with all these different governing bodies. It took them forever to sort out which one would be recognized by the IOC [International Olympic Committee], and by the time they finally did, I was off to cycling to make my Olympic bid there. . . . That was the big thing, that was what made me switch.

"The thing about life is that you're always met with these intersections. Sometimes it's a two-way, sometimes it's a five-way, and you've got to decide which way you go. Do you decide you want a sport or academics? If you choose sport, which sport? And then you just meander through that maze: swimming, cycling, triathlon, or running. And where do you go from there?

"There's so much pressure to be an athlete in one of the mainstream sports. But if I had succumbed to peer pressure, I'd have been trying to play baseball and basketball, and I would have completely sucked."

Pressure aside, Lance knew what he wanted. "I can remember Lance was at the house one afternoon," says Jim Hoyt, "and he said, 'Man, I wanna try road racing.' He was riding for us in triathlons at that time."

To compete in cycling, Lance applied for a racing license from the U.S. Cycling Federation. As a beginner, he was given the lowest category, a category 4 junior. His first race was a short, multilap, closed-circuit event, called a criterium. It was held on the Lennox Loop in Richardson, just up the road from Hoyt's Bike Mart. Locals call it the Tuesday Night Crit.

"I knew the people at the registration table," Lance recalls, "and they said, 'You have a cat. 4 license, but we'll let you ride with the cat. 1, 2, 3s; but whatever you do, you can't win the race.' That would give them a lot of grief. So I said, 'Okay. Right!'"

Hoyt was watching the race with his wife, Rhonda. "In the first five minutes, I remember Rhonda said to Lance, 'Go!' and he took off like a rocket." One of the category 1 riders, Kevin Cameron, latched on to Lance's back wheel.

Lance was still very much a triathlete, and he had just fitted to his handlebars the latest item in aero technology, the Scott U-shaped clip-on, which gave him a time-trial-like position on his regular road bike. That helped him pull away from the field, towing Cameron behind him.

"Kevin's a really nice kid, six years older than Lance," Hoyt adds. "He's short and was always powerfully built, and he was good at fighting the winds of Texas on the flat roads at high speeds. That boy could flat-ass turn it on. He's a bike racer, not a bike rider."

Despite Cameron's speed and experience, he soon realized that Lance, the total beginner, had a lot more power than he did. "Kevin said, 'I won't sprint, I won't sprint,'" Lance says. "So if he wasn't gonna sprint, I was gonna win. I considered that for about five seconds and thought, 'Screw it. I'm just gonna take the win.' They can figure out if they want to punish me.

"I ended up winning, and of course the referee realized that I was a cat. 4, and his initial reaction was, 'We're gonna suspend your license.' They discussed it for a couple of weeks and in the end decided that they'd just upgrade me to cat. 3. That was my very first bike race."

So Lance the triathlete, who knew nothing about the tactics and protocol of bike racing, won the race—and his cycling career was launched.

Lance didn't abandon triathlon immediately because he was making good money there, and he knew that paying his own way was important to his mom at a time when her marriage was on unsteady ground. For the same reason, when he wanted to trade up from his Fiat convertible to something more powerful, he turned to his bike sponsor, Hoyt, who guaranteed the car loan for a Chevy Camaro, while Lance made the monthly payments. And when Hoyt put him on a pearl-white Schwinn Paramount OS—"a really fine steel bike; I sold a hundred twenty-five of those rascals that year"—he also fitted Lance's car with a Yakima bike rack to safely transport the new Schwinn.

Benefactors such as Hoyt helped Lance move forward in his chosen sports and took pressure off his mother, who was then working overtime to advance in her job. Lance's mentors also offered emotional support, which helped him get through some hard times in his youth and the pain he felt around Terry and Linda's marriage.

After Linda discovered that Terry was seeing other women—which Lance had suspected ever since he retrieved Terry's love letters from the trash can in the Dallas airport—Linda eventually summoned the courage to tell her second husband to get out of the house and out of her life. When she called Lance and told him what had happened, he says he was "downright joyful."

But Linda regrets that the hypocrisy Lance had witnessed steered her son away from religion. "Terry Armstrong was a preacher's son, and the unfortunate experience that we went through was the hypocrisy," she says. "Those were very formative years for Lance, and I think the pain of what I went through in that marriage and the infidelity that Lance saw gave him a bad taste in his mouth about religion. For that reason, he has a difficult time with his faith journey."

For Linda, faith has always been a source of strength. "No matter what, I always turn to that," she says, "and it's gotten me through a lot." It worries her that Lance doesn't have that to lean on, but she understands why. "You lead by example," she says, "especially with children."

Terry has regrets as well. "If I'd have stayed in church and stayed true to my faith, the infidelity would have never happened," he tells me, his voice quavering. "Do I regret that? Absolutely. And do I regret the way I brought Lance up? Absolutely not."

Terry says he always wanted the best for Lance and always will. "When Linda and I were going to sign our divorce decree," he says, "she asked me, 'Shall we sell the house?' And I said, 'Absolutely not. Lance is going to stay in that house until he graduates from high school. But then, afterwards, the house should be sold.'"

Watching his mother go through the pain of divorce, Lance became more hardened against Terry and increasingly devoted to her. "He saw her struggles, and it made him want to succeed," says his old friend Boggan. That connection was evident that fall when Lance competed in the U.S. national triathlon championships in Hilton Head, where, on the back of his jersey, he had emblazoned these words: "I Love My Mom."

But nothing would make his mother prouder than to see Lance graduate high school and go on to college—a dream that was denied her by a teenage pregnancy. And as he began his senior year at high school, Lance seemed to have both goals within his grasp. Graduation was rarely denied an athlete as talented as he was, and his swim coach, Chris MacCurdy, said he would likely earn an athletic scholarship for college—and might even make the next Olympics in swimming. But Lance had other plans.

Already, local cycling experts felt that Lance had the ability to make a breakthrough at the national level. They were proven right when his mom took him to Moriarty, New Mexico, to race on the fastest time-trial course in the nation. There was an early-morning chill at the event's six-thousand-feet elevation, so Linda gave him her little pink windbreaker to wear in the race. "My mother had become my best friend and most loyal ally," Lance said. "She was my organizer and my motivator, a dynamo." With her cheering him on, Lance raced the 20 kilometers (12.5 miles) at an astonishing 30 miles per hour in a time of 25:03, smashing the national junior record by a stunning 44 seconds.

"He was still a kid, and he hadn't spent a lot of time road riding," says Lance's one-time training partner, Craig Staley. "But the thing about watching him race in those early days was that he had no limits in his mind. He was racing against riders that might have had ten years' experience and who were quite mean and bitter about it—and tough. But there was nothing stopping him. Every other racer was held back by fear or fatigue or whatever, but he had no limits."

Those qualities were also seen by Bart Knaggs, the Austin athlete who first saw Lance at the Waco triathlon and who was now one of the state's top cyclists. "We were in a really hard road race west of Austin," Knaggs says. "Lance got stuck with the main group, and he pulled us all the way in to the finish. He was very upset with how the race turned out. So we were all sitting around recovering, drinking water, and Lance comes out in this frigging bikini, and he goes for like an hour's run—to train for some triathlon! He just had all this energy."

Staley agrees. "What struck me early on about Lance, what really set him apart then and was going to set him apart in the future, was that 'no limits' feeling, that mindset he'd get."

Lance kept racing with that mindset, and in the spring of 1989 it helped earn him an invitation to the tryouts for the U.S. national junior cycling team at the Olympic Training Center in Colorado Springs, Colorado. But because that trip would mean taking a leave of absence from school during the second half of his senior year, the teachers at Plano East warned that it might keep him from graduating—especially since he had missed some classes in his junior year when he was busy traveling to triathlons. Lance heard what they said, but he still went to Colorado.

"I rode the trials because I thought it would be pretty neat to go to Russia as a seventeen year old," Lance says, referring to the world junior cycling championships that July. All he had to do to get on the national team was prove that his reputed bike-racing strength and time-trial speed were for real. The federation coaches saw that quickly enough. "When he was up there on a training camp, he lapped the field," says Hoyt. Lance's reward was a trip to the 1989 worlds in Moscow, along with his friend Chann McRae, who also made the team. But there was bad news as well: The high-school staff decided that the time the two seniors had spent away from school disqualified them from graduating.

"They got railroaded!" their classmate Wilk says. "Because at that time there was another senior, a kick-ass swimmer, that also got selected for worlds. It was okay for *her* to go, but Lance and Chann were told, 'You guys can't do this. You're gonna fail on us.' I think it was more because they were troublemakers, and the girl was a good student."

Lance was infuriated by the school's decision. But his mom kept her cool, and she did everything she could to find a school outside the Dallas public school system that would help her son graduate. She finally found one, Bending Oaks High School, which would help him make up the missed courses so he could get his diploma. The tuition fees were in the thousands of dollars. Ex-husband Terry says that Linda wrote him to ask if he'd help. "I did, and I still have the cancelled check," he tells me.

Terry holds onto that check and to memories of his son. But both Lance and his mother have tried hard to forget that part of their lives and to disown Terry and Eddie, the two men who had married Linda and been a father to Lance. They never see them and rarely speak about them, as if that alone could make them disappear. "I was completely loved by my mother, and I loved her back the same way, and that felt like enough to both of us," Lance has written. But curiously, the two men they reject remain close by.

After leaving south Dallas, Lance's biological father, Eddie Gunderson—whom Linda calls "Eddie Haskell" in her book—made his home in Kemp, Texas, just a fifteen-minute drive from where Lance's grandfather, Paul Mooneyham, lives on Cedar Creek Lake. Eddie went into selling real estate, remarried three times, and had two more children. His life has been lived below the public radar, with a minor blip on January 21, 2008. On that evening, Eddie was stopped by the police after a witness saw him driving erratically, veering into oncoming traffic, about twenty minutes from his home. He failed a sobriety test, and when the officer searched Eddie's Jeep Cherokee, he discovered a large quantity of marijuana and hallucinogenic mushrooms. The Jeep was impounded, and Eddie was taken to jail.

Eddie's mug shot shows a heavyset man in his mid-fifties, with brown eyes, blond shoulder-length hair, and large rimless glasses; he looks confused. First held on bail, he was released on probation after a plea bargain.

As for Lance's stepfather, Terry Armstrong—whom Linda refers to only as "Sales" in her book—he returned to his Christian faith some fifteen years after his divorce, and soon after, met the woman who became his second wife. Terry presently attends a Baptist church in the Plano neighborhood where Linda now lives, worshipping only five minutes from her home.

"You know, there's not a day goes by when I don't pray for Lance," Terry tells me. We are sitting in his office, where pictures of Lance and a painting of Jesus hang on the walls. "The last time I saw him, he was seventeen—I think I'd been gone then three or four months—and I went over to the house and dropped off a birthday present. I believe I gave him a hundred bucks. He was very hateful, very vindictive, due to the circumstances. That was the last time I saw him."

And so, by age seventeen, Lance had everything he wanted: the fast car, the pretty girls, and national acclaim in swimming, triathlon, and cycling. But he was wrong about one thing—it didn't all come easy.

CHAPTER 5

MOVING ON

My high-school buddies all still as heck live in Plano.
I couldn't get out of there quick enough.
—LANCE ARMSTRONG

WITH THE IRON CURTAIN still pulled tightly around the Soviet Union, Lance Armstrong went to Moscow and unveiled his bike-racing strength to the world. He was seventeen when he competed at the 1989 world junior cycling championships. It was his first trip to Europe and his first time competing against an international field. He didn't win, but his performance garnered him more attention than was given the winner, Swiss rider Patrick Vetsch, who led in the mass-sprint to the line.

Before that race, few people outside Dallas had ever heard of Lance. And even during the race, not too many cycling fans were paying attention—since it happened while Greg LeMond was battling to an epic eight-second victory at the Tour de France.

But some key people did take notice. One was Chris Carmichael, a recently retired professional cyclist from Florida. "I was just getting into coaching," Carmichael says, "and I had heard about this kid who was ungodly strong. Most people said, 'He's a triathlete; he's stupid; he doesn't know how to ride his bike.' Then I read the race report in *VeloNews* of the junior world championships."

Another person who noticed Lance was the U.S. team's physician in Moscow, Andy Pruitt, an influential figure in the sport. When Pruitt first saw Lance ride, he thought, "This kid was definitely different. He had the loner mentality of a triathlete; and when we were riding the course beforehand, it became obvious to me that he was superhuman."

Lance's performance in Moscow also made a deep impression on one of his U.S. teammates, Dede Demet, who was there for the junior women's event. Demet won a gold medal in that race and went on to become one of America's most successful female bike racers. She still has clear memories of Lance from that trip to Russia two decades ago.

"He was stocky and strong looking, but lean. He was pretty brash. I remember he attacked only a kilometer or two into the race and rode off the front all day with one Russian guy. Lance got caught in the last kilometer, but he was the workhorse of the duo, and it was really an impressive ride. I think maybe he'd done only five bike races before that, and that made it all the more impressive."

Something else struck Demet at the time. "Lance was still doing triathlons," she says, "and he was very serious about his training. There was a big triathlon [the USAT sprint championships], which he won the year before, that he was preparing for at the end of that summer. I remember being in shock that he did like a ten-mile run with Chann McRae only a few days before the championship race."

Professional bike racers just don't do that; their mantra is: Walk rather than run, sit rather than stand, and lie down rather than sit. Lance and Chann's long run was the exact opposite of that dictum—and it didn't please one of the U.S. team coaches, Connie Carpenter, an Olympic gold medalist in 1984.

"Connie made some pretty strong comments about it, trying to stop them from doing that," Demet remembers. "Connie tends to take control of situations, and so even though she wasn't the men's coach, she wanted them to prepare more like cyclists. But it didn't work. They did what they wanted to do, and that's very much in Lance's character."

The Moscow race was held on the same roller-coaster circuit as the 1980 Olympics. "I prerode the course with Connie," Demet says, "and she told me a specific point on a specific lap to attack, and to sit in the group until then. So I attacked where she told me to, and I rode away and won the race. I was really lucky to have someone like Connie to give me advice and tell me how to race. I don't think Lance had the same kind of advice from the men's coach, Bob Bills."

But at this early point in his cycling career, Lance wasn't listening to *anyone's* advice. His only plan was to blast out of the pack and try to hang on till the end. "I went out way too aggressively," Lance now admits, "and I didn't eat. And that's a weird course in Moscow. It's relentless but not that hard, just those little bursts."

After being out front for more than two hours, Lance was caught and passed by the tight, fast-moving pack on the final lap. He eased back and crossed the finish line in seventy-third place, more than four minutes behind the winner. "At the end of that race I had all kinds of pain," he says. "I was standing up and stretching to ease the back pain, probably due to not having the best position on the bike."

"We had some laughs and tears after it was over," Pruitt recalls. "Lance couldn't figure out how he got beat. He knew he was the strongest guy in the race, but the masses had overcome him. There was some arrogant anger there, especially when Dede went on to win, and the spotlight shifted to the girls' race, and we had a big celebration around Dede in the hotel. He was a pretty arrogant young man. But it was obvious after that foray that there was a great future for him."

Nearly twenty years later, Lance still remembers the "baby-face, doughy-looking" Soviet who stayed with him, lap after lap, during their long but fruitless odyssey on that Moscow course. "It was Heinrich Trumheller," he says, revealing his uncanny memory for people and names. "All he wanted to do then was trade jerseys. I told him to get outta my face. I was bummed out. He had dual Russian-German citizenship, and he raced for the Telekom team as a pro. He was not very good as a pro. That's like a lot of good junior athletes—gone in their early twenties. Guys get distracted . . . girls, alcohol. . . ."

Besides the empirical reason for Lance's defeat in Moscow—group tactics generally overcome individual strength in cycling—Pruitt had another theory. "There are people who perform well when they're angry," he says. "Rocky Balboa talks about the 'eye of the tiger,' and everybody's eye of the tiger comes from a different place. I think Lance grew up mad, and he grew up to show the world whatever he wanted to show them. But in Moscow, he wasn't mad at anybody.

"When he *does* focus his energy, there's not many people gonna get in his way. His eye of the tiger is anger."

Richardson bike-shop owner Jim Hoyt also saw that anger. "Coming back from Moscow, he was having a little trouble with teammates," Hoyt remembers. "In one of the Tuesday Night Crits, his teammate Max Miley beat him in the sprint, despite Lance shoving him and trying to cut him out. So Max slipped off his bike and jumped Lance like a cowboy, got him on the ground. Lance was just mad as a hornet. He called me out, and I ended up taking back his bike. That was the Schwinn Paramount I'd put him on—and on which he did the world junior championships."

Lance was furious about losing his bike, but Hoyt had had it with Lance's shenanigans. Earlier that year, Lance and a friend had borrowed a motor scooter from Hoyt's bike shop to do some motor-paced training; and after they crashed the scooter, Lance put it back in the warehouse without telling Hoyt. "That's what I call a rascal," Hoyt says. Then Lance returned from the Colorado training camp without the $500 bike rack Hoyt had fitted on his car. "He told me so-and-so needed it," Hoyt says. "We had a bit of fuss about that, and I got over it."

But it wasn't so easy for Hoyt to get over the next incident.

It was past midnight when the speeding white sports car raced through the intersection of Interstates 75 and 635 in north Dallas. Within seconds, a police officer had thrown on his car's flashing lights and wailing siren and taken up the chase. The four kids crammed inside the Chevy Camaro IROC-Z28 had been partying at a nightclub in Deep Ellum, the trendy warehouse district east of downtown Dallas.

As soon as they heard the police siren, one of the kids shouted, "We've gotta stop! We've gotta stop!" Instead, the IROC driver, Lance, gunned the throbbing five-liter, 190-horsepower engine, and his car roared toward its top speed of 130 miles per hour. "That thing was fast, Dickens too fast," says Adam Wilk, who was in the passenger seat that night. "And we were drinking."

Maybe Lance thought he could outrun the cops. In a minute, he'd be through the Dallas city limits, into Richardson and hurtling past Hoyt's Richardson Bike Mart. It might have flashed through Lance's mind that Hoyt had enabled him to buy the IROC. ("I cosigned a note for him on that car," says Hoyt. "What I didn't realize was the car was in my name.")

But as he raced through Richardson, Lance's attention was focused on controlling a charging, two-ton mass of metal at a speed he'd never driven before. And even though there was little traffic at that hour on I-75, temporary construction walls restricted the roadway to two lanes. "It was real narrow," remembers Wilk, growling to mimic the sound of the IROC's revved-up engine bouncing back from the concrete walls.

Lance and his three buddies were soon out of Richardson, but a third police car was waiting for them as they entered the city of Plano. On familiar roads, only three miles from home, Lance knew where to exit the highway, and he knew there was a friend's party going on that night not far from the Collin Creek Mall, which they were just passing.

"We ditched the car at the exit right before Park Boulevard and jumped out," says Wilk, "because there was nothing out there back then, just a few houses. Lance and I got away because we weren't that drunk. We could run. We just went and hid in the field. Laid low. The two other guys were blitzed. One guy didn't get out of the car, and Steve Lewis got caught at the McDonald's on the corner."

One of their other buddies, John Boggan, remembers, "I was at the high-school party Lance was coming to. I think he made it on foot." "If it hadn't have been for his legs," Terry Armstrong says, "he'd have been in the hoosegow."

While Lance was hanging out at the party, the police were trying to locate the owner of the abandoned car. "At about three o'clock in the morning, the Richardson police pulled me out of my house at gunpoint," Hoyt recalls. "Lance and his IROC had outrun them, so the police impounded the car and found it was in my name. I was not real happy about that."

Hoyt wasn't taken to the police station that night, but that wasn't the end of the story. "A week later," he says, "I was downtown working with the chief of detectives and chief of police on a bicycle safety program. I was planning to get the car out of the pound and drive it home. But after the two chiefs leave, an officer comes out the door—and they arrest me! They said there were outstanding speeding tickets. Lance was notorious for his speeding tickets. Also, I didn't realize my own insurance was tied to that car, too, which explained why my insurance rates kept going up. . . . I spoke to Linda, his mother, and said Lance doesn't get the car back until he talks to me, and see if we can iron this out."

It would be a while before that would happen. Wilk says Lance disappeared for a couple of weeks after ditching the IROC. And what went down next is told to me by Bob Mionske, a friend Lance would make on the national cycling team.

"I'll tell you the quick version of what he told me about that car," Mionske says. "Lance said he never apologized, and a couple of weeks later he's racing at the Stockyards in Fort Worth. It was a criterium, and he was a junior at the time. Before the start, and within earshot of Lance, Jim Hoyt says, 'There's a hundred dollars to the first guy that takes Armstrong down.' The other kids in the race are probably like, 'You're kidding, right?' But Lance heard that, and he lapped the field twice. And when he was on the podium, he was like, 'I want to dedicate my win to Jim Hoyt.' And he looked right at him, and Jim's just glaring back, because Lance had turned it on him."

Hoyt and Lance wouldn't talk to each other again for almost ten years. Hoyt kept the impounded IROC for seven months before taking it for a short drive—"It was so powerful I spun it around in the street," he says, "and so I sold it."

When Lance turned eighteen, his life was in transition. High school was finished, and college wasn't on his agenda. He was still competing in triathlons and doing well. "He destroyed everyone at the national sprint championship in Ventura, Florida, that fall," recalls his one-time mentor Scott Eder, who by now was in Lance's rear-view mirror. "But he was already into cycling pretty big time." Not only into it, but winning practically every race he entered. Lance knew that his future was in cycling. If things went the way he hoped—and he could overcome his mother's reluctance on his choice of careers—he would compete at the 1992 Olympics before becoming a full-time professional.

It was around that time I interviewed Lance, the up-and-coming racer, for the first time. It was also the first time I received a letter from an interviewee's mother. Linda wrote to thank me for the story I wrote, and, specifically, for not portraying her son as just a cocky young kid. As Lance was gaining more recognition, he was also getting advice from all quarters on how to advance his career. This was the era before cell phones and e-mail, when people communicated by old-fashioned phones, faxes, and U.S. mail. I was then editing America's main competitive cycling magazine, *VeloNews*, and I received a fax from two of Lance's cycling friends in Dallas. They asked if I could help Lance find a European team so he could learn how to race in the sport's traditional home. I wrote to Swiss cycling guru Paul Köchli—he directed Greg LeMond to his first Tour de France victory—and said, "What can you do for this young guy from Texas? He's not built like Greg, but he could well be America's next Tour winner. Can you help?"

I got a fax back from Paul, who was then the sports director of a Swiss pro team, Helvetia. He said he could get Lance into a French club team, the U.S. Creteil-Lejeune, which he was using as a feeder for his pro squad. It could have been a terrific start, but Lance's life was heading in a different direction.

Word of his potential had spread rapidly through the inside network of American cycling. Among its more respected leaders was Eddie B—short for Borysewicz—a Polish émigré who arrived in the United States in 1976, became the first full-time national coach at the U.S. Cycling Federation, and coached the 1984 U.S. team that won America's first Olympic cycling medals in seventy years. He left the federation three years later to get into pro cycling and, for 1989, he set up a team with the help of Thom Weisel, a successful financier (and amateur bike racer) who ran a San Francisco brokerage firm, Montgomery Securities. They obtained title sponsorship from a Japanese car company, Subaru, which was just establishing itself in the North American market. Eddie B and Weisel's goal was to grow Subaru-Montgomery into a team that could one day race the Tour de France. They started out with a modest budget and were building a roster of experienced pro racers and emerging amateur talent.

One of the calls they received was from Mike Fraysse, an official with the cycling federation, who had helped Eddie B get established in the United States a dozen years before. Speaking in his clipped, heavily accented English, Eddie B recalls, "Mike call me and told me, 'Eddie, you always looking for talent, there's some animal in Texas'—that's exactly his words—'so would you like to check him out?' And he give me his telephone number.

"So I call Lance and tell him I'm going to be in Austin for a race. So I went to race, and after race we talk. One of my questions was about his health: 'Have you had some sickness in the past?' He told me, 'No, never.' He never was sick. Okay, did you have the flu? No. A headache? No. So I say, 'Man, that's impossible.' And mom was with him, and mom say, 'No, he was never sick.' How about dental stuff? 'My teeth is perfect.' So I talk a little bit with mom. I introduced myself as I'm looking always for young guys for develop. And I say to him, talk to your mom, talk to your friends, and when you like to be with us, give me call."

Now in his mid-sixties and working as a consultant and part-time coach, Eddie B lives in a rural part of Southern California, near Escondido. Continuing his story about Lance, he says, "He send me blood test and VO_2 test in one week. So when I receive this I said to him, 'Get to Escondido, because we have a clubhouse. Live over there with a few guys like Mike McCarthy [who raced in the 1988 Olympics].' And he show up, and when we talk I say, 'We can offer you twelve thousand dollars.' He was very honest. He told me, 'I not deserve that.' I say, 'You resolve, not deserve.'

"And I said, 'That's deal, huh? To have food on the table and don't be worry about money.' Because at this time, he was poor guy. So must give him money to be comfortable and think only about cycling. And we start work together. He was very coachable, very nice, very honest. All the time, I have good feeling about him."

The feeling was mutual, so Lance signed with Subaru-Montgomery. In addition to the stipend, he would be given team bikes and clothing and have his travel expenses reimbursed. Linda realized her son would need a credit card, which was then virtually impossible to obtain for a teenage kid without a real job and no equity.

"I said to Lance, 'Why don't I write my American Express company and ask if I can co-sign for you to get a card, and I'll send them a copy of your contract.' Well, lo and behold, they sent me a credit card with the name 'Lance Armstrong' on it. And that was during a time when people didn't really have credit cards," Linda says. "Today, he's got this black American Express card, and I've still got the regular one. And the black card is apparently carte blanche—you can buy the moon if you want to."

Shooting for the moon was the credo for young Lance. "When he came back from seeing Eddie B in Escondido," Linda recalls, "he says, 'Mom, I'm probably gonna live in California.' And, of course, I wasn't ready to think about him leaving, let alone move to California. That was way too far."

Lance was attracted by the climate, the hills, and the ocean of Southern California, but he wasn't sure if he should move there—and eventually decided against it. All he really knew was he didn't want to remain where he was, in the fast-growing northern suburbs of Dallas. "My high-school buddies all still as heck live in Plano," Lance says. "I couldn't get out of there quick enough." He was about to meet the man who would help him make that move.

John Thomas Neal was one of the most influential players in Lance's life. He was also one of the quirkiest, smartest, and most gregarious people he'd ever meet. J. T., as everyone called him, was short and sprightly and had a bouncy quality about him. He walked fast, talked fast, and seemed to smile and talk at the same time. "A world-class character," Lance says.

A graduate of the University of Texas law school, J. T. practiced as an attorney before becoming a real estate entrepreneur in Austin. He lived with his wife and children in an upscale neighborhood west of town; and his wealth enabled him to do the things he loved: giving massage and looking after swimmers, triathletes, and cyclists who came through Austin.

"I met J. T. at the 1990 Tour of Texas. I just came out to watch the race," Lance says. "J. T. was the massage therapist there for Subaru-Montgomery. Then I saw him at the state championships. 'Listen,' he said. 'I've got this place that's becoming available for rent. It's open in June.' I said, 'I'll be there.'"

Lance's aunt remembers how his mom reacted to Lance's move to Austin, the Texas capital, which is 220 miles south of Plano. "When Lance left, I sensed Linda's sorrow, her loss of him not being there," Debbie says. "But he had to move on. That was critical.

"I don't think she really knew if he could make something of it. But he believed in what he was doing all the time. And then he had that braggadocious side, that cockiness—and that provoked everybody, my dad as well. When he moved out and went down to Austin, that hurt! Linda was smashed by that."

Linda admits, "It left a hole in my heart. It wasn't that I depended so much upon him; it was just all the wonderful, fun things that we did together. I'd never been alone, and I didn't have any hobbies, didn't have any real outlets because nights and weekends were devoted to Lance, and then I worked in the day."

Lance says he had no idea Linda would be upset by his move. "That was a hard day for my mother. She was very upset," he says. "I didn't think it would be like that."

"Still," Linda says, "I realized it was a good stepping-stone for both of us. And as much as I was sad, I was so happy for him. First, I knew he would be in good hands with J. T.—J. T. was just a gem. And I think those first two years that he was in Austin, had it not been for J. T., I don't think it would have gone so well. So J. T. gets every bit of the credit. He was his 'mom' down in Austin."

Lance felt in sync with J. T., more than he ever had with his stepfather, Terry, or early mentor Eder, or bike-shop owner Hoyt. "J. T. was funny. He bitched about everything but in a sweet way," says Lance, who then goes into a riff, perfectly mimicking J. T.'s mannerisms and high-pitched Arkansas accent. "'Lance, you're drinking too much. I *know* you're drinking too much. It's wintertime, you're out there with your buddies, you're drinking all that beer' . . . 'Goddamn it, you're looking *fat*, Lance, you're looking fat, boy.' And he'd go on about the girls. 'Lance, too many girls around. You gotta get serious now.' . . . Or I'd take a leak for him for analysis. 'Look at it, goddamn it, you're not drinking enough water. Your piss is *yellow*, Lance. You've got to drink more.' For me, it was like, what-*ever*. He was a great, great character."

Besides taking care of Lance and giving him massages, J. T. helped him settle in his new hometown. "J. T. just liked to help," Lance says, "and he didn't need to be rewarded financially. His wife was like my mother. I was over there all the time when I first moved here.

"Back then, Austin was really cool. The original Whole Foods was there, a little dumpy place on Lamar. I'd walk down there from my place. J. T. and I were always hanging out at a diner near there, having lunch together."

Austin was also the hometown of Bart Knaggs, who'd been in a couple of races with Lance and finally got to meet him while riding home from a local Tuesday night race. Five years older than Lance, Knaggs had already graduated from college and was working a full-time job. His intelligence and maturity helped their relationship develop, as did Knaggs's knowledge of all the best back roads for training in the Texas Hill Country—which was a huge improvement over the flat terrain Lance used to ride in Plano. And the more the two rode together, the closer they became.

"One of the hardest things about being a bike racer is finding someone you can manage to train with," Knaggs says, "because training takes so much time. It's four or five hours side-by-side for five, six, seven days a week. It's good if you can still talk and tolerate each other . . . and we got on really well."

Knaggs summarizes the Lance he met then as being "really tough-minded, didn't have excuses, didn't believe in God, didn't need this or that, didn't need his father, didn't need resolution with his dad, and was very mature. He was a man at eighteen or nineteen."

"Also," Knaggs adds, "Lance didn't know that he was smart then because people told him he was dumb. But when you got started talking about anything, he'd go straight to the heart of it. He would go, 'What the fuck, why was that, what about that, who's this guy, why didn't you do this, how does that work?' He would have so many questions.

"You just knew that this guy was going to achieve what he wanted to achieve. He never thought he was the ideal cyclist, but a close-enough fit. He was insatiable about the shit he cared about, and there were three pretty simple things at that time: girls, business, and biking. On our rides, he didn't want to talk about biking because that's what you do. No, he wanted to know, for example, what's going on with Whole Foods, what's their stock up to? He wasn't consumed with bikes."

Linda still wasn't sure that Austin was the best choice for her son. "It suited Lance's lifestyle, let me just say that," she says. "J. T. ran a lot of interference for him, like I did up here. . . . But it didn't feel good to have to lose Lance. I'm sure I was in a state of depression. It seemed that the only true happiness I ever had back then was when the two of us were together."

Soon, though, Linda realized one great benefit of Lance's move: J. T. Neal. "I really think had it not been for him that Lance could never have found his way," she says softly, remembering the upbeat man who would die young. "It gave me comfort to know that J. T. was there, and we got to be close. I just loved him, loved him."

"If there's one common thread to Lance's story, it's Linda," Debbie says. "But J. T. played a huge part."

CHAPTER 6

HERE COMES THE KING

Physically, you've got it. But until you understand how the intricacies of bike racing work, you're never going to be able to win a world championship.

—CHRIS CARMICHAEL

LANCE WAS ANGRY when he first met Chris Carmichael. The date was June 11, 1990; the place, Chicago's O'Hare International Airport. They were headed in opposite directions. Carmichael was on his way home from two weeks in the United Kingdom, where he coached the U.S. national A-team at the Tour of Britain. Lance was on his way out, to compete with the national B-team at the Tour of Sweden. Both were feeling their way in new careers: Carmichael as the national team coach, Lance as a full-time amateur bike racer.

"Lance was upset at me because he was put on the B-team, and Bobby Julich went on the A-team, and they were the same age, two juniors moving into the senior ranks. He thought *I* did that," says Carmichael. "I explained to him, 'Look, I came on as the national coach after this selection was made, so I'm inheriting this. And I don't care if Bobby Julich is getting favoritism, because now I'm the national coach, and if you want to go to the A-team, you've got to prove yourself.'

"Lance said, 'You know, I'm gonna make you eat your words, Chris Carmichael, because I'm gonna prove to you that I'm the best damn rider there is out there.' And I said, 'I'm looking forward to that.' He thought I was gonna be angry with him, and I wasn't. I just said, 'Please show me.'"

It was a challenge Lance couldn't resist. "I was pissed that I was put on the B-team," he recalls. "I was super-motivated to prove people wrong. That's the reason I was at the Tour of Sweden."

But stepping up from two-hour junior events to four-hour senior amateur races takes most athletes several years' of adjustment. And in that first year, Lance not only had to cope with longer distances but he was also being thrown into pro-am races, competing against hardened professionals. That was the case at the Tour of Sweden, a week-long stage race that began a few days after his airport conversation with Carmichael. Several of the teams were even using the Swedish race to prep for the Tour de France.

"We were racing against guys like Jean-François Bernard," Lance said to me, soon after competing in Sweden, referring to the French star who was third in the 1987 Tour and won a stage atop the mythic Mont Ventoux. "I really fell in love with the sport at that race," Lance added, exhilaration in his voice. "I love the whole 'rock and roll' business in Europe. It's a big scene, and I want to be part of it."

That Lance would eventually become part of the European scene, where cycling champs are treated like rock stars, seemed inevitable.

He quickly realized that his new sport has the same sort of magic and mystique across the Atlantic that baseball and football do in America. But he also saw that behind the glamour of bike racing is a dogged, blue-collar harshness that he experienced for the first time in Sweden.

"The hardest pro or high-level experience I've ever had was at that Tour of Sweden," Lance says. "I would lie in bed at night and just go. . . ." He hangs his head, not finishing the sentence. "I was so dead. My body was constantly resisting the urge not to get on the bike the next day. It was an out-of-body experience."

It was a tough race for an eighteen-year-old kid, but for him just to finish was impressive. Good results were not that essential in this early period of Lance's international career. More important, he needed to learn how to race like a European in these high-level cycling events. As a triathlete, he would race "at the redline," at the point of exhaustion, from start to finish. Now, he would have to change from expending a steady, high level of energy in a mostly solo effort to conserving energy in the shelter of the pack, or *peloton*, as it's universally called, until the defining moments of a race. Lance would have a hard time learning that essential lesson.

A keen observer of Lance's naïveté was Len Pettyjohn, who was a Denver University professor before he became one of America's top cycling team directors. In 1990, he was directing the Coors Light pro squad that competed in most of the American races that Lance rode with Eddie B's Subaru-Montgomery team.

"My first impression of Lance was just another brash, inexperienced national team guy," Pettyjohn tells me, as we sit on the porch of his neo-Victorian home in Boulder. "We used to make fun of kids like that—'just another pony head'—because they would ride up to the front of the peloton and kind of get in the way. He was a little distinctive in that he would just charge off the front. It was almost always inappropriate. You could see that he had a pretty big motor, but no control, no real consideration or thought of what he was doing. After one race, somebody asked Lance why he attacked when he attacked—because he was alone for a long time off the front, and then he got caught and was dropped. Lance's comment was, 'I felt good.' Hearing this as he walked by, one of the guys on our team goes, 'Yeah, everybody felt good then.'

"The point was, you don't attack when *everybody* feels good. We kind of chuckled about it, and he kept doing it, race after race. But you could see he was gonna be the strongest guy on the national team."

Pettyjohn says that Lance's arrival on the national squad—he was soon upgraded to the A-team—was difficult for some of the older, more experienced team members to accept. This was so for John Lieswyn, one of Pettyjohn's amateur team members. "Lieswyn had this impression of himself as being equal to or better than anybody else, and he couldn't accept or understand why all of a sudden Carmichael and all of us looked to Lance as being the best guy on the team."

One rider who had no problem accepting Lance's leadership role was Bob Mionske. Mionske was the reigning U.S. amateur champion, and he had finished in a brilliant fourth place at the Olympic Games road race in 1988. "It didn't bother me if one of my teammates was the best guy in the world," Mionske says. "I think that was different for Bobby Julich, Chann McRae, and the other guys. They were a little envious, whereas I was just glad to be where I was. That gave me the ability to talk more easily to Lance."

Mionske, who's now an attorney, was not a typical Olympic athlete. Nine years older than Lance, he had a degree in psychology before becoming a full-time bike racer. His intelligence and openness were attractive qualities to a young kid.

Mionske meets me at a San Francisco café to talk about Lance. He's wearing jeans, a faded World Peace T-shirt, and dark glasses, and he starts off by recalling their first encounter.

"We were driving down to training camp in Austin on the Interstate going eighty to ninety miles an hour over these rollers," says Mionske, who speaks with a deep Midwest accent. "Lance was driving his late-model BMW, and we were telling each other stories, trying to feel each other out. We have similar backgrounds. We both had young moms, and dads that abandoned us, and both of us were sort of alpha males and never backed down to anybody. He had a lot more physical ability on a bike, but I have physical ability in other ways.

"My mom was a waitress in Illinois and gave me up to foster care. I ended up living with my cousins, and when I finally got back with my mom she had married an ex-convict who beat up a cop. So it's been an adventure, you know. He was very aggressive, and I learned to stand up to him. Kids at school never beat me up after that because I was never frightened. And if you're not frightened, no one bothers you. I've used that the rest of my life . . . and I think Lance has, too.

"So Lance and I were driving down the Interstate, speeding, and a cop coming the other way put on his lights and turned around. I just said, 'Go, go!' We took the first exit and screamed down this country road. It dead-ended in the parking lot of a boy's camp, where we came skidding to a halt, and everyone's looking at us. We'd lost the cop, but we sat and cooled our heels for half an hour just to make sure."

After that initial bonding, Lance and Mionske deepened their friendship in the two-year build-up toward the Barcelona Olympics. Lance proved he was there for him, Mionske says, once in a race and once in a personal crisis. "I had to get from Dallas to San Jose in a hurry," he says, starting off with the personal. "I'd broken up with the woman I was dating, when she agreed to take me back. And Lance promised to give me a ride to the airport from the house I was staying at. Anyways, I'm waiting and waiting, and I'm getting panicked.

Finally, I run inside to call for a taxi just as he comes ripping around the corner in his BMW.

"We throw my stuff in the back, and he drives through every stop sign in Highland Park, a real tony neighborhood in Dallas. We're soon flying down the Interstate until we merge onto this other highway. The cars are stopped as far as you can see, and he felt guilty for coming so late. And he's like me—he just goes for it. He steered onto the shoulder and just floored it, right alongside a retaining wall. It's three lanes of stopped traffic and we're passing them at seventy-five miles an hour on the inside! We were driving through dust and dirt, and it was kicking up a fog. When you looked back you couldn't even see the cars; it was just dust. I thought, 'This might not end well,' but we just kept the hammer down anyways. I really wanted to make that flight, and I ran straight through the airport on adrenaline. I ended up seeing my girlfriend . . . and marrying her. Thanks to Lance."

Then there was the deed Lance did for his friend at an early-season Texas bike race called the Primavera. Mionske says he had pretty good form, and even though he was weakened by a stomach virus, he hoped to impress the rep from his team's new sponsor who was watching. It was the last stage of the multiday race, and Lance needed to gain some time to overcome two national team veterans, Kent Bostick and John Frey. Mionske had a plan: Make a surprise early attack to take advantage of a wind that was blowing sideways after a stormy night.

"I told Lance, 'Let's put it in the gutter right off the bat,'" Mionske says. "And when he came through for his pull, I could see he was gonna really floor it, so I moved up and got right on his wheel. He only gave me about an inch, and he just kept it floored for probably two, three miles. When I turned around, I could see a long ways behind us, and we'd dropped the whole national team *and* all the other teams. The only guy still with us was Bostick, and he was just about hanging on.

"Lance would even pedal on the downhills. I was tucked in behind him, almost touching his wheel, but I was convinced that my brakes were rubbing because I couldn't feel the draft. I realized when we dropped Kent on a downhill that there was nothing wrong with my brakes. Lance was just going ultrafast. So then it was just Lance and me.

"I started flagging because my dysentery started to hit, and I told Lance, 'I've gotta win this race because the sponsor's here. And that's the deal.' He said, 'Yeah, whatever.' I never asked for a race my whole life, and I didn't really ask for it then, but he understood. Then we were about four hundred meters from the line—and he goes flying by me! But then he sits up, turns around, and gives me a big smile. He could have just ridden away from me, but he let me have it . . . though I still had to sprint really hard to get the win."

While Mionske embraced Lance as a leader of the national team, others were put off by the guy they considered a Texas cowboy. "There was a lot of resistance from the older guys," Carmichael says. "They didn't like him. And there were a lot of reasons *not* to like him. First, they were scared of him because he was very, very strong. And he was aggressive—he'd say, 'I wanna kick your butt.' He was just a young kid coming in, and he dressed different to how they dressed. There was this generation gap."

Carmichael, who'd eventually become Lance's personal coach before founding Carmichael Training Systems, is speaking to me at his company's Colorado Springs headquarters, a converted grain warehouse. He's probably the least pretentious CEO in the country, typically wearing jeans, casual shirts, and a baseball cap. He's in his late forties, but a wave of blond hair flopping over a smooth forehead gives him a boyish air.

"I was still an athlete in 1989 when I became national coach," he recalls, "and I knew there was a lot of feeling to keep the old team together. But I followed a similar tactic to Eddie B when he first came into U.S. cycling: Focus your efforts on the youngest athletes. So I decided not to put much effort into the older guys, but help the younger group led by Lance, Chann, and Julich."

The season highlight for the national team was always the world amateur road championships, which in 1990 would be held in Utsunomiya, Japan. The previous year, the U.S. team had placed fourth in the 100km team time trial—an event in which the four-man teams start at three-minute intervals and race as fast as they can for that 60-plus-mile distance. The best time wins.

"We had a team time trial camp going into the Japan worlds," Carmichael says. "Lance was the strongest guy in the tests, so I kept putting him in situations where he could challenge the older group of riders, by rotating them in two-man time trials. And Lance was always coming out on top. When it came to doing four-man trials, they wanted to keep their old team intact, and they didn't want to bring Lance in. So I said, 'Look, I'm sorry, we're bringing Lance in. He's continued to perform the best. This is the team.' And only John Frey didn't have a problem with it. So we put Lance in that team time trial, and he blew the whole team apart. Those guys were begging for mercy.

"It was clear that Lance should go to Japan. And once he gets himself situated, he's very much a team player. As a first-year amateur, age eighteen, there was a lot of concern: Could he ride both events, the team time trial and then the road race? A lot of the coaches thought it was too much to ask of a young guy. And it was. But we had two riders break collarbones in a preparation race, so Lance did both events. If nothing else, he'd gain experience."

Staging the world championships in Asia for the first time demonstrated how the European sport of cycling was finally reaching out to the rest of the world. It was a process that would accelerate through the 1990s as satellite television and then the Internet brought cycling to an ever wider audience. The tradition-bound sport was changing fast, and it was searching for a personality who could offer global appeal—someone like Lance.

Already, he was making a big impression on those who came in close contact with him. One of these was Dede Demet, who, like Lance, had stepped up from the national junior team that went to Moscow to the senior squad headed for Japan. She explains why, as Carmichael suggested, not everyone on the team was happy with Lance's arrival.

"On the trip to the world championships in Japan," Demet says, "everybody started calling him the King. It was almost like a joke. He *was* pretty loud in terms of giving his opinion, and he always had a stronger voice. A lot of the older riders were taking the piss out of him because they thought that Lance *thought* he was the King. But I think Lance kind of liked that."

The older riders may have been mocking Lance before the competition began, but by the end of the week he had their respect.

The first event was the team time trial, which is extremely demanding. Each of the four riders takes his turn at the front to relay his teammates at more than thirty miles per hour for almost two hours. Lance says it's still his favorite event in cycling, partly because of its toughness, and also because each man has to implicitly trust his three teammates in what is essentially a demanding team-building exercise.

The team time trial requires an almost military approach, which is why teams from the Soviet bloc countries usually dominated the worlds through the eighties and early nineties. They were expected to dominate again in Japan.

That didn't deter Lance, despite being the youngest rider in the field. His teammates were all eight to ten years older, yet he was the leader of the U.S. foursome, the one who dictated their pace. Two of his teammates, Jim Copeland and Nate Reiss, were, like Lance, also on Eddie B's Subaru-Montgomery team; the other team member was Nathan Sheafor.

"Lance was very strong in the team time trial, and the whole team rode great," Carmichael recalls. In fact, at half distance, the four Americans were winning, with a clear lead over the Soviets and East Germans. It looked as if they were on the verge of one of the greatest performances in U.S. amateur cycling history—until two mechanical problems cost them a couple of minutes, and they ended up in seventh.

Lance had only two days to recover from that extreme effort before tackling his main event, the 115-mile road race. Carmichael spoke to him before the start. "I told Lance, 'The goal is to get through this road race and not just go to the halfway point, not to look at it just as experience. So I want you to go into this road race with the mindset to be the world champion.' And he says, 'That's the way I will do it.' I think he liked me telling him that."

For Lance, his "no limits" mindset meant making an early assertion of his strength—just as he had done a year before in the junior championship in Moscow. He figured that it was smart to race from the front on a nine-mile circuit that included a really steep hill they had to tackle twelve times.

"Lance should have won that race," Demet says. "He was clearly the strongest rider, but he just rode really stupid again. Gave too much too soon. He went very, very early in the breakaway, and still finished eleventh. That was the best any American had done at the worlds in years, but he was super frustrated. I can remember Chris Carmichael being pretty proud of him, though, because he showed he had the strength to win. We all went for a beer after the race, and Chris was pleased at how strong Lance was. He told him, 'You've got to refine your skills and learn how to race tactically. But there's no reason why you can't win the worlds one day.'"

Carmichael confirms that conversation, saying he told Lance, "You had a good race, but you've got to change how you ride this thing; you can't do this in the future. Now, everybody knows who you are, so you've got to up your game and realize that there's a whole mental aspect to this. Physically, you've got it, and we need to keep developing that aspect. But until you understand how the intricacies of bike racing work, you're never going to be able to win a world championship or an Olympic Games."

The only way an American racer can learn "the intricacies of bike racing" is to compete in Europe. Traditionally, cyclists from English-speaking countries have based themselves in Belgium and the Netherlands, where there are races almost every day through the spring and summer. That's where Carmichael went as a young racer in 1981—and won nine times—but he had a different plan for Lance.

"Going to Europe was a big turning point in Lance's career," Carmichael says. "I took him to Italy on the national team when he was nineteen. A lot of people thought he should have gone to race in Belgium because it suits a big guy like him. But he needed to learn finesse. He grew up in Plano, Texas, which is dead flat with a lot of wind. And going to Italy really teaches you to become a professional bike racer. He would have to get over big climbs and learn how to position himself in the peloton. He could really evolve there, whereas Belgium is a specialty type of racing, with cobblestones, narrow roads, lots of rain and wind."

Lance agreed: "I've got to learn to be smart, and I started to learn that under Carmichael."

The highlight of the national team's Italy campaign in April 1991 was a multiday stage race called the Settimana Bergamasca. It would prove to be a milestone in Lance's amateur career, teaching him the skills of racing as Carmichael expected, while also offering insights into loyalty, backroom deals, and the politics of the sport.

Besides having to compete against Italy's top amateur racers, including a young upstart named Marco Pantani, the U.S. national team had to contend with several pro teams. This was a transitional period for cycling, when there was a clear divide between amateur and professional cyclists, and they could only compete against each other in officially sanctioned pro-am races, like this one in the Bergamo province of northern Italy.

A situation like this could sometimes cause conflict-of-interest problems—as it did for Lance at the Bergamasca. He was racing there for the U.S. national amateur team, but also in the field was the Subaru-Montgomery pro squad, directed by Eddie B—who had nurtured Lance's talent and shared his wisdom with him and who was paying him a thousand dollars a month. One of the men on the Subaru-Montgomery roster was Reiss, a rider who had raced with Lance in the team time trial in Japan the previous year. As a result, the situation in Italy was potentially explosive—for Lance, Eddie B, and Carmichael.

"When I started in cycling at sixteen, seventeen years old, I was on the national junior team," Carmichael says, "and Eddie B was the coach. I was one of those younger athletes under Eddie, along with Greg LeMond, Ron Kiefel, and Davis Phinney. Now here I am, thirty years old, I'm the national coach, and Eddie is Lance's coach at Subaru. That proved a bit of a tug-of-war—especially at the Bergamasca."

While Subaru and the other pro teams stayed at nice hotels, Carmichael's national squad was surviving on a shoestring budget. When several of his riders fell sick, the coach called in Massimo Testa, a young family practitioner from nearby Como. Testa had worked for the 7-Eleven team as a sports doctor and unofficial trainer when Carmichael was on the team.

"I drove over to see them after work, so I got there at about 9:30 at night," Testa recalls. "They were all piled up in one room, six riders in the room—Lance, Chann McRae, Fred Rodriguez, Steve Larsen, and two others—sharing bunk beds. It was above a pizzeria that was very loud. And three or four of them were sick, so I had to go to a pharmacy to get some antibiotics."

Despite their lowly accommodations, the young guys in the Stars and Stripes managed to be competitive in the ten-day race. After five stages, Italy's Mariano Piccoli was firmly in the overall lead. "Then there was this stage where real nasty weather blew in with rain and sleet," Carmichael says. "We were well prepared, and Lance did well and went up to second on the General Classification [GC], right behind Nate Reiss." Reiss took over the red-and-yellow leader's jersey—the equivalent of the *maillot jaune* at the Tour de France—because he was third on that stage; and Piccoli, who didn't race well in cold weather, lost several minutes.

"The next day, Eddie B told Lance he should work for his Subaru-Montgomery teammate Nate Reiss, and Lance came back to me in the follow car and told me that," Carmichael says. "And I said, 'No, you're not. You're here racing for the national team."

Lance confirms the conversation. "I didn't have any problem in not working," he says, "and I said, 'Look, Eddie, I'm not going to work against him, but I'm not going to kill myself to make him win.'"

When I ask Eddie B about the incident, he recalls it somewhat differently. He remembers his Subaru team defending Reiss's lead against the Italians for the next few stages and doesn't mention asking Lance for any support. But Carmichael insists that "Eddie confronted me after one of these stages, and he said, 'Lance rides for me. He rides for my team. I pay his salary.' And I said, 'Eddie, this is the national team. He doesn't ride for you. He rides for the U.S. team here.' It was very confrontational.

"Eddie had developed a close relationship with Lance, and he felt betrayed. We talked about it, and there was a tough mountain stage coming up, and Lance says, 'There's no way Nate Reiss is gonna be there. He's not gonna be there. I don't even need to attack him.' I said, 'Well, you know, personally, I think you should attack if you want to win this race.' And he says, 'Look, I plan to.'"

Until late in the decisive stage, Reiss was still in with a chance of holding on to the race lead. Then, according to Eddie B, he had some bad luck. "Nate had flat tire," Eddie B says in his clipped Polish accent. "So we change wheel—and all Italian professional teams go to front and hammer."

The pro teams' acceleration began to split the race apart, and that made it tough for Reiss to chase back to the leaders on his own. He needed help, so Eddie B drove up to the main pack to speak to his other riders—this being before radio communication existed. When he finally reached the peloton, he told his entire team—but not Lance—to wait for Reiss.

Lance saw it differently. "Nate Reiss and I never got on that well," Lance says. "He was in the leader's jersey and got dropped. And they wanted me to wait for him."

"The finish was on circuit," Eddie B goes on, "and after full lap chasing very hard, my guys bring Nate back to peloton."

"Nate ended up catching us," Lance confirms, "but then there was a lot of fighting. The Italians kicked one of the Subaru guy's bars and he fell off his bike, and other Subaru riders kicked back."

"It was last lap and uphill finish," Eddie B continues, "and Nate was tired because he work hard; he lost about forty seconds to stage winner. And Lance, because he started day in second overall, became leader of the race."

"After the stage, when I took the jersey," Lance adds, "Eddie B launched into me. He said, 'We're not going to pay you, and we'll kick you off the team.'"

Eddie B says, "Of course, Lance not help my guys chase, which was fine, because he was second guy on GC. The problem was, did he want to be with my team or be with national team only? Then, because he was race leader, he didn't want to do any team work. So I say, fine, okay."

Lance took the overall race lead, but he had just a few seconds' advantage over his nearest challenger, Fabio Bordonali, a seasoned Italian pro. And because the U.S. amateurs were all getting tired by then, it looked likely that Lance would need some help from another team to hold off the aggressive Italians.

It often happens in stage races that one coach makes a deal with another coach to help out at times like these—perhaps with a team that's out of contention, or even with a theoretically friendly team, such as Subaru. Eddie B says that's just what happened.

"At first, Carmichael made deal with Russians," he says, "but Russian team blow up. Next with Czechs, and Czechs same thing. Carmichael finally come to us, with Lance, and asks for help. Some of my guys were upset. I explain that he is young, not experienced, but he's our boy. Everybody can make mistakes, and I say, 'You have to work' . . . and the team did very good job."

But even before the final day of the race, news of the dispute between Lance and Eddie B reached Subaru team owner Thom Weisel in San Francisco. Lance says that one of the Subaru team riders had gone home early after dropping out of the race, and he had shared the story with the team's senior rider, Thurlow Rogers, back in California.

"So there was this whole drama back home," Lance says, "with Thom and the team, and Eddie having his ear. And Thurlow called Thom, going, 'This is complete bullshit.' Those were hard times for me. I was scared to death. This team was threatening to kick me off, and I was thinking, 'They're not gonna pay me. How am I gonna live?' I didn't sleep the last three nights of the race, and I was sick as a dog.

"There were no cell phones back then, and I didn't know how to call anybody from Italy. Finally, I got a call through to my mom from the pay phone at that little place we were staying at. She said, 'Do what you've got to do.'"

Coming up was the final day of the race. It had two stages, a long road race in the morning and a demanding uphill time trial in the afternoon. The night before, Dr. Testa came to check up on his new patients. "The sickest was Lance," he says. "At first I tried to discourage him from racing the next day, because the weather forecast was again very bad—cold, rain, and snowing. But he was in the overall lead. So he said, 'No way. Give me the biggest antibiotic you have.'"

Lance managed to keep his slender overall lead in the ninety-mile road race—with or without Subaru's help—and he then faced the closing time trial. It was nothing like the completely flat time trial where he set the national junior record a couple of years before. It was only seven miles long, but it zigzagged up a narrow, mountain road to the summit of the Colle Gallo.

The riders started at one-minute intervals for their solo efforts against the clock, with Lance starting one minute after Bordonali. The Italian had placed first and second on the Bergamasca's two most difficult stages—ahead of Lance both times. Also, Lance still had a disadvantage climbing mountain roads because his heavy triathlete's torso weighed him down, especially compared with the skinnier, lighter riders. Another handicap for Lance was the effects of the antibiotic. He would just have to grit his way through the time trial, using his inherent power and drive in an attempt to hang tough for the overall victory.

Testa was on the Colle Gallo, helping Carmichael by taking time splits and letting him know how Lance was doing compared with

Bordonali. Knowing about Lance's sickness, Testa says, "I was impressed by the determination of this nineteen-year-old kid. He was going head-to-head with one of the best Italians, and he gave everything in this uphill time trial. He was so sick at the finish, and yet he held onto the leader's jersey—and won."

Bordonali had started fast, but faded near the top to finish the overall race thirty-five seconds behind Lance, while Reiss was fourth overall, two and a half minutes back. No American had ever won the Settimana Bergamasca before, so this was a huge breakthrough for U.S. amateur cycling, as well as for Lance. Eddie B saw it differently. "Lance won this race, okay," he says. "But when he came back from podium, he never said, 'Thanks team for your help.' My guys very, very upset . . . and that was problem, the friction in team with Lance."

"Lance felt betrayed," Carmichael explains. "He felt the way it was handled wasn't good. That cemented our relationship, and we spent a lot of time together that summer. He talked with me about his childhood and well beyond. Yeah, we bonded in Italy, and there's no question I helped him with his cycling. But he was a young man who was trying to create his identity and also struggling with the things he faced when he was growing up."

One person who watched Lance close up at that time was Demet, who observes, "Lance was clearly a super talent. But I honestly think that what he would achieve in his career was mainly because he was so mentally strong and had so much confidence in himself. Also, he was able to work really hard. Those characteristics showed from a very young age. He never lost them, they never changed, and he never let anything get in his way."

CHAPTER 7

THE ROAD TO BARCELONA

He saw that you let the terrain, the distance, and the other riders slowly soften up the field, and you save yourself for that perfect moment to make your move.
—CHRIS CARMICHAEL

THE RIFT THAT OPENED between Lance and Eddie B in Italy effectively ended the coach's plans to groom him for Olympic stardom—but instantly made Lance the most sought-after young racer in America. At the time, other than Eddie B's Subaru-Montgomery program, only two U.S. teams were capable of supporting such an ambitious athlete as Lance. One was Len Pettyjohn's Coors Light squad, which, with the help of its 1984 Olympic medalists, Alexi Grewal and Davis Phinney, was dominating the domestic racing scene. The other was Motorola, a Tour de France team directed by Jim "Och" Ochowicz, who founded the team ten years earlier with sponsorship from 7-Eleven. Both Och and Pettyjohn coveted Lance.

"I told my sponsor, 'This kid is the best young rider I've ever seen,'" Pettyjohn says. "I'd watched LeMond grow up as a junior and what he became, and I said this kid will be every bit as good as Greg but in a different way. So I made this plea: 'You need to come up with some supplemental sponsorship because this guy is not going to stay with Eddie B.' But the sponsors turned me down; they said they were happy with the program as it was."

In contrast, Och had a far bigger budget, and he was always willing to talk to talented young riders recommended by national coach Chris Carmichael—who raced for Och's 7-Eleven team for most of his pro career. So, less than a month after the Bergamasca race, Lance and Och met following an early stage of the 1991 Tour DuPont, which was then America's biggest multiday race, played out in the Mid-Atlantic states.

"My first impression of him was pretty strong," Och says. "He said his goals were to be a pro, to race in the Tour de France, and to be one of the big riders. Right away, we knew we trusted and liked each other, and I was pretty convinced I wanted to take him on." Three months later, Lance signed for Motorola. The contract said he'd retain his amateur status and receive a stipend until the 1992 Olympics, and then turn professional at full salary and race with the team.

Och and his squad had their first look at Lance the racer in that '91 Tour DuPont. Sean Yates got to see him best when he and Lance were part of a three-man breakaway at an evening criterium stage in Richmond, Virginia, where thousands of spectators chanted "U-S-A, U-S-A" for their Olympic prospect.

"I'm not one for talking much," says Yates, one of the most down-to-earth characters in pro cycling, "but I did talk a little with Lance in that break. Och said this was the big guy, and we were going to have him on our team the next year."

The veteran English pro says he first saw Lance's willingness to ride hard and work for a colleague on that warm night in Virginia, when Lance helped his U.S. national teammate Nate Sheafor win the stage. Partly because they shared these good team traits, Lance and Yates felt a mutual respect and would become firm friends over the following years. They were still close two decades later, having hooked up again at the Astana team, where Lance began his 2009 comeback and Yates worked as a sports director. Lance, who's ten years younger, refers to Yates as the big brother he never had.

Yates tells me about his young bro' as we sit outside his team's equipment truck on a warm summer's day in the French Alps. The tall Brit, now in his late forties, still has the ultralean legs of a racer. He speaks with a blunt, rural accent, having been raised by hippie parents in the Ashdown Forest, an area of steep, bracken-covered hills and narrow back roads in southeast England.

"We seemed to hit it off straightaway," Yates says, referring to his first sit-down meeting with Lance at the Motorola team training camp in Santa Rosa, California, in January 1992. "We ended up riding quite a lot together, just me and him. One day, on a six-hour training ride, we were riding along when he made a joke about someone in the street, and he started laughing and laughing. I just turned around and said, 'You won't be laughing like that when you're pro, boy!' And he always brings that up, every time I see him."

Yates was warning the fledgling Lance that life would soon be getting a lot harder. Pro cycling requires a racer to gain and perfect countless skills, despite any physical excellence he may have. One important lesson he needs to learn is how to fearlessly race a bike down mountain roads at speeds of up to seventy miles per hour. Yates was regarded as the fastest descender in all of cycling, and he began to teach Lance those skills at that California training camp.

"We were testing these new Specialized tires," Yates recalls, "and they were not at all good for descending, especially when it was wet.

And so he was asking me how he should descend. He'd follow me, and I'd show him the lines and tell him to relax. He's a confident guy, and if he could watch me going down the hill ahead of him, he would think, 'Well, Christ, if he can do it, why can't I?' So he learned not to bottle out—or, as Americans say, chicken out. And soon, you get a feel for the corners, how far you can push it, and then it's not so hard."

While Lance's new teammates were teaching him the skills he would need in pro racing, he was also still learning from Carmichael, his national amateur team coach. "Throughout that winter we talked a lot," Carmichael says, "and I started really training him. Before I began working with him, his longest ride was like four hours, and I was having him do five- or six-hour rides. Part of that was for him to slim down. 'You're gonna get skinnier,' I told him. 'You're gonna look more like a real road cyclist by training like a road cyclist and not doing that other stuff, like running and swimming, that triathletes do.'

"He was a strong guy; he could time trial well, and he climbed well for a big guy. Now I wanted him to work on his sprint. That wasn't important in triathlon, but it's a skill he was gonna need in bike racing because a lot of races come down to sprints. He started getting better at sprinting, and he liked that because he began to see how tactics worked. He saw that you let the terrain, the distance, and the other riders slowly soften up the field, and you save yourself for that perfect moment to make your move.

"You have only two bullets in your pistol, not six, only two. One is to attack or bridge to an attack, and the other is to win an eventual sprint. He's a smart guy, so given that, he started to look at how the terrain and the distance would weaken people. So when he attacks four hours into the race, it's a lot more effective than attacking two hours into the race."

Lance continued to get advice from Carmichael, Yates, and his teammates at Motorola, but he didn't always listen. That was the observation of Motorola team leader Andy Hampsten, the first U.S. winner of Italy's Giro d'Italia, in 1988, and twice a top-four finisher at the Tour de France. He saw that Lance had a distinct way of acquiring knowledge. "He was very active about experimenting and learning, even with his arrogant attitude," Hampsten says. "And he wouldn't be arrogant for arrogance's sake. He genuinely didn't know things, but instead of admitting it and asking about it, he'd go and find out for himself—and learn the first time.

"I'm not going to say that's the best way to learn, but that's the way Lance Armstrong needs to learn. Other people can ask, they can watch, they can read books, they can watch bike-race videos and learn the same things. Or they can hang out with their teammates and have it explained to them. But he cultivated this brash attitude."

When I asked Lance about his reputed arrogance at the time, his answer was quick but not defensive: "I don't feel I'm arrogant or cocky. I just think I have a lot of self-confidence. I don't know if it was anger or aggression or what. I was just motivated to prove people wrong."

Some of Lance's rivals were so blinded by what they saw as arrogance that they failed to notice the Texan's amazing potential. That was the case with Alexi Grewal, the only American to have won the men's road race at the Olympic Games, in 1984, who was on Pettyjohn's Coors Light squad in '92. "My first impression of him was: How can this guy be any good? He was pretty rough, he had a young physical body, and he was pretty strong. But he pedaled squares," Grewal says, using cycling slang for a less-than-smooth pedaling style. "That changed over time as I watched him race and raced against him. But I would never have guessed he would be the rider he was, never in a thousand years."

Grewal's boss, Pettyjohn, saw "another telling side of Lance's personality" at a stage race in Colorado where Lance was seen as a threat to his team. "One stage was a criterium in Vail. Coming down to the finale, Lance was away with two of my riders, Davis Phinney and David Farmer. I signaled it was time to get rid of him," Pettyjohn says, alluding to a familiar tactic when a team has a two-to-one advantage in a breakaway. "They knew you don't take a dangerous guy like Lance to the finish line. So Davis and Farmer started attacking Lance. Whoever attacked, Lance would jump after them until the next stab came, and he'd counter that, and he'd chase him down.

"After two or three times of that, Davis rode up to Lance and goes, 'What are you doing? Because we're just going to attack you until one of us gets away. You just need to sit up.' And then Farmer jumped, and Lance chased him down again, and he turned around to Davis, and he goes, 'Fuck you!' Then Davis attacked—but they couldn't drop Lance. His attitude was: 'I don't care what conventional wisdom is in this sport. Fuck you!' That was Lance. He was the brash, arrogant, I-don't-care-what-you-do guy from the very start."

In his build-up to the Barcelona Olympics, Lance raced exclusively for Carmichael's national team—in Europe through the spring and at domestic races in the early summer—before final preparations in Spain. The intention was a gradual progression to the Olympic road race on August 2, with Lance holding back his power in preceding events. But it was tough for Carmichael to keep his reins on Lance. And while the hot-headed Texan didn't attempt to defend his title at Italy's Settimana Bergamasca, he couldn't be stopped from winning one of the stages, making a huge effort to overcome two powerful Russians.

Two weeks later, Lance was back home for a Grand Prix race in Atlanta. He was competing, as an amateur, against the U.S. pro teams, headed by Coors Light. That team's Phinney, the favorite to win the race, remembers that Carmichael's national team had just received a wireless radio system, manufactured by Motorola, which enabled the coach to talk to his riders during the race. "They were the first ones to have that communication," Phinney says, "and it helped them win the race.

"Lance got away in a break with our Greg Oravetz, who won the USPRO Championship a few years before that. It was just the two of them. Greg was a bit like Lance, big and strong and confident. He thought he was going to win. Carmichael was behind in the team car, talking to Lance on his radio. Chris could see when Oravetz was gonna jump, and when he did, Lance was able to go at exactly the same time—and he beat Greg in the sprint to the line."

It was soon after the Atlanta race that Lance and his U.S. national team again rode the Tour DuPont, and this time he paced himself to an excellent twelfth-place finish. The overall winner was Greg LeMond, while another Tour de France winner, Laurent Fignon of France, placed eighth; and the then-reigning world champion, Gianni Bugno of Italy, finished eleventh, just ahead of Lance.

Following that tour's final stage, a time trial in Washington, D.C.'s Rock Creek Park, Lance was riding the teams' hotel elevator with Grewal. It seemed like a good opportunity for the aspiring Olympian to ask Grewal about his gold-medal victory at the Los Angeles Games. Instead, according to the Colorado native, Lance wanted an explanation for something he saw as inexplicable: the fact that Grewal took a spectacular stage win the day before in Richmond and followed it by finishing last in that day's time trial. "I can't figure it out," Lance said to Grewal. "You win one day, you're dead last the next day. What happened?"

"Dude," Grewal replied, "I'm tired. Here's your reason why I was dead last. But at least I won yesterday."

Recalling that conversation sixteen years later, Grewal says that being that tired was a concept that seemed hard for Lance to grasp.

The eleven days of hard racing at the Tour DuPont gave Lance excellent form for a pro-am race in Pittsburgh the following weekend, when the U.S. national amateur team was pitted against the best American pro teams. The 115-mile Thrift Drug Classic, named for its pharmacy-chain sponsor, was regarded as the toughest single-day race in America. Held on an eight-mile circuit of city streets, it took in a steep, corkscrew hill that climbed three-hundred-fifty feet in six-tenths of a mile to the top of Mount Washington. The race was made even tougher that year by cold, wet weather that forced much of the field to abandon early on.

Given his growing status as an Olympic favorite, Lance was considered one of the riders to watch, as Coors Light's Pettyjohn confirms. "We had a team meeting before the race, and I said to my riders, 'You just can't let Lance ride away,'" he says, adding that he hoped two of his best men, Stephen Swart and Scott Moninger, would put in strong performances.

"So Lance attacks on the hill, and we chase him down. Lance goes very quickly again, and we cover that move. Lance goes a third time, and this time he's gone. Everybody else is now completely in the red zone. At first there are eighty guys in the race, then there are twenty, then there are three, and then he rides away alone.

"I roll up in the car to the chase group that Swart was in and say to him, 'What the hell are you doing? You can't let him just go away like that.' Swarty looks over at me and he goes, 'You fucking chase him!'

And I see he is absolutely cross-eyed. So I'm like, 'Oh, you're not back here because you let him ride away. He *rode* away.' And there wasn't anything we could do about it."

Pettyjohn's best finisher that day was Moninger, more than four minutes behind Lance.

"It was clear that Lance had more power, especially on the climb," Pettyjohn says. "And what was really dramatic was he had the ability to recover so fast from a max effort and do it again and again. It was like Lance was doing a Wingate test over and over. That's a test done in the lab to measure your maximum power and see how fast you can recover from that kind of max effort. It's the *hardest* thirty-second test that anybody ever does on a bike."

Any athlete who has taken that test can attest to the pain. Lance's high-school friend, Adam Wilk, says that his coach Erin Hartwell, an Olympic medalist, took the test in which "you try to produce the most lactic acid you can," and scored an improbably high rating. "He did the test and literally fell over," Wilk remembers. "He was in the fetal position for an hour and a half; he pushed himself that hard!"

Lance's capacity to resist pain better than most athletes developed along with his career; and it was soon evident that his ability to make repeated efforts at maximum power was much more important than his having large lungs or a bigger-than-average heart.

Pettyjohn's team would again confront Lance and his U.S. Olympic squad a month later at the four-day Longsjo Classic in Fitchburg, Massachusetts. After two stages, a time trial, and a circuit race, Lance led the race by four seconds over Coors Light's Swart. To win the race overall, Lance and his teammates would have to keep Swart in check on a hilly ninety-mile road race that finished atop the two-thousand-foot-high Wachusett Mountain.

Midway through the stage, Lance was in a small group five minutes behind a six-man breakaway that contained his teammate Darren

Baker and Swart's teammate Phinney, whose career highlights included two stage wins at the Tour de France.

Phinney, noting that the national team was again using its radio communication setup, describes what happened to his six-man breakaway group. "I saw the national team rider, Baker, listening to his earpiece and then go to the back of our group. There were cars coming up from behind us honking, and this rider comes up and goes straight by, going five miles an hour faster than us—it was Lance! He went by us on an uphill, not that steep, but very hard. Baker then sprinted from behind us and went with Lance. It was as if they were in a different race; they finished five minutes ahead of us.

"In the hotel after the stage, I called Lance and went to chat with him in his room. I was the elder statesman of the peloton, and he was the young punk, cocky and self-assured. He was focused on Barcelona at that point, and he said, 'I sort of wish the Olympics were today.'"

The morning that the Olympic Games began in Barcelona, Lance was sitting quietly in the pit area of the Catalunya motor-racing circuit before the start of the first cycling event, the 100 km team time trial. Sporting a small goatee and with a somber look on his young face, he seemed despondent that he wasn't racing for the U.S. team that day. He was cheered by the arrival of some family and friends—his granddad Paul, his mom and her new husband, John Walling, and his high-school friend John Boggan—but Lance looked bored. He was kicking his heels against a concrete retaining wall as he watched his four teammates get ready for their race. At age twenty, he may have been the country's strongest team time trialist, but Coach Carmichael had decided to have Lance rest up and focus on the road race the following weekend—where he had the greatest chance of a medal.

Lance loved racing, and training for and being in the team time trial might have lifted his spirits and strengthened his form. Instead, he just had a daily diet of training rides from the U.S. team's hotel in the Penedès wine country west of Barcelona. They were staying there because the Olympic Village had too much traffic for safe cycling. Lance, who thrives on excitement and activity, said he would have much rather been with the thousands of other Olympians than staying at a distant hotel. But he could overcome a little boredom if it meant he'd be better prepared for his shot at an Olympic gold medal, his major goal since he left triathlon for cycling two years earlier.

Lance was a focus of the media at the road race course in Sant Sadurni d'Anoia, a dusty town of ten thousand people that produces *cava*, Spain's premier sparkling wine. But there'd be no clinking of champagne glasses for the U.S. team on that stiflingly hot day in the rolling vineyards of Catalonia.

The odds seemed stacked against the Americans from the start. Because of race rules, the sixty-one countries represented were allowed just three riders each. To give him the best support, Lance wanted his two strongest national teammates, Darren Baker and Bob Mionske. Mionske was there, but an antiquated U.S. Olympic Committee regulation decreed that one of the three riders had to be an automatic selection from the Olympic trials. The surprise winner of that spot was the internationally inexperienced Timm Peddie, of whom Carmichael said, "I think Timm realizes that he's not ready for this."

Another detrimental factor was the course: With only two short hills on the ten-mile circuit, which was lapped twelve times, it lacked challenge. Lance needed power climbs to show his true strength, and this was a course for subtle tacticians.

In the end, the Italians rode the smartest. They put their 1991 world amateur champion Mirko Gualdi in the day's main breakaway—which was instigated by an inspired Mionske—and then counterattacked with Fabio Casartelli, who escaped with two others on the final lap to win the gold medal. A half-minute later, Germany's Erik Zabel took the sixty-eight-man field sprint, with Lance coming in twelfth, Peddie thirty-seventh, and the weary Mionske seventy-fourth. Mionske had suffered from heatstroke. Peddie said he "slowly deteriorated." And Lance confessed, "I wasn't having one of my better days. I rode at the front to keep motivated, but it was obvious my legs weren't turning."

At the finish, Mionske says, "We were crushed. And when we were sitting in the team tent afterwards, Lance was really down. He didn't say much. So I made a point of telling him, 'If you had had good form today, you would have just ridden away from those guys. You're way stronger than them.' If I hadn't have been sick, I think I could have hung with them pretty easily myself, and maybe even won. But because I was in that break, I knew they weren't riding strong—even excellent riders like Erik Dekker. Compared to Lance, I was a 30cc moped, those guys were 50cc scooters, and he was a 500cc motorcycle."

Knowing he had that power, Lance had hoped to end his amateur cycling career with a gold medal around his neck. Instead that went to Casartelli, the promising Italian who'd be joining Lance on the Motorola team in a few years' time. As for the Texan, he headed straight from Barcelona to Spain's Basque Country to contest his first race ever as a professional. And it wasn't just any race, but a World Cup event, 145 miles long, the Clásica San Sebastián. A tough entry into the pro peloton for the rookie from Plano.

CHAPTER 8

A ROOKIE IN ORBIT

My first impression of him was the same as everybody's: this guy with the big mouth and a little bit of attitude. But you could definitely see there was something special about him.

—JOHAN BRUYNEEL

IT RAINS MORE in the Basque Country than in almost any other part of Spain. And on August 8, 1992, as Lance headed up the steep early switchbacks of the Jaizkibel, the major climb of the Clásica San Sebastián, a violent thunderstorm unleashed another downpour. "It was the worst weather I've ever raced in," said the seasoned Mexican Raúl Alcalá, who was with the leaders and already over the 1,460-foot crest of the cloud-cloaked mountain.

The dire conditions were taking their toll on the field of 207 starters. Just before that last climb, a mass pileup on the slick roads brought down twenty riders, including Spain's Miguel Induráin, who'd won the Tour de France for a second time two weeks earlier. Another former Tour winner, Stephen Roche of Ireland, lost control on a dicey descent, crashed into a rock, and needed stitches in his face.

Too scared, too fatigued, or too demoralized to continue, ninety-six men pulled out of the race. But Lance, riding solo well behind the other survivors, plowed on through the stinging rain. Perhaps he was remembering his mother's words: "Son, you never quit." Or maybe he was thinking of the words spoken to him a little earlier by Hennie Kuiper, the team's assistant manager. When Lance lost contact with the peloton, Kuiper drove alongside him in a team car, rolled down the window, and said, "Push yourself, Lance! What you do now will only benefit you later."

Kuiper, one of the wisest old-timers in pro cycling, was perhaps the hardiest racer the sport has ever seen. A world and Olympic champion, this stoic Dutchman won the toughest one-day classics and twice finished second at the Tour de France. Perseverance was his greatest strength, and that's the gritty quality Lance was now displaying as he pushed on through the storm.

While he was still struggling, his Motorola teammates had finished the race and gone to their hotel to get out of the rain. One of them, Andy Hampsten, says, "We were just worried about where he was." There was no way of knowing Lance's whereabouts because mobile phones barely existed then, and the range on the team's radio system was very limited. Lance later admitted, "I would've abandoned if I'd have been there alone." But he wasn't; a second Motorola team car had been designated to stay with the rookie in case he needed help.

Kuiper stood at the finish line, which had emptied out after Alcalá received the winner's trophy. "I was waiting for half an hour," Kuiper said. "Somebody asked me what I was doing. I said I was waiting for someone. Then the police lights came . . . it was totally dark . . . and then there was Lance, the last man. But he was still riding hard."

Hampsten says, "I thought it was pretty cool that he finished his first race when almost anyone else would have quit. It was a really long race, six hours or more. I remember Lance being very impressed by how hard it was and being a little afraid of it as well. But that was a good baptism for him."

It was a tough baptism too. "I wanted to give up cycling that day," Lance says.

"By evening, after a good meal, he pulled himself together," Hampsten adds, "and he was looking forward to the next race."

Refusing to drop out and finishing last at San Sebastián might have revealed more about Lance's personality than any other performance. That's the opinion of his early benefactor, Jim Hoyt, who was following Lance's career from afar. "Mentally, one of the qualities that made Lance such an incredible champion was his fear of failure," Hoyt says. "Just look at his first pro race. . . . Having respect for failure, and being able to fail, is very, very important."

Riding in such testing conditions and completing all 145 miles—the farthest he'd ever raced—enabled Lance to begin his next event, the Tour of Galicia, with his pride intact. This second pro race, also on the rugged coast of northern Spain, started two days later. It offered Lance five days of less intense racing, a chance to find his place in the pro peloton, and a platform to begin living up to the hype that preceded him.

"Everybody had been reading about Lance because he was fresh off the Olympics," says Johan Bruyneel, then a twenty-eight-year-old racer on the top Spanish team, O.N.C.E. "My first impression of him was the same as everybody's: this guy with the big mouth and a little bit of attitude. You could definitely see there was something special about him."

Many years later, Bruyneel would become Lance's team director and confidant. Coincidentally, they became statistically linked in that

1992 race in Galicia: In the final standings, Bruyneel finished thirteenth, and Lance was fourteenth, three seconds behind him.

It was a great result for Lance in his first pro stage race. What's more, he did it by getting stronger each day. On the fourth stage—a sixty-two-mile run from Tuy, a town on the Portuguese border, to Cangas, a fishing port on the Atlantic coast—Lance took his first victory as a professional. He got a big boost from his Canadian teammate Steve Bauer, who had already shown Lance how to win by taking the second stage in a mass-sprint finish. Bauer guided Lance through the final kilometer in Cangas and enabled him to use the sprint skills Carmichael helped him with earlier in the year. Lance easily beat the vaunted English sprinter, Malcolm Elliott, who was second. Then, on the next day's final stage from Cangas to the city of Pontevedra, in another sprint finish, Lance was runner-up to Peter De Clercq, a Belgian who'd just won a stage of the Tour de France.

With his confidence restored and his ambition stronger than ever, Lance the rookie left Spain and headed to Italy and then Switzerland for some much bigger races, including one that would lead the influential French sports daily, *L'Équipe*, to headline its report: "Armstrong Is in Orbit."

Lance was fortunate when he turned professional. That year, the Motorola team included three of the most talented and successful pro cyclists ever produced by the British Commonwealth: Phil Anderson from Australia, Bauer from Ontario, and the Englishman Yates. All three were in their thirties and nearing the ends of their careers, and between them they had more than thirty years of pro-racing experience. "They were great mentors for Lance," says team boss Och, "because they were open to sharing their knowledge." Just as important, they could communicate with him in English. Had Lance joined a top European team, the advice provided by three equivalent veterans would likely have come in French, Italian, or Spanish—languages he did not understand.

The gregarious Anderson, from suburban Melbourne, was a true pioneer: the first Australian cyclist to wear the yellow jersey at the Tour de France and the first to win a one-day classic race—the equivalent of an Olympic or world championship road race, usually on a point-to-point course raced annually for many decades. Anderson was a good role model for Lance because he had similar physical gifts and could perform well in any type of race.

Bauer, who grew up in the village of Fenwick playing hockey on frozen ponds, turned to cycling in his teens and took a silver medal at the 1984 Olympics before turning pro; he finished as high as fourth in the Tour de France. Bauer's calm disposition, intrinsic honesty, and utterly unshakable resolve were all qualities that Lance would admire.

And then there was Yates, the dependable teammate, who would do anything asked of him, no question.

Besides its team members sharing a common language, Motorola was more freewheeling than the European squads. Traditionally, the *directeur sportif* would impose his will on his team without much discussion. Motorola was different. "We weren't some big-pressure team," Yates says. "And Och wasn't one to be screaming down the headphones. But we still had a lot of wins. I was motivated by riding for the others, and Lance coming there was perfect.

"We roomed together from the start. I'm a no-nonsense type of guy, and he was pretty similar, and that's why we probably got on so well. We always had a laugh, and he would like me to tell him stories before he went to bed. Stories about bike racing, like leading out someone for a sprint, or whatever."

Yates, Bauer, and Anderson all raced with Lance on Motorola for several years until they retired from the sport. During that time,

Coors Light's Pettyjohn was a keen observer of how they interacted. "I don't think there was any doubt that Yates was the biggest force, the one Lance trusted," Pettyjohn says. "He kind of shepherded Lance around and through the peloton.

"What Lance needed was somebody who was really powerful that he respected. So he didn't see Yates as a competitor; he saw him as somebody he could get something from, and he also had the demeanor to communicate it to him. I think that's really critical, because Lance wouldn't listen to many people at that time—I'm not sure he *ever* did. So I would say that the single most important person in Lance's life, as a competitor, was Sean Yates.

"I watched them together during races. Sean would ride up to Lance, and you could see him lean over and say something. And over the course of a couple of years, you saw Lance make fewer and fewer mistakes. The more Yates got in his ear, the more Lance got to the point where we could never drop him. And probably because Yates was delivering the right message, Lance would attack at the right time, and we never would catch him."

"With Lance, it was always a situation of holding him back," Och says, referring to the rookie's youthful tendency to charge away too soon in a long race. The counsel of Anderson, Bauer, and Yates was starting to have its effect, though, and that was apparent in Lance's second World Cup race, the Championship of Zürich, two weeks after his last-place finish in San Sebastián.

Curiously, in his coauthored autobiography, *It's Not About the Bike*, Lance writes this about the Zürich race: "I attacked from the start and stayed on the attack for practically the entire race. I had little or no idea tactically how to ride in the race—I just put my head down and bulled through it." But that's the exact opposite of what actually happened.

On a gray and rainy August Sunday, over six laps of a twenty-five-mile circuit north of the Swiss city, Lance—far from attacking from the start—stayed sheltered in the peloton for nearly the entire race. He then followed the advice of his teammate Bauer, who'd won the Zürich race three years' earlier, and waited till the final lap to join a seven-man attack. Then, on the appropriately named Regensberg ("Rain Mountain"), Lance broke clear through the swirling mist with Russia's Viatcheslav Ekimov and Belgium's Jan Nevens. Both of those hardened pros had won stages at the Tour de France and were accustomed to racing over long distances, but Lance managed to stay with them.

Och, who was driving the Motorola team car behind the three riders, recalls, "After the Regensberg, it was downhill a lot, on little roads, and we didn't catch up with them until the last ten kilometers. Then I had an accident. The front of the car was banged up, and the radio was starting to go, and I wasn't sure that I would make it to the finish.

"The heater was redlined, and then the radio stopped working. I was driving through to the front, and I was gonna tell Lance to stay on Ekimov and forget about Nevens because Eki's the smarter guy. But just as I rolled down the window, and Lance came back to me, I didn't get one word out of my mouth before the car just went 'pffff' and stopped. With no radio, Lance was on his own, and what happened next is exactly what I thought was going to happen. The other two took turns at hitting him, and finally, with two kilometers to go, Ekimov got a gap and that was it. Lance finished second."

It was still a tremendous performance by the twenty-year-old American, and it resulted in a gushing half-page profile in the August 25, 1992, edition of *L'Équipe* that said: "As Greg LeMond continues to make little impression, his young Texan compatriot arrives as his possible successor. He was the sensation by finishing second at Zürich. Immediate take-off!"

A week later, Lance won a second pro race at Marostica, near Venice, Italy. It was a highly contested event, in which riders—including Lance—were vying for places on their national teams for the world championships. The very competitiveness was an elixir for Lance. He managed to break clear with ten others and was so confident of beating them that, when the team car came alongside, Lance just whispered to his Motorola boss, "Och, you can relax, man."

"He just looked at me," Och says, "and that's all he said. So I told him to attack, and—bang!—he hit 'em, and they couldn't do anything about it. He was strong that day."

There were expectations that Lance could cause an upset at his first world professional road race championship in Benidorm, Spain, five days later. But he was caught up in a crash and had to pull out of the race. His injuries also hampered his performance at the immediately following Tour de l'Avenir—an eleven-day version of the Tour de France for young riders—that took place on the hilly roads of Brittany in western France. Nonetheless, he distinguished himself by taking a couple of top-three stage finishes, wearing the green jersey of most consistent rider for six stages, and ending up with the red-and-white polka-dot jersey as the race's best climber.

Lance's hectic year, including two months as a full professional, came to an end in early October when he placed seventeenth at a World Cup race in Montreal, Canada.

Few cities are more different than Plano, where Lance was raised, and Como, where he would come to live at the outset of his European pro cycling career. While he was growing up, Plano exploded from a small town of 20,000 people to a modern community of 260,000 that the U.S. Census Bureau calls America's most affluent city. In comparison, Como's stable population of 80,000 works in silk factories and the tourism industry. And whereas Plano is bland and as flat as its Spanish name indicates, steep mountains dip straight into the stunningly beautiful Lake Como—where celebrities such as George Clooney, Madonna, and Sting own lakeside villas.

Home to dozens of Italian pro racers, Como is the place where Och decided to base his 7-Eleven team in the mid-1980s—because of the mild weather and because it was the hometown of Dr. Massimo Testa, the pro team's first physician and trainer. Testa was the doctor who treated Lance in 1991 at the Settimana Bergamasca race, and he would become his trainer in early '93.

In Como, Lance linked up with two of his new teammates, Detroit native Frankie Andreu, who was five years older than Lance, and a quiet Norwegian rookie, Bjorn Stenersen. "Those three guys got an apartment together," Och recalls. "It wasn't such a nice place, but they were just starting out, and it was all they could afford."

Lance began spending most of his time with his housemates and the other six Motorola riders living there—training, going to races, or just hanging out.

"When he was in a group, Lance was great. He always had a good attitude," Testa says. "He was probably missing a little bit of social life as Como's not the place you can go out much; the people are kind of quiet. And while the first group of American riders who moved here—like Andy Hampsten, Davis Phinney, and Ron Kiefel—became friends with Italian families, the Lance group always went out together. They saw the language as a big barrier. This second generation was not so much into learning languages like Andy, Davis, and Ron were. It was also the time when the Internet came, so they were spending time on their computers.

"In one way, compared with a young Italian kid, Lance had no social skills at interacting with different people. But in terms of self-confidence and independence of judgment, he was already very mature. He had no rules, and that's what I appreciated. He was completely different. He was a nice guy to have around, with a lot of energy."

As for Lance's progress as an athlete, Testa tells me: "We were still in the early phase, and I was not trying to be too serious with him about training. I didn't want to burn him out. We were very, very conservative, and I hope he appreciates that. Those years were very important . . . when we were holding him back to save for later in his career."

Motorola team leader Hampsten—the only American to have won the Giro d'Italia—lived five miles away from Como, just across the Swiss border. "It was kind of fun hanging out with Lance," Hampsten recalls. "He'd come over for dinner, or we'd have little barbecues for all the guys in the area, and we trained together some. He and I both worked with Massimo Testa.

"That first spring, I remember Lance saying to Massimo, 'I just got beat in a sprint, Max. I want to learn how to sprint! What training do I do?' Then he went out and did that training—and he won all the sprints he needed to from that point on. He was able to really focus his body on what he wanted to do and accomplish it."

Jim Ochowicz has a soft spot for the Laigueglia Trophy, a mid-February race on the Mediterranean coast that opens the Italian cycling season. "That's where we first won a race in Europe with Ron Kiefel," Och says, sitting on the back porch of his home in Palo Alto, California, and remembering his 7-Eleven team's pro debut in 1985.

"We would go to the same café before the race every year. We'd pull in there with the cars, and the guys would be having coffee and putting muscle rub on their legs. It had that very Euro feel. The teams don't do that anymore because they all have buses. I think we had a lot more energy and feel for the atmosphere back then. Lance loved that scene."

At the start of 1993, Lance wanted to show the cycling world that he was not just another brash American racer. He planned to be a team leader who wins the sport's most esteemed single-day races, the so-called classics. Laigueglia wasn't a classic, but its winner generally goes on to be a favorite at the season's first such event, Milan-San Remo. By racing at Laigueglia, Lance was showing that he wanted to be a serious contender for the upcoming classic. And he raced with confidence and character, getting into the day's main breakaway on the second of two hilly loops in the one-hundred-mile race. With him were his Motorola teammate Andy Bishop, two Belgians, a Venezuelan, and three Italians—including the country's big classics star, Moreno Argentin.

In his typically aggressive style, Argentin powered away from the breakaway group on the last major climb and took a half-minute lead with two other riders. Och was watching the action from the Motorola team car with Testa. "Jim was telling Lance not to go after Argentin," Testa recalls. "He said, 'Only go if someone comes with you.' And Lance said, 'I wanna go.' Two times he called the car saying, 'Please, Och. I wanna go.' And Jim said no. And when Lance went anyway, Jim was like, 'Aagh! This guy has no experience, he's gonna blow up.' And then the race radio says: 'A Motorola rider is approaching Argentin . . . Argentin is waiting . . . the Motorola rider is attacking Argentin.'"

Pier Bergonzi, a sportswriter from the main Italian sports newspaper, *La Gazzetta dello Sport*, vividly recalls the latter stages of that Laigueglia race. "Argentin deliberately provoked Lance," he says. "Because Andy Bishop was one of the few Americans we Italians knew in that team, Argentin said to Lance, 'Go Bishop! Go Bishop!' And when Argentin said that, Lance said back to him, 'Go Chiappucci! Go Chiappucci!' Claudio Chiappucci, of course, was a big rival. Argentin was furious."

With both men fired up by their verbal exchange, they dropped down to the coast with their two breakaway companions and then headed for the line. "Argentin started the sprint," Bergonzi tells me, "but when he understood that Lance would be too strong for him, he stopped pedaling, so he would finish fourth. He didn't want to meet Lance at the anti-doping control—only the first three were tested."

By defeating Argentin, one of the world's best ever single-day racers, Lance was warning the Italian peloton that he'd be ready for Milan–San Remo. At 185 miles, this is the longest classic, but its mostly flat course makes it one of the fastest too. Two moderately difficult climbs—the Cipressa, 20 miles from San Remo, and the Poggio, 3 miles before the finish—provide the more aggressive riders with a chance to attack. But a big group usually reaches San Remo intact, resulting in victory for the fastest sprinter.

Lance hoped to buck that trend and perhaps emulate the sport's most prolific winner, Eddy Merckx of Belgium, who was one of the few men to win Milan–San Remo on his first attempt. Merckx did that in 1966, at age twenty, and went on to win it a record seven times in eleven years. He scored most of those victories by making solo attacks on the switchback descent from the Poggio and gaining just enough of a gap to hold off the sprinters.

After retiring from racing, Merckx founded his own bicycle company, which by the early 1990s was supplying racing bikes to several pro teams, including Motorola. As a team sponsor, Merckx showed up at training camps and races, and, through team manager Och, he soon struck up a close relationship with Lance. Merckx was happy to share his knowledge with the young Texan, and knowing how to race fast downhill was one skill he advised him to acquire.

Lance had already received a few lessons in descending from Yates at the 1992 training camp in California. He would get more advice from his teammate Phil Anderson while training on the French Riviera before the weeklong Paris-Nice, which serves as a warm-up for Milan–San Remo. Motorola team leader Hampsten remembers one particular descent in Paris-Nice, which drops precipitously from Tanneron, a Provence hill town, to the Mediterranean coast.

"I remember Phil instructing Lance on how to dial in the descent," Hampsten says. "And they were going much, much faster in training than I was going to risk going down it in the race itself. I was dead impressed by how fast Lance accomplished that skill just a few days after he said, 'Okay, now's the time I want to concentrate on descending.' He wasn't a great bike handler, but Phil really showed him how to do it, and Lance had it nailed. It went from this kid who didn't handle his bike very well when he first rode with us to mastering how to descend and sprint within a year."

Lance demonstrated his improved downhill skills on the sixth stage of Paris-Nice on that very descent from Tanneron. "He took off just over the top and dropped everyone," Hampsten continues. "He went screaming down that hideous descent. It was dry, but the really tight turns were slicked down from car tires and oil. In training, Phil and Lance took about fifteen seconds out of me; but in the race, Lance took thirty seconds out of *everyone*. That's a huge amount in a descent of only three miles."

Lance finished second on the stage, and the self-assurance he gained there would help him at Milan–San Remo the following week. He knew he had no chance of winning the Italian classic in a mass sprint; only a few sprint specialists could do that. Lance would have to tackle it in the more daring style of his new adviser, Merckx.

The Motorola team decided on a dual strategy for San Remo: Lance would attempt a solo attack on one of the two last uphills—or descents—while his Italian teammate Max Sciandri would aim to stay with the other leaders and use his inherent finishing speed in the final straightaway.

Four of their teammates paced Lance and Sciandri through the opening six hours of the race, keeping them sheltered from the wind and fresh enough to follow the attacks on the climb to Cipressa. Then, to the shock of the millions watching the live telecast, Lance bulled his way to the front and broke clear on the downhill. Using the skills he'd learned from Yates and Anderson, he gained a second or two on each of the tight, plunging turns and reached the flat coastal road with a good solo lead.

But Lance's audacity would not be rewarded on that March day. He was caught by a powerful chase group of thirty riders just as he began the final climb of the Poggio. Still, the new pro was strong enough to stay with the leaders until the end of the seven-and-a-half-hour classic, placing twenty-second, while teammate Sciandri finished an excellent third.

Lance had come far since his first race as a rookie back in San Sebastián, and there were many who helped him along the way. Not the least of these was Hennie Kuiper, who had shouted out unforgettable advice in that Basque thunderstorm: "Push yourself, Lance! What you do now will only benefit you later."

CHAPTER 9

BREAKTHROUGH

If I don't cut it this year, I'm gonna go back and go to college.

—LANCE ARMSTRONG

LOSING WAS NEVER EASY for Lance. Winning was what excited him and fired him up. "My whole thing growing up and my whole thing through the early years was, 'First is all there is,'" he says. "Second really sucks." So he had a hard time when his results steadily worsened in the spring of 1993. The nadir came on April 4, the day he first contested Belgium's Tour of Flanders.

Only a handful of one-day races are considered true monuments of the sport: four major classics in the springtime, the world championships in late summer, and one more classic in the fall. And, like golf's majors, cycling's classics are all about winning.

Belgium's Tour of Flanders is the most demanding of the spring classics. It traces a labyrinthine, 163-mile course through the Flemish hinterland, seeking out the steepest hills and most jarring cobblestone roads. Lance loved the challenge, but the challenge proved too much. On that sunny April day in bike-crazed Flanders, he lost contact with the pack on a cobbled climb and became one of the seventy-eight nonfinishers.

"He was very ambitious for the Tour of Flanders, and he couldn't understand why he was dropped like that," says teammate Sean Yates. "I told him most guys have been trying for years just to finish that bloody race." Still, Lance was distraught with his performance. "If I don't cut it this year," he told Yates, "I'm gonna go back and go to college."

This wouldn't be the last time Lance would have second thoughts about racing bikes at what he then called "shitty races" in Europe. It was tempting to think of living a collegiate life like his old friend John Boggan, whom he'd hang out with on his trips back to Austin. Maybe only rugged characters like Yates had the grit to persevere with such demanding work. The easygoing Englishman accepted the privations of a nomadic life in Europe, even reveled in them, while Lance needed a constant connection with his home country.

"He was always on the Internet," Yates says about his roommate, "maybe doing some investing. And he always watched CNN. I was completely different. I didn't have a computer—didn't know how to turn one on—didn't have any stocks and shares or anything like that. I was completely antitech."

They did share a few things, though, besides their chosen sport. Each had a passion for speed: Yates loved taking his supercharged motorcycle to the racetrack, and Lance had his fast cars. And they both had a high tolerance for pain, with Lance embracing it and Yates accepting it.

"When I was ill, I suffered," Yates admits. "Or if I had a bad back in the Tour de France—'Christ, here we go again' type of thing. But it's soon over, and the bad days are forgotten. You don't remember the pain once the day's gone. And when I look back, riding a bike a few hours a day is a bloody luxury compared to working a proper job, like digging holes ten hours a day or cutting hedges, day in, day out."

Yates has experienced both: Between cycling seasons, he cut hedges and dug holes; and after retiring from racing, he worked as a gardener for several years until he was offered a job in cycling team management. But Lance was never one for manual labor, and there was a reason.

According to Andy Pruitt, who set up a medical program at the U.S. Cycling Federation in 1992, "Lance started to complain early on about his back. He'd seen multiple chiropractors, and his back would still go out. We discovered he had a spondylosisthesis, which in his case was a congenital fracture at the base of the spine."

Pruitt is a specialist in treating cycling-related injuries by using advanced bike-fitting techniques, and he's one of the few people who's aware of Lance's problem with his back. "His L5 vertebra is in two or three pieces, like large free fragments, so the majority of the vertebral body can slip forward and actually be out of place," Pruitt explains. "So when his back would go out, and the chiropractors would adjust it, he would get only temporary alignment. I came up with a plan to ease his pain."

Nonetheless, Lance says, "chronic back pain was a huge problem from 1990 to '96. We had to look at my cleats, position on the bike, seat height, fore-and-aft seat adjustment, and handlebar height. So for most of my career, I rode on the tops [of the handlebars], very rarely on the drops, just to ease the pain."

When the speed in a race climbs to thirty-five or forty miles per hour on the flats, most riders grab the "drops," the lowest parts of the handlebars, to be as streamlined as possible; but Lance has to remain on the "tops" because of his back, even though this demands more power and a higher threshold for pain. However, being able to ride at high speeds in this slightly elevated position means that his chest is less constricted, which allows him to take in more air with each breath, a possible advantage in races that last six or seven hours.

This advantage wasn't enough, though, to pull Lance out of his spring slump. Finishing classics, let alone winning them, wasn't going to be easy—which is what he initially believed after his second-place finish at the previous year's Championship of Zürich, a relatively minor classic. Looking back at that race, he now said, "I got robbed. I was completely clueless. People watching on TV saw 'this kid is getting screwed' by the two veterans. But I was so excited about second place, I didn't see what was happening."

Lance was beginning to see that he would continue to "get screwed" in the classics, where tactics and knowing the pitfalls of every race course are just as important as being strong and on form. Even European racers at the height of their careers have a hard time winning a classic. Realizing that it could be years—if ever—before he'd win one, Lance decided to also focus on developing his skills in multiday races. His 1991 victory at the Settimana Bergamasca, when he was still an amateur, showed his potential to succeed in long stage races. And before his disappointing 1993 spring classics campaign, he had performed extremely well in his first major weeklong race, Paris-Nice, where he almost won a stage and placed ninth overall. Therefore, Lance saw no reason why he shouldn't make his debut that year at the longest and grandest stage race of all, the legendary Tour de France.

His team boss, Och, wasn't so sure. "We hadn't even talked about the Tour," Och tells me. "In fact, we *avoided* talking about it. The other riders didn't want him to do it because they thought Lance was too young, only twenty-one. And I agreed with that early on that year."

Tackling the Tour as a rookie is rarely attempted. Two of the most gifted racers since World War II, Eddy Merckx and Greg LeMond, who'd both win the Tour de France multiple times, were pros for almost four years before making their Tour debuts. Yet Lance felt he'd be ready only ten months after turning pro.

If he were to start the 1993 Tour and be competitive, he would need to put in a few thousand miles of racing in the next two months—and start chalking up some wins. Fortunately, his next event was the Tour DuPont, the East Coast race he had entered twice as an amateur for the experience. Now, as a pro, Lance felt ready to shoot for overall victory. For sure, it was no Tour de France, but it was the biggest race in America.

Lance stepped up to the challenge brilliantly, waging a race-long duel with Raúl Alcalá, the Mexican who'd won the San Sebastián classic on Lance's pro debut nine months earlier. The Texan scored a spectacular win on a stage through the Blue Ridge Mountains—his first victory in three months—and he was second overall, only nineteen seconds behind Alcalá, going into the final stage, an individual time trial at Greensboro, North Carolina.

Lance shone in this discipline as a junior racer, when he set a national record over 12.5 miles. But the DuPont time trial was three times that distance. With his bad back, it would be tough for Lance to stay in the low-down time-trial position for that long. And he was facing Alcalá, a gifted time-trialist who three years earlier won a Tour de France time trial, ninety seconds ahead of Miguel Induráin, the Spaniard who'd go on to win five Tours.

Alcalá beat Lance by two minutes in Greensboro. The result was not surprising to the sport's insiders, but Lance was bitterly disappointed. He retained second place overall, however, proving himself as a leader to his Motorola teammates.

"Lance was very ambitious, and he obviously had great talent," Yates says. "For me, that was a perfect combination. Ever since I turned pro in '82, I was always motivated to ride for others. It's nice to have ambitions within the team and a leader who has objectives—and Lance was that guy. He allowed me to do what I like doing most, and that's riding on the front."

Andy Hampsten, Motorola's designated leader for the upcoming Tour de France, also recognized that Lance was quickly acquiring the tactical skills of a winner. "With the help of Bauer, Yates, and Anderson, he was learning things like who's going to work in a break," Hampsten says. "He's very good at anticipating other people's moves, and he was very interested in characters—how people want to race, how they psych other people out—to watch for that and anticipate it. And he's brilliant at making the break in really difficult situations and reading the politics in a race to make things happen."

Lance would need all these skills in the weeks ahead, starting with three races that offered an inspiring challenge.

The challenge was called the Thrift Drug Triple Crown. If one athlete won all three races—the Thrift Drug Classic in Pittsburgh, the Kmart Mountain Classic of West Virginia, and the CoreStates USPRO Championship in Philadelphia—he would be awarded a check for one million dollars. It would be the biggest payout in the sport of cycling; the winner of the Tour de France earned only one fifth that amount. But the chances of someone taking the Triple Crown were considered so slim that Lloyds of London insured the race promoters for the million bucks.

If Lance needed more motivation, this was it. When his mom heard about the prize, she asked him, "What are the odds that you can do that?" "Pretty good," he replied. "I'm gonna *win* it." "Okay!"

she said, knowing that when her son went into a challenge with that attitude, he usually came out on top.

Still, Lance knew it wouldn't be easy to win three such difficult and diverse races. The easiest for him would be the first, the Thrift Drug Classic in Pittsburgh. As an amateur, he won this multilap race the year before by making repeated attacks on the circuit's vicious climb up Mount Washington. "That was a hard hill, steep, with a little bit of cobbles at the top," Lance says. "That was the best race America had back then."

This time, he raced even stronger. "We saw at Pittsburgh that this guy was something special," says Len Pettyjohn, manager of the rival Coors Light team. "When he attacked, he literally rode away, and there was nothing we could do. We could organize a chase, but he was gone."

Next up was the Kmart race in West Virginia, a six-day stage race that included a slew of tough climbs in the Appalachians. "Our Scott Moninger had won there the year before," Pettyjohn says, "and we thought we had a great team for this race. It's a hard one, but Mike Engleman, our other climber, was in top form."

The event began with a short time trial, known as a prologue, of one and a half miles. Lance won it in dominant style ahead of a former Olympic track gold medalist, Steve Hegg, and he felt ready to win again the next day. Anderson, who was Motorola's road captain and responsible for making tactical decisions, recalls that Lance was wired with ambition on what was the event's most challenging stage. "He just wanted to go on the attack," Anderson says. "He would come riding up to me and say, 'Can I go now?' I'd say no. Then he would come again: 'Can I go now?' 'No, not yet.' Then we were coming to the bottom of this steep hill, and he comes up again: 'Can I go now?' I said yeah, and his eyes lit up, his whole body came alive, and he shot away up that hill faster than anyone I've seen."

Lance sped up to an earlier breakaway group, blew it apart, and bolted clear. "I felt like I could ride through a brick wall," Lance says. "I remember in West Virginia riding away from people just like a motorbike." Only one man could stay with him: Coors Light's Engleman. Engleman was strong that day, but Lance was stronger. He took the stage and finished two minutes ahead of the rest. The Texan was in power mode, and four days and four stages later he took the overall victory in the Kmart race well ahead of Engleman. It was now two down, one to go, in the Triple Crown.

The final event, in Philadelphia, was still a week away, so rather than contest a couple of midweek races, Lance returned home to Austin to focus on recovery and rebuild his form. He did motor-paced workouts behind J. T. Neal's motor scooter and went for five-hour rides in the Texas Hill Country. It was a smart decision: He gained a week of low-key training and avoided the growing East Coast media buzz surrounding his potential lottery-sized payday.

Lance flew back on the eve of the race to attend a press conference where he made the statement that would soon follow him everywhere. When a reporter asked if he was "the next Greg LeMond," Lance replied, "I'm flattered by the description, but I'm on the Lance Armstrong agenda."

If any man was qualified to assess whether Lance would follow in LeMond's footsteps and win multiple world championships and Tour de France titles, it was Pettyjohn. The Coloradan had helped LeMond in his comeback victory at the 1989 Tour, and he had a close-up look at both athletes during the formative times of their careers. "My assessment of Lance at the time was that he was every bit as good as Greg in terms of his power, his tenacity, and his singular focus on being the best," Pettyjohn says. "He had the personality of a really arrogant guy who you knew was gonna die on the bike before you beat him.

"What Lance had at that point was explosiveness, an ability to light it up for a short period of time when the race was really hard, beyond what I ever saw Greg do. Also, by training year-round he was far more disciplined than Greg, who had no discipline in the off-season."

For Lance, year-round training seemed natural; it was what he had done as a teenager and triathlete. And the previous off-season, he had trained in Como under Massimo Testa. "I introduced him to rowing," Testa says. "I'd have my guys rowing on Lake Como from October through December. It was great cross-training before they got on the bike."

Lance might have remembered that training as he test-rode the Philadelphia course, looking out at the varsity crews on the choppy waters of the Schuylkill, the day before the last leg of the three-race challenge. The race's ten laps of a 14.4-mile circuit (followed by three short, finishing loops) take in Kelly Drive, Fairmont Park, and the blue-collar neighborhood of Manayunk, which features a formidable hill known as the Wall. This was the setting for his chance at taking home the Triple Crown—and a million-dollar check.

By the 9 a.m. start of the CoreStates USPRO Championship on June 6, 1993, tens of thousands of spectators had already gathered along Philadelphia's Benjamin Franklin Parkway, where the race would begin and end. A cool northerly breeze rustled the flags of the nations posted along the four-lane boulevard; a second-grader sang the National Anthem; and the U.S. riders in the 125-strong field placed their right hands over their hearts. Besides being an internationally rated event, this was also the national pro road championship, and the first American to finish the 153-mile race would be awarded the coveted Stars-and-Stripes cycling jersey.

Lance was up early that day and breakfasted on pasta and eggs before heading to the start. In the staging area, he flashed a confident smile and said he wasn't at all nervous about the six hours of racing that lay ahead. He then talked to me about his planned tactics, knowing that this relatively flat course favored a mass-sprint finish. But, he added, after riding the circuit the day before, he thought it possible for a solo rider to make a successful breakaway. Motioning with his hand, the rookie pointed out that the wind was blowing from the north. "That wind makes it hard for a solo rider up by the river," he said. "But if you get away on the Wall on the last lap, you have a tailwind blowing you back to the finish."

His theory was sound, but for 99 percent of the starters such a bold tactic was an extreme long shot; every race in the event's history had seen the finish contested by a small group or even the whole peloton. Then again, to become the first rider to pull off a solo victory was exactly the type of challenge that inspired Lance.

The gun was fired, the race began, and there were the expected early attacks leading to a long breakaway; but the field was back together with fifty miles to go. Lance had been easily following his teammates' wheels for more than four hours, and then his Aussie mentor Anderson made a strong surge over the cobblestone streets of Manayunk to split the pack—with forty miles remaining. With Anderson's impetus, Lance launched himself up the half-mile Wall, urged on by thousands of partying fans.

"No one was gonna stop Lance that day," Yates says. "I couldn't stay with him on the hill, and that was a good hill for me. He was riding at a whole other level. He was turbo."

Only five men did manage to catch Lance over the hilltop, including Roberto Gaggioli, an Italian sprinter on the Coors Light team. All six riders—three Americans, three Italians—were still together as they headed into Manayunk for the tenth and final time, now two minutes ahead of the Motorola-controlled peloton.

Pettyjohn picks up the story: "It was the last lap, we were rolling along the river, and Gaggioli came back to the car. He looks at me, and he goes, 'I hope Lance doesn't attack again.' I said, 'What do you mean? He *is* gonna attack.' He goes, 'I can't follow him.' And when Lance went away, the others were all looking at each other, all cross-eyed, and Lance rode away alone."

Racing as ferociously as he did in his key uphill attack in West Virginia, Lance gained almost thirty seconds in that half mile up the infamous Wall. And he knew he'd be racing solo with no one to help him over the remaining seventeen miles. Just as he predicted, Lance was riding with the wind at his back toward the finish line. He'd soon be passing the Philadelphia Museum of Art, where Rocky Balboa ran up the steps to the triumphant rhythm of the "Gonna Fly Now" theme song: "Trying hard now / won't be long now / flying high now / gonna fly, fly, fly."

At a crossover point on the course, where Lance could see his pursuers, his old friend Bob Mionske, riding in the opposite direction, gave him the thumbs-up. "He told me later he thought that was pretty cool," Mionske says.

Lance's mom had flown in for the day. She was standing by the finish line when her son came cruising down the Parkway with his arms thrust high in celebration. And she joined Lance on the podium as he received the national champion's jersey and a giant facsimile check for a million dollars.

At the time, there was some talk that deals had been struck between riders on a few teams to help Lance win the million-dollar prize, but nothing was ever confirmed. However, fifteen years later, Grewal tells me that after the race he received “a sealed envelope with two grand in crisp one-hundred-dollar notes.” He explains that the deal—whereby he and his Coors Light teammates each got a share of the big payout—was first discussed at the Kmart Classic in West Virginia, soon after Lance decisively won that race’s first two stages.

With Lance in a commanding overall lead after those two stage wins, his Motorola teammates faced a formidable task: riding hard at the front for the remaining four days to stop any threatening breakaways and to keep Lance fresh enough to respond to attacks. Riding “tempo” all day is a difficult assignment for a nine-man team at the Tour de France; it was almost as tough in this American race where there were only six on a team.

The Motorola guys were understandably exhausted at the end of the first of those four days, after pulling the peloton for more than six hours on an undulating course of 137 miles. They weren’t too eager to repeat this for three more days, and so they looked for some help.

It’s not uncommon, though rarely discussed, for two teams to work together in a stage race if both sides can benefit. The helping team might get support in a future race or take a piece of the prize-money pie. Such a deal was proposed after that third day in West Virginia. One of the Motorola men went to a Coors Light rider and suggested that their two teams share the workload for the remainder of the Kmart race. If they did, it virtually guaranteed that Lance and Coors Light’s Engleman would remain in first and second places for that event. The Coors Light riders knew that their leader had no chance of making up time on the formidable Lance. So a deal was struck, and Lance went on to win that second of the three Triple Crown races.

On the morning of the final race in Philadelphia, the Coors Light riders met to discuss their tactics for the day and to decide if they would extend their West Virginia pact to favor Lance winning the

Triple Crown. "I wasn't against it in the pre-race team meeting," Grewal tells me, "as I knew Lance was gonna win anyway."

Only one man at the meeting opted out of the deal. That was Davis Phinney, who had won the USPRO title two years earlier. "I got wind of some deal-making. I didn't want to hear or know about it. And I still don't know the details," Phinney tells me. "So in the room, I made my famous statement: 'I'm here to win the race, I will do everything I can to win the race, and I hope you will support me in trying to win the race.' And then I walked out."

Was the race fixed? No. In baseball, basketball, or soccer, match-fixing is relatively easy because only two teams are involved, and one of them can throw the game. But in a typical pro bike race, there can be twenty teams, each with eight riders, so it would be hard to pull off. Nor would there be much of an incentive once you divided the prize money one-hundred-and-sixty ways.

At that Philadelphia race, the Coors Light riders had no way of guaranteeing a win for Lance, but they could improve his odds by a few percentage points. That's why the potential cut for each of the deal participants would be only $2,000 if Lance won. And with ten teams vying for the win, including five European squads that flew in just for this race, that was a big "if."

"I was so new to cycling," Lance says, "I wouldn't have known whether Och made a deal or what. In cycling, you're always making allies on a daily basis. But the fact of the matter is, it would be hard to rig a race like Philly."

Phinney was emphatic that Lance would have won the Triple Crown, deal or no deal. "I don't think it affected the race," he says. "Maybe some guys benefited from doing nothing. . . . I was right alongside Lance before the Manayunk Wall. There was Malcolm Elliott, myself, and one or two others; all of us were right at the front. He just motored away and then turned and gave us what would become 'the Look.'

"I remember thinking, 'That's it! There goes the future, and I'm not part of it!' He just took off like a rocket. It was not like anyone was holding back. We were just toast. He won that race so fair and square. Lance always had that extra gear. He could do something that 99.9 percent of the population was incapable of doing."

Lance's teammate Anderson says that his eventual split of the Triple Crown prize money, divided among the entire Motorola team roster of eighteen and support staff of twelve, was $15,000. Because the prize was taken as cash and not spread over twenty years, the million dwindled to $600,000, which was then subject to deductions by the U.S. Pro Cycling Federation and the Internal Revenue Service.

But Lance left with something more: As the Triple Crown winner, he now had an aura of supreme confidence and the Stars-and-Stripes jersey on his back; and he'd be wearing those prestigious colors at his first Tour de France the following month. "Lance started pressing me hard for a Tour start at the DuPont race," Och says, "and by Philadelphia he was winning everything, so I couldn't *not* give him his chance. But it came with a restriction: I was gonna pull him out of the race not long after we got to the first mountains."

Andy Hampsten twice finished fourth at the Tour de France and made the race his main season goal after 1988, when he became the first American to win the Giro d'Italia, a race second in prestige only to the Tour. In 1993, the blond, straight-backed Coloradan was the undisputed leader of Motorola's Tour team, while a recent addition to the squad, Colombian Alvaro Mejia, was his first lieutenant. Lance was there to get some experience, help Hampsten as much as he could, and perhaps shoot for a stage win.

After his solo victory in Philadelphia, Lance had returned to the

Tour of Sweden, the race he did as an amateur three years before. That first time, he barely survived; this time, he won a stage and placed third overall, a minute behind the winner, his Australian teammate Anderson. Their colleagues Max Sciandri, Frankie Andreu, and Yates also finished in the top ten, boosting the team's morale ahead of the Tour de France.

After a short training camp in Normandy, where Motorola's nine Tour riders tested their aero' bikes and scouted the Tour's upcoming team time-trial course, they headed to the start at Puy du Fou in central France. Lance was getting his wish to race in cycling's premier event, and he was finding the Tour to be everything he hoped for. As the youngest man in the race, he was psyched to be in the nighttime presentation of the twenty teams on a lake fronting a medieval castle; he was motivated by the prologue circuit that included a hill just like the Wall in Philadelphia; and he was astounded by the 150,000 fans who showed up on prologue day to watch the 180 starters ride their individual time trials at one-minute intervals.

Knowing he had great form, Lance expected he'd be one of the protagonists in the prologue. But like an overeager beginner, he went too fast, too soon; and when he hit a headwind on the exposed half-mile climb, he slowed to a crawl. Far from making a glorious debut, Lance was upset to learn that eighty men finished ahead of him; and Miguel Induráin, the winner and defending Tour champion, went forty-seven seconds faster than him in just four miles of racing.

Lance's excitement was revived at the fifty-mile team time trial four days later, when he helped Motorola place third, the best ever by a U.S. team at the Tour. After pulling his teammates up a long hill to the finish in Avranches, Lance said, "I felt okay, but I had a bad stretch in the middle. I just can't do the sixty kilometers an hour on the flats yet." That wasn't surprising; even Hampsten had problems staying with the near-forty-mile-per-hour pace set by the dynamos of the team, Anderson, Bauer, and Yates. "I was pretty hammered at the end," Hampsten said.

Hampsten has better memories of the Tour's second weekend, in northern France, when everyone was talking about the Motorola team. On that Saturday's hilly stage, three of his teammates made it into the winning seven-man move: Anderson, Sciandri, and Mejia.

"With three out of seven in the break, we should have won the stage," says team boss Och. "But it was tough because we were riding to get Mejia time for the overall. This meant that Anderson and Sciandri had to ride a lot harder than they would have in the break," rather than saving something for a sprint win.

In the end, Sciandri unexpectedly lost the sprint to Danish rider Bjarne Riis. "Sciandri was very embarrassed not to have won," Hampsten says, "and Anderson was pretty pissed about it."

So was Lance. "I couldn't believe how a donkey like Riis could beat a thoroughbred like Sciandri," he said.

"Lance just rolled by at the end and shook his head at the guys," Och recalls.

"And Lance doesn't like Riis, never did," Yates says. "And then for him to beat Max when we had three in the break . . . that pissed him off. His attitude was: I'll show 'em how to bloody do it on me own! That's what he said he'd do the next day, and he had the legs to pull it off."

The next day saw a NATO commander, General Charles Boyd, riding with Och in the Motorola car. "I was notified by the State Department that he wanted to see a Tour stage," Och says. "The four-star general pulled in with two armored cars just before the team meeting. He wanted to know every strategy. He picked that stage because it finished at Verdun."

The Battle of Verdun, in 1916, was the most deadly military confrontation in history. Almost a quarter of a million French and German soldiers were killed, and another 400,000 men were injured. As a mark of respect for the fallen, the Tour organizers banned the raucous publicity caravan from driving through the battlefield. For the racers, though, the tens of thousands of white crosses dotting a grassy hillside were a backdrop to a fierce fight for supremacy.

The Tour's top contenders—Induráin of Spain, Tony Rominger and Alex Zülle of Switzerland, and Claudio Chiappucci of Italy—quickly responded to each other's accelerations on the steep climb to the battlefield's highest ridge. And right up there with them was Lance, who'd been helped all day by his teammates to keep him ready for this moment.

At the twelve-hundred-foot summit, a crash sent Zülle tumbling to the ground and splintered the field. Lance managed to stay in the front group of thirty with Induráin, Rominger, and Chiappucci. Then, weaving his way forward in the fast-moving line of riders, Lance spotted three men jumping clear. "Shit, I've gotta get up there," he told himself. He did, but he took two men with him: his Tour DuPont rival Alcalá and Frenchman Ronan Pensec. The six leaders soon joined forces and headed into Verdun with a fifteen-second gap on the chasing group.

Lance followed the other five as they tried, separately, to escape for the win; but they were still together entering the streets of Verdun. "I was at the back of the group and to the right," Lance recalls. "Pensec was ahead of me and moving right, toward the barriers." The only chance Lance had of winning as they raced into town at forty miles an hour was to get through the narrowing gap between Pensec and the metal crowd barriers. And if Pensec blocked Lance, the Frenchman could be disqualified for interference since they were less than two hundred meters from the line. "So I started yelling at him," Lance says. "I thought, 'He's gotta stop moving over.' And he did."

Lance stood on his pedals, pumped his legs with maniacal energy, and threw his bike from side to side as he burst between Pensec and the metal barricade. He knew he was winning, and before crossing the line two feet ahead of Alcalá, who'd made a late rush on the other side of the street, Lance lifted his hands from the bars, thrust out his chest, and raised his arms in triumph.

At that moment, in a living room in Germany, an American athlete watching the race live on television suddenly leapt up from a couch, threw *his* arms in the air, and began shouting at the top of his voice—much to the German family's surprise! The athlete was Mark Allen, the superstar triathlete and Ironman world champion, who competed against Lance six years' earlier when Lance was a teenage prodigy.

"I saw the entire stage, so I'd seen how difficult it was," recalls Allen, who was in Germany for an Ironman race. "It wasn't like at the very end he outsprinted everybody; it was just one attack after another after another after another. This was before the Tour was live in the States, and I was in Europe, so I was one step closer to the reality.

"Lance seemed to be in every single attack. It's getting toward the end of the stage, and the attack group's getting whittled down, fewer and fewer guys. All of a sudden, Lance is one of the last guys left, and he comes around this French guy and wins the stage. I was off of the couch screaming 'Lance!' It was very impressive, and for him to win a stage in the Tour at that age, that was the real beginning."

It's been said that Lance, at twenty-one, was the youngest athlete to win a stage of the Tour. In truth, the youngest was Frenchman Henri Cornet, who was only nineteen when he won a stage at

Toulouse in 1904. More important than Lance's age, though, was the fact that he had made a breakthrough before a world audience.

"That was a big day for Lance," Och says. "That really was the start of who he was and where he was going. His wins in Philadelphia, Laigueglia, and elsewhere, they count . . . but a legitimate stage win at the Tour was so much bigger."

Lance winning a Tour stage in the Stars-and-Stripes jersey of U.S. champion produced massive worldwide publicity; it also generated effusive praise from the influential General Boyd. Both factors contributed to Motorola extending its $3 million-a-year team sponsorship; in addition, Och raised Lance's next-year salary to $500,000. It was heady stuff for a young man of college age, but it didn't stop him from extending his Tour into the mountain stages, where he would discover how this race can bring you to your knees.

His team trainer, Testa, remembers exactly how Lance fared. "When we hit the Alps, Lance said, 'I want to do at least one day in the mountains; I'm not tired at all.' And we told him, 'We don't want to see you in the lead group or the second group, but in the third group, where most people ride. Just look for Yates.'"

On the first of these alpine stages, Lance rode with Yates for the entire six hours and over three mountain passes—including the legendary Galibier Pass, which climbs 6,890 vertical feet in 22 miles—and the two men finished strongly in the second group, twelve minutes ahead of the main pack and twenty-one minutes behind the leaders.

"Lance did a great stage, really up there in the second group," Testa says, "and he said, 'I want to try one more stage to see how I recover overnight.'"

The next stage was an even tougher 127 miles, with four giant climbs, and Lance struggled on the concluding 10-mile ascent to the ski resort of Isola 2000. He rode the final switchbacks in the shelter of his teammate, Anderson, and finished almost twenty-nine minutes behind the stage winner. On crossing the line, Lance headed straight to the team's hotel.

"I was looking for him after the stage because he was going really hard at the end, and he was fatigued," Testa says. "I wanted to see how he was doing. He was in like room 11,000. I eventually found it, and I opened the door, and everything is like empty, untouched, and the shades are still down. I thought, there's no one here. So I go in and look around, and it's like a dorm, with three small rooms, each with bunk beds.

"In one of the rooms I see something moving under a blanket. It was dark. I go in and touch the blanket, and it was Lance. Outside it was super-hot, but he was in bed with two or three sweaters on and a wool hat. He's under this blanket, and he was shaking. That's what happens when you're dehydrated. So I say, 'Hey, Lance, how do you feel?' He said, 'Doing great. Tomorrow, I want to try another.'"

Despite finishing almost half an hour behind the best, Lance had still completed that stage ahead of fifty-four riders, while another twenty men had quit the race on the two brutal days through the Alps. The young Texan had proven himself to be, as they say, a true Tourman. "He's exactly the opposite of the complainers," Testa says. "For him, the little problems are no problem, and the big problems actually charge him up to go harder. That's a unique combination of physiology and mental attitude."

Lance had completed twelve of the twenty-one stages, and he probably could have continued. But his Austin friend J. T. Neal had arrived at the race, and he would drive Lance back to Como the next morning as had previously been arranged. In Como, Lance would start preparing for another challenge: the world championships. He was back on the road to winning, and that's just where he wanted to be.

CHAPTER 10

THE RAINBOW AND THE GOLD

> It was a very simple place, just an empty room with his bike and somewhere basic to sleep.
>
> —PIER BERGONZI

FOLLOWING LANCE'S PLANNED DEPARTURE from his first Tour de France, Motorola's team boss Jim Ochowicz and trainer Massimo Testa were concerned about their young star's next goal. "Max was nervous, and I was nervous, that Lance would actually *win* the worlds," Och says. "It's hard to be the world champion at twenty-one and deal with all the accolades that go with that title. What are the expectations after that? Could it be the end of his career?"

The two men were questioning the benefits of Lance taking the world pro title, which reaps massive prestige and publicity in Europe. The championship is normally won by an established star, someone who has the stature to take in stride one more honor. What concerned Och and Testa was the chance that being rewarded prematurely with the sport's supreme title could stunt Lance's development or even end his ambitions. They both knew that cyclists who win too much, too soon, can lose their appetite for the laborious training that is necessary for continued success.

Nonetheless, in that summer of 1993 before the worlds in Oslo, Norway, Och and Testa decided to "get behind Lance 100 percent."

No event in cycling is more dramatic than the world professional road race championship. It's one race on one day and produces one winner. The outcome is rarely known until the last few seconds when the strongest survivors sprint for the line and one of them gets there first. Occasionally, the event produces a lucky winner—perhaps because the course is not selective enough or because the race comes down to a mass sprint and the one who takes the most risks wins.

But more often, the race rewards the strongest, most enterprising rider, an athlete who has won or goes on to win other major races, the one who truly is the world's best cyclist: an Eddy Merckx, a Greg LeMond, or perhaps this year, the man who'd just won his third straight Tour de France, Miguel Induráin.

The winner of the worlds is awarded a gold medal and a simple white racing jersey that has a rainbow hoop around the chest made up of blue, red, black, yellow, and green bands, representing the five continents. The rainbow jersey is worn by the champion in every race for the following year, which adds greatly to his visibility—and to the burden of living up to his newly won reputation.

As Lance prepared for the 1993 worlds, he reviewed his previous attempts to become a world or Olympic champion. At the junior worlds in 1989 and at the senior worlds the following year, he made the mistake of burning all his energy too early in the race. At the 1992 Olympics, he simply had an off-day, while his first stab at the pro title ended with a crash. Now, a year later, he knew two things: the need to focus his training on still being competitive at the end of a race lasting six or more hours, and the need to have his final preparations include training on the actual course.

While his teammates were still racing the Tour, Lance trained alone in Como, where he had an informal routine with Testa. "Almost every morning, he came to see me at my family practice on the Piazza Volta in old town Como," Testa says. "He would come to the cappuccino place next door, and if it was rainy I'd put my head out the window and tell him, 'Okay, today, four hours, and go do this climb, or go hard on this one.' I knew all the roads."

After the Tour finished—with Motorola's Alvaro Mejia in fourth and Andy Hampsten eighth—Lance had some company for his rides. "A couple of times," Testa says, "I joined him on my scooter with Mejia and Andy to do uphill motor-pacing. When I blew on my whistle like a soccer coach, they had to jump hard up the hill. So one jumps, the second one jumps, then the third one. And Lance made it look easy. He had really trimmed down since riding the Tour, and he was climbing much faster. He also had good acceleration."

The training paid off for Lance in a series of World Cup races that August. In these six-hour events, he was usually the most aggressive rider. He placed thirty-fifth in Spain's Clasicá San Sebastián (a year after finishing dead last), fifth in Britain's Wincanton Classic, and fourteenth at Switzerland's Championship of Zürich, his last race before the worlds.

"He should have done better in Zürich," Och says. "Once again, he didn't wait long enough before making his move." It was a tactical mistake that Lance would discuss with Och the next morning, when they took a short training ride together in the pouring rain, a ride that almost ended in disaster.

"We were coming back into Zürich, flying down this hill, and as we were coming around a turn, I could see some rail tracks ahead," Och says. "I didn't see the tracks were running along the street until too late. As I hit them, my wheel got caught in the tracks, and I went down hard. The impact burnt the watch off my wrist. Lance saw I was coming down, so he went to the left of the island and into the traffic coming the other way."

It could have been the end of Lance's hopes for the following weekend's world title race, but he swerved out of danger before coming to a halt. Besides showing his presence of mind, the narrow escape demonstrated just how much his bike-handling skills had improved.

Lance's mom arrived from Texas to watch her son race in Oslo. "I was there for a week," Linda says, "and I could see him getting a little quieter each day, going into that certain mental state, like a winner."

Thanks to good weather, Lance was able to follow his pre-worlds training goals. On the easy days, he rode with Och. For some of the longer rides, he trained with his mentor Anderson, who'd be racing for the four-man Australian squad. In theory, Lance and Anderson should have been rivals in the race, but afterward Lance revealed, "Phil was looking out for me all the time. He was wearing an Australian team jersey, but he was still a Motorola rider, and he was there for me—which was great!"

At that time, the American and Australian national pro cycling federations had very few licensed racers, and there was no money to pay the men selected to ride the worlds. Och says he even paid the week's hotel bill for the U.S. team. In contrast, the well-funded European federations each had a pool of cash to pay big bonuses to their riders should one of them take the title.

The Italian team was considered the top favorite to win. It was led by three former world champions, Moreno Argentin, Gianni Bugno, and Maurizio Fondriest, and also included Claudio Chiappucci, who was fresh off winning the Clasicá San Sebastián. Then there was Spain's Induráin, who was eager to add the worlds' rainbow jersey to his collection of three yellow jerseys from the Tour.

Lance, the youngest man in the event, was considered to have at best a 5 percent chance of winning—although his odds increased slightly when the week's sunshine was replaced by a steady drizzle on the morning of the race. "Lance didn't *like* to race in the rain, but he didn't mind it," Och explains, "and he knew that 50 percent of the field was done when it rained. . . . The strategy we'd agreed with Lance was: Don't make a move until two laps to go; that's the very soonest you try to go with a break."

Lance's most experienced teammate for the race was Hampsten. "We felt really good that Lance was our protected man," Hampsten says. "He had really good form, and we knew it would be a race of attrition. I had the role as captain as far as orchestrating what the team was doing."

As the 171 riders lined up for the fourteen-lap, 160-mile championship, anxiety was etched on their faces. They wore plastic rain jackets over their colorful national team jerseys, knowing that the rain had set in for the day. They also knew that the roads would be treacherous, especially on the painted white and yellow street markings. "I'm not sure the course will be that easy," Lance said, in a blend of bravado and understatement, as he waited for the starter's pistol.

Once the race began, so did the crashes. More than a race of attrition, it became a race of survival. "The roads were so slick and there were so many crashes, it was hard to keep track of what was going on," Och says.

"We didn't know it was going to be that slippery," Hampsten adds. "It was really chaotic, a lot of fear, a lot of stress amongst all the riders. And I remember watching the Italians freaking out—Gianni Bugno just stopping in his pit saying, 'I'm done, I'm done,' and his mechanics letting air out of his tires because of the slick turns, and then pushing him back in the race.

"Because of the weather, we said, 'Let's just keep an eye on Lance.' It's not like we could lead him up to the front, riding in the wind to protect him all the time. And he told us he didn't want to be ferried around. We just stayed some distance behind him in the peloton, so if he crashed we wouldn't be in the crash.

"And he did crash—a couple of times. But we didn't panic or try to get him up to the group immediately. By now we'd figured out where we could ride hard, which road surfaces we could go fast on. I remember people saying, 'Lance's down again!' We would try not to do a huge show with everyone coming back to help him, but with two or three guys coming back on the flats and getting him to where we wanted him to be."

As more and more riders crashed out or quit, Lance sat quietly in the peloton remembering Och's advice to wait. "I was trying to be patient and control myself," he said. "I knew that if a winning break was going to happen, it would happen on the last lap."

The end game actually began on the penultimate lap when Induráin responded to an acceleration by Chiappucci. Lance quickly closed on them, followed by about a dozen others. A counterattack then came from local hero Dag-Otto Lauritzen and Dutchman Frans Maassen, and they began the final lap four seconds ahead of twelve chasers. The winner would be one of these fourteen men, who came from ten different nations. Lance was the only non-European.

None of the leaders wanted to risk making a winning effort too soon, so they waited. But when Lauritzen dropped Maassen on the longest of the course's two hills and began to move out of sight of the group, Lance grabbed the opportunity. "The peloton was racing negatively, and I knew I had to go then," he said. "So I did."

With nine miles to go, Lance sped away up the climb. Maassen latched onto his wheel, and they caught Lauritzen by the top of the ridge. Ahead lay a tricky descent before the last short climb, followed by a longer downhill and then a fast, flat run-in to the finish.

"Lance just bombed that first descent," Hampsten says. "He did some brilliant bike-handling to make it safely around a little left-hand curve where there'd already been about forty crashes. That downhill was so crucial, and he had all this momentum and the power to carry his speed into the last hill and to kick it over the top. It was tremendous!"

The Induráin group chased and caught Lauritzen and Maassen by the final summit, and they were now furiously racing after Lance—who disappeared into the heavy rain, riding along a straight, flat road across a plateau before making the fast, curving descent toward the gray waters of the Oslo Fjord.

Watching the race at the finish line was the U.S. team physician, Andy Pruitt, who had been working on Lance's back problem that week. He remembers thinking, "This kid's back was out, and he attacks the powers-that-be of cycling, riding the tops of his handlebars. He just rode away from them. It was phenomenal! Our jaws were on the ground."

Induráin and the other superstars continued to chase, but Lance increased his lead on the downhill from ten to twenty seconds. Once he made it down to sea level and completed the last of the treacherous turns, he took a quick look back. "I turned around to see if the peloton was there," he said, "but I couldn't see them."

Then, after he swept down the straightaway with only seven

hundred meters remaining, he looked behind again, and yet again—still no one. He knew he had it won. All the way down that finishing stretch, Lance celebrated his astonishing success: He waved, shouted, blew kisses, and bowed to the crowds standing under umbrellas. The fans from all over Europe and a handful of Americans, including Lance's mom, responded with loud cheers and thunderous applause as the new champion thrust his arms high above his bare head and pointed his index fingers toward the clouds.

"People think I'm cocky because I get so emotional in my victories," Lance later said. "They think, 'Who does he think he is? Is he trying to rub it in the other guy's face?' That's not the case. It's not something I can control. I have to do it with emotion or I'm not gonna win."

Induráin, one of cycling's all-time greats, led home the chasers for second place. "I started feeling better towards the end, and I was strong for the sprint," the Spanish rider said. "But that was all I was good for. To win the title is a whole other thing."

A frenzied mass of reporters and television crews chased Lance beyond the finish line, but his trainer, Testa, was the first to reach him. They hugged excitedly, and "the first thing Lance said was that he was kind of shocked that he'd beaten all those big guys."

Afterward, Testa says, the officials "wanted to take Lance to see the Norwegian king, but they didn't want his mom. Och and I were working as mediators with the officials, and Lance said, 'Max, bottom line, I don't want to see the king; it's the king that wants to see the world champ, right? So if he wants to see me, my mom comes with me. Otherwise, they won't see either one of us.'

"So his mom went in with him. . . . If I was twenty-one and they said you can't take your mom to see the king, I would accept that as being the rules. But not Lance."

Had he known he has Norwegian blood in him, Lance might have been more eager to meet the king. Lance's dad's great-grandparents,

Martin and Marie Gunderson, were born in Oslo, and left Norway for Texas toward the end of the nineteenth century.

But the only family connection Lance felt on this momentous day was with his mom, who says that her son winning the world championship remains the happiest moment she has shared with him. "That was an absolutely amazing time," Linda says. "He wanted that so *bad.*"

At twenty-one, Lance was the third-youngest world pro champion in the race's history. And like all new world champions, he was about to receive his full share of adulation.

With the rain still falling, Lance stood on the winner's podium, a gold medal hanging from his wide neck and the rainbow jersey stretched over his broad chest. The U.S. anthem was playing, and hearing it made him remember the path that brought him to this point. "I was thinking about growing up, watching the Olympics on TV," he said. "That was my dream, to be on the podium and hear the national anthem. And for me to hear it here in front of thousands of foreigners was pretty special. It certainly made up for the Olympics."

Barcelona had been a big disappointment, so for Lance and Linda, Oslo was their breakout moment. "I later framed the world championship jersey and the gold medal," Linda says, "and then put pictures on either side to make a little shrine to Lance."

After partying all night in Oslo with his American teammates, Lance had only two hours' sleep before taking a charter flight to the far west of France for a special invitation race. As the new world champion, he was the star attraction, greeted by tens of thousands of French cycling fans in the town of Châteaulin. He was also given a huge appearance fee, more money than he earned in a year just two seasons earlier.

When he returned to Como, Lance was feted like a hero. Neighbors in his apartment complex had decorated the building and hung banners greeting *nostro campione* ("our champion"). The European media soon arrived to interview the young American phenomenon. And when Lance went for a short training ride, the townspeople chased after him, clamoring for his autograph.

"My life has changed forever," Lance said. "Whether or not I like it is pretty irrelevant, because now I am the world champion."

Among the media that came to see Lance in Como was Pier Bergonzi, a reporter from *La Gazzetta dello Sport*, the top Italian sports daily. He and a photographer spent the day with Lance, shooting photos of him in different parts of town and conducting an interview at his two-bedroom apartment—"It was a very simple place, just an empty room with his bike and somewhere basic to sleep," Bergonzi says. The day ended with dinner at the elegant Villa Flori on the palm-fringed shore of Lake Como. Lance and the journalist were the guests of Och and the Motorola corporate brass, who were staying at the four-star hotel.

Everyone at that dinner was excited for Lance. He was at the pinnacle of his sport only a year after turning pro. But the nervousness that Och expressed before the worlds was still apparent. "Lance was already starting to think about the next year," he says, "riding with the rainbow jersey and always having that attention and the pressure of being the world champion." Bergonzi asked Testa what he saw in Lance's future. "I said that he was a former triathlete and swimmer," Testa says, "and so he had a big upper body—all muscle, no fat. So you can only get his body lighter by remodeling the muscles. Because of that, I said, I can't see him winning the Tour de France."

Now practicing sports medicine in Utah with orthopedic surgeon and Olympic great Eric Heiden, Testa knows that a true contender has to have a light upper body to be competitive on the Tour's giant mountain climbs. In 1993, Lance weighed 174 pounds. That was slightly more than Merckx when he was winning his five Tours, but Lance is two and a half inches shorter than the Belgian superstar. So for an equivalent weight-to-height ratio, Lance would need to shed at least 8 pounds; and Testa said the only way for Lance to lose that weight would be to remove mass from the muscles of his upper body. Not an easy task.

Lance, too, was asked whether he could see himself ever winning the Tour. He replied, "Later in my career, if I feel I can focus on my time-trialing and climbing, I don't know why I can't be up there in a grand tour. But for now, I am happy with being world champion."

Despite the celebrity status he acquired in Europe, Lance was relieved to get back to Austin by mid-September. Here, only true cycling aficionados knew or cared that they had a world champion living in town, so Lance was able to return to the low-key life he preferred. He had a few months to kick back, eat some Tex-Mex food, drink some Shiner Bock with his friends, watch the University of Texas and Dallas Cowboys football games, and even get back with one of his high-school girlfriends, Sonni Evans. While visiting Plano, he went to see another old buddy, Adam Wilk.

Lance was itching to spend some money, Wilk says. "He starts telling us, 'I've been getting like twenty . . .' He hesitates, then continues, 'I'm not bullshitting you, I've been getting twenty-five-thousand-dollar appearance fees, and they've been giving it to me in a paper bag.' Then he says, 'Let's go buy a car.'

"So off we go, these two punks in T-shirts, baseball caps backwards, just stupid stuff. He wanted to look at two sports cars, the Acura NSX and the BMW 8 series. First we go to the Beemer place, they don't even look at us . . . so we go down the street to the Acura dealership, and luckily the saleslady's husband was kind of into cycling, and so she'd heard of Lance. We did a test drive, and he writes a sixty-eight-grand check! He pays cash for a car! I was just like, damn!"

The NSX, which has a top speed of 140 miles per hour, is a road version of the Formula 1 race cars then driven by world champion Ayrton Senna. Wilk says that Lance called him a few weeks later to say he had burned through the first set of tires in eight hundred miles and that the custom tires cost $1,200 a piece. "So he didn't go so crazy with that car after that," Wilk says. "That was a twenty-one-year-old with a lot of money. Life's been good. Life's been *real* good."

Back in Austin, Lance was able to hook up again with his friend and massage therapist, J. T. Neal, and his old training partner, Bart Knaggs. But he didn't have a resident trainer or coach in Austin as he did in Italy. So he contacted his national team coach, Chris Carmichael, in Colorado Springs.

"Lance had just become the world champion, and he really wanted me to move to Austin," Carmichael says. "He said, 'You can work with Motorola, and Och will have you as an assistant director. You can move to Austin, and we can work really closely.' And he'd say, 'Damn, then you could motor-pace me, you can do this and that.' But it's not the motor-pacing I was worried about; it would be, 'Hey, can you stop and pick up the dry cleaning?' Because I had seen things evolve like that with other people. So I was like, 'I'm your coach. I'm not gonna pick up your dry cleaning. I'm not moving to Austin.'"

Lance was disappointed by his coach's decision, but it helped Carmichael earn his rider's respect, and that enabled them, eventually, to work together much more closely. For now, though, Lance would be coached from long-distance, and he'd get his daily feedback from J. T. and Knaggs, the two people he most relied on and respected in Austin.

"Lance was a tough judge of people," Knaggs says. "Instantly, he had an opinion on guys—he respected you or he didn't. And it took a lot to get his respect. If you asked him what he thought of someone, he'd say, 'He's a chump' or 'He's a bad-ass.' There was no in-between. And maybe he was wrong with his judgment sometimes. But he judges himself hard, and he doesn't have a separate way to judge everybody else."

Knaggs, whose mix of thoughtful demeanor and street talk appealed to Lance, says that one immediate connection between them was that they both came from broken families. "Lance is a lot like urban athletes that come from a shitty background, don't fit into school, and get chips on their shoulders," Knaggs says. "Maybe his whole cocky thing was false bravado. He was just used to fighting his way through shit."

Knaggs is not surprised that Lance was able to win cycling's elite world title in his first full season as a pro. "Anyone who's raced a bike knows the hardest thing is what goes on between your ears," he says. "There's so many physically talented people, but few of them truly succeed in sports. It's the mental side of it that matters. And the first check box is, can you suffer like a frigging pig?

"You can either take that as being some elegant, meditative state where you try to disassociate pain—that's what an Andy Hampsten does. Or you can be Lance. I think Lance conjured up all the pain he could muster and then burned it off. There's been other guys equally talented, but in the early years he just said he's gonna get to the last thirty miles, last twenty miles, last ten miles . . . and then I'm gonna out-*will* you!"

Back in Europe, people were still talking about the young upstart who somehow won a stage of the Tour de France and then the world title. Not everyone was pleased. The European peloton is a close-knit community where different teams spend hours riding together almost every day. They respect each other, the traditions of the sport, and the wisdom of their older riders. Enter Lance, the brash cowboy from Texas, who knew it all and did it his way.

One of the older riders the twenty-one-year-old Lance offended was the usually genial Allan Peiper, a Belgium-based Australian, who's now a well-regarded team director. At that year's Tour, Peiper had just retired from racing and was having a hard time doing his first assignment as a television reporter. He ran into Lance in Paris on the Tour's final weekend. "Lance had won his stage and left the race, but he had come back to Paris to celebrate with his Motorola teammates," Peiper says. "It was 11:30 on the Saturday night before the finish. I'd gone out to dinner with my camera crew and they were still at the table drinking when I left to look for a taxi. As I left the restaurant, I bumped into Lance. He was standing on the corner with a chick on each arm and two bottles of beer in each hand, and he said, 'Come and have a beer.' And I said, 'Nah, I'm going back to the hotel.' There were a lot of people where we were standing and he just yelled out, 'Peiper, you're a fucking pussy.' In Lance's way, maybe he was being friendly, trying to make contact. I didn't say anything. I just turned and kept walking."

Peiper adds, "Lance was an angry young man when he turned pro. He didn't have many friends in the bunch because he had no respect. He was this cocky young American who knew he was gonna make it."

Lance *was* making it, and now that he'd won the worlds, there was no more talk of fixed races or fluke wins. Instead, the talk centered on one question: Who *was* this American kid and how far could he go? One star thought he had the answer. Italy's Claudio Chiappucci boldly proclaimed, "One thing is certain: He will never win a major Tour."

CHAPTER 11

A SHADOW AND A CURSE

The sport changed a lot in one year. I'm not going to say why it changed or how I think it changed, but I will say that it changed a lot—and a lot of guys got a lot stronger and a lot faster.

—LANCE ARMSTRONG

PRO CYCLISTS TALK about the Curse of the Rainbow Jersey. The legend started in 1965, when British star Tom Simpson broke his leg skiing a few months after winning the world championship; and it grew in 1970, when world champion Jean-Pierre Monseré was killed in a race accident the following year. Other world champions have suffered serious accidents or an undue share of bad luck. And over the years, the curse has come to imply that whoever wears the rainbow jersey has trouble winning. That was the case with Lance. But even more, a shadow seemed to be cast over his year, a sense of uncertainty and confusion that affected his career, his relationships, his sport, and his spirit.

There were still high points, though, starting with a stellar performance in the spring classics.

Racing through the medieval streets of Liège, Belgium, on April 17, 1994, Lance looked set to win his first classic. Only two miles remained in the centennial edition of Liège-Bastogne-Liège, the oldest of Europe's most challenging one-day races. It covers 166 miles on a course of steep hills and deep valleys in the Ardennes region, where Patton's army won the Battle of the Bulge in World War II. Now, another American, wearing the rainbow jersey of world champion, was seeking a victory. Lance was in a lead group of five that had ripped the field apart and looked set to contest a sprint finish. "I knew I was the fastest finisher," Lance said, "and there was only one climb left."

Several world champions before him had won this classic, and Lance was aiming to join their prestigious company. But two riders posed a real danger. Both were members of Italy's Gewiss team: Giorgio Furlan, an Italian who had already won that year's Milan-San Remo, and his Russian sidekick, Evgeni Berzin. Lance expected the two men to deploy the well-known tactic of taking turns to accelerate and making their three rivals chase each time, until one of the two would eventually spring clear.

The Russian made the first attack—and that was it! He went so fast that none of the others could follow him. At the finish line, Lance was faster than the other three lead riders to take a hard-earned second place, but he couldn't understand where Berzin had found all that zip after seven hours in the saddle. "When Evgeni Berzin takes off with a mile to go and puts a minute thirty on four guys, that's not normal," Lance said. "I'm concerned about that."

His bewilderment only grew three days later when Berzin, Furlan, and a third Gewiss team rider, Moreno Argentin, left the rest of the pack in the dust at another hilly classic race in the Ardennes, the Flèche Wallonne.

Lance, Andy Hampsten, and their Motorola teammates, along with all the other teams, could do nothing when, with forty-four miles still to race, the three Gewiss men disappeared into the distance. A twenty-strong group chased hard after the trio, but could make no impression, while the peloton fell farther and farther behind.

"I was in the main pack of *sixty*," Hampsten says, "and we finished almost half an hour behind the three Gewiss guys—and we weren't going slow. For me, that was the pivotal moment with drugs. I'd heard tons of stories, secondhand—because bike racers never talk to each other about what they're doing—but this was actually happening."

After Argentin, Furlan, and Berzin swept the top three places, race followers claimed they must be doping. All the rumors centered on a banned, undetectable drug, recombinant erythropoietin (EPO), which augments a rider's natural erythropoietin to boost his red-blood-cell count; it's said to improve performance by as much as 25 percent. Perhaps, some reasoned, this explained all the victories being racked up by that year's Gewiss team.

Put on the spot, the team's Italian sports doctor and trainer, Michele Ferrari, held an impromptu press conference. "The journalists asked how I could explain the team's success," Dr. Ferrari said in a 2001 interview with a Danish newspaper. "I said it was due to training and diet.

"Then they asked where is the boundary between doping and non-doping. I said that anything that isn't *prohibited* is permitted. But the next day they wrote erroneously that I said that anything that can't be *detected* is permitted. They asked for my thoughts on EPO, which *was* prohibited, and I said it isn't dangerous to use but dangerous if it is abused. There are many physiological reasons why I said that, but it would take hours to explain.

"During the interview, I was drinking a glass of orange juice, and I used it as an example. Drinking orange juice in and of itself isn't dangerous, but if you drink ten liters it can be dangerous—you could get diarrhea. The Italian media quoted me as saying that EPO is no more dangerous than orange juice; only *L'Équipe* in France quoted me correctly."

After reading his words in the Italian press, the Gewiss team bosses sacked Dr. Ferrari, though there was no proof of any wrongdoing. At that point, Ferrari was a decade into his career as a sports doctor and trainer. He had worked closely with his university mentor, Professor Francesco Conconi, who heads the University of Ferrara's Biomedical Sports Research Center. Conconi researched and tested so-called blood-doping methods before the practice was banned in the late 1980s.

The talk of undetectable drugs being used in pro cycling in 1994 put the sport's governing body, the Union Cycliste Internationale (UCI), or International Cycling Union, in a dilemma. Its president, Dutchman Hein Verbruggen, publicly denounced doping but said the UCI was helpless to take action against the alleged cheats because it had no way of proving that someone was using banned substances such as EPO or human growth hormone. The media sharply criticized Verbruggen when he refused to condemn the Italian teams. Like millions of bike-racing fans around the world, Verbruggen wanted to believe that the improved performances were due to better, more scientific coaching methods—and that was partly true.

Traditional training, based purely on riding the bike, was augmented with more scientific methods throughout the 1970s and '80s. And to keep on top of the latest innovations and put them to practical use, teams began hiring sports doctors, who created more targeted training schedules based on lactate threshold, oxygen uptake, power output, body weight, fat percentage, pedal cadence, and other such parameters. Some of these sports doctors, it was rumored, were also instigating the use of drugs.

Doping was nothing new in sports. It can be traced back to ancient Greece, where athletes were sometimes caught cheating in the original Olympic Games. In the nineteenth century, strychnine, cocaine, opium, and alcohol were openly used to help athletes get through long-distance walking, running, and cycling events. Following World War II, amphetamines and steroids became the illicit drugs of choice. But none of the cheats were punished in those days because antidoping controls were not legislated until the mid-1960s. And none of the drugs then used had EPO's formidable powers to improve performance and damage the sport.

EPO, a genetically produced drug, was first introduced to medicine in the late 1980s to treat anemia in dialysis and cancer patients, whose ability to produce natural erythropoietin is limited by kidney malfunction or chemotherapy. But sports scientists such as Professor Conconi quickly realized that injections of EPO could boost the oxygen uptake in athletes and improve their performance by significant percentages. And although EPO was soon added to the list of prohibited substances in Olympic sports, including cycling, no viable test to detect the drug in blood or urine analysis would exist until 2000.

Because it was undetectable and could be bought over the counter in Europe, EPO soon became widely used in sports, especially running, cycling, and cross-country skiing. Years later, a number of retired professional cyclists—including Denmark's only Tour de France winner, Bjarne Riis—would reveal that they began using EPO in 1993. But back in the nineties, there were only rumors of its use; and those rumors gained traction in April 1994 with those two races in Belgium where Lance was baffled and beaten.

"The sport changed a lot in one year," Lance told me at the time. "I'm not going to say why it changed or how I think it changed, but I will say that it changed a lot—and a lot of guys got a lot stronger and a lot faster."

"We were all concerned," Hampsten says about the mood within Lance's Motorola team. "Collectively, we believed that a lot of riders on other teams—it wasn't everyone—were doing EPO, testosterone, growth hormones, and other things, because that's what we were hearing . . . from pretty reliable reports within the peloton. And the differences were phenomenal. When I'd hear the data about how much a person's hematocrit would increase with EPO use—from a normal level of 45 up to 50 or 60—you can relate to how much their power output improves."

A male athlete's normal hematocrit level—the percentage of oxygen-carrying red-blood cells—is between the high 30s and mid-40s. (Lance's hematocrit varies between 39 and 46.) Increasing that percentage to 50 or more improves the athlete's oxygen uptake, which allows him to work less hard at a certain speed or go faster at a normal workload—but not without risks. One danger of raising the hematocrit level to 55 or beyond is increased viscosity of the blood, which can cause a heart attack or stroke, especially when the heart rate is low. There were reports of dozens of young athletes dying in their sleep in the early nineties, but no proven connection was made with EPO. It wasn't until 1997 that the UCI mandated a maximum hematocrit level of 50 percent. Cyclists who tested above that level were not allowed to compete for at least two weeks, or until their red-blood-cell count returned to a normal level. (A small percentage of pro cyclists, especially those who live at a high elevation, have a natural level above 50 and qualify for an exemption certificate.)

"Before EPO," Hampsten says, "we knew we were always racing against guys on drugs, but I don't think those drugs gave them more of an advantage than the advantage we had knowing they're gonna come crashing down. We didn't lose energy worrying about what other people were doing; we just focused on ourselves, and we didn't need to win every race."

The American squad's "higher ground" attitude began to change in 1994. "There was a lot of grumbling on the team," Hampsten says, "and we did get technical data from Massimo Testa because he would talk to his colleagues on other teams. He was always straight with me. 'Sure enough,' he said, 'if so-and-so who you raced with for eight years and you always dropped on the climbs, if that guy's beating you now, his hematocrit is 15 points higher, and he's gonna kill you in the mountains.'"

Hampsten would experience this firsthand at that year's Giro d'Italia, a race he had won six years earlier. "I was in the same condition I usually was for the Giro, but this time I was so far down in the General Classification that I was just trying to win a stage. . . . Well, it got to the point where I just wanted to be in the top *ten* in a stage. And I *couldn't*, not even when I was in a five-man breakaway with a two-minute lead at the base of a climb.

"Fortunately, our sponsors were very understanding. We would still win big races, and we were aiming to win the Tour de France. For myself, I couldn't dwell on what other people were doing, positive or negative, because it affected my results."

Lance was as frustrated as Hampsten about the situation. "I ain't pointing fingers, that's the responsibility of the UCI," he said. "They should be interested in at least checking, and if there is a problem, there should be some sort of controls. People question why I haven't had a great year, and all I can tell you is I'm doing my best."

Besides the possibility of a new rival—EPO—other factors were behind Lance's relatively poor year. His natural talent was still there, and his results would have looked terrific for any other twenty-two-year-old, but he was having a tough time trying to repeat the phenomenal success he had in 1993. He had known that racing as the world champion would be burdensome, partly due to high expectations and also because wearing the rainbow jersey made him more visible, a marked man. And then there was the legendary Curse, which seemed to be at work. The year Lance wore the rainbow jersey was the only time in his racing career that he wouldn't win a single European race. Finally, there was Lance's own immaturity, which kept him from having the balance and focus he needed.

Perhaps his biggest mistake was starting off the season in Mexico. The Motorola team had recently recruited Raúl Alcalá, the Mexican who'd beaten Lance at the 1993 Tour DuPont, who would now ride for Lance, Motorola's team leader for most stage races. To show support for him, in turn, Lance and a few teammates traveled in January to Alcalá's hometown of Monterrey to start the pro-am Ruta Mexico. They helped Alcalá win the two-week stage race, but Lance said that "doing the Tour of Mexico threw off my whole year."

Besides losing focus in his racing program, Lance was having a hard time in his personal life. Over the winter, he had reestablished his relationship with Sonni Evans, a former high-school sweetheart who had graduated from Southwest Texas State University. "She's very loyal, very caring, very supportive," he said before leaving for Italy with her to share a new apartment in Como. "She knew me when I was struggling, before I was 'Lance Armstrong, world champion.' That means a lot to me."

But it wasn't enough.

To avoid spending too much time alone in a foreign city, Evans would drive behind Lance when he went on long training rides with his Como-based teammate Frankie Andreu and their new rookie colleagues, George Hincapie and Kevin Livingston. Hincapie, who'd go on to become Lance's longest-serving team member, remembers one particularly difficult ride.

"It was cold that day," Hincapie tells me. "We were riding a six-hour loop through Bergamo, and there were some icy sections on the mountain roads. Sonni did not know how to drive on the ice, and a couple times Lance got so mad he had to get in the car and drive over an ice patch for her. Then a car with some Italians in it started honking at us.

"Well, Lance couldn't accept people honking at us to get out of the way—we would get into arguments once a week, and cars would stop, and an enormous fight would break out. Anyway, Lance was not having a good day that day in the mountains, and the Italians got out of the car, and they and Lance started pushing each other. One of the guys went after Lance, and he kept falling down because of the ice. Finally, we had to break it up.

"We got out of that situation, but Lance was so mad that he rode crazy hard the rest of the day. It was like two and a half hours home, and he made it brutal."

Times like that hurt Lance's relationship with Sonni, and she soon packed her bags and returned to Texas.

"Lance's results weren't too good that spring," Hincapie says. "He trained super-hard but he just wasn't happy because he wasn't killing everybody like he did before. We'd get weekly tests for lactate and power with Max Testa, who was always so positive about our prospects. But Lance would want to know, 'Why are *they* so much better? Why are *we* getting our butts kicked?'

"Max would say, '*Tranquillo, tranquillo.*' That was his favorite word. 'You guys are still young, you're gonna be good . . . and you're world champion, Lance, don't even stress.' We didn't know that much about training or about our bodies as we do now. Back then, we would basically train hard all year long, and you just went from race to race and hoped you'd feel good at the races."

While Lance did not win any races in the first four months of 1994, his near-miss at Liège in Belgium allowed him to earn the respect of his teammates. "Lance was always confident he was gonna win," Hincapie says. "Even when he lost a race he'd say, 'I'm gonna beat that guy next time.'"

With the spring classics over, Lance headed home for a month of domestic racing. "His main goal was to win the Tour DuPont," Hincapie says, referring to the multiday race that Lance lost in '93 to Alcalá. "Lance was super-pumped for that race, and he was such a great leader at DuPont. He'd always motivate us to pull hard for him, especially on the climbs."

"If I don't win this year, I'll be devastated," Lance admitted before the race began in Wilmington, Delaware. "I didn't come here to be second again." His confidence was high because, besides having Alcalá on his side this time, he also had the support of his three strongest teammates, Phil Anderson, Steve Bauer, and Sean Yates, who were absent from the previous year's race.

The team did well and helped Lance win the hardest climbing stage in the Appalachians, but once again he finished second overall after losing the final time trial. This time, the winner was Viatcheslav Ekimov, the Russian who'd defeated him at the Zürich classic two years earlier. This latest loss *was* devastating to Lance, who finally realized that no matter how strong he was in the regular road stages, he would keep on losing the overall victory if he remained subpar in the time trials.

The French call the time trial *la course de vérité*, the race of truth, because it separates the riders who have true greatness from the journeyman professionals. If Lance wanted to be one of the greats, as he had told Och before he signed for Motorola, he would have to improve his time-trialing strength. To do that, he would need to not only train more specifically for the event but also go to the wind tunnel and seek out the most aerodynamic position on the bike. Such detailed preparation would demand more patience from Lance, who still had an impetuous riding style and who had barely changed his riding position since his days in triathlon.

Another option was to give up on winning stage races like the Tour DuPont, focus solely on the one-day races—the classics, the worlds, and the Olympics—and take his money and run. That seemed to be the way he was thinking at the time. During a one-on-one interview at that 1994 DuPont race, after J. T. finished massaging him, Lance told me, "I'm out of here in two years." He said he was seriously thinking about quitting pro bike racing after the 1996 Olympics in Atlanta—where the cycling events would be open to professionals for the first time, and he'd get a second chance to fulfill his longtime dream of winning an Olympic gold medal. And since the one-day classics were the events most similar to the Olympics, he saw tackling them as a way to the gold.

In Steve Bauer, Lance found a perfect mentor for the classics. The Canadian was smart and strong, and he had the mental boldness to astound his opponents. What Bauer didn't have was luck. In the grueling Paris-Roubaix of 1990, the photo finish showed he had lost that most-coveted classic by less than a centimeter. He also had near misses at the Olympics and worlds. But none of his losses deflated Bauer's upbeat spirit, a spirit that lifted Lance when things were down.

"I got pretty close with Steve," Lance said in 1994. "I spent a lot of time with him in Austin. And when I've got two guys to hang out with, Yates and Bauer are my number-one and number-two guys."

Lance's Austin friend Bart Knaggs remembers the good times he had with Lance and Bauer when the Canadian came to town. "We'd go out to dinner every night, have a few beers, listen to some music, stay out till twelve or two," Knaggs says. "Lance wasn't gonna shy away from the training, and he wasn't gonna shy away from the living. He wasn't into that monastic sacrifice. He was just like a boxer: 'I'm a hard-headed guy. If you punch me on the nose, I'll punch you on the nose, and guess what? At the end of the day, I'm gonna beat you if I've had six beers the night before or none.'"

Knaggs describes a typical training session the three guys took part in after one of those nights out. "It was a group of six of us on kind of a shitty day. We picked out this six-hour loop and headed east. We'd been out two or three hours, hadn't stopped, when this rolling road turned into dirt. It was probably a three-mile section of dirt road.

"When you hit a different surface like that, you suddenly go a lot slower. Bauer was pulling, and I don't think he even shifted gears. He just powered away in his super-compact, egg-shaped style. He wasn't visibly strained, and he just dropped us all. We were skidding around and chasing our balls off after this guy, and it looked like he wasn't even trying.

"Lance got closer to catching Bauer than all of us, and when we re-grouped, he was like, 'Congratulations, Steve.' Not real public and not over-the-top, just, 'All right, that's a man.' And Bauer was like, 'I just ride hard when I see dirt, eh?' This guy's one of the legends. He was the pro.

"It was also like that when Yates came into town. They were clearly the hard men that Lance loved. You could tell he was just watching, and he wanted to pay attention; he was like a puppy dog with them."

Yates and Bauer traveled to Austin with Lance right after the '94 Tour DuPont. "We went riding, water-skiing on the river there, driving around on his Harley-Davidson, and playing pool," Yates recalls. "Just enjoying ourselves like guys do."

Their five days together was a pleasant interlude in a year that didn't have too many celebratory moments. Lance managed to win two more races on that American sojourn—the Pittsburgh event for the third time and a stage of the West Virginia race—but he and the team soon returned to the daunting reality of a drug-tainted sport in Europe.

The Tour de France, Lance's second, was the main item on the Motorola team's agenda. As preparation, Lance placed seventh in the ten-day Tour of Switzerland, his best overall performance yet in a major European pro stage race. At the Tour de France, he failed to win a stage as he had done the year before. He rode strongly, though, especially in the team time trial, in which he, Yates, Bauer, Andreu, and Anderson powered Motorola to second place, only six seconds behind one of the Italian teams, GB-MG. That result helped boost Yates in a later stage, when he got into a break with Andreu and wore the yellow jersey for a day; but that was the team's only highlight in the Tour. Without its expected Tour leader, Hampsten, who didn't start because of an injured knee, and minus Lance, who left after completing fourteen of the twenty-two stages, Motorola disappointed its sponsors.

Midway through the Tour, Hampsten visited his teammates in hopes of boosting their spirits. "When I arrived, it was like going to a funeral, their morale was so low," he says. "The '94 Tour was an extremely hard Tour, and there was an elevated pace compared with earlier years—probably because of the drugs becoming more prevalent. The team was really concerned about how uncompetitive they were."

Lance's biggest shock in that Tour came in stage nine's time trial on a broiling day in the Dordogne region. On a forty-mile route—the longest individual time trial of his career—Lance started two minutes ahead of Miguel Induráin, Spain's defending champion. Before half-distance, as he pounded up one of the course's many short hills, Lance was stunned when Induráin came sweeping past him like a tornado. "I knew Induráin was gonna catch me," Lance said, after finishing the stage more than six minutes slower than Induráin, "but I didn't think he could do it that fast. I tried to match his speed, but he was just like a motor. That was a bad idea, and I blew up at the end. I barely made it to the finish." Still, Lance finished the stage in a respectable thirteenth place, and even stage runner-up Tony Rominger conceded two minutes to the untouchable Induráin.

Lance's erratic year continued with another high point: second place in a classic. This time it was the familiar Clásica San Sebastián, where he made his pro debut. It was a great performance, but as at Liège in the springtime, he was beaten by someone who normally wasn't at his level. The winner by two minutes was Armand De Las Cuevas, a Frenchman who worked as a support rider for Induráin at the Tour. Once again, the media was skeptical about the winner's performance, especially when they discovered that De Las Cuevas was a client of the sacked Gewiss team doctor Michele Ferrari. And once again, there were whispers about doping.

Lance then defended his world title in Agrigento, an Italian city on the island of Sicily. He prepared just as hard with Testa to be on the same form as in '93, yet he was weighed down this time with a new concern: How many of his rivals were fueled by EPO? Lance rode a strong, smart race to be with the leaders on the final lap, but he simply couldn't go with the attacks on the long climb to the finish, and the best he could place was seventh. The winner and new world champion was Frenchman Luc Leblanc, who, like the bronze medalist Richard Virenque, was a member of the Festina-Lotus team. Neither of them had ever performed so well in a major one-day race.

There were suspicions that these two medalists were not riding "clean," but with no viable test for EPO, nothing could be proven. It would be another six years before the suspicions were confirmed when a French court revealed that the Festina team had engaged in organized doping since 1993. At that December 2000 tribunal, Leblanc admitted using EPO in 1994 at the Tour of Spain and Tour de France, but denied using it at other races. However, one of the other witnesses, who worked for the team throughout the nineties, testified that "all the Festina team riders at the world championships [in 1994] were given the same preparation: EPO with supplements. Luc did the same as everyone else."

Further insight into how some teams introduced EPO to their "medical programs" was offered the French tribunal that investigated the inner workings of Festina-Lotus. Prior to the 1993 Tour de France, the tribunal's report states, "the team riders who had yet to use EPO were growing impatient to get access to it several days before the start . . . The main reason had to be that other teams were already administering this substance. The EPO arrived the day before the start . . . and each rider had the right to one dose of 2,000 units per day, and then one dose every other day until a week before the finish."

Lance had left the 1994 worlds disappointed that he hadn't earned a medal but pleased that he'd found a new girl: Daniëlle Overgaag, a flaxen-haired racer on the Dutch national women's team, who went to stay with Lance in Austin that fall. Being an athlete as well as a fledgling model—she would go on to become a popular television personality in the Netherlands—Overgaag seemed to fit in perfectly with the flashy Texas lifestyle. Yet like many of Lance's relationships, this one would last less than a year.

The possible loss of that relationship was just one of many things on Lance's mind that winter, as he tried to cope with the new demands he faced as a rising star. He was deeply concerned about the direction pro cycling was taking in Europe; he lost a number of his valued Motorola teammates as they switched teams or retired; and he was worried about several aspects of his private life. "A lot of things were happening with me and the sport, and I let a lot of things go, including my relationships with a lot of people," he said in November 1994. "I didn't communicate as well as I should have because I was much busier, and a lot of times I was confused by that busyness. I didn't communicate enough with my mother, or with J. T., and darn sure not enough with Carmichael. I let those things slip and I paid for it.

"These people made me what I am. I realize relationships change as people mature, but I need J. T. on a personal level and Carmichael on a training level. And with all these changes to the sport, I've gotta be focused, I've gotta know what I'm doing."

One of the changes that troubled him most was Phil Anderson's messy departure from the team. The pony-tailed Aussie had been a guru to Lance through his first two pro seasons, but things started to sour between them when Lance left the '95 Tour a few days earlier than planned. It got back to Lance and team manager Och that Anderson was displeased about Lance cutting the Tour before his teammates expected, and that upset Lance. Anderson was due to retire at the end of that season, and he was hoping to make his farewell appearance at the Paris-Tours classic, a race he had won at the height of his career. But Och did not select him for the French race, saying the team was focusing instead on its younger riders. Anderson was even asked to return his team bike before riding his final race, at the Commonwealth Games in Canada. "I didn't understand why they didn't let me ride Paris-Tours," Anderson says. "I'd been racing in Europe for more than fifteen years and I just wanted to say goodbye to my mates."

Hampsten, who transferred to another team the following year, was dismayed by how Motorola treated the Australian. "They were shameful in my opinion how they discarded Anderson," Hampsten says. "He saved us a couple of years running with his wins, and at management's behest he completely put himself at Armstrong's disposal. It's still difficult even to imagine the way they treated Anderson. It was so unnecessary."

Lance had strong and mixed feelings about losing his teammate. Anderson had given him so much, but Lance felt hurt and betrayed by his mentor's recent criticism—of him and, later, of the team. And for Lance, any sense of betrayal is hard to forgive. After his adoptive father, Terry, betrayed his mom, Lance put Terry out of his life and out of his mind. Now, it would be a long time before he'd again speak with Anderson.

"Phil was great. I loved that guy," Lance said shortly after Anderson left. "I listened to everything he said; and whatever he thinks, I still listened to him this year. I really need a relationship like that, and I'm gonna miss not having a mentor like Phil. But after what he has said and the way he went out, I don't know if I'm gonna miss him."

Today, Anderson says he has a cordial relationship with Lance. They reconciled at the Tour Down Under in 2009 when Sean Yates brought the Aussie around to Lance's hotel. But when they parted in 1994, it was hard for both of them. Underneath the young star's anger, there was loss: The man he had looked to for answers and strength was leaving in a time of uncertainty. For Lance, the greatest uncertainty was whether his relatively poor season, the team's lack of top results, and especially the growing EPO problem in Europe would force Motorola to pull its title sponsorship. But a determined

Och convinced their sponsor that Lance's talent was so huge that the team did not need to risk what the Italian teams were allegedly doing with banned drugs, and it would be a mistake to pull out of cycling. Motorola renewed its contract for another two years, which would carry Lance at least until the Atlanta Olympics.

That was a huge relief for Och and Lance as they planned their future together. It helped that they had an Italian team doctor and trainer, Massimo Testa, who had a deep understanding of the sport and was recognized as one of the strongest anti-doping voices in the peloton. Testa also recognized Lance's ability and potential. "From day one, Lance Armstrong was different, unlike any of the other riders I've known. I saw results I'd never seen in any other rider," he says. "What he did in those early years was already kind of special—and I know there was no cheating at that time."

As Lance prepared for his next season of pro racing, he felt almost relieved to have the rainbow jersey—and its Curse—off his shoulders. But he knew that the shadow over his sport was not about to lift. EPO wasn't going away. And neither were uncertainty, change, and loss.

CHAPTER 12

ENDINGS AND BEGINNINGS

It was the hardest day of my career, bar none. Even though they were going easy, it was hot, and physically it was damn hard. Mentally, I was just so far away.

—LANCE ARMSTRONG

IN HIS QUEST to be one of the stars of professional cycling, Lance had established himself as a team leader and earned the respect of the European riders. And in a dangerous and demanding sport—where life-threatening crashes, debilitating illness, and broken bones are common—he had led a relatively charmed life. But by 1995 Lance had to address some hard questions: How could he stay competitive in a sport that had a growing doping problem? How would he replace the valued teammates who had left his team? And how could he repair the personal relationships he had let slip?

There were no immediate answers, though at least some progress was made on the team front. It had been a blow to Lance that year to lose longtime team leaders Andy Hampsten and Max Sciandri to rival squads and to have senior riders such as Phil Anderson and Raúl Alcalá retire from the sport. And with a relatively small budget, Motorola team manager Jim Ochowicz could not afford to hire ready-made stars; instead, he was adding promising but largely untested young riders. Lance's friend George Hincapie had already arrived, along with two other recruits Lance knew from the U.S. national team, Bobby Julich and Kevin Livingston. Then there were the Italians Fabio Casartelli and Andrea Peron, who both came from the Como area, the team's base in Europe.

Lance connected most with Peron. A sharp dresser with fashionably long sideburns, he was the same age as Lance and spoke fluent English. "Lance tried to speak Italian," Och says, "but he wasn't great." Lance had seen Peron's strength in various races and had been pressuring Och to hire him. "I always wanted him on the team," says Lance, who believed that Peron would be a powerful rider on his own as well as someone who could help him when needed.

Team doctor Testa had recommended Casartelli, and the 1992 Olympic road race champion was as traditional as Peron was flamboyant. "Fabio grew up in a cycling family," Testa says. "He had just married, and his wife was expecting their first baby. They were living at his parents' place." The twenty-four-year-old Italian impressed his teammates by his efforts to learn English with them, and he lifted their spirits with his big happy smile.

None of the newcomers had the experience or knowledge of the veterans who had left, but Lance was excited by the new talent. On reviewing the overall team roster of twenty riders, he told me, "I think we're on the verge of having a great year; but we've got to win."

Lance showed the way by taking a solo stage victory at Paris-Nice in March—his first success in Europe since the 1993 world championships. A month later, he again targeted Liège-Bastogne-Liège, where he rode strongly but was dropped from the winning break and finished sixth. Back in the States, Lance finally pulled off the overall win at the Tour DuPont. He won two mountain stages by wide margins and even took one of the three time trials, leaving old rival Viatcheslav Ekimov two minutes behind in second.

Almost as important as Lance's breakthrough victory in the American race was Peron's performance. The Italian proved to be a powerful team worker and also managed to win a stage and finish third overall. As for Casartelli, he had a slower start to the season, mainly because he was recovering from knee surgery to correct an injury he had incurred at the previous year's Tour de France. But Och and Testa were confident that he would benefit from Motorola's supportive atmosphere. "He was an up-and-comer," Och says.

Both Casartelli and Peron were selected for Motorola's nine-man Tour de France squad, where their main task was to help Lance complete the whole three weeks, and perhaps help him win a stage along the way. With those two goals in mind, Lance rode conservatively for the first week. He had targeted the seventh stage into Liège, Belgium, for a possible win. His Austin friend Bart Knaggs was watching the stage from the finish line hoping to see Lance finish first. "It was looking good," Knaggs says. "Lance was away with a bunch of riders, and Miguel Induráin of all people goes across and blows by, and only one guy stays on his wheel, Johan Bruyneel. Lance tried hard to join them, and he didn't quite make it. So there was big Induráin with little Johan tucked in behind him. At the end, Johan came around Induráin, just barely, to win the stage. That moment probably put something in Lance's brain: 'Johan was smarter. He took my prize.' And at the finish, Lance was pissed. He wanted to win."

Lance was disappointed again in the next day's time trial when he placed nineteenth, five minutes behind Induráin. Then the Tour headed to the Alps, where Lance did a little better than he had in his first two Tours. He even made a solo escape on a long downhill. But he was caught as soon as the road tilted upward, and he again realized that his heavy upper body was a handicap on the high-elevation alpine passes. That was frustrating after he had shown such great climbing form at the Tour DuPont, where some of the hills were as steep as those in the Alps, though roughly half the length. On his first encounter with the legendary climb to L'Alpe d'Huez, Lance placed 56th out of 143 finishers, almost nineteen minutes behind stage winner Marco Pantani, the skinny little Italian climber Lance had first faced as an amateur.

Peron finished a few minutes ahead of Lance on the Alpe, with Casartelli a couple of minutes behind him, and the two Italians continued to ride well on the rolling stages between the Alps and the Pyrenees. Lance was again looking for a stage win, and he almost pulled it off. He powered a long-distance breakaway on the stage to Revel, but was too confident in a two-man sprint finish and narrowly lost to Ukraine rider Sergei Uchakov.

Showing his anger, Lance rode straight past the awaiting media, stormed off to the anti-doping control, and then rushed to his team car parked in a backstreet before saying anything. "It's terrible, just terrible," he said. "I felt for sure I was going to win." Had he won, it would have lifted the spirits of his entire team. Instead, they now faced three painful days in the Pyrenees where their only mission was survival.

The second of those days began on a misty morning in St. Girons, a market town where ancient arched bridges cross fast-flowing streams. Ahead lay a monster stage of six mountain passes through the heart of the Pyrenees. The fog was still lifting as the peloton am-

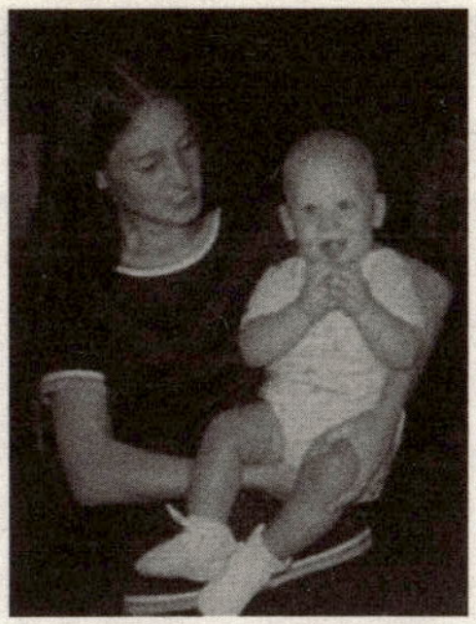

Held by his mother, Linda, baby Lance is already looking big and strong at seven and a half months. (COURTESY LINDA KELLY ARMSTRONG)

Linda's sister, Debbie, always had an affection for her first nephew, here at age 3. (COURTESY LINDA KELLY ARMSTRONG)

At 4, Lance loved his pet cats, Tootsie and Tommy. (COURTESY LINDA KELLY ARMSTRONG)

On his 8th birthday, Lance proudly shows off his first BMX bike with his Uncle Alan. (COURTESY LINDA KELLY ARMSTRONG)

He was named after a Dallas Cowboys football star, but at age 8 Lance played for the Oilers, the nickname of the Garland YMCA football team that was coached by his adoptive father, Terry Armstrong (*top left*). Lance switched to the Armstrong Middle School squad in fifth grade. (PHOTOS COURTESY TERRY ARMSTRONG)

After Lance expressed interest in BMX racing, his parents bought him a new BMX bike for Christmas in 1981. (COURTESY TERRY ARMSTRONG)

At 13, Lance swam with his buddy John Boggan on the City of Plano Swimmers team. At 16, he was already ahead of the pack when he helped his high-school cross-country team win the Dallas district championships. (PHOTOS COURTESY HAL BOGGAN)

At an awkward age, Lance posed with his mom and adoptive dad Terry Armstrong in 1986. (COURTESY TERRY ARMSTRONG)

A more sophisticated Lance posed with his first girlfriend Gina Di Luca. (COURTESY HAL BOGGAN)

Lance's mom, Linda, missed out on her own senior prom, so Lance took her to his, along with his date, Tracey Parrent. (COURTESY LINDA KELLY ARMSTRONG)

At his first triathlons, Lance had help from his mom. (COURTESY HAL BOGGAN)

Early mentor Scott Eder was thrilled when Lance won the 1988 Tulsa Triathlon (TULSA WORLD PHOTO)

Richardson Bike Mart owner Jim Hoyt supplied Lance with the white Kestrel tri bike he used to win his first bike race. (COURTESY JIM HOYT)

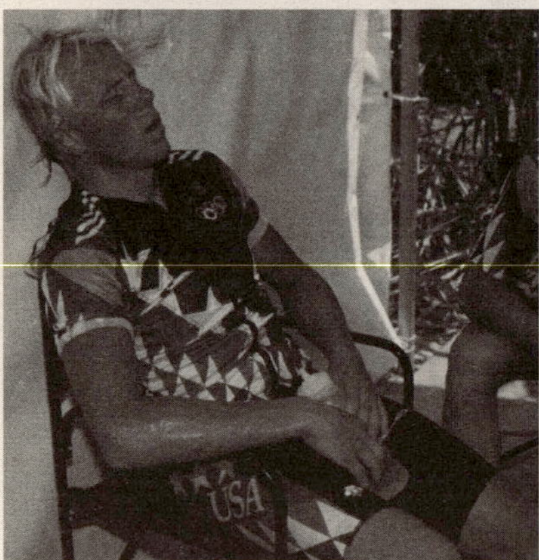

Lance took advice from U.S. team coach Chris Carmichael before the Barcelona Olympics road race began ... but he and teammate Bob Mionske were devastated at the finish. (GRAHAM WATSON PHOTOS)

Brit Sean Yates was like a big brother to Lance when the Texan first turned pro.
(GRAHAM WATSON PHOTO)

In his first full season of pro racing, Lance, at age 21, won the Verdun stage in his Tour de France debut and celebrated with his mom after claiming the world champion's rainbow jersey in Oslo, Norway. (GRAHAM WATSON PHOTOS)

After his highly successful 1993 season, Lance earned enough cash to lay down $68,000 on a 140-mph Acura NSX sports car in Plano, Texas. (COURTESY HAL BOGGAN)

The 1995 Tour de France peloton honored the memory of fallen colleague Fabio Casartelli by allowing his Motorola teammates (*l to r*) Steve Bauer, Alvaro Mejia, Frankie Andreu, Andrea Peron, Steve Swart, and Lance to reach the Pau finish line ahead of them. (GRAHAM WATSON PHOTO)

Lance further honored Fabio by winning the stage into Limoges three days after the Italian's death. (GRAHAM WATSON PHOTO)

Motorola team manager Jim Ochowicz (*l*) and team doctor Massimo Testa guided Lance through his first four years as a professional bike racer. (GRAHAM WATSON PHOTO)

J. T. Neal was a father figure to Lance; shortly after he and Lance enjoyed a boat ride on Lake Austin, they were both diagnosed with cancer. (GRAHAM WATSON PHOTO)

Austin urologist Dr. Jim Reeves said Lance had one of the worst cases of cancer that oncologists had ever seen. (COURTESY DR. JIM REEVES)

After surgery to remove two lesions from his brain, Lance was left with a U-shaped scar. (JAMES STARTT PHOTO)

Less than two years after rigorous chemotherapy, Lance returned to racing 13 pounds lighter and more determined than ever to conquer the world.
(GRAHAM WATSON PHOTO)

The European press constantly questioned the methods of Lance's Italian trainer Dr. Michele Ferrari. (GRAHAM WATSON PHOTO)

U.S. Postal team director Johan Bruyneel took Lance to innovative pre–Tour de France training camps in the Pyrenees and the Alps. (GRAHAM WATSON PHOTO)

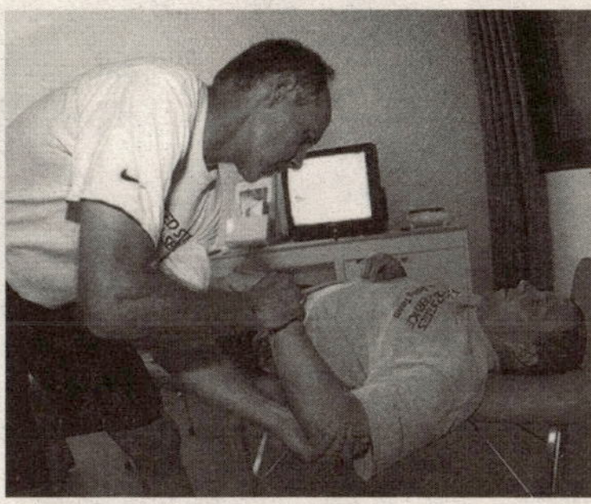

Starting in 1999, chiropractic doctor Jeff Spencer used state-of-the-art recovery techniques to keep Lance in his best form throughout every Tour. (GRAHAM WATSON PHOTO)

Lance celebrated his first Tour victory with his wife, Kristin, and his mother, Linda, in Paris. (GRAHAM WATSON PHOTO)

Three former race winners Lance, Jan Ullrich, and Marco Pantani faced off at the start of the 2000 Tour. (GRAHAM WATSON PHOTO)

A formidable duel between Lance and Jan Ullrich at the 2003 Tour saw Lance recover from a series of near-disasters to overcome Ullrich on Luz-Ardiden (*left*), while the desperate German gave his all in the race's final time trial, but came up short.
(GRAHAM WATSON PHOTOS)

In 2005, Lance celebrated his seventh consecutive Tour de France victory with his friend and team director Johan Bruyneel (*above*), while Lance's three children, Luke, Grace, and Bella, shared the podium with their dad on the Champs-Élysées (*below right*). (GRAHAM WATSON PHOTOS)

American teammate George Hincapie helped Lance win all of his seven Tour victories. (GRAHAM WATSON PHOTO)

On a December 2007 USO trip to entertain the troops in Afghanistan, Iraq, and Kuwait, Lance posed with an injured soldier, U.S. Army corporal Chad J. McNeeley, along with his co-celebrities Robin Williams (*front right*), singer Kid Rock (*top right*), comedian Lewis Black, and former Miss USA Rachel Smith. (COURTESY DEPARTMENT OF DEFENSE)

Austin lawyer Bill Stapleton has been Lance's only agent. (GRAHAM WATSON PHOTO)

Training partner and Austin friend John "College" Korioth was the first manager of the Lance Armstrong Foundation. (ELIZABETH KREUTZ PHOTO)

Constant adviser and friend Bart Knaggs is now one of Lance's closest business partners. (ELIZABETH KREUTZ PHOTO)

They had a challenging relationship, but no one questioned the love Lance and Sheryl felt for each other. This picture was taken only two months before they called off their engagement in January 2006.
(GETTY IMAGES PHOTO)

Fatherhood has been one of the joys of Lance's life. His children Luke and twins Isabelle ("Bella") and Grace are respectively seven and five in this April 2006 picture.
(GETTY IMAGES PHOTO)

On his comeback to pro cycling in January 2009, Lance was once again ahead of the pack.
(GRAHAM WATSON PHOTO)

bled over the flat opening roads that weaved past fields of corn. Church bells greeted the riders as they entered each village of stone-and-slate cottages. On leaving the last of these, Portet d'Aspet, they felt the sun break through as the leaders accelerated up the opening slopes of the stage's first climb.

The compact group stretched into a long line over the crest of the Col du Portet d'Aspet before heading down the steepest descent of the Tour. It's only three miles long, but pitches downward at a giddy 15 percent grade. Although the day's breaking action had yet to begin, gravity pulled the riders' downhill pace to forty miles per hour as they swooshed around the turns.

Casartelli was riding a new titanium bike for the first time that day. It was lighter than the alloy steel one he'd been riding for the first two weeks. A lighter bike makes the long mountain climbs a little easier, but it can also make a fast descent harder to control, and when Casartelli took a long, curving left turn on this first descent, something went terribly wrong. Riders were falling all around him. One of them was forced to the right, hit a line of two-foot-high concrete blocks guarding the outside of the bend, and was launched into the trees below. Another rider, Frenchman François Simon, was riding behind Casartelli and described what he saw: "Fabio's front wheel suddenly stopped and he went headfirst over the bike." Casartelli fell heavily and ended up unconscious, lying on the road about three feet from the line of concrete blocks.

It's not clear what happened in the split seconds after his front wheel locked up. It is known that none of the riders involved in the crash were wearing helmets; they weren't made mandatory in pro cycling until 2004. It's also known that the front part of Casartelli's bike was smashed. But it's unclear what caused the front wheel to lock up so abruptly. Many believed that he hit one of the concrete blocks. More likely, the cyclist in front of him skidded, swerved, or dabbed on the brakes, causing Casartelli to pull sharply on his brake levers. And being on a new bike, with new brake pads and a different dynamic from his old one, he may have pulled too hard.

When Casartelli went over the handlebars, his head collided with a sharp object, probably the edge of a concrete block. "When we went past, it was just a mess, bikes everywhere," says Lance, who had been behind Casartelli in the peloton and was planning to wait for him. "I sat at the back just waiting to check in, and the Dutch rider Erik Breukink came up to me, and I'll never forget him saying, 'You don't need to wait back here.' He was thinking bad crash and Fabio not getting back in the bike race."

First on the scene of the accident was race doctor Gérard Porte, who reported that Lance's teammate was losing "an enormous amount of blood" from severe lesions on the right side of his head. The initial medical report described a craniofacial traumatism, a deep coma, and multiple skull fractures. And the veteran Belgian rider Johan Museeuw, who was also lying injured on the road, later said, "I lay there for five minutes watching him die."

Casartelli's death was reported several hours later, after the twenty-four-year-old Italian suffered three successive heart failures during attempts to revive him on the helicopter ride to the hospital in Tarbes. Some of the riders were given the tragic news as they were climbing the fourth of the day's six mountain passes. Others, including Lance's Colombian teammate Alvaro Mejia, didn't find out until they finished the stage. Mejia was sobbing and shaking when he sat down in the backseat of his team car, and then buried his head in a towel.

"That night, we were in this little hotel and everybody was shaken," Testa says. "Some of the riders were breaking down. They were ready to go home. I thought we should pull out of the Tour as a sign of respect. I said to Jim, 'What about we all go home to Como and see the family? They've got this three-month-old baby.' Lance was the one who started to push us to stay on. He said, 'I don't think we can make it better by pulling out. We have to stay here and see if we can win a stage or something.'" Lance felt that staying in the race would be the most fitting way to honor Casartelli. And if he could win a stage in his name, it would be all the more a tribute. "That was the biggest sense of loss that I'd ever felt," Lance says.

"Fabio's death hit him hard," Chris Carmichael confirms. "Lance called me from the Tour. The tough thing about the Tour is you're living together with all these guys. You share a room with someone. Every meal's together with your team, and then you come down to dinner and there's an empty seat at the table, and it's because he died. That's a pretty tough thing to take."

It was hard on everyone to remain in the race. But it turned out that Lance was right in insisting the team carry on. He seemed to grasp instinctively the historical significance of honoring a fallen colleague. The last time a rider died in the Tour—Englishman Tom Simpson collapsed while climbing Mont Ventoux in 1967 after suffering a drug- and sunstroke-related cardiac arrest—the peloton slowed en masse the next day to allow Simpson's friend and teammate Barry Hoban to ride ahead alone and win the stage.

Casartelli was given a similar tribute in 1995.

Black patches were stitched to the left arms of the blue-and-red team jerseys of Motorola's remaining six riders before they pedaled to the start of the Tour's sixteenth stage in Tarbes. And the bicycle that Casartelli had ridden for the first two weeks of the Tour was attached to the team car that would be following the peloton all the way to the finish in Paris.

The black patches and the bicycle helped Peron, Casartelli's Tour roommate, find some resolution to this unthinkable loss. "Today, Fabio will be on his bike beside and within me and like that all the way to Paris," he said. "He'll be within me in the month ahead. All my life he'll be with me."

Another Motorola man looking for closure was Stephen Swart, a big, blond-haired New Zealander. Like Casartelli, he was already a father, and this was the second Tour he was riding with the team. After signing the day's official start sheet, Swart went to sit in the shade of the covered marketplace in Tarbes. He wanted his solitude, but he took time to say a few words. "When I signed in, they'd blanked out Fabio's name," Swart told me, his voice quivering with emotion. "That's when it really sunk in. Not yesterday when we were told during the race, or last night at the hotel. It didn't really sink in—until now. We have to face up to it one day, so it's probably better to do it right away."

Swart and Peron then took their places at the head of the silent peloton alongside Lance, Mejia, Steve Bauer, and Frankie Andreu. They bowed their heads as a minute's silence was called to honor Casartelli. Then, along with the rest of the field, they slowly set off on a stage that the senior riders soon decided should not be contested. Instead, everyone cycled at a processional pace on the 147-mile mountain stage through the Pyrenees, and they donated the day's prize money to Annalisa Casartelli, Fabio's widow.

It was a painful journey for Lance's men, not only because of the marathon ride in searing heat, but also because of the grief that memories of Fabio evoked. "There were 120 guys there, and about 115 of them didn't say a word for eight hours," Lance said two days later, the first time he would publicly speak of the death. "It was the hardest day of my career, bar none. Even though they were going easy, it was hot, and physically it was damn hard. Mentally, I was just so far away. I don't ever want to have a day like that again."

Just as the 1967 Tourmen allowed Hoban to go ahead of the pack to honor his compatriot Simpson, so the 1995 peloton silently slowed coming into the stage finish at Pau to allow Casartelli's teammates to ride through the streets six abreast. As a final gesture, Peron's five colleagues stopped pedaling in the last meters to let Casartelli's close friend and roommate lead them across the line amid the applause of the respectful spectators.

"It's not easy to concede a stage of the Tour de France. That's a stage somebody could have won," Lance said, "could have made their career. And for everybody to sit up and say this is not a day to race, this is a day to mourn . . . that says a lot. Certainly my attitude toward the peloton completely changed that day. I was impressed by their class."

When Lance had argued for the team to stay in the race as a tribute to Casartelli, he'd also said he might try to win a stage in Casartelli's honor. Lance knew he wouldn't be able to win the flat stages into Bordeaux and Paris, where the sprinters would rule, nor the final time trial. So he had just one option: the rolling 104-mile stage across the foothills of the Massif Central to Limoges.

Lance wasn't the only one wanting to win this stage. Despite blazingly hot temperatures, dozens of riders were soon instigating breakaways, chasing them down, and then starting another. After two hours of this attack and counterattack, Lance's old Russian rival Ekimov went clear with five others; and a mile later, they were joined by another six-rider group, which included Lance, his ex-teammate Max Sciandri, and Bruyneel, the Belgian who had beaten Induráin on the stage into Liège. Having ten teams represented in the twelve-man move meant there were ten teams in the peloton with no reason to chase. And so the dozen riders moved ahead by one minute, then two, then four . . . and the gap kept growing. The leaders knew that one of them would win.

At twenty-three, Lance was the youngest and least experienced rider in the break, yet he was telling Och on the radio that he felt incredibly strong. "I had Fabio on my mind the whole time," Lance said. And if he were to honor him with a win, he knew he couldn't wait for an eventual sprint and risk losing like he did in Revel the previous week. He would have to make a solo move. But when?

If Lance went from a long way out—ten miles or more—he would have a hard time holding off the others, who would join forces to chase him down. Still, he figured that Ekimov would likely wait until the final couple of miles to attack; that Sciandri and Bruyneel would stake their chances on a sprint finish; and that none of the others expected anyone to make a long-range attack.

Unfortunately, there were no more climbs for Lance to try one of his trademark uphill surges. And so, with almost twenty miles remaining, he did something he'd never done before. With a long, flat stretch of road before him, he bolted from the front line of riders and sprinted away as if the finish were only a quarter-mile away. He shocked all of them; they were slow to react, and he quickly took an eighteen-second lead. That wasn't much of a gap, though, against eleven guys working together to chase him down.

But Lance kept pounding his heaviest gear for the next half-hour, and he kept on gaining time. He was told he had one minute on the group as he raced into Limoges, still riding at thirty-five miles an hour—a formidable feat on a regular road bike, not a custom time-trial machine built for speed. He still had about five miles to go, including a long haul up to the finish above the town. "It was very, very hard in the last bit," he said, "but I kept thinking about him. The people at the side of the road wouldn't let me forget. There wasn't a minute went by I didn't hear '*Pour Fabio.*' I was possessed."

Lance couldn't let Fabio down or disappoint his mourning family, who were watching the race on the live telecast at their home in Como. With them in mind, he charged on. Inside the final mile, he looked back for the first time and saw . . . no one! He knew he was winning, and he knew he could have celebrated like he did when he won the rainbow jersey in Oslo two years before. Instead, Lance now rode with a different emotion. There was no showboating. He pointed toward the open sky with his right index finger and pumped his black-gloved hand as he looked upward. Then he pumped both hands, still pointing to the heavens, as if to direct everyone else's gaze there, too. When Lance pedaled up the slight incline to the finish, he repeated his gesture of homage to Casartelli. Then, on crossing the line, he made one perfunctory clap of the hands above his bare head. That short clap was for him; the rest of the day was for Fabio.

Fifteen years later, Lance tells me, "That was my greatest victory."

Bruyneel, who four years later would become Lance's team director and closest confidant, was astonished by Lance's performance. He had a long conversation with him on that Tour's last-day ride into Paris. The Belgian remembers it well: "I told Lance, 'When you went, I thought, You're crazy, you're going way too early.' And he said, 'I knew who I was riding for, and I knew from the moment I had twenty meters that nobody would see me anymore.'

"I then told him I had exactly the same experience in '93 when I won a Tour stage at Amiens. My father had died three or four weeks before the Tour; he died of a heart attack at the end of a bike ride only two kilometers from the house. He was fifty-three years old. And I told Lance that I also went quite early in my break, and when I had ten meters, I told myself, 'This is it, nobody sees me anymore.' I just rode to the finish with . . . call it a state of grace.

"They were really very similar experiences, and that was a moment that brought us close together—very personal, very emotional, very deep experiences that stay forever.

"For me, the purest experience of my career were those twenty kilometers of breakaway into Amiens. And Lance says the same thing about his win into Limoges. That's something very, very connecting. It's funny, because after that we never spoke about it anymore. But there are some things you don't have to speak about. . . ."

Casartelli was neither the first nor the last Tour athlete to have his life or career ended by a high-speed crash—that's a risk that all racers are aware of when they take the start.

Closure on Fabio Casartelli's passing came for his family and the Motorola team that November, when Lance assisted in the unveiling of a massive white marble memorial sculpture to Casartelli close to the spot where he died. Fabio's wife, Annalisa, and son, Marco, were there, along with his parents, Rosa and Sergio. "Lance would always be there for the family," says Och, who helped coordinate the funding and erection of the memorial. The Tour de France organizer Jean-Marie Leblanc said in a brief address, "Thanks to this memorial, no one will ever forget Fabio or his wonderful smile."

By finishing the Tour—in thirty-sixth place, almost ninety minutes behind Induráin, the winner for the fifth time—Lance proved he could not only get through the three weeks of racing but could also be competitive in the final days. Granted, winning a stage was a far more limited achievement than contending for the yellow jersey. But by completing one whole Tour after two planned "half Tours," he was carefully acquiring the knowledge he would need to take a larger role in cycling's premier race. In fact, Lance was already progressing faster than Induráin had at the same age.

Like Lance, the Spaniard entered the Tour in his rookie season, but he got no farther than the fourth stage in his first attempt (Lance did eleven stages); and the following year he pulled out after eight stages (Lance did fourteen). Both men completed their third Tours, Induráin in a lowly ninety-seventh place, Lance in thirty-sixth. After that, Induráin continued to improve: He finished forty-seventh in his fourth Tour, seventeenth in the next, and tenth in his sixth Tour. Given this comparison, it seemed that Lance had plenty of time to emulate Induráin, who eventually won the Tour in his seventh attempt.

And when it came to the one-day races, Lance was about to surpass Induráin, who was twenty-six when he won his only classic, the Clásica San Sebastián, in which Lance finished last on his pro debut. But now, three weeks after the Tour, Lance took another shot at this same race at age twenty-three, and this time he was one of the leaders over the Jaizkibel—the mountain on which he struggled alone through a rainstorm in 1993. He took command of the race on the steep, twisting descent, and only two riders could follow him. After one of those two stopped with a flat tire, Lance had just one man to contend with, French star Laurent Jalabert, one of the world's fastest sprint finishers. "If he was on his worst day and I was on my best," Lance said, "then maybe I could have beaten him in the sprint."

But it didn't come down to a sprint. Lance had some good fortune when a small chase group caught him and Jalabert about three miles from the finish. And when Italian rider Stefano Della Santa immediately sped away, only Lance responded. It was an instinctive move that confirmed how much tactical progress Lance had made. He then worked hard with Della Santa to establish their breakaway before focusing on the final sprint—which he easily won.

From dead last to glorious first in just three years, Lance was the first American in history to win a European cycling classic. The Spanish race lacked the renown of major classics, such as Milan-San Remo, the Tour of Flanders, or Liège-Bastogne-Liège. But winning San Sebastián wasn't a bad place to start.

Eddy Merckx won all the major classic races multiple times, besides scoring five victories in the Tour de France. As the biggest winner in cycling history, Merckx is lauded wherever he goes in Europe, yet he's the antithesis of a celebrity. Now in his sixties, the Belgian superstar lives with his wife of almost forty years in a quiet suburb of Brussels. Merckx is a big man—over six feet tall—and has an imposing presence. Until 2009, he owned an artisan bike-manufacturing business in a converted brick-built farm, and he still provides commentaries for the major bike races on Belgian television. Merckx doesn't like talking about his own achievements, but he's always willing to give advice or be sharply critical of others. Lance was one who benefited from his critiques, especially in 1995.

Merckx came to see Lance at that year's Tour when the race was in Belgium, and he made a point of following Lance in the time trial, watching him with Och from the Motorola team car. The Belgian wasn't impressed with what he saw when Lance was only nineteenth, five minutes slower than Induráin.

After the stage, I asked Merckx to comment on Lance's ride. The great man shrugged, pursed his big lips, and puffed out his cheeks before saying, "His position on the bike is not the best. And he has to be more specific in his training and lose a lot of weight if he wants to do better in the Tour."

In an intense pro career that burned him out by age thirty-two, Merckx had trained harder and longer than any of his rivals. Now, he wanted to help Lance. So he called the coach he thought could best harness the enormous physical and mental talents of "this animal from Texas," as Lance had once been called. That coach was Dr. Michele Ferrari, the controversial Italian sports doctor.

"Eddy Merckx insisted for a long time that I have a meeting with Lance in order to rearrange his training schedules and lifestyle, although I was not very convinced about it," Dr. Ferrari tells me.

"Lance didn't strike me as a cyclist that could be suitable for my training methods. Eventually, though, I accepted to meet and test him."

The meeting took place that November in the sports doctor's office in Ferrara, Italy, while Lance was in Europe to attend the Casartelli memorial ceremonies. "I could immediately see he had talent, with a particularly high anaerobic threshold [AT]—around 420 watts if I remember correctly," Ferrari says, referring to a number that distinguishes Lance from most other athletes. "But he was definitely fat, as well as being quite big muscularly. We discussed a training program for the winter period, and nutrition."

Only a few people knew about that initial meeting between the sorcerer and his new apprentice; and, except for a brief mention by a cycling magazine in 1997, Lance's association with Ferrari was not made public until some five years later when David Walsh, a sportswriter for *The Sunday Times* of London, wrote about it in a full-page article that attempted to link Lance with doping.

Motorola's team doctor and trainer Massimo Testa was one of the first to hear about Lance's 1995 meeting with Ferrari. "I didn't learn about it from Lance," he says. "I learned from an Italian rider I'd worked with since he was a junior. He said he went with his team to see Dr. Ferrari, and he saw Lance there. I was not upset—but to be honest, I was not too happy.

"I'd spent some time with Ferrari because we both started working in pro cycling at the same time on the Chateau d'Ax team [in the late 1980s]. We would run together sometimes after races, but we never became really connected. In those years, he was kind of controversial in his role with teams because he started to work with individual athletes from different teams.

"I never really believed too much what they were saying about him. He was considered one of those magic doctors where you would go see him and boom! So I was a little skeptical about that, and I was not too happy to have a rider of our team involved with him because I didn't really know what was going on."

What Testa did know was that Lance needed a dedicated coach. Carmichael was an ocean away, still working with amateur racers on the U.S. national team, and Testa himself was taking care of a team of twenty riders. "I realized I was kind of the family doctor of the team," Testa says. "I was working in my spare time to do training programs for Lance and the others, but my main work was as the family doctor. So my time with them was not the time that Ferrari or some other coach could spend. I realized Lance wanted more attention."

Once Ferrari took on Lance as a client, he ran tests with him every three to four weeks, and from those results he adapted his training loads, both in intensity and volume. "Lance was quite scrupulous and full of enthusiasm," Ferrari recalls, "but his weight was not dropping that much. He kept around 80 kilograms [176 pounds], while his AT was constantly improving: It was up to 460 watts [in early 1996], or 5.75 watts per kilogram." By comparison, Induráin scored around the same level early in his career, and he only began winning the Tour after he lost about fifteen pounds over a number of years. At his peak, the Spaniard's AT was close to 7 watts per kilogram—hence Lance's need to reduce his weight while retaining the same level of power. Those were the goals that Ferrari could help Lance attain.

When later asked to evaluate Ferrari, Lance said, "Michele's a bright, bright man who's brutally honest. He's also an incredibly misunderstood person. He's made some bad mistakes in terms of the press and interviews and in the way he's reacted to certain questions. If he gets asked a question, he's going to give a very direct, intelligent answer—such as that whole orange juice quote." Lance was referring to the answer Ferrari gave after three of his riders shockingly swept the podium at the 1994 Flèche Wallonne.

Nonetheless, because of the perception that Ferrari was a "doping" doctor, Lance didn't want to publicize his new relationship—even though, ironically, his intention was to get the best possible trainer to help him combat those riders who *were* doping. And even though the man who introduced him to his new trainer was the most revered person in all of cycling: Eddy Merckx.

Lance had addressed many of the questions he had faced a year earlier, but none were yet settled. His and Och's efforts to rebuild their cycling team and have powerful new teammates were ongoing; Yates was still around, but Bauer decided he had done his last season of European racing, and Casartelli's death had left a deep hole within a team seeking cohesion.

In his efforts to compete in a peloton apparently rife with EPO, Lance had been somewhat successful: He had won three races in Europe that year, including his first classic, and he had taken a bold, perhaps risky, step in hiring Dr. Ferrari as his new European trainer.

As for relationships back home, Lance had a few ideas to improve them. His biggest decision was to build a house in Austin; he'd had enough of rentals. It would be his first real home, and he was going to help in its design. Furthermore, he would name it Casa Linda for his mom. That was one way to reaffirm his closest relationship, while he would cement another by having his pal J. T. Neal oversee the construction of the lakeside villa. And though Lance had broken off with Dutch girlfriend Daniëlla by the end of the season, he expected that a new relationship would soon begin. His Austin riding partner Bart Knaggs had just introduced him to John "College" Korioth, who ran

The Cactus Room, one of the most popular bars in town. "I think Lance thought, 'This is the guy to hang out with because he knows all the beautiful women,'" College recalls. He was right.

CHAPTER 13

ROLLER-COASTER RIDE

I came crashing down on the last stage and didn't finish.
I was really bad . . . with the wet and cold . . . it was terrible.
—LANCE ARMSTRONG

"Lance and I did everything together," John "College" Korioth says about the fall and winter of '95. "We rode together, vacationed together, and connected on a lot of issues. And at that age, the issues were chasing women, riding bikes, getting drunk, and having a good time."

Four years older than Lance, College was best friends with Bart Knaggs in kindergarten; they played basketball through high school; and then Knaggs got into bike racing, met Lance, and introduced him to College about ten years later. "I was still in love with basketball," College says. "But I tore my knee up when I was twenty-seven, and

Bart told me to get a bike to stay in shape. One night, Bart brought in Lance to The Cactus Room. We got talking, and when he asked what I did, I said, 'I get up in the morning and ride my bike. . . .' And he was like, 'You *ride?* I'll go riding with you.' He needed someone to train with because Bart was doing his MBA then.

"The only people I'd ridden with were Bart and one local amateur. I'd never done a race; and Lance had just got done with the Tour de France. But from that day on we rode virtually every day he was in Austin."

College, who's six-foot-two, has a long face, close-cropped gray hair, and a strong baritone voice. We meet at Jo's coffee shop in downtown Austin, four blocks from the Six Lounge, a nightclub he now co-owns. "Back in '95, we had very little responsibility, no big bills, just a simple life. Things were great," he says, while eating yogurt and granola. "Lance would hang out in the bar a lot. I remember one night he must have said something smart-alecky to two of our bouncers; they were bodybuilders. They had him pinned up against the wall, like wrestling with him, and Lance couldn't do anything about it. But it was all in fun. By then, Lance was part of our family in that bar."

Knaggs introduced Lance to someone else that winter: a local lawyer, Bill Stapleton. Knaggs thought that his friend was big enough now that he needed an agent.

"I'd started a sports agency with a junior partner in a big Austin law firm," Stapleton tells me. "We were doing it on the side, working nights and weekends. One day, my old law professor at the business school called to say there was a guy called Bart Knaggs in his class who was trying to find an agent for Lance."

Knaggs had already contacted some of the country's largest sports agencies, including Leigh Steinberg of Los Angeles and Advantage International of Washington, D.C. "And I was just this young lawyer in Austin," Stapleton says. "We eventually set up a meeting with Lance and Knaggs at my old firm, Brown McCarrol. I had Shiner

Bock on ice and everything he might possibly want. It so happened that my partner had one of our football clients in: James Patton, a defensive tackle with the Buffalo Bills, who'd just been in the Super Bowl. We talked about having James drop by and say hello to Lance. Thought Lance might be impressed."

Knaggs takes up the story: "When he heard the name Patton, Lance acts like he's seen a ghost. He sits straight up and says, 'You fucking kidding me? He's coming in here? Keep him away from me.' Bill is like freaking out and pops a beer. 'I'm kinda screwed here,' he says. 'What's going on?' 'Well,' Lance says, 'I mean, we were kind of seeing the same girl, and this guy tried to rip the door off my house just five days ago!' Patton was this big, huge monster-masher guy and he'd scared the living shit out of Lance."

Stapleton adds, "So I said to Lance, 'If you want to get the hell out of here that's fine; just go down that back elevator.' He stayed while I went to give my partner the scoop, but the meeting just sort of disintegrated after that."

Knaggs and Lance left the building. On their way out, Knaggs recalls, "I'm thinking I'm screwed because Lance was gonna leave the next day for Europe, and I'm like, 'All right, my fault.' The worst client pitch meeting you could ever imagine. So we're walking along and Lance, in his way, says, 'You know what? I like that guy.' 'Really?' 'Yeah, you know man, that was a tough situation, and he just came straight up, like a good guy. Yeah. I think that's my guy.'"

A deal had yet to be struck, but Stapleton persevered. He went to a race to see Lance compete, gave him some help with a small contract, and saw what a great client he could be. Then he spoke with J. T. Neal, whom Stapleton knew from the days when he was a swimmer. "For me, trying to sign this guy was the most important thing in my life. I'd even left my firm," Stapleton says. "For Lance, it was, 'I don't know if I need an agent; Knaggs thinks I do.' Then I went to lunch with J. T., and a couple days later Lance calls me and says, 'If we're gonna do this, do we sign a contract? Do you have one I can look at?' Well, yeah. So I faxed one to him in Europe and a couple days later it comes back signed. And that's the same contract we have today: two pages saying you can hire me when you want, you can fire me when you want, and this is how you pay me. So basically it's a handshake deal."

The first thing Lance asked Stapleton to do was "get a Nike deal," because Lance had written the sportswear giant asking for support when he was a triathlete in high school—and been turned down. Stapleton says he put in some fifteen calls to Nike before getting a response, but he managed to get a three-year contract that paid Lance $30,000 a year. That was the first deal in what would be a long and successful partnership between the young lawyer and his bike-racing client.

Life was good for Lance. He had a great contract with Motorola, his new agent was starting to make side deals, and his relationships with J. T. and his mom were again strong. On the racing side, he was following the training schedules dictated by his new trainer, Michele Ferrari, and also keeping in touch with Chris Carmichael and Jim Ochowicz to fine-tune his preparation for what they all hoped would be his best season. Because Motorola's title sponsorship was up for renewal at the end of 1996, Lance's targets for the year were winning another classic, repeating his Tour DuPont victory, riding well at the Tour de France, and becoming an Olympic gold medalist in Atlanta.

To help him achieve those ambitious goals, Och beefed up the team. He brought back Max Sciandri, hired some solid European support riders to work with Andrea Peron, and gave more responsibility to his other American riders: Frankie Andreu, George Hincapie, Bobby Julich, and Kevin Livingston.

The changes worked out well. Lance began the year's campaign at Paris-Nice, where he put in his best yet performance in a European stage race. He fought a weeklong battle with the world's number-one-ranked cyclist, Laurent Jalabert, excelling in both the time trials and mountain stages, to place second overall behind the French star. Lance then showed improving form in the spring classics. He even survived the cobblestone climbs of the Tour of Flanders for the first time, albeit finishing twenty-eighth, four minutes behind the winner.

Next up was the Flèche Wallonne, the hilly Belgian classic where Dr. Ferrari's three Gewiss team riders had swept the podium two years before, amid rumors of doping. It wasn't a major classic, but the Flèche had a much longer history and greater prestige than the Clásica San Sebastián that Lance won in 1995. The course for this sixtieth edition was made up of three separate loops that each culminated on an ultrasteep hill called the Mur de Huy ("Wall of Huy"). Part of the Flèche's notoriety was due to this narrow, twisting ascent to the finish, which is lined with a dozen ancient brick shelters that house tableaux depicting Jesus Christ's path to Calvary: the Stations of the Cross.

On race day, after 125 miles of fierce competition, Lance was one of two men who arrived at the foot of this Belgian *Via Dolorosa* well ahead of the rest. His rival was a Frenchman, Denis Rous, who was on the best form of his life after two wins and a host of top placings that spring. They climbed side by side, standing on the pedals, around the hill's two steepest switchbacks. Then, as they passed the sixth Station of the Cross, Lance sprang away from Rous and held strong to the finish to score a dramatic win. He was pumped. The world's best riders had been left in his tracks.

In contrast to most major sports events, there were few official press conferences in cycling at that time. So reporters at the Flèche were thrilled when Lance came to see them in the makeshift press-room—a school classroom—and sat down at a small wooden table to answer questions. A score of plump Belgian, Dutch, and French sportswriters, their pens and notebooks poised, instantly gathered around the exuberant Texan. As the first American to win a traditional spring classic, Lance was asked what changes he'd like to see in pro cycling. Hesitant at first, he replied, "Cycling has a lot of tradition, and it's still a very simple sport." Then, warming to the subject, he said, "If I could make changes, there'd be better hotels and maybe team planes. I'd like to see the sport at a much higher level—like soccer, tennis, and Formula One car racing. If this were Formula One, we wouldn't be sitting around this little wooden table. . . ."

Not wanting to offend the Europeans, he caught himself, smiled, and said, "This is a great table! I don't want to change this sport one bit!"

The journalists cracked up, appreciating Lance's humor and frankness. The American then showed his growing knowledge of cycling's traditions by pointing to the race number he had just worn to victory in the Flèche: number 51. He said he had heard that morning from Eddy Merckx's wife that 51 was a lucky number—the one that her husband had worn in his first Tour de France, which he brilliantly won.

Commenting on his own win, Lance said, "I certainly came for the victory, but my main goal today was to race smarter. I've had some good results, but I've not had *enough* results. Patience is still hard for me."

He then spoke about the two decisive moments in the race, perhaps remembering Chris Carmichael's advice many years before: "You have only two bullets in your pistol, not six"—when you break or bridge to a break, and when you make a late attack or contest a final sprint.

Lance fired the first of those bullets after ascending the Wall for the second time, chasing six men who had broken away. "I was five or six seconds back," Lance said. "I felt that was the race, so I had to go . . . and it took me about five hundred meters to cross. It seemed like a long time." Lance's explosive power took him across the gap with his heart-rate monitor showing more than 200 beats a minute—just below the 209 maximum he had recorded in 1990. He then set about working with the six Europeans, helping them build a one-minute lead over a fifty-strong chase group.

Lance fired his second bullet near the top of the Ben-Ahin hill, the last climb before the course descended into Huy for the finish. As the steep grade eased, he accelerated, and only Rous could follow him. "At that moment, I think everyone was like this," Lance said, making a throat-cutting gesture.

Lance made a similar attack four days later in his bid to win the much longer Liège-Bastogne-Liège. Just after the summit of the rugged La Redoute climb, with twenty-three miles to go, his attack drew out two Swiss riders, Mauro Gianetti and Pascal Richard, from a lead group of fifteen. The trio would go on to fight out the victory. Lance was strong enough to counter separate attacks by Gianetti and Richard on the long climb to the finish in Ans. But despite their being on different teams, the Swiss pair seemed to have ganged up on the American. "I didn't like their monkey business," Lance said about his rivals forcing him to lead out the final sprint into a headwind. Then the wily Richard sprinted by to take the win, leaving Lance in second. An hour later, in the locker room, Lance said, "I thought I had it won with fifty meters to go, but I didn't have that extra gear. I wasn't super today."

Lance's next seasonal goal was to win the Tour DuPont. And just like the year before, he dominated the race, taking five stages, including both time trials. He won by wide margins, some three minutes ahead of Frenchman Pascal Hervé, with Swiss star Tony Rominger—

a Tour de France runner-up and Giro d'Italia winner—in third, five minutes back. Lance's former teammate Andy Hampsten, now riding for the fledgling U.S. Postal Service squad, finished sixth. He was impressed by the improvements he saw in Lance. "His time-trialing was really solid," Hampsten says. "Also, instead of just breaking away to win stages, he was very good at focusing his team on wearing other people out so he could attack at the crucial time. And when Lance kicked it on the climbs, all we could do was watch him ride away; he would shake Hervé off his wheel, then he and Rominger would disappear, and he would beat Rominger when they were out of sight."

In the final day's time trial at Marietta, Georgia—just north of Atlanta, where he'd be shooting for Olympic gold three months later—Lance beat Rominger by half a minute. It was an extraordinary margin in less than ten miles of solo riding.

Perhaps he went too hard, though, in an eleven-day race he had virtually wrapped up by the seventh stage. After Lance crossed the finish line, a seasoned American sportswriter, John Rezell, saw something unexpected. "I was the first reporter running at his side," Rezell says, "and for the first time in the four years of covering him, something wasn't right. I wrote down: 'Instead of the energy-packed, fist-pumping celebration that has been his trademark in such breakthrough victories, his eyes were bloodshot, his face beet-red . . . he looked wasted.'

"I wrote those words, then read them over and paused. The only cycling fans I saw that day were cheering wildly, oblivious to any difference in Armstrong's demeanor, attitude, or spirit. But I could see it in his eyes, more than anything.

"I struggled with that lead more than any other I have written. Maybe I was focusing too much on the final moment, rather than the entire scope of the race. But each time I wrote an alternative effort, it felt shallow, as if I had decided to hide something. In the end, I closed my eyes and relived those moments: running alongside Lance down the street, seeing his shoulders slumped, his head down, his eyes drained. I had never seen him like this. I let it stand as written."

Lance didn't race for the next four weeks. He returned to competition at the Tour of Switzerland, a ten-day race that takes in some of the longest and highest mountain roads in the Alps. "It was tough to be thrown back in there and have that be such a hard race," Lance said. "I was coming up, and coming up . . . and I had two good stages . . . but then I came crashing down on the last stage and didn't finish. I was really bad . . . with the wet and cold . . . it was terrible."

Other than planned exits from his first two Tours de France, this was the first pro stage race Lance had quit. He still had a week in Como to make final preparations for the Tour, but the weather didn't improve and neither did Lance's condition. "I didn't feel good in training," he said. "The whole week was bad."

The awful weather continued for the Tour's first week on mainly flat roads through the Netherlands, Belgium, and northern France. Not inspired by any of the courses, Lance finished near the back of the peloton every day. "It was such a hard, hard Tour," recalls George Hincapie, Lance's young teammate, who was riding the Tour for the first time. "I didn't want to quit so I was hoping to crash. I was hurting so hard, I thought it would be better to crash and injure yourself than just quit. I remember Lance being kinda quiet, and I was wondering, did he have a cold?"

The weather worsened on the sixth stage, which headed south to Aix-les-Bains on the eastern edge of the French Alps. Low clouds swirled around limestone peaks, heavy rain lashed the riders in their plastic rain jackets, and strong crosswinds made it tough to stay with the fast-moving pack. Lance was one of those having problems, and after forty miles of groveling at the back, he fell behind with five others.

A few miles later, on a long rising road and with the pack more than two minutes ahead, Lance, shivering from the cold, coasted to a halt and dropped out of the race, just as he had in Switzerland two weeks before. "Och came on the team radio and said Lance is quitting," Hincapie recalls. "Lance didn't say anything; he just turned around, and then he was out."

After the stage had finished, I went to the hotel where Lance was staying to find out what went wrong. In the lobby, a TV crew was waiting to interview that day's winner. No one was interested in Lance now that he had quit. I went up to his room. The television was tuned to CNN; Lance was tuned out. His eyes were lusterless and he seemed morose. He was waiting to see the team doctor, and even before I sat down he blurted out, "I'm bummed!"

"My team knew I'd been bad, but I haven't come right out and said that I'm sick," he told me. "I don't want to say that because I never get sick, I mean, very rarely. I don't even remember when I last had a throat or respiratory problem.

"I woke up several times in the night feeling under the weather. I think I had an infection set in yesterday. I woke up and couldn't swallow. In this weather it's hard to fight. I had no power . . . couldn't breathe. I thought it was just allergies, or the weather, or blocked . . . I'm disappointed. I didn't expect to come here and get sick. But I am, so what can I say? I have to stop and try to fix it."

Lance seemed downcast and confused, and when I asked him more questions, he grew impatient. "The reason I'm bummed out is that I'm still here, still around, still answering questions. . . . I need to get out, get better, get busy. . . . It doesn't do me any good to sit around here and do interviews about why I'm stopping. I've gotta get home and start focusing on the Olympics."

Atlanta '96 was planned to be the high point of Lance's season, if not his whole career. It was a once-in-a-lifetime opportunity to compete at the Olympics in his own country. His agent, Bill Stapleton, was in town, hoping there'd be some endorsement opportunities should his client win gold. But because Lance had left the Tour early, he wasn't as racing fit as his opponents. "I trained harder than I've ever trained in my life," Lance said. Still, it's difficult to replace three weeks of intense pro racing with just training. And Lance had to know that riding some minor American races, training at home, and having a week in Birmingham, Alabama, to acclimate to the expected heat of Atlanta wasn't the ideal preparation before heading to the Games.

"We stayed at this secluded estate in rural Georgia, which wasn't ideal," recalls Andy Pruitt, the U.S. team physician. "Lance was struggling on his time-trial bike, and he said, 'Andy, my back's out.' I tried all the tricks that my dad, a chiropractor, had taught me, but I couldn't resolve his issue. I knew he needed a certain manipulation to put this free fragment at the base of his spine back in its normal place. We were a day away from the time trial, and the chiropractor in the Olympic Village couldn't fit him in, so I went through the Yellow Pages and called all the chiropractors until I found one that sounded reasonable. I told him I was bringing an Olympic athlete.

"So we drove an hour south to a strip mall with a neon sign outside, and this guy had gotten his entire family in there! We signed autographs and took pictures, even though they had no idea who Lance Armstrong was. The guy took the X-ray, manipulated his back, and all was good."

Pruitt admired Lance's perseverance and ability to rise above pain. However, he points out, "I don't want to paint the perfect picture because it has been difficult to work with Lance at times. He could be somewhat secretive, wanting his own people. And there were lots of times when he could test you, too."

At the Atlanta Olympics, Lance placed only sixth in the 32-mile time trial, more than two minutes slower than the winner, Miguel Induráin. And in the 140-mile road race, he was a marked man. He did make a solo breakaway with 24 miles to go, but after he was brought back, he missed the vital attack. His teammate Frankie Andreu said he suggested to Lance that they try to bridge to the leaders, "but he said, 'I'm pretty knackered. I don't think I'll be able to make it.' And anytime Lance did make a move, the others reacted. He was so marked."

"I was hoping I'd feel a little stronger when I went," Lance said after placing twelfth. "I definitely didn't feel super. I mean, I was strong when I started to go away, but I couldn't roll it like I'd hoped. When I was caught, I realized I was in a little bit of trouble. Of course I would have liked to have won, but I have to be realistic. It's been a long year."

It was unusual for Lance to make excuses; he had clearly lost some confidence after his string of poor performances that summer. The lack of good results meant that Motorola would not renew its title sponsorship for the following year, and the team that Och created would disband after twelve years in the pro peloton.

"There were several reasons for Motorola dropping out," Och reveals. "Internal politics, management changes, and a policy difference. They wanted to do soccer, not cycling. They made a big mistake in my opinion. It was a pity because we had the next generation coming through. I was disappointed."

Och's loss—he never found a new sponsor and eventually changed careers—meant more work for Stapleton. And Lance saw just why he *did* need an agent when he obtained a two-year, $2.5 million contract with a French team, Cofidis. Stapleton's negotiations allowed Lance to take Andreu, Julich, and Livingston with him to the new squad, while Hincapie went to the lower-budget U.S. Postal Service team. "I was a little upset that he didn't take me to Cofidis," Hincapie says.

Lance would race a few more events in Europe that fall, including a two-man time trial in mid-September, his final race with Sean Yates, his longtime friend and mentor. Yates retired a few days later, and Lance returned to Austin. There, he would celebrate his twenty-fifth birthday, the new contract, and a new girlfriend that College had introduced him to at The Cactus Room: Lisa Shiels, a blonde engineering student at Austin's University of Texas. He was also excited about his new house, a lakeside Spanish-style mansion whose tall windows overlooked the pool and whose dock already moored a motorboat and jet ski. J. T. oversaw its completion, Linda got it ready, and Lance was eager to make it his home.

A few days after Lance moved in, J. T. came to see him, and the news he brought was not good.

"J. T. had cancer," Linda says. "Leukemia. He wasn't gonna tell anybody, but I guess he sat down with Lance when Lance moved into Casa Linda. It was like J. T.'s house too; he had a key because Lance was on the road all the time." J. T. wanted Lance to know about his illness, but he downplayed it and maintained his lively spirit. He even attended Lance's birthday party.

A few days after that blowout bash in his new villa, Lance called his mom in Plano. "He wanted to know where his flashlight was, because I had unpacked everything in his home," Linda says. "I took a week's vacation, working night and day to get that house ready. So I told him where to find the flashlight, and then he told me about having headaches, blurred vision, and not feeling well. He thought he might have partied too much on his birthday.

"He had promised Nike he would go up to Oregon and ride with this group that was doing research on a new cycling shoe, but he said, 'Ma, I think I'm too sick. I don't wanna go.' And I said, 'You can't let these people down. They're counting on you. You really need to go.' And he's like, 'Well, I'll go to the doctor and get a shot.' Some kind of steroid shot that'll make him feel better, you know."

Although steroids are banned for competition use by the International Cycling Union, athletes are permitted to use them for therapeutic purposes and often do. Lance was no exception. "If his back was out and his doctor Max Testa wasn't there he'd have him call me and say what he would prescribe," says U.S. team physician Pruitt. "I was never asked to do anything illegal, and I did have to record a few of the steroid injections that we'd give Lance because of his back pain. So the four years I spent in close contact with him, I never saw anything that I was upset about . . . but I would get the phone calls from Max, not from Lance."

Just before Lance traveled with his new girlfriend, Lisa, to Bend, Oregon, for the Nike weekend, his old high-school friend Adam Wilk came to town with his wife. "We were at his house for dinner with him," Wilk says. "He wanted to show me this Harley he just got and the Porsche 911 turbo. A buddy of his, the motorcycle world champ Kevin Schwarntz, had recommended it. Lance took my wife out on the motorcycle, and I drove the Porsche. He never said anything to me about feeling bad."

Despite having to leave Och and his American team, and despite having to deal with the sad news about J. T. and get over feeling sick, Lance was relaxed and convivial in Bend. He chatted with the Nike people about the prototype cycling shoe they were building for him, and he went for a two-hour bike ride with them and a group of journalists who'd been invited for the product launch. After the ride, Lance relaxed with a beer on the deck of his rented cabin. While Lisa cooled off in the pool, he chatted with me about his season and the year ahead. He said that his new team wanted him to perform at a high level at the Tour de France in July rather than at the Tour DuPont in May. I asked him how he felt about the French team's sports director, Cyrille Guimard, who had coached Frenchmen Bernard Hinault and Laurent Fignon to Tour de France victories in the 1980s. "Guimard thinks that I could win the Tour someday," Lance said. "I don't even know if *I* think that. If I took my DuPont form and put it into the Tour de France, I'd probably be pretty good. I just have to move that form from May to July. And in July, the weather is much better suited to me . . ."

Lance was looking forward to being back in Austin, he said, enjoying his new house, hanging out with his buddies, and riding again with College.

"I remember leaving him one day that fall," College recalls. "We had ridden and he was standing right in front of his new house doing this Superman, Hercules pose, and I was laughing about it, razzing him. He was on top of the world."

CHAPTER 14

A STEEP HILL TO CLIMB

> Things went from bad to worse. I don't know of anybody that could have had that much bad information in three months.
>
> —LINDA ARMSTRONG

On Wednesday morning, October 2, 1996, Lance and College were halfway through one of their regular training rides when, according to College, "a really weird thing happened." They were climbing a long, steep hill called Crumley Ranch Road in the Texas Hill Country. Suddenly, College says, "I started to ride away from him. That had never happened before, this local amateur rider dropping the number-one pro racer in the world. I'd never seen him hurting that bad. I looked back at him and I was like, 'What is your problem? Wow, you really are hurting aren't you?' I had to wait for him at the top of that hill."

Just one day before, after Lance returned from the weekend in Oregon, their ride had been very different, the norm. "I was fit, really bike-racing fit, and we went out and did a three-hour ride, and he was in the saddle just killing me." College says. "We were going up these hills and I'd never seen him this strong."

But after College dropped the pro on Crumley Ranch Road that Wednesday, Lance had something to say to his friend. "He told me that after the bike ride the day before he had coughed up some blood. I was like, 'Really?' And he starts telling me that his testicle 'is absolutely killing me.' I said—and what did a young kid like me know?—I said, 'Have you been having too much sex lately?' And he was like, 'No, a little bit, but nothing crazy.' And talking like that with another man is a sensitive subject, and he was shy to talk about it. I was thinking, 'Oh, your testicle hurts, tough it out, big deal.'"

Lance says he was on the phone with his agent Bill Stapleton when he had that coughing attack. He put down the phone and rushed to the bathroom. In his book, *It's Not About the Bike*, Lance wrote: "I coughed into the sink. It splattered with blood. I coughed again, and spit up another stream of red. I couldn't believe that the mass of blood and clotted matter had come from my own body."

Unsure of why this happened, Lance hung up with Stapleton and called a neighbor he'd recently become friends with, Dr. Rick Parker, a plastic surgeon. By the time Parker arrived at the house, Lance had flushed away most of the blood. So seeing only a small residue, Parker said it was probably a cracked sinus; he knew Lance often suffered from allergies.

To get a second opinion, Lance dialed his old team doctor Massimo Testa in Italy. "He called me to say he had this pain," Testa says. "He described to me what he had. I was afraid about the swollen testicle. It was a new thing? 'No,' he said, 'It's been like this several months.' So I said, 'You know what, you need to go to see a urologist.'"

On Wednesday morning, Lance still had the testicular pain. "I'd actually had that pain for a long time," he tells me. But that didn't stop him from rendezvousing with College at the Hula Hut restaurant for their usual 9 a.m. ride. On getting home, after his embarrassing chat with College, Lance says he "called Parker again. I said, 'Something's not right. One of the things bothering me is a little weird; I don't want to talk about it.' Parker didn't even come down; he wanted me to go and see a urologist, Dr. Reeves."

An appointment was made for later that afternoon. Before then, Lance drove to see J. T. at their regular hangout, The Tavern, a popular sports bar up the street from Whole Foods. J. T. later told a reporter that over lunch Lance told him he "felt pain in his abdomen and that it hurt him to walk." After driving to a local mall, J. T. said Lance complained again. "We thought it was a hernia," he said. Lance got back into his Porsche and drove through the University of Texas campus to reach the urologist's office.

Dr. Jim Reeves, a well-regarded Austin urologist, is now retired and lives with his wife in the Texas Hill Country. Their house overlooks fifteen hundred acres of ranchland that has been in the family for four decades. His full beard gives Reeves the air of a frontiersman, an image reinforced by the homemade traps he sets to catch wild hogs. Born in Wisconsin, he has the midwesterner's penchant for understatement, but there's no mistaking the authority in his deep but quiet voice when he recalls the patient he saw that October afternoon more than a decade ago.

"Dr. Rick Parker said he had a friend he needed me to see . . . a famous bike rider. But I hadn't heard of him," Dr. Reeves says.

Lance didn't like seeing unfamiliar doctors; he had bad memories from age four, when he fell off a little Tonka truck and ended up in an emergency room. Now, twenty-one years later, he was having to strip, don a surgical gown, and lie on a paper-covered exam table. Dr. Reeves didn't like what he saw: a "softball-size" right testicle.

"Apparently he had ridden the Tour de France with this enlarged testicle, so he'd had it at least three months," Dr. Reeves says. "The miracle is he had enough stamina to keep going with a testicle that big. How in the world was he able to ride at all on that itty-bitty bike seat in those tight britches?"

The long-established urologist wanted tests done before he could give a definite diagnosis, but, he tells me, "I saw this was cancer, no question about it." Not yet sensing what was wrong with him, Lance dressed, drove his car around the corner to a lab on Medical Arts Square, and underwent an ultrasound. "The radiologist called and said the ultrasound was positive," the doctor continues. "That means the lungs are full. So I said, 'Get a chest X-ray, too.' At that point it was apparent that there was a lot of cancer, widespread. I knew he would need chemotherapy. Dudley Youman was an oncologist I'd used a lot, and I knew he was a serious bike rider—a good match. So I called Dudley and scheduled Lance for surgery the next morning before he even came back from the lab to see me.

"It was the end of the day by then. I called Rick and said, 'Lance has testicular cancer, and I want you to come over and be with him when I tell him because that's gonna be real important. This is a big deal.'"

After studying the test results and chest X-rays, Dr. Reeves confirmed the diagnosis with Lance and Dr. Parker: a fast-growing form of testicular cancer that had metastasized from the malignant testicle to the abdomen and lungs—which were filled with golf-ball-sized lesions he pointed out on the chest X-ray.

"I said to Lance, 'I'll leave you alone with Rick for a while, let y'all talk.' So I shut the door and they talked for a while," Dr. Reeves says. "Apparently, Lance was able to express his emotions, but when I came back in he was all business. He said, 'I'm ready, let's fix this, what shall we do?' I said, 'Well, I have you scheduled for surgery tomorrow morning at 7 to remove the malignant testicle.'"

Lance says he was stunned and confused when he left Dr. Reeves's office that evening and began the five-mile drive home. The sun was setting beyond the golden dome of the Texas State Capitol. Bill Stapleton had just turned on the lights of his downtown office. College was greeting the night's first customers at The Cactus Room on Sixth Street. Bart Knaggs was working late at his start-up tech company. And Lance's mom was at home in Plano kicking back after a tough workday.

Lance remembers driving slowly and obsessively thinking, "I won't be able to race my bike again," before he picked up his car phone and began making calls. At that time, most of his friends had only pagers; very few had cell phones. One of the first people he got through to was Stapleton, who still remembers his words. "He said, 'I've got some really bad news, Bill.' I started thinking, 'Here we go, he doesn't want an agent anymore. I'm getting fired.' And he said, 'I've got cancer; I don't need an agent anymore.' He was obviously in shock. So he wasn't able to explain a lot. He said, 'I'm driving home.' So I went there immediately."

College was wondering why he hadn't heard from Lance. "Normally he paged me like once or twice in the afternoon to see what I was gonna do that night. And I looked down and I didn't have my pager. Around 7 o'clock I had to go into the cooler, and I found the pager caught on a case of beer. There are something like eight pages from Lance, so I call him, and he says, 'Where the hell have you been?' I explain about the pager, and he says, 'I've gotta tell you something. I'm just gonna come right out and say it to you.' And I said, 'All right.' And he said, 'Testicular cancer.' So I said, 'That's what J. T. has?' And he says, 'No, that's what I have.'

"I was standing in the office, and that just buckled me at my knees. I collapsed in this chair. I was clueless to what that was, clueless to cancer. 'So what does this mean?' I ask. It's a very difficult conversation for two best friends to have. 'I have to have an operation tomorrow morning at 7.' We said we loved each other . . . and I was there at St. David's Hospital the next morning. I was scared to death . . . scared for Lance, scared for myself."

When Knaggs got the news he immediately started researching "testicular cancer" on the Internet and printed as much useful information as he could to take to Lance that evening.

When Lance reached his house, Parker was waiting at the door and offered to call Linda because Lance was too emotional to tell her he had cancer. "I was working on a big critical project that day," Linda says, "and I'd just got home. I was sitting outside, trying to unwind from the day and reading a cycling magazine when the phone rang. I knew Rick Parker and all of Lance's new neighbors because I'd spent a whole year building his home down there. Of course, my heart sank down to my stomach, and it occurred to me, 'Wow, how quickly your life can change.' They got a flight for me, and Bill picked me up at the airport. It was all so fast that you really didn't have time to think. But I wasn't going to let myself think that I was going to be seeing . . ."

Linda doesn't finish the sentence, indicating that imagining her son to be terminally ill was too much to bear. "Everything we had been through from the very beginning when I was pregnant at sixteen, to knowing that child growing inside of me was gonna be my stability and my salvation . . . and I was just not gonna give in to that," she continues. "You've gotta put on a happy face, this positive face that I've always tried to put on for Lance. I just wasn't going to give in to the fact that he'd die.

"And you go from the middle of the rat race, pouring your heart and soul into your job, and suddenly you're gonna have to care for your only child. And as hard as it was for me to fear that I would lose my job, it didn't matter. I'd find a job because I knew I would be there for my son."

So Linda joined Stapleton, Knaggs, and Lance's other close friends at the lakeside villa, where the phone calling continued. Och was contacted in Milwaukee, where he was out to dinner with his family, and Carmichael called in from New York, where he was on his way to Switzerland for the world championships.

Och was all business and said he'd fly in the next morning, while Carmichael couldn't believe the news was real. "I got six or seven phone calls from Bill Stapleton to call him," Carmichael says. "I couldn't reach him, so I called Lance's house, and Bill picked up the phone and said, 'Lance was diagnosed with testicular cancer.' I said, 'You're joking,' I think I repeated that ten times, 'You're joking, give me a break.' Then he said, 'Lance is here, let me hand the phone to him.' And I heard his mom in the background, and I was like, 'Holy shit!' I said to Lance, 'Do you want me to come back there? What do you need?' But everything was pretty well set." Carmichael made plans, though, to be there as soon as he could.

"It was a crazy night. Shocking," Stapleton says. "And we all had to be at the hospital early."

By the time the operation was over, Och had arrived to be with Linda, Stapleton, and the others. "They brought Lance from recovery with the oncologist," Och says, "and the doctor who did the surgery was grim. It wasn't a good message he gave us . . . he said it had metastasized . . . and there were other issues. He was kind of not very confident. But Lance was sitting up in the bed, and one of the first things he said was: 'I'm gonna beat this thing.'"

The chances of a cure for Lance's cancer were given to the media as "sixty to sixty-five percent." Not great odds. But when I ask Dr. Reeves what he and oncologist Dudley Youman found out that October day, his words are chilling.

"We found mostly embryonal cells," he says, "and those at that time were essentially not curable. They're blood-borne and keep spreading; they'd spread everywhere. More surgery wasn't good, and radiation's not good, not for that kind of cell. So I spoke with Dudley and we were saying, this is what we've got, and what should I tell him? And he said, 'Well, tell him 20 percent.' I said, 'Okay.' But in my view, the chances were zero, or almost zero. In those days, chemotherapy was good, but with that much cancer, there was no way . . . this thing was incurable.

"After we got the path' report back and studied all the X-rays and test results, we told Lance 20 percent. But he wasn't happy with 20 percent. I don't think he ever accepted any percentage of cure short of 100 percent—in his mind, that is."

Dr. Reeves says he'd never seen any other testicular cancer patients with that much density of embryonal cells. "It was just top to bottom," he says. "The lungs were solid. With some other kinds it's easier to cure, but not embryonal cells. If a physician looked at those X-rays—I mean, if you had that kind of cancer yourself—you'd start getting your affairs in order; you really wouldn't think about winning this one."

Whatever the odds, Lance and his support crew vowed to approach this latest challenge with the same professionalism and passion they had displayed throughout his already astounding cycling career. The doctors were somber, but Lance's friends and family remained as upbeat as possible. Linda's instinct was to keep Lance's spirit intact. "I tried to encourage him," she says. "I told him to go out and ride your bike, go walk, do something, don't change anything."

Having College to ride with would boost Lance's morale, and even in the hospital on that dark morning, College brought lightness to the group. "When two nurses came into the room at separate times to check up on Lance," College says, "each of them looks at me and says, 'Oh, hey John!' I knew both of them from the bar because I have to check customers out before they're allowed in.

"And this is the first time I really met Linda. She and Och must have been wondering how he knows every girl in town. I didn't want to give a bad impression. Also, we were worried that the more people who saw Lance in the hospital that word would get out about his cancer, but the staff there had been instructed not to say anything."

Stapleton admits that he also began to worry. "I was thinking, 'How's this gonna get announced?' I didn't want it to leak out," he says. "So we made calls over the weekend to sponsors, and we planned a press conference for the Tuesday."

That was the earliest that Lance's cancer could be announced to the world because the doctors, knowing the urgency, moved up Lance's first bout of chemotherapy to Monday. And that weekend he was driven to the state's nearest sperm bank, in San Antonio, to preserve some of his semen in case the chemotherapy made him sterile.

Journalists and invited guests were patched into the October 8 conference call/press conference, so details of Lance's cancer soon reached a lot of people. "Having that press conference was a smart thing to do," Och says, "because it put the word out on the street. And because the Internet was still in its infancy—not everybody had it—the right people got the message."

Knaggs had been researching the best cancer care available, and the initial data pointed to Houston, Texas, and the M. D. Anderson Cancer Center, which was regarded as the premier cancer hospital in the United States. Lance and his friends visited the facility. It wasn't a good visit. "The toughest news was the M. D. Anderson guys saying, 'Probably, you're not gonna make it.'" Lance says. "We were scared shitless."

Lance didn't like that prognosis, nor did he like the form of chemotherapy the doctors there were recommending: Bleomycin. It might kill the rampant cancer calls, but it could also have damaging side effects for an athlete by weakening his lungs.

"Lance had just gotten back from M. D. Anderson when I arrived in Austin," Carmichael recalls, "and that was not a good mindset because the prognosis and treatment options they gave him were not very favorable.

"But Lance gets this interesting e-mail the next day. It was from Dr. Stephen Wolff, who was an oncologist and a cyclist. He wrote: 'You don't know me from Adam, but you should be aware that the leading oncologist in testicular cancer is Dr. Larry Einhorn, who's based out of Indiana University. You should do everything you can to go see him for treatment.'

"Lance asks, 'Do you think this guy's for real?' The e-mail said Vanderbilt University in Nashville, so I said, 'Let's call him up.' So he calls Stephen, who says he'll get Einhorn's phone number. That was just random. Lance was getting a lot of e-mails.

"So Lance went up to see Einhorn, and it was a whole new outlook. He told Lance there's another way to treat this that potentially could spare your lungs. He didn't say that he could cure it, but the chemotherapy wasn't going to fuck him over forever, and it wasn't gonna do what Bleomycin does, damage the lungs. Einhorn said, 'I can't guarantee you that you're not going to have residual effects, and they may prevent you from returning to the physical level you were at, but it's a lot better than this other stuff.' That gave Lance a lot of confidence.

"At the same time, all these other things were coming along. It didn't all happen at once. He'd do another test, come in the next week, and then the results would take another three days. You felt you were making headway, and then you get hit with worse news."

Despite the severity of the chemotherapy Lance would undergo in Indianapolis, he remained optimistic about the outcome and continued riding his bike when he was back in Austin. His old Motorola teammate Frankie Andreu came to visit and ride, while Kevin Livingston, who had moved to Austin, was a regular training partner.

"Maybe I did too much sometimes," Lance said, recalling one particular ride with Livingston. "I had to get off my bike and lie in a yard. After thirty minutes riding, I was just wasted . . . completely exhausted . . . almost like deadish. Kevin was scared. He was ready to get a car, but I rode home; just needed a rest."

While his friends and teammates did all they could for Lance, his American sponsors also stood by him, even though none of them knew whether Lance would ever return to pro cycling. "Oakley gave him a gas-powered remote-control car as a gift," College recalls. "It was a toy dune buggy that could do fifty miles per hour. He called me to say, 'You gotta see it. I'm having a blast with this thing.' I couldn't go right away, but I called him later to see if he wanted to go to dinner, and Lance's girlfriend, Lisa Shiels, answered. I asked, 'Where is he?' And she said, 'He's out there playing with that fucking car. I hope it goes in the fucking lake.' Lance called me later and says, 'I need your help. I turned off the remote-control unit and went to turn off the car, and it took off and went in the lake.' Lisa was laughing, and Stephanie McIlvain, the Oakley rep, was there and she thought it was hilarious. But Lance took it seriously because it was a gift. It was too dark for me to find the car that night, but I managed to fish it out of the lake in the morning. If I could do anything like that to support Lance, I did."

Losing the toy car was a distraction, but during the first week after his diagnosis Lance says he was scared he was going to lose everything. "He sold his Porsche the next week because it freaked him out," his Plano friend Adam Wilk says. "It was like the money's gone, everything's gone, I'm done; and that car was the first possession he sold."

Through the long days and nights that followed his diagnosis, Lance had his mom to lean on. "I took every bit of vacation day and personal day I had," Linda says. "I never knew anyone that had cancer, so I'm sitting there reading a paper saying that only six thousand men a year are affected by this testicular cancer. Why my son? So there's anger, and then there's fear—a lot of that!—and then there's all kinds of sadness. I'm getting people to come and stay with him, and we're taking calls; I had this revolving door going on for three weeks for him. We talked about the future, what it would be like for him to marry one day, and have a child."

That same week Linda received other news, from her sister Debbie. "At exactly the same time Lance was diagnosed with cancer, I found out that I was pregnant," Debbie says. "And as he was going through his treatment, I was going through my pregnancy. It was really an emotional time on all fronts, and I was spending a lot of time on the phone with Linda. So when I was forty, I had another baby."

News of her sister's pregnancy gave Linda some solace, but Lance's diagnosis was tough to handle. "When that door shut at night and I'd go to bed, I'd cry myself to sleep," she says. "And that job as a caregiver I did not interview for, nor did I want. But your life can change in a beat, go in another direction . . . so that was a very, very dark time."

Once Linda returned to her full-time job in Plano and Carmichael was back at his national coach's office in Colorado Springs, the caregiver role was passed on to Och, who'd just overseen the Motorola team's final race in Europe. "My plan was to stay with Lance the whole time," Och says. "When we originally went to Indianapolis, I checked into the hotel; he checked into the hospital. We met his doctors, Lawrence Einhorn and Craig Nicholls, but when they started the first chemotherapy protocol, they discovered he had a brain tumor."

This was the most traumatic news yet: two lesions had metastasized on the top part of Lance's brain and would have to be removed. "That brought a lot of worry and depression," Och says. "He already knew he had a big lump in his stomach and all the spots on his lungs, but the brain tumor scared him. They had to postpone the second chemo session to schedule surgery. And Dr. Scott Shapiro, who was going to do that surgery, came in to visit before Lance went back to Austin. They wanted him to recover a little bit from the chemo and build some strength back. He was riding his bike, and he was pretty much okay."

Lance says the exercise always cleared his head and helped him focus on the positive. Rather than obsess on the upcoming surgery, he was relieved that his spiraling blood counts had been slowed by the first chemo sessions. "He'd live or die by the cancer numbers, the markers that would come back from the blood tests," Carmichael says.

When Lance, his girlfriend, Lisa, and Och returned to Indianapolis for the surgery, they were joined by Linda, Carmichael, College, and Livingston. "Lance liked people around him at the hospital," Carmichael says. "It's funny, because I don't think my character would have liked that . . . but he liked having people around."

"Lance's hair was already starting to fall out," Och says, "and what was left they shaved off and got him ready for surgery with this big crown on his head. The day before the surgery, he heard about a twelve-year-old around the corner that was gonna have to do the same thing. He wanted to visit this kid, so we went into his room and Lance sat down on his bed next to him, both with their crowns on. I think that got Lance thinking for the first time about giving something back in the cancer space. Because this kid was in worse shape than Lance was, and that was the first time he saw someone in that situation who was a kid. It moved him."

That night, Lance seemed more relaxed than the close friends gathered around his bed. "Dr. Nicholls had just walked in and said the brain operation was like cutting a pumpkin," College says. "He said, 'We just cut in a little hole and it pops right out, and then we put the pumpkin head back on.' That freaked me out. So Lance slapped me on my knee and said, 'It's gonna be okay, College.'"

On October 24, Lance had the brain surgery.

"When he went in, he was worried, but I got scared," Carmichael says, lowering his voice to a whisper. "At this point, I thought I was going to his funeral. I never said that or anything, but I was thinking, 'Am I gonna go to this guy's funeral?'"

"The surgery was pretty tough on him," Och says. "Dr. Shapiro removed the tumors, but Lance now had big scars on his head. It took a bit of recovery. And the treatment was always getting deeper, harder; he was sleeping more and getting all the symptoms: nausea, the mouth sores. . . . Right after the brain surgery, we went for a walk outside. We tried to move him around, but he didn't even want to do that then. Pretty surprising for a guy like that.

"That was the only time he ever said to me that he thought he might die from this experience. We were sitting outside and he said, 'Right now, I'm not sure I'm gonna beat this. And I don't wanna die.' But I never thought he was gonna die. I don't know why. He certainly looked like it."

Lance recalls a later meeting with his cancer doctors, including Shapiro, Nicholls, and Einhorn. "They'd seen more cases than anybody, literally seen tens of thousands of international cases," Lance says. "I asked, 'How bad was it? Worse than 50 percent of cases you'd seen?' Worse. 'Worse than a quarter?' Worse. 'Bottom 10 percent?'

Worse. And I got it all the way down to the worst 2 or 3 percent they'd ever seen. Fuck."

"That was a hard time," Linda says. "I was in a bad marriage [with John Walling], and I was the only one working. You're in a bad relationship, the man was an alcoholic that I was supporting, and my only child is sicker than a dog, and I can't be there for him. It was just wrong. And things went from bad to worse . . . next . . . next . . . next. I don't know of anybody that could have had that much bad information in three months."

"You could tell by the second round of chemo that it was starting to wear him down," Och says, "because he slept more and ate less. We had a routine: Boom! Seven o'clock I'm there, we're down in the cafeteria, apple fritter, cup of coffee, rolling him back to his room. And then he'd do his medication with LaTrice Haney, his nurse, and then he'd sleep, the doctors would come in, ask him questions, give him numbers. When they walked in he was like at attention; he wanted to hear what they were saying, and he only wanted to hear good things.

"After the third round of chemo he was in that curve . . . where the numbers were starting to work in his favor. That was a big motivation for him. What also kept him going was when he went back to Austin—Motorola loaned us their corporate jet one time. The first couple of days he wasn't so good, but by the end of the week he was super-recharged.

"That was when Eddy Merckx came over from Belgium to do a local team time trial with Lance in Gruene, Texas. Eddy rode with Lance, I rode with Kevin Livingston, and Bart Knaggs rode with College. That was a big deal. Lance and Eddy started in front of us, and Eddy was scared to death that Lance was just gonna drop dead on the bike because he looked so bad. Eddy was still heavy then, and we came up on them fast, and Eddy was dropping Lance. We were both like, 'Whoa!' But Lance wanted to do that, and Eddy was a big trooper to come over there to see Lance. Eddy's more of a father figure than a mentor. That meant a lot to Lance.

"But the next round of chemo was the hardest. He was hoping it would be the last one, and it was. That last day in the hospital they had to get the catheter out of the chest, and they had a hell of a time getting that thing out. Lance said, 'God, this is harder than the chemo!' It was in the artery, and it had got all closed up. But they got that out, and it was finally over. The numbers were where they were supposed to be on that last round. They can't be one or two; they've gotta be zero. He got it back to zero, which was a miracle. Really was a miracle."

Dr. Reeves would agree. He says that Lance overcame one of the most advanced cases of cancer that anyone has ever overcome but believes he had not done it alone. He had his family, his close friends, hundreds of acquaintances, thousands of bike-racing fans, and millions in the general population all helping him recover.

When I ask Reeves what qualities he saw in Lance that enabled him to get through such a severe form of cancer, he says, "Determination. Total determination. . . . The average person would say, 'I don't want to be that sick, or the chemotherapy's not helping me any, why would I do that?' And he got four courses, and some of the most severe chemotherapy there is."

"But," the doctor adds, "you'd have to consider it a miracle—with a lot of help. The universe needs help to work its miracles. It can't do it by itself. And all along he had increasing support from people. I think if you have that many people who almost on a daily basis are thinking about you, putting that much energy into your welfare . . . I think that had great bearing on his healing."

Besides the thousands of goodwill messages that Lance received at his home, countless groups around the country were praying for him to recover. Some of those groups were started by family members he no longer saw. Lance's paternal grandmother, Willene Gunderson, said, "When Lance was sick, we had a special prayer for him every Sunday morning" at the Four Mile Lutheran Church in Cedar Creek Lake, Texas. "The church was founded by some of his ancestors." And Lance's adoptive father, Terry Armstrong, tears up when he tells me, "In Paris, Texas, my dad had over five hundred people in prayer chains, daily. And I would pray every night. . . . And I'd get the reports of the cancer's severity, so I guess there is power of prayer."

Dr. Reeves is one of many doctors and researchers now looking into the healing power of prayer. He's a member of the International Society for the Study of Subtle Energies and Energy Medicine, which in 2007 held a symposium called The Science of the Miraculous.

When I point out to Reeves that Lance is not religious, he says, "You can have miracles, and you don't have to be religious—I prefer the word spiritual—you don't have to be spiritual; the prayer still works. Just his mother alone praying for him—that would add incredible force to the spiritual thing. But all those people holding him in their hearts and wanting him to get well—that's immense energy in one person's direction."

CHAPTER 15

NEW BEGINNINGS

I've never seen you afraid of anything,
but if you ask me, you're afraid of trying.
—CHRIS CARMICHAEL

SOME PEOPLE BELIEVE that Lance is a freak of nature, gifted with a body that's capable of extraordinary feats. His critics are convinced that his success is due to drugs, even though chemical enhancement cannot explain his sustained athletic brilliance. But what many tend to ignore is Lance's unwavering spirit, a spirit that enabled him to emerge from cancer and leap straight back into action.

Less than two weeks after the chemo catheter was yanked from his chest, Lance spent Christmas week at his mother's home in Plano. When he arrived, Linda was taken aback by his appearance. "It was just so sad to see him," she says, "the dark circles under his eyes, white skin, no hair, no eyebrows . . . and to see that his body was giving out." She was equally taken aback by his setting up a wind trainer in the bedroom so he could ride his bike. "I went to check on him upstairs, and he was on that wind trainer, just pedaling his heart out, dripping with sweat."

Lance wasn't riding his bike for fun or exercise; he had a challenge. In two weeks, he planned to travel to France, attend the Cofidis team's media presentation, and ride with his new teammates at a three-day training camp—to prove he was still a cyclist, not a dead man. Cofidis had signed its multimillion-dollar deal with Lance before he was diagnosed with cancer, but after Alain Bondue, the team manager, visited Lance in the hospital, he was unsure about the Texan's future.

"I'll never forget the look on Alain Bondue's face when he walked into that hospital room and saw Lance Armstrong," Och recalls. "Lance was lying there, hooked up, bald, scars on his head. Bondue didn't think he was going to live, let alone ride a bicycle again."

Bondue had made the trip from northern France to Indiana with Paul Sherwen, a former Tour de France rider and current television commentator, who had worked for six years with Och's Motorola team as director of public relations. An Englishman who speaks fluent French, he had become one of the people Lance respected the most. Sherwen was also friends with Bondue, having raced with the tall Frenchman for several years on the same pro cycling team.

"I was going over to the States for Thanksgiving," Sherwen tells me, "so I said to Bondue, 'Why don't you come with me, and we'll go and see Lance.' Alain knew Lance liked wine, and he brought him a very special bottle, a 1994 Château Mouton Rothschild. We visited with him and Och for an hour or so, and Lance was in and out of sleep; he would close his eyes and wake up and close his eyes again."

Sherwen's most vivid memory from his hospital visit was "seeing this skinny guy walking down a corridor, wearing black tracksuit pants and pushing a drip, and he had this thing fixed in his arm. I thought that was going to be my last image of him."

Also visiting with Lance that day was his agent, Bill Stapleton. "When Lance got cancer, I thought Bill was gonna be out of there," Chris Carmichael says. "Because if Lance isn't getting paid, *he's* not getting paid. But Bill didn't waiver. He was there, not within one iota of leaving."

Stapleton says, "Lance was a friend by then. He needed someone to manage the people that had deals with him, like Cofidis, and there was no telling if he was gonna need someone to do another deal for him."

So Stapleton thought he should take the opportunity to shake hands with Bondue and perhaps discuss Lance's Cofidis contract that was about to become effective. "I knew he wanted to talk," Stapleton says, "and I ended up in a hotel room with him and Paul Sherwen. I didn't realize until we had the conversation that his contract, like any professional athlete's contract, was subject to a medical test. And they said they were going to make him do it, so we had a heated argument. I got pretty fired up, and I told him to fuck off. I just couldn't believe they were doing this now. I said, if you guys want to get a guy who's on the third round of chemo to do a medical exam for sports, then go right ahead."

Sherwen, who was translating, remembers things differently: "It was at Stapleton's suggestion that we sat down and had a meeting, and he came up with the idea of renegotiating the contract. I am absolutely certain that Alain did not have it in his mind because Alain's not a lawyer, he's not a negotiator. And the Cofidis boss, François Migraine, is a businessman who has a soft spot for cycling; his first thought would not have been, 'Shit, I've got to renegotiate the contract.' His first thought would have been, 'Shit, I wonder if this guy's gonna live.' I was caught out. I was a French-speaking person so I had to be there to facilitate. I was a bit shocked. A guy's in bed dying and people are renegotiating his contract."

That heated exchange in a hotel room may have soured Stapleton's future dealings with Cofidis, but the result was a not unreasonable deal for a cyclist who might have raced his last race: The team would honor the original $1.2 million a year contract for the first six months and then reduce it to $400,000 a year for the remaining eighteen months.

Lance, though, believed as Stapleton did that Bondue had come to appraise his condition and change their contract if what he saw looked grim. So it was in his "I'll show the French" frame of mind that Lance pounded the pedals on his wind trainer that Christmas in Plano. And to further get him into some kind of shape for the January training camp, he turned to his coach, Carmichael. "We talked about two weeks before the camp," Carmichael says. "He was just over his chemotherapy. He rode a little bit in between the chemo sessions, but he'd ride like five miles and stop twice and be out of breath. He couldn't ride with anybody. We were talking about it, and he said, 'You've got to get me the schedule. What are these fucking guys gonna have me do?'

"Alain Bondue faxed me the schedule, and luckily the camp was at the Cofidis headquarters in Lille, not far from Belgium, so it was gonna be cold, and they couldn't ride all that much. It was like 60K one day, 80K the next, and then 140K the third day—a three-day block of training. Still, I was thinking, 'Holy shit, this guy can't ride five miles without stopping twice. And in two weeks he's got to go to ninety miles—and with a *pro* team?!'

"I knew Maurizio Fondriest [a former world champion] and Tony Rominger [a Giro d'Italia winner] were on the team, and they're not gonna go at Lance's pace, so we had a plan. For the 60K, just sit in and do the first couple of turns at the front in the first half hour—

because he'll have the most energy in the first half hour, and it shows he has a presence—and don't go to the front again the rest of the way. And then the 80K was like, try to get back to the follow car during the ride, try to get some water bottles, try to hold on. . . . For that longest ride, the 140K, I said, 'You can't waste any energy. None. Don't go to the front. Don't do anything,' because he hadn't ridden more than twenty minutes in God knows how long. 'Just stay at the back. And that morning you've got to eat a lot and make sure you start with a full tank of carbohydrates. And use your momentum wherever you can. Try to get to the front before a climb, drift back on the hills . . .' And we were plotting all this stuff out, all this stupid stuff just for a training ride!"

Their plan gave Lance enough confidence to show up at the camp—much to Bondue's surprise—and to ride with his new teammates. Every night he checked in with Carmichael. "For the 60K ride, he was okay. The 80K, he was like, 'Man, I was dragging that last bit. I dunno. . . .' 'So this is it, man, you've gotta do it tomorrow.' And he was like, 'Fuck, I'm gonna do it. Those motherfuckers aren't gonna take me out on 140K.'

"He called me afterwards, and I asked him, 'How did it go?' 'I wasn't the last guy,' he said. 'Two other guys got dropped. I didn't do squat! I hid . . . I used momentum . . . I used every trick I could think of. I was eatin' all the time.' Imagine that. There are two guys that couldn't even stay with a guy who's got cancer! He was like, 'All right!'"

It's hard to imagine anyone else surviving three months of aggressive chemotherapy and invasive surgery and within weeks be riding a bike for four hours with some of the best pro racers in the world. It was a quintessential example of what sets Lance apart: an astounding ability to focus his mind and body to achieve impossible feats.

Carmichael believes that what most motivated Lance at that training camp was his perception of what transpired between Stapleton and Bondue at their meeting in Indianapolis. "It fits the pattern," Carmichael says. "When people betray Lance, he always gets stronger from it. . . . I went to see him two or three times in Austin that spring, and he was getting pretty damn strong. But he didn't have much desire to return to racing. The team wasn't giving him full support, and he was trying to figure out what was going on with his body. The doctors didn't want him to overdo things while he was still recovering from the cancer."

While Lance was in Europe that January, he went back to Como and saw his former trainer Massimo Testa. "I had dinner with him, his girlfriend, Lisa, and Jim Ochowicz. Jim was flying all over with him," Testa says. "Lance showed me all the pictures, the sequence from when he started chemo, day by day. Lisa took the pictures of him; she was very supportive during his cancer treatment."

There were other, less visible changes in Lance that people were noticing—changes in his character. He appeared more humble and less brash. His old swim coach, Chris MacCurdy, noted this when Lance was in Plano over Christmas. "He came by one morning," MacCurdy says. "My wife got him breakfast, and she had a way with him. She had him out front planting pansies. I couldn't believe he did it. 'He planted *pansies?*' That's another side of him—good guy, great guy—he'd become real down-to-earth."

Back home in Austin, Lance embraced chores he'd never found time for before. Rather than engage gardeners, he tended to the landscaping himself and planted new trees. It was as if he were sowing the seeds of a new life. He just wasn't sure what to keep from the old one.

His mother saw more clearly than anyone else what Lance was going through at that time. "When you've gone through a terrible illness like he did, and gone from being at the top of the world and then gotten cancer and almost died, you look at life differently," Linda says. "I remember Lance saying, 'I wanna simplify.' And he went through all of these material things he worked so hard for, and he decided, 'I don't need this.' Like the Porsche. He was so proud of that car.

"But coming off something as hard as he'd been through, you can't make big decisions in your life. I look back and think, you've got to let yourself heal, mentally, not just physically. To make big decisions throughout that healing time . . . it can be good, it can be bad; but a lot of times I don't think you have a clear mind."

Lance's biggest dilemma was not knowing if he wanted to return to the peripatetic life of a pro bike racer. His monthly MRI checkups were all clear, but a relapse was still possible, and he was scared that racing—or even training—could bring back the cancer. "You have to heal," Linda says, "and that was part of the healing: 'Why do I have to do this again?' My comment to him was 'This is all you ever knew. This is what got you up every day.' And I told him, 'If this is something you don't get up every day and feel good about and say I love my job, then do something else.'"

It was during that time of uncertainty that Lance did find something else, a project that excited Linda as well. "What was good that came out of those three months of treatment, and now that he was cancer free, was his wanting to start this cancer foundation," Linda says. "We just sat on the floor and read letters every night, cases of them. Sometimes jokes, sometimes information about the treatment he took. . . . Both of us not being readers, once you are forced to get in that situation, you're like a sponge; you want to soak up everything around you. And he said, 'You know, I want to start this foundation, and I want to give back.' I never was involved in philanthropy or helping people because it was just a struggle to do the things I was doing. But when we decided to start the foundation, and he taught me the importance of giving back, that was a key lesson that Lance showed me."

Lance wasn't sure yet what focus the foundation would take; but having personally suffered from the lack of public awareness and knowledge of testicular cancer, that seemed like a place to begin.

The cancer foundation was still a tenuous concept that January when Lance was sitting around with his friends Stapleton, Knaggs, and College. Also there was Bill Cass, a product manager at Nike who's a talented artist. He had created an illustration for a get-well card that College describes as "a cartoon of Lance on a bike racing down the hallway of a hospital in his gown and the doctors pulling him back." So, given their intention to raise the awareness of testicular cancer, College said, "You know what, we ought to use this as a poster for a race or a bike ride." When the others said they'd already been talking to Nike and Oakley about putting on a ride, they set a date to meet over dinner at Z'Tejas, a Mexican restaurant, where the Lance Armstrong Foundation was essentially born. (The table where they met was later donated to the foundation and now sits in the foyer of its Austin headquarters.)

The group agreed that a charity bike ride would be a great way to kick off their project. College said he was thinking of quitting his bartending job and volunteered to be the organizer of what would be called the Ride for the Roses. "I met with Stapleton and he said we need to get a title sponsor," College says. "I had no clue how much we'd need, so Bill says, 'What about $25,000?'

"Out of the blue, I get a phone call from a woman at a PR firm. She says, 'I have a client looking to do something in the community, and we hear you're all gonna do something.' The client is Ikon Office Solutions. So I met with the president of the company's Austin branch, a guy named Milo Bump. I gave a horrible pitch, but he says, 'Sounds great, man, let's do it.' I was like, 'Wow!' Then I thought, 'Oh shit, now we're actually gonna have to put on this ride.' I ended up doing a lot of the work with the PR girl and her colleague, Kristin Richard—and that's how Lance met his wife-to-be."

The inaugural event for the foundation was a press conference at the Shoreline Grill restaurant on Austin's Town Lake. "I met two amazing women there," Lance says, "one was former Texas governor Ann Richards [who would die from esophageal cancer in 2006] and the other was Kristin."

The foundation was giving Lance a purpose in his post-cancer life, but it was too early to know if he still had a future in cycling. Perhaps there were other things he could do. He loved the music scene, and he'd just met Michael Ward, the lead guitarist of one of his favorite groups, The Wallflowers. Ward was an amateur cyclist and he readily agreed to take Lance on the road with them for a week. Lance biked with Ward in the day, watched him perform at night, and sometimes joined the group on stage playing guitar.

"We would play a show and get in the bus at 1 or 2 in the morning after all the parties are done and drive overnight to the next town," Ward tells me, "so you're either sleeping on the bus or maybe get to a hotel at 4 or 5 in the morning. We'd been doing this night after night for about a week, and Lance was still taking naps during the day, tired and worn out from chemo. We were sitting up one night and he told me this story: 'You know what, man? I read this article recently in a magazine, and they polled really successful people, like doctors, lawyers, and the like, and they said if you could do anything else, what job would you trade it for?'

"And he said, 'Nobody said movie star, nobody said astronaut, everybody said rock star.' And he goes, 'You know what, man? Let me tell you something. Your life is shit. This is terrible. Why would anybody want to do this?' And I say, 'Oh man, it's not that bad.' And he says, 'No, it's shit! I'm telling you right now! It's ridiculous man, bouncing around all night on some bus, checking into a hotel at 5 in the morning, and trying to go back to sleep. This is awful. Everyone thinks this is great. But this is fucked up!'"

It made bike racing look good.

In the decade since Lance had abandoned his Camaro sports car after a police chase and left bike-shop owner Jim Hoyt to sort out the mess, he had bumped into his old benefactor only once. "It was in Lajitas, Texas, at an early-season mountain-bike event," Hoyt recalls. "I'm up real early in the morning looking for a cup of coffee in this tiny western town. I come walking up from one end of the street with a cup of coffee, and coming the other way on a bike is Lance. Just he and I. I'm thinking, 'Oh shit, I really don't want to deal with this.' He just rolled up and says, 'Hey dude.' We chatted a bit, but we didn't connect. Lance has trouble saying I'm sorry."

The next time they met was in the spring of 1997 at the first Ride for the Roses. "The day before the ride, Lance was signing autographs with two other cycling stars, Sean Kelly and Davis Phinney. I got in line with everyone else to get their signatures," Hoyt says. "Lance saw me, stood up, and waved me to the front, but I shook my head and just went through the line. He stood up, stuck his hand out, and says, 'I'm sorry,' and I said, 'Apology accepted.' Then I wrote a check to the Lance Armstrong Foundation for five thousand dollars"—roughly the amount Lance had spent on the car payments.

That check was a big chunk of the twenty-five thousand dollars the foundation made on that first event. "We thought we'd give a lot of the proceeds to the American Cancer Society," College says. "We met with them, and they started asking Lance for all these appearances. I was taken aback. I was thinking, 'Wait a minute, you've done nothing here, and I never even knew about testicular cancer and that's your fault.' That motivated us. I said after the meeting, 'We can do this, and we can do a better job.' And there were days I regretted saying that; we had some hard days ahead. But that's what started the evolution of the foundation."

What also helped the project evolve was the charisma that people were now seeing in Lance. His Plano friend Adam Wilk, who was at that first Ride for the Roses, recalls, "There was a party afterward at Lance's place. We were sitting and talking with him in front of his house when a couple of kids walked up, bald heads, cancer kids—and Lance was so different. My wife went to me, 'My God, has *he* changed!' People have to touch him now, like Jesus . . . he's such a beacon of light to people. Kind of freaky if you're with him in person. I just stand back. They're mesmerized by him."

It often happens that a couple breaks up after going through a traumatic experience like a life-threatening illness. That's what happened with Lance and his longtime girlfriend Lisa Shiels. The emotional toll sank in deeper once the experience was over, and they slowly drew apart.

Lance had little energy to put into anyone or anything at this time, although he was pursuing the development of his foundation. It was that work that initially brought him closer to Kristin, who represented the sponsor of the charity ride. As they grew to know each other better, Lance saw a woman who was as tough and independent as he was. He was taken with her humor, her intelligence, and her beautiful smile.

Kristin was equally taken with Lance's smile. "I thought he was cute," she says, recalling their first meeting; and she was soon attracted by his other qualities. "He was a rare combination of being both strong and vulnerable in the same moment . . . he was charming . . . charismatic. He has a magnetism that attracts people. I think I was curious about him on a lot of levels.

"He didn't have a lot of pretense and variance about him because of the place where he had just walked, and it was very easy to get to know him. We were both at a period in our lives where we were open;

it was a hopeful time to be that age. And for him, with everything he had just done, it was one of those times that's really special."

By that summer, Lance and Kristin were in love and traveling together through Europe, taking in the marvels of Italy, Spain, and the South of France. It was on that trip that they stopped by at the Tour. "When we get out of the car at the start village," she remembers, "Lance is completely bombarded by photographers and microphones and everything, and I thought, 'Why are they so interested in him?' It was very amusing as I had no idea of his accomplishments and knew nothing about cycling."

Lance took the opportunity to chat with journalists and visit with his Cofidis teammates Frankie Andreu, Bobby Julich, and Kevin Livingston. But he wasn't showing any enthusiasm for racing his bike, despite urgings from Stapleton, Knaggs, or even Coach Carmichael, who felt Lance needed to get his life back on track. Only Kristin seemed to be getting through to him, Carmichael says. "She was like, 'So what's this guy gonna *do?* He's twenty-five years old now, and he's gotta do something with his life. He should at least try to figure this out.' I think she was trying to help him along."

Stapleton wanted Lance to commit to his return to racing so he could get back to Cofidis. He and Lance had already traveled to France in April when they had lunch with the team's bosses, Migraine and Bondue. "They were putting all this pressure on Lance to ride the Tour in July," Stapleton remembers, "and it was really uncomfortable. Lance was just getting his hair back."

Lance was all too aware of how cancer had ravaged his body and threatened his life. He got more reminders through his regular blood tests and reports, and he had a real fear that any kind of overexertion could make the cancer recur. His doctors had told him to use the year to rest and heal and put off racing. But, he has written, "Chris thought I seemed empty without it. He thought I needed a push, and our relationship was always based on his ability to give me one when I needed it."

To give him that push, Carmichael flew down to Austin in early August, ten days after the 1997 Tour de France, which was won by a young German, Jan Ullrich. "I told Stapleton that I was going to tell Lance he needs to race his bike," Carmichael says. "And Bill said, 'Good luck, man. He doesn't want to hear it.' I told Lance, 'We gotta talk. We're gonna have dinner together. Just you and me, no Kristin.' Because they were, like, so much in love. So we went to Chuys, a Tex-Mex place; we sat outside.

"I said to him, 'Bobby Julich just took fourth in a time trial at the Tour de France. And you're ten times the rider of Bobby Julich. You gotta get back to racing, Lance. Whether you make it back or not, I don't care, but you're gonna need to know if you can come back.' The Julich thing kinda bugged him. He says, 'I don't need to return to racing. I've done what I need to do. I don't owe anybody anything.' So I say, 'Sure, you don't owe anybody anything; you owe this to yourself, to see what there is. You've got all this in you . . . and it's still there. You remember I told you in Bergamasca six years ago, someday you'll win the Tour de France? You know, that stuff is there. And the only person who's gonna know whether it got taken away because of your cancer is you. And the only way you're gonna know is to try. I've never seen you afraid of anything, but if you ask me, you're afraid of trying. I can't blame you. I'm just telling you. You're afraid of trying to get back to it.'

"It wasn't a great conversation, and he wasn't ready to hear it. But all weekend, I was saying to Stapleton, 'Bobby Julich had a frigging great time trial.' And I think Lance started trying to figure it out."

Lance could never resist a challenge, and soon after that meeting with Carmichael, he gave Stapleton the green light to call Cofidis and say he was ready to start racing. "I told them I'd like to come over and talk about next year, talk about his schedule, what the doctors are saying," Stapleton says. "I flew to Paris, drove up to Lille, and we had this stupid, super-long lunch before we even talked. And then they pointed out a clause that if Lance didn't race in four international races they could terminate his contract. And they said they'd decided to go in another direction and were going to focus on Bobby Julich, and they were going to terminate Lance. I was like, 'Is there some reason I had to fly from Texas for you to tell me this?' Our talk ended abruptly, and I called Lance from a pay phone in Paris to tell him we'd have to start looking for a new team."

This proved to be a tougher proposition than Lance or Stapleton imagined. Lance felt humiliated when virtually every European team failed to respond to Stapleton's inquiries. So Och was enlisted to help them contact his former colleagues in the peloton. "Cees Priem of TVM was the only one to offer Lance a contract," Och says, "but it was too little."

Stapleton didn't fare any better. "I faxed every team, and one of the few that faxed back was the Mercatone Uno team of Marco Pantani. Lance even spoke to Pantani, but when it came to talking money, they just evaporated. One after the other they turned us down. We were still talking to Saeco-Cannondale—Scott Montgomery of Cannondale bikes had approached us the previous year—and we scheduled a meeting at the Interbike show in Anaheim, but he stood us up."

It was at the Interbike show that Stapleton and Lance also ran into Mark Gorski and Dan Osipow of the U.S. Postal Service team. "But we never really considered them an option," Stapleton says. That's because six years earlier Lance had split acrimoniously with the Postal team's predecessor, Subaru-Montgomery, after a falling-out with coach Eddie B and team owner Thom Weisel. Still, when Stapleton was in San Francisco the following week, he had second thoughts and set up a meeting with Weisel, the CEO of Montgomery Securities, and Gorski, Eddie B's replacement as team manager.

"In the meeting, Thom was motivated to get Lance on the team," Stapleton says. "I told him we had talked to Cofidis about doing a two-hundred-thousand-dollar deal for '98, and I led them to believe we were interested in that offer. So I told Weisel we wanted two-hundred-thousand dollars but with an upside—a thousand dollars for every UCI point, with no limit." The UCI awarded points on a sliding scale, from 10 points to the winner of a minor race up to 500 points to the winner of the Tour de France. In 1996, before cancer, Lance had scored 1,315 UCI points, which would have earned him 1.3 million dollars had this proposed clause been in his contract.

"Gorski said their budget will never support that," Stapleton continues. "He said, 'We want him, but. . . .' Thom then looked at me and said, 'I'll cover that if we have a deal.' I said I needed five minutes to call Lance, and that was it. We didn't have an alternative, so we took the deal."

At that point, Postal wasn't even ranked in the top twenty of the world's best teams, and it had just competed for the first time at the Tour de France—where the American team placed its French leader Jean-Cyril Robin in fifteenth overall, almost an hour behind winner Ullrich. The Postal Service is an independent agency of the U.S. government and was sponsoring a cycling team to spread international awareness of its global brands; competing successfully in Europe was one of the team's major priorities. By taking on Lance, the team sponsors (and Thom Weisel) were investing in a young man who had shown he was capable of doing amazing things and who they hoped would do even greater deeds in the future. To reintroduce Lance to the national media, Postal planned a September press conference in New York City.

One of the invited guests to the press conference was a retired Austin venture capitalist and amateur cyclist, Jeff Garvey. He had met Lance through his massage therapist after he told her he wanted to get involved in philanthropy. "Lance came to my house for lunch,"

Garvey tells me. "He showed up in a pickup truck, and when he took his hat off, he was as bald as I am, but for very different reasons. I'd heard stories about him, and not many of them were great: a cocky Texas kid that had some negativity attached to his boldness. But he couldn't have been more cool and calm. We had a four-hour lunch, and what shocked me was that he knew more about Austin Ventures, my firm, than the companies which we had financed. I wanted to get involved in philanthropy because my mother and father both died of cancer, and my wife's parents both died of cancer. So he asked me if I would help with his foundation, which was still an idea."

Six months later, the foundation was still little more than an idea. "The office was in my condo," College says. "I'd roll out of my bed into the desk chair. Lance came over one day, and I still had all this race crap from the Ride for the Roses. It looked like hell, so he said, 'We've got to get you out of this place.'"

The night before Postal's New York press conference, Lance and Stapleton asked Garvey to dinner at their hotel. "Lance was nervous," Garvey recalls, "so it was Bill who met me first and asked if I would consider being chairman of the Lance Armstrong Foundation. I said sure, I'd be flattered, and when Lance came down to dinner he said, 'Are you gonna do it?' I didn't know Lance that well or what this foundation was gonna do, not a clue. They had ten thousand dollars in the bank, no employees, no mission, and no purpose. And I said I'd be the first chairman."

The next day's press conference was very important to the Postal Service brass, but Stapleton warned them that there'd be little interest in Lance from the national media, that he was no longer a big name. He was right. "There was just a smattering of reporters and a couple of cameras," Stapleton says. "There's nobody there. Lance held up his Trek bike, and we had a short press conference. That was it."

College, who had been trying to drum up donors for the cancer foundation all year, knew all about Lance's lack of name recognition.

"This was my pitch for the year," College says. "'My name's John Korioth and I'm from the Lance Armstrong Foundation. Maybe you've heard of Lance? No? You haven't? Well, uh, he's the cyclist who got cancer. Heard of him? You haven't? He . . . uh . . . have you ever heard of Greg LeMond? Okay. Lance's kind of like Greg LeMond, but he hasn't won the Tour de France. Okay? Yeah, he's the guy that got cancer. Yeah, that guy. Can I come and talk to you about some stuff we've got going on?' My days were filled with cold-calling like that. No one really knew him."

Lance's old days of glory were now forgotten. But October '97 was a time of new beginnings. Tests showed that he was completely cancer-free on the one-year anniversary of his diagnosis. The cancer foundation held its first board meeting, where College saw that "when you get the right people in the room, you figure out what to do. That was the turning point for the organization." And later in the month, Lance's willowy blonde girlfriend, Kristin, accepted his proposal of marriage. "I was at that place in my life where I didn't know if I'd see another year, another five years, or another ten years," Lance tells me. "I mean, you want to put together the all-American dream, so I wanted the house with the white picket fence, the 2.3 kids, and the SUV." And he wanted to share that dream with Kristin.

As for Lance the cyclist, he had a new team, an incentive-based contract, and a renewed appetite for pro racing. All the ingredients were in place for his first big comeback.

CHAPTER 16

FALSE START

The truth was, nobody had heard of the Ruta del Sol, and announcing "I'm gonna ride my bike again" is not a comeback.

—BILL STAPLETON

ANXIOUS. CONFUSED. CANTANKEROUS. That's how his friends described Lance as he approached his return to the European peloton. He was full of doubts. How could he not be? Other athletes had returned after serious injuries or illnesses, but Lance was the first in an endurance sport to survive a near-fatal cancer with its months of debilitating chemotherapy and then attempt a comeback at the highest level.

Following the one-year anniversary of his cancer diagnosis, he had four months to prepare for his comeback race. The first two months were spent training in Santa Barbara, California, where he rode every day, talked with his coaches, and received daily massage from Shelley Verses, a former massage therapist at Motorola. (By now, his Austin friend J. T. Neal was too sick with leukemia to continue working as his personal soigneur.) Evenings were spent with his fiancé, Kristin, in a rented beachside cottage that overlooked the Pacific Ocean; they liked the town so much they decided to get married there the following spring.

Santa Barbara was also proving to be a great place to train, and Lance felt his strength returning at a surprising rate. After one long ride into the rugged Santa Rafael mountains, he told Verses, "I'm thinner than I've ever been. I'm so strong I don't know *what* my body can do."

Dr. Michele Ferrari, Lance's Italian trainer, remembers seeing him that autumn. "He was definitely lighter, around 74 kilograms [163 pounds]; he had lost a lot of muscle mass and a lot of strength. Without cancer he could never have lost that much." Lance was roughly 13 pounds lighter than he weighed in 1996.

A lighter body can dramatically improve a cyclist's performance on steep, long mountain passes; but to reap the benefits of carrying less weight, Lance would need to recoup the power he had before cancer—and Chris Carmichael was ready to help him. "He trained a lot better that winter than he'd trained in a long, long time," his coach says. "He was excited . . . but something wasn't right in him, and I knew it in Santa Barbara. He was training well, and he was obviously in love with his fiancée, but something wasn't right."

What was missing was a calm state of mind. "He struggled a lot," Bill Stapleton notes. "Part of the struggle was the anxiety he showed; he was very cranky and not really ready to race again."

Lance and Kristin were both ready, though, to start a new life, and they were excited as they left for Europe. Settling in France, they rented an apartment in upscale St. Jean-Cap Ferrat, a seaside town outside Nice. Kristin set up their new home and began taking French classes; and Lance hooked up for training rides in the Alpes-Maritimes with his ex-teammate Kevin Livingston, who was still on the Cofidis team and living in Nice.

Speculation about Lance's return was high in the European media. They wondered whether a cancer survivor could reclaim the position he once held in the world's toughest sport. To find out, reporters traveled to the Spanish city of Seville for the opening stage of the Ruta del Sol on February 15, 1998. "I didn't like it," Lance said about his first day of racing. "There was a lot of attention and a lot of pressure that I was uncomfortable with, and my expectations were probably too high. In hindsight, I should have never put any pressure on myself."

Despite the external and internal pressures, Lance held his own in the peloton, climbed with the best riders on the third day's uphill finish, and managed to finish the five-day race in fifteenth overall. It was a strong result for his first race back, but he wasn't pleased. Stapleton puts it this way: "With the comeback came all the expectations, and Lance expected corporate sponsors like AT&T would be lining up by February. But the truth was, nobody had heard of the Ruta del Sol, and announcing 'I'm gonna ride my bike again' is not a comeback."

Lance's next chance to shine came at the Paris-Nice race, which he'd almost won two years earlier. "He went there with big hopes," Carmichael says, especially since the weeklong stage race would finish in Lance's new hometown, where Kristin would be waiting. But the week started badly. At the opening time trial in a frigid Paris, Lance did no better than nineteenth; that was even behind his young teammate George Hincapie. As a result, the Postal team's sport director, Johnny Weltz, decided to make Hincapie his team leader for the race. So when Hincapie was stopped by a flat tire during the next day's long, flat stage to Sens, all his teammates, including Lance, were told by Weltz to wait for Hincapie and pace him back to the field.

"Having to wait wasn't a known position for Lance, especially having to wait for me," Hincapie says. "I felt bad about it. And it was cold and windy. Lance was pulling the hardest of anybody, but it was hell coming back. We never made it back to the first group, and there was a hard circuit waiting at the end."

The weather was bitter cold, and the racing was typically unforgiving, but no one expected Lance to suddenly stop pedaling, pull to the side of the road, and quit the race. "I saw him at the hotel," Hincapie says, "and he was like, 'I'm done, I'm not ready for this sport.' He was not happy to be back in Europe, suffering like that, and not winning, and staying at this shitty hotel. He just packed up and left. We were all shocked."

This wasn't how things were supposed to start out—or end.

"I thought that was the last time I would ride a bike in Europe," Lance admits. "I was pretty convinced of that. Again, I was confused. But I felt a certain sense of relief that night flying home to Nice."

Kristin also believed that this was it for Lance. "He called me when I was in the supermarket, but he didn't have time to tell me why he was coming home early," she says. "And when he got back, he wasn't sure what he wanted to do with his life. That's where the confusion culminated, and he just had to step back. He was pretty sure he was going to retire."

Back in Colorado, the phone rang at Carmichael's house in the middle of the night. "It was Lance calling me from Nice," the coach says, "telling me he had quit bike racing and was flying home. 'I've got Kristin here,' he said. 'I took her out of French class, and we're leaving. I'm done.' When I heard that, I said, 'Look, I'll come down to Austin when you get back, and we'll chat. I'll give you a few days.'"

John "College" Korioth now had a real office for Lance's cancer foundation and two employees, who were busy preparing for their big fundraiser, the second Ride for the Roses. A couple of days after

Lance and Kristin returned to Austin, a third worker showed up. "It was Lance," College says. "I found him in the mail room stuffing envelopes for the ride entries, and I said, 'Dude, what in the fuck are you doing here?' He said, 'I'm stuffing envelopes. I'm helping.' And I said, 'We don't need your help. Go get back on your bike.' And he said, 'That's the very last thing in the world I want to do right now.'

"I was thinking, 'He's just blown a gasket and he'll get back on the bike in a couple of days.' But then I knew, 'Oh man, it's real bad. He can't just do nothing.' That's when Kristin had a long talk with him. She said, 'If we're gonna get married, I want to know what you're gonna be doing. I can't live my life in limbo.'"

"I think that he was really kind of lost," Kristin says. "You can't have two people lost at the same time. I knew that regardless of what my feelings were at the moment, whether I was disappointed or frustrated or whatever, I knew he needed me to be strong, to be there for him, and be a rock. He needed steadiness because everything else was spinning out of control for him."

With her strong will and strength of character, Kristin was not unlike Lance's mom. And being a devout Catholic, her religion, like Linda's, gave her added strength and faith. "It was not so much that I had a faith in Lance, though I definitely believed in him, but it was far bigger than that," Kristin says. "Otherwise it would have been insufficient for us both to get through that time."

Lance had asked College to be best man at the couple's wedding, which was planned for early May, and College had asked Lance if he was going to ride again—at a very specific race. "I had come up with another crazy figure, one hundred thousand dollars, to sponsor a downtown criterium race as part of the Ride for the Roses weekend the night before the charity ride," College says. "And Lance had said, 'You won't get that for a local crit!' When I called him later to say I got the hundred grand from Sprint, he didn't believe me. 'I'm looking at the check right now,' I said. 'Get ready to ride your bike.' The sponsorship was tied to him racing his bike in that downtown crit, and now it was looking like he's not gonna compete, and I'm gonna have to answer to Sprint."

College's dilemma gave Lance some focus and a sense of purpose. For the first time, he wasn't thinking of racing for himself, but for a cause, and the two parts of his life began to merge. "I knew there was the Ride for the Roses and the race there. So I knew I would have to train for that," Lance said. But he couldn't see any further than that when it came to racing.

"That was when there was a sort of summit meeting between me, Bill, and Kristin," Lance says. "They sat me down and said, 'You can't quit like this, you've got to get moving. You've committed to your cause and your team, and you're just home playing golf with your buddies and drinking beer.' She was not nice about that. It was like, 'You get your fuckin' ass going.'"

"I had a very vested interest," Stapleton admits, "and in my view and Kristin's view, Lance was not a quitter. But there was really no master plan, so we told him, 'You can't quit like this. We need a doable exit to end your career properly.'"

Carmichael, who'd spoken with Stapleton and Kristin before the meeting, says that Lance, who hadn't touched his bike in three weeks, was adamant. "He said, 'Fuck it, I ain't goin' back to Europe.' That's when I came up with the idea of his riding the USPRO Championship in Philly as his farewell race. And he said, 'Okay, I'll do the Pro Championship, and then I'm done.'"

No one wanted to push Lance, even if they could. And no one really knew, even if he resumed racing, whether he could regain the drive and fire that characterized his racing before cancer. But Lance knew that after his failed European comeback he needed to be more cautious and tamp down his own expectations.

"I eventually unpacked my bike," he said, "and started to train two hours a day with friends. Then Chris got this idea of doing a training camp."

They decided to go to Boone, North Carolina, the small town in the Blue Ridge Mountains where Lance had won stages of the Tour DuPont in the mid-nineties. To make his time there less lonely and more productive, Lance invited another racer to join him: Bob Roll, a former Motorola teammate, who's known for his wild humor. "We had terrible weather," Lance recalls. "It was in the forties and raining for eight days, but we had fantastic training. I wanted to see if I *wanted* to do it again, and I discovered there that I do love the bike, and I can get through awful conditions. And it didn't hurt to have Bob, who was keeping me entertained the whole time. That, for me, was the turnaround. I left there a different person."

Lance says his form improved so much that week that when he was tested in the exercise physiology department at Boone's Appalachian State University, "I broke their machine." His power wattage was off the charts, and Lance was on track once again. "I had dinner with him right after the camp and before he flew out of Charlotte," teammate Hincapie says, "and he was super-motivated to be back into cycling."

Charged with enthusiasm, Lance took a detour before heading home: He flew straight to Atlanta, where he was a last-minute entry at a 120-mile circuit race. For the first time in almost two years, he was having fun riding a bike, and his good mood carried over to his friends and family, just in time for his and Kristin's May wedding.

Held in Santa Barbara, the wedding was serene and traditional. In the grace of an old Spanish-style church, Kristin in a long white gown and Lance in black tie and tux were married in a Catholic ceremony. A dance party followed. "It was fun, a great time," College says, "and Lance was on the comeback." So much so that he continued training throughout his California honeymoon. His foundation's Austin race was less than two weeks away.

The race was held on a balmy Texas evening on a course only two miles from Dr. Jim Reeves's office, where Lance had been diagnosed with cancer. On that night nineteen months before, he had driven home slowly, not knowing if he would live or die. Now, he was vigorously racing his bike against a field of American pros, celebrating his return to the life he loved best. "I hadn't done a criterium in years, and I'd never done one at nighttime," Lance says about the thirty-five-mile race on a four-turn circuit. "I suffered bad. I really had a hard time."

Lance gritted his teeth every lap as the peloton climbed a block-long hill and sped under streetlights along Sixth Street, where live music boomed from the bistros and bars, including The Cactus Room. Thousands of Austinites were thrilled to be watching their local hero race in his hometown for the first time in his pro career. From a viewing platform at the start-finish line, Kristin couldn't contain her excitement as her husband moved toward the front of the pack in the final laps. And when he burst out of the darkness into the bright glare of camera lights to win the race by a second, she screamed with delight. Lance was equally excited. "That was the first time I'd felt that rush from the crowd since winning the Flèche Wallonne about two years earlier," he says. "That was a long time to wait."

There was a special guest at the race, five-time Tour de France champion Miguel Induráin, and he presented Lance with the first-place trophy. The popular Spaniard had retired from cycling the previous year, and his appearance in Texas had been arranged by Paul Sherwen, media director of the old Motorola team. With Sherwen's wife, Catherine, translating, Lance and Induráin met that weekend to discuss racing, training, and the Tour. "Miguel explained to Lance his technique for pedaling fast up mountains," Sherwen says. "Miguel was the master of it, and as far as I'm concerned, it was there, at that Ride for the Roses, where Lance first grasped its importance."

Climbing mountain roads on lower gears at a higher pedal cadence, rather than overcoming steep gradients using pure power with a heavy gear, is a technique that Lance was just beginning to learn; but because of the false start to his comeback, he hadn't practiced it that often. His Italian trainer, Dr. Ferrari, was a strong advocate of this climbing style. "Already in the early nineties with Tony Rominger, I had started working on pedaling cadences higher than the average," Ferrari says, "so with Lance it was a deliberate choice. We started him training with varied cadences at different intensities. Such specific training included lots of long climbs at medium pace with pedal cadences of between 60 and 90 RPM [the number of pedal revolutions per minute], as well as workouts around the anaerobic threshold at 90 to 100 RPM."

Anaerobic threshold (AT) is the point at which exercise becomes much harder for an athlete because he is then producing lactic acid faster than he can metabolize it. The athlete's body functions more efficiently below his AT, hence the need to raise that number by specific training. For cyclists, using high power to pedal faster reduces the amount of force needed for each pedal stroke. This allows a rider to conserve energy, which can be significant on long mountain climbs, especially when there are three or more climbs in a single day. But spinning the pedals uphill for long periods is a difficult technique to master. It's easier if you have a high AT.

The studious and athletic Dr. Ferrari, whom Lance describes as "a brilliant mathematician," says that Lance's AT that summer of '98 "was back to the values he had before cancer, around 460 watts, but his lower weight brought the watts per kilogram up to 6.21 [Induráin's was close to 7 at his peak]. Lance was now riding faster uphill than before the illness."

Len Pettyjohn, the highly regarded American team manager and trainer, believes it was Ferrari who most helped Lance with a focused training regimen. "In terms of how to train, it clearly came from Ferrari," he says. "And Lance didn't get it until after cancer. The interesting thing is that nobody in cycling back then really knew the science of training; that came from other sports, from track-and-field and Nordic skiing. Ferrari had the more broad-based perspective on how to apply that and use it for a cyclist. What Lance learned was how to train smarter and when to apply the force in races. He began to understand the discipline of training *and* the discipline of racing. Prior to that he had no discipline, just like a lot of strong guys—feel good, go hard."

Lance's buddy College also noticed a significant change in Lance's approach to racing. "I don't think that guy counted anything except his money prior to cancer," he says. "But once he learned how to count red and white blood cells, he learned how to count calories, watts, and all the scientific things he needed to apply to his sport."

It would be a while before Lance could fully apply his and Ferrari's more scientific techniques to races in the high mountains. But following his Austin criterium victory, he felt ready to again tackle the European races. Kristin happily agreed to head back with him to France, and a plan was put together with his coaches. After the USPRO Championship race in Philadelphia, he would compete in two stage races that his Postal team had earmarked as preparation for its Tour de France squad—but July's Tour would not be on Lance's agenda. Because of his lack of recent racing, they would test him out instead in September's Tour of Spain (the "Vuelta"), a three-week race like the Tour but with a weaker field. The Vuelta would also be a good lead-in to the end-of-season world championships.

Lance was unexpectedly successful in these first few races. His goal in Philadelphia was to help his Postal teammate Hincapie become the national champion because Lance himself lacked the training miles to be competitive in a 156-mile race. "I felt sluggish, as though I was dragging a manhole cover," Lance said at the time. Hincapie says Lance "did an awesome job at the end of the race. We had three guys up there [Lance, Frankie Andreu, and Tyler Hamilton] doing the lead-out train for me, and I won the sprint. Lance was so happy; I'd never seen him that happy."

That infectious spirit carried over to his next race, the multiday Tour of Luxembourg, Lance's first European race since he "quit the sport for good" three months before at Paris-Nice. But in Luxembourg, Hincapie says, "it was back to the old Lance. He got into the break the first day and won that stage. Everyone was surprised he was so strong just a couple of days after flying to Europe."

His opening-day win, when he outsprinted Lauri Aus of Estonia and finished four minutes ahead of the field, was reason for celebration. But Lance's reaction seemed unusually tempered. He confirmed that weeks later when I met with him and Kristin for an interview. "When I called Kristin after winning, she said, 'You don't sound very happy,'" Lance said. "I, of course, was screaming when he rang up," Kristin interjected. "Winning is just not the same as it was before cancer," Lance continued, "but I think that's a good thing. It comes back to balance. Before, when I'd win, I'd be so, so high, and then I'd come down too low. It was difficult for me to be consistent. In Luxembourg, it was nice to win against a European professional field, but I knew I had to defend the lead for four more stages."

Lance's fired-up teammates were ready to ride hard for him the rest of the week to keep him in the lead. "We worked our butts off," Hincapie recalls. "He didn't want to lose that race." But Aus didn't give up easily; he picked up a couple of time bonuses in the sprints and was leading Lance by two seconds heading into the final day. That was when the Postal team showed its growing unity. Andreu cleverly went with the key breakaway to take the pressure off his teammates. They could bide their time until Lance was ready to make a strong uphill attack that would lead to Aus being dropped. Andreu easily stayed with the leaders and won the stage, while Lance gained enough time to win the overall—his first victory as a pro in a European stage race.

Two weeks later in Germany, Lance won the second of the two pre-Tour stage races. "After that win, I remember trying to convince Lance to do the Tour," Hincapie says, "but he already had a plan. He wanted to go home and train and then prepare for the Tour of Spain. He could probably have done fine at the Tour de France that year, but he didn't want to do it."

It was Lance's good fortune to skip the '98 Tour since that was the one devastated by doping scandals. The trouble began before the start when the French police discovered a trunkload of banned drugs in a Festina-Lotus team vehicle. Festina was one of the world's highest-ranked teams, and its nine riders were pulled from the race once their manager admitted that his team had set up an internal system of doping. What ensued was a witch hunt. Police ransacked hotel rooms and searched team vehicles for drugs. The riders staged a couple of sit-down strikes; one stage was cancelled; six of the twenty-one teams pulled out of the race in protest; and only half of the 189 starters reached the finish in Paris.

During the worst of that dark Tour's scandals, Lance was in the United States, where he took in Oregon's Cascade Classic stage race as part of his training program. He won the hilly five-day event before heading back to Nice, where the Armstrongs were buying a beautiful home on a hillside overlooking the city and the sea. To ramp up to European race speeds, Lance entered a couple of August's one-day classics and the Tour of the Netherlands—where he finished fourth overall after working for his new Russian teammate, and former rival, Viatcheslav Ekimov—before heading to Spain for the Vuelta. That's where he would test his still-developing fast-pedaling style on true mountain climbs. And that's where he would have a fortuitous meeting in a Barcelona hotel, a meeting that would fundamentally shape his career and his life.

It was on the Vuelta's rest day in Barcelona, four days before his twenty-seventh birthday, that Lance took a phone call from Johan Bruyneel—the Belgian racer he had an emotional conversation with after dedicating his 1995 Tour de France stage win to Fabio Casartelli. Bruyneel, after a dozen years of high-end racing, was about to retire from the sport, and he was coincidentally in Barcelona to interview with officials of the professional riders' union, who were looking for a new president. But when he was offered the job, the Belgian said that before deciding he wanted to talk to some riders. "The first guy I put on my list was Lance. I don't know if it was because of A for America, or whatever," Bruyneel says. The two men met and talked at Lance's hotel.

"The day after," Bruyneel continues, "he called me at my home in Spain to see if I was really committed to this riders' union presidency. 'You know,' he said, 'we're also looking for people, and our team needs to restructure.' So I said, 'Okay, well maybe I can do something with the media or whatever.' And he asked if their team manager could call me.

"Mark Gorski was the Postal team manager at that time, and when he called he immediately started to talk about the job of directeur sportif. So I said, 'Well, I didn't think about that.' And he said, 'Well, Lance told me that you wanted to be the directeur sportif.' And I said, 'I didn't tell him that.' So I asked for some time to think about it—and I accepted a week later. Postal was just a second-division team then, not first division. It was an interesting challenge, and I had nothing to lose."

By the time Bruyneel had accepted, Lance had ridden well in the Vuelta's first mountain stages, and he got stronger as the race went on. His best ride came at a stage finish on a seven-mile climb in the mountains north of Madrid. In freezing fog, Lance climbed better than ever, taking fourth place in a front group of five. "I've never climbed in the first group before," Lance said. "So much of this sport is about confidence and believing you're going to be there and that you deserve to be there. Now, if I can come to a race like this with the confidence and with a strong team, I think anything's possible."

The next day, Lance placed third in a flat twenty-four-mile time trial to finish the Vuelta in fourth overall. And the following week, he took two more fourth places—in the time trial and road race at the world championships in the Dutch city of Valkenburg. They were outstanding performances, and they helped Lance amass 1,024 UCI points for the year to add a million dollars to his salary. Still, as his agent Stapleton pointed out, "Fourth place at the worlds and fourth at the Vuelta is not a comeback." Lance was going to need something better if his return from cancer was going to have any resonance with corporate sponsors in the States.

That "something better" was already being conceived by the man who was about to become the Postal team's sports director. Bruyneel came to Valkenburg for his first official meeting with Lance and Gorski. "I told Lance I was going to accept the job," Bruyneel says. "And one of the first things I said to him was that we should focus on the Tour de France and that I thought he could be a contender. He was kind of surprised about that. He thought I was crazy."

CHAPTER 17

YELLOW JERSEY

We can try and break down a Tour de France that's been around forever . . . or we can try and repair it. I want to be part of the renovation.

—LANCE ARMSTRONG

JOHAN BRUYNEEL IS BOTH CHARMING and tough, with a disarming smile and a steeliness in his eyes. "Some people think he has no compassion or just doesn't care," Lance says. "But that's just his style. He's very direct." The self-assured Belgian is always on the move yet always at ease, particularly with his peers in the pro cycling community, conversing effortlessly in French, Spanish, Italian, English, or his native Flemish. He has a European understatedness that's the perfect foil to Lance's American glitz. But, like Lance, he's a controversial figure. Many regard him as a genius organizer, a multitasker who can orchestrate all it takes to get a win. Others don't trust him at all; put off by his secretiveness in the past—something he now regrets—they believe he can be underhanded and cut corners to get where and what he wants.

When Bruyneel became U.S. Postal's sports director, he brought a discipline that the team had previously lacked. He also brought together the disparate parts of Lance's racing career, coordinating with coach Chris Carmichael, trainer Dr. Michele Ferrari, and Lance's various equipment consultants and suppliers. Lance had wanted Bruyneel to direct his team because the two men shared a winning attitude and both are, as Lance says, "information junkies."

Lance told me an incident that revealed another similarity. "I was on two phones," he said, "so when Johan called on a third phone, my teammate Christian (Vande Velde) answered it and said, 'Oh, Johan, he's on two phones. He's just like you. You must be brothers.'"

Once the two "brothers" started working together, they communicated with a constant stream of text messages, phone calls, and e-mails to discuss every facet of their plans and aspirations. Bruyneel had entered Lance's life at a propitious moment, when all the stars were lined up in the Texan's favor: He was back 100 percent as a pro cyclist; his cancer foundation was firmly established; his marriage was flourishing (a first baby was on the way); and his recovery from cancer was no longer a top concern.

"I never thought of him as a guy who had cancer," Bruyneel says. "I just saw him as an athlete. In '99 he still had to have his checkup early that year. He was nervous about it, and I was nervous about it, but when that checkup was done and everything was fine, I never thought about it anymore." What Bruyneel and Lance *were* thinking about was the Tour de France.

"Lance told me that winter he wanted to try and win the Tour," Dr. Ferrari says. "I was not that convinced at first, but Bruyneel said it was possible." The Italian trainer was skeptical because of his experience with his prize pupil, Swiss rider Tony Rominger, considered one of the sport's greatest riders. Under Ferrari's guidance, Rominger had won the Tour of Spain three times and the Giro d'Italia once, but he never did better than second at the Tour de France—losing to Induráin in 1993. So while Lance had proven he could climb with the best, Ferrari knew you could be a great rider and still not win the Tour. And although he recognized, like Massimo Testa before him, that Lance had exceptional physical qualities, he didn't know if Lance could translate that potential into brilliance at the Tour.

Bruyneel was more confident about Lance's odds because he had watched him develop as a fellow racer, and he had his own experiences as a prominent Tour rider to draw on. Lance returned that confidence: He believed that Bruyneel could develop a team for the Tour: one that could unite around a strong leader. "As a rider, Johan was a better-than-average talent who got really good results from racing smart," Lance says. "He knew modern cycling. He also spoke a bunch of languages so he could talk to all the different guys on the team."

And Bruyneel had a plan. It developed after Lance told him, "I've ridden all these climbs in the Tour de France, but I was always at the back in the mountains, and I didn't really pay attention. So I don't *know* those climbs." They decided to overcome this lack of knowledge by having Lance train in the mountains through the spring and preride all the Tour's mountain stages in early summer. Bruyneel also put fewer races on Lance's '99 schedule to make room for Tour-specific training camps.

Although climbing strength is key, a true Tour contender also needs to master the time trials, a contest of pure speed, where riders start at intervals and the fastest finisher wins. One key to success in these races against the clock is acknowledging that the bike can play as big a part as the rider. To help develop a better time-trial bike, Lance had two experts he had worked with since his late teens: John

Cobb, an aerodynamicist in charge of wind-tunnel testing, and Steve Hed, who manufactures fast wheels and aerobars. He also had a long-time relationship with Japanese company Shimano, which manufactures bicycle *gruppos* (cranksets, chainwheels, pedals, derailleur gears, brakes, and handlebars), and a new relationship with the Postal team's cosponsor Trek bicycles, whose designers impressed him from the start. Other companies on Lance's aero team were Nike (shoes and skinsuits), Giro (helmets), and Oakley (glasses).

Using cutting-edge technology to get the fastest bike was the first step to Lance's time-trial success; the next was a tough training regimen to get the best out of his body. By the spring of '99, Dr. Ferrari says, Lance's aerobic threshold (AT) number "was already high enough to perform good time trials, but we worked on his position, too, to find a good compromise between power output and aerodynamic efficiency. A position that is aerodynamically extreme doesn't allow the athlete to develop the same amount of watts, especially on rolling courses such as the ones in the Tour de France. A slightly higher position that allowed Lance to push the same watts as he was pushing on the climbs was the best choice. So a typical training session was to repeat three to four times a climb of three to four miles at 5 to 6 percent gradient, riding his time-trial bike at a cadence of between 100 and 105 RPM."

Those numbers are startling. Only riders at the level of a Rominger or an Induráin can turn the pedals that fast on a long climb. Lance concedes that this type of training wasn't easy, but it helped him improve his power while getting more used to riding in the stretched-out position on a time-trial bike. "For me, at least, the time-trial position isn't natural; it's uncomfortable, and a lot of times you want to get up out of the saddle and you want to move around," he says. "But if you can do a climb in that lower position, repeat climbs, day in, day out, then when you get into a flat time trial, it feels a little easier." As for his perennial lower back pains, Lance says they eased after cancer, which made it easier for him to adapt to a more radical position in time trials.

Ferrari's uphill time-trial training methods forced Lance to practice the fast-pedaling climbing style that Carmichael had recommended and which Bruyneel was helping him perfect. "Every time I was on the phone with him I was really annoying, to the extent that we would have a fight about it," Bruyneel says. "I'd say, 'Be sure to use small gears and don't stand up.' And when we did training camps, when it was just him and me, I made him wear a radio to constantly remind him every time he was tempted to use big gears—until he didn't have to think about it anymore."

For Lance to focus his Tour de France preparation on training rather than on racing was a radical departure from tradition. All the great champions raced in arduous multiday races like the Giro d'Italia to improve their form for the Tour. Lance did compete in a handful of one-day classics and stage races that spring, but his limited schedule was further restricted by a series of minor crashes. He had only one win in four months, and that was in a flat ten-mile time trial at a second-tier race in France.

At first, Lance wasn't convinced that training camps were the best preparation. "On one of the rides," Bruyneel says, "he came back to me on the radio and said, 'Okay, we'll do this because we started it, but next year I'll focus on the classics again.'"

It wasn't long, though, before Lance saw the benefits. "At both camps, in the Alps and Pyrenees, I lost weight because there was so much riding," he said. "I gained form and lost weight." He continued to lose weight when he was at home, where with Dr. Ferrari's guidance, he "weighed the cereal, pasta, bread, everything, with a little digital scale."

Kristin watched him "add up every calorie he ate, then calculate all his output to make sure that was more than he was eating. He was like a mathematician with the calculator every day. It was crazy, but it worked."

Besides helping him burn calories, the training camp rides were building up Lance's confidence and stamina. Both Lance and Bruyneel have vivid memories of one mammoth ride—Lance on his bike, Bruyneel in a follow car—which covered six steep climbs in the Pyrenees. Lance would race this stage to Piau-Engaly two months later in the Tour. "It was raining and cold," Lance recalls. "Johan said, 'No, you can't get out in this. We'll just drive.' We started to drive part of the course, and I said, 'Stop the car. Let me out. This is ridiculous.' So I rode the rest of the way. He couldn't believe it."

"It was so cold," Bruyneel says, "that the motorcycle driver of a photographer with us that day quit his job. So what I saw Lance do, by himself, seven hours on the bike, all these climbs, and how he was still performing at the end, I just had a feeling. . . . And knowing how *I* would have felt after seven hours, I thought if somebody's going to beat him in July, that rider will have to be *really* good. When he finished that stage to Piau-Engaly, I said for the first time, 'This guy's gonna win the Tour!'"

Even Dr. Ferrari was beginning to see Lance as a contender. "All winter and spring we worked hard with the focus of repeated long climbs typical of the Tour de France," the Italian trainer says. "Lance was living in Nice and he often trained on the same climb where Rominger used to test himself: the Col de la Madone, which is almost eight miles at a 7.7-percent average gradient, a typical Tour de France climb. Tony lived in Monaco, which is closer to the Madone [than Nice], and he climbed it hundreds of times. His best time was 31:30."

About five weeks before the Tour, Lance had managed to get within a minute of that time on his monthly test ride up the Madone, which climbs three thousand vertical feet from the coast at Menton. Then, following a trip back to Texas for the Ride for the Roses weekend—which this time raised a million dollars for his foundation—Lance returned to France for two final stage races that June.

At the eight-day Dauphiné Libéré, which is considered a mini Tour de France in the Alps, the Postal team was outstanding. Two things were now evident: how much the Postal riders had come together as a team under Bruyneel's guidance and how much Lance's form was coming on for the Tour. Lance won the Dauphiné's short prologue time trial; and his teammate Jonathan Vaughters, a skinny climber, took the overall lead after a prestigious victory on Mont Ventoux. Lance placed fifth, a minute slower than Vaughters, while Postal's two other mountain goats, Kevin Livingston and Tyler Hamilton, also finished top ten. These four would form the core of the Postal team at the Tour, along with three other Americans: Frankie Andreu, George Hincapie, and Vande Velde.

The team was upset when Vaughters lost the Dauphiné on the last mountain stage, despite Lance working hard for him; but Vaughters made amends by winning the following Route du Sud, a four-day event that closed with a summit finish at Plateau de Beille in the Pyrenees. It was on this bleak, windswept peak that Lance scored his first-ever mountaintop stage victory in Europe, breaking clear with just Vaughters and finishing two minutes ahead of the field.

This was a huge morale boost for Lance, who went back to Nice to be with Kristin and have a final week of training before heading to the start of his fifth Tour de France and his first since cancer.

There was time for one last test ride up the Col de la Madone. At the end of a five-hour training ride on a hot, muggy day, Lance and Livingston did the climb together, riding side-by-side up the narrow back road that zigzags across a steep mountainside. When Livingston stopped with a flat tire, Lance continued at race speed to the top, where he punched the time button on his bar-mounted computer and saw: 30:47. He had broken Rominger's record by a remarkable forty-three seconds—more than five seconds faster for every mile!

"Lance did that ride on a standard bike with a bike pump and spare tube included," Dr. Ferrari says. "His AT was 490 watts, his weight 74 kilos, and his watts per kilo 6.72." That was on par with five-time Tour champion Induráin. From every angle, Lance looked ready to be a challenger at the Tour.

Lance's return to the Tour de France was significantly low key. The European media knew nothing about his test on the Madone; few reporters even bothered to check out U.S. Postal, which was ranked nineteenth of the twenty starting teams; and the race wasn't yet being broadcast live in America. "We were the smallest team in the Tour," Bruyneel recalls. "We had a $3.5 million budget, no team bus, just two shitty campers, and we didn't even have a press agent."

Because of his past Tour record—he had finished only one of the four Tours he started—Lance was not considered a real contender. And despite his much-improved performance in stage races, most of the media and the public still thought of him as a one-day classics specialist. Much greater credence was given to his former teammate Bobby Julich, still with Cofidis. The Coloradan was given race number 1 because the top two finishers from the previous year, Marco Pantani and Jan Ullrich, were not racing, and Julich was third overall in 1998. Germany's Ullrich was on the injured list, and Italy's defending champ Pantani was in disgrace after exceeding the UCI's mandatory 50 percent hematocrit limit in a surprise blood test at the Giro d'Italia. There was still no valid test for EPO, but anyone testing above the hematocrit limit was regarded as a likely doper.

Ironically, several of the Festina-Lotus riders who confessed to EPO use at the 1998 Tour were back at the race after serving their suspensions. These included Switzerland's Alex Zülle, the 1995 Tour runner-up, who was again regarded as a top contender. Also tipped for a high finish were the Spanish riders Fernando Escartin and Abraham Olano, Italy's Ivan Gotti, and Dutchman Michael Boogerd.

By coincidence, the '99 Tour opened at Puy du Fou, the historical theme park in west-central France where Lance started his first Tour in 1993. The prologue time trial was being held on the same four-mile circuit, featuring the same half-mile-long hill where Lance had faltered and faded to a dismal eighty-first-place finish. His expectations for this year were much higher, much closer to the top.

Showing his new attention to detail, Lance spent a couple of hours the day before the prologue just circling the course with teammate Hincapie. They rode each turn at race speed to find the fastest line and decided that the most critical section was the corner at the foot of the main climb, where they could choose to keep the chain on the bigger of the two chainrings and risk being overgeared on the climb, or shift to the small chainring and risk losing speed at the foot of the hill.

They first tried the big-chainring option. "We were probably doing thirty-five miles per hour going downhill into the right turn," Hincapie recalls. "Lance was looking down at his gears and all of a sudden the Telekom team car pulled out from a line of vehicles right in front of him. I was just behind so I yelled 'Lance!' And he looked up at the last second."

In an instant, Lance saw the car—and the possible end of his Tour dreams. "As soon as I looked up it was too late," he said. He swerved instinctively, just as he did when a car sideswiped him as a kid in a Dallas street. "I smacked the side of the car and went flying over the handlebars. I caught the side mirror on my right ribs . . . but because

I had speed when I hit the ground, I just slid. I had a bruise on my ribs, and the next day I was sore all over."

Lance's narrow escape shook him up, and he was uncharacteristically nervous before the next day's prologue. But true to his nature, he didn't let the pain affect him. He was ready and anxious to cash in on all his time-trial training on the hills of southern France. In the minutes before climbing the steps into the start house, Lance pedaled slowly around a warm-up zone like a stalking cat, eyeing his former teammate and now rival Julich, who'd start a few minutes later. The large crowd applauded when Lance, introduced as the man who'd beaten cancer, sped down the start ramp. His Tour had begun.

When he reached the turn where he'd been hit the day before, he was in second place, three seconds slower than Olano, who was the reigning world time-trial champion. Then, climbing the hill, Lance picked up the pace. He spun a low gear on the steepest pitch, shifted up to power over the ridge, and sped downhill toward the final tight turns. When he crossed the line with what proved to be the fastest time, the crowd's applause changed to wild cheering.

Lance looked stunned. He couldn't believe he'd actually won, beating runner-up Zülle by an astounding seven seconds, with Olano in third. The media, shocked that a cancer survivor had beaten all the race favorites, immediately dubbed him the Miracle Man. And when Lance stepped onto the awards platform and pulled on the Tour leader's *maillot jaune*, the yellow jersey, he wasn't the only one crying.

"It was like he had just *won* the Tour," Hincapie says. "We were all hugging each other, we were so happy. But then we were scared shitless. In previous years, our only concern was getting *through* the Tour de France. Now we were going to have to defend the yellow jersey and pull the peloton around France. How the hell were we gonna do that? We were all in shock."

Even the thoroughly organized Bruyneel was feeling the heat. "I wasn't prepared for all that pressure and attention, Lance wasn't prepared, and the team wasn't prepared."

Despite the team's misgivings about the long, tough journey ahead—"It seemed like Paris was years away," Hincapie says—the riders and staff were inspired by Lance's yellow jersey and ready to do all they could to protect it. They got their first chance on the second stage, when they faced the opening week's toughest challenge: a narrow, two-mile-long causeway, the Passage du Gois, which connects the island of Noirmoutier and the mainland. Built centuries ago, the Gois crossing is flooded at high tide, leaving puddles and patches of mud when it's open to traffic. At their pre-stage team meeting, Lance and Bruyneel told the others to race at the head of the peloton before reaching the causeway to ensure that Lance remained near the front. This would help him avoid getting caught up in possible crashes on slick sections of the crossing.

The Postal riders kicked up the speed on a bridge to the island; then, on the two miles before the causeway, Hincapie says, "I took Lance to the front, and I really put myself in the red. We were going so hard, and there was no shelter from the wind, that we assumed there wouldn't be many guys left with us. There were only fifteen in front after the Gois," including Olano.

Behind them, a big pileup on the causeway saw some riders skidding off the road into the mudflats. Postal's best climber, Vaughters, was a crash victim, splitting his chin open; he continued riding for a few miles but, losing blood and in great pain, he was forced to abandon the Tour.

With shrewd advice radioed from Bruyneel, Hincapie and Lance slowed down after traversing the Gois to allow a thirty-strong chase group containing three of their teammates to join them before they picked up the pace again to gain time on the rest of the field. Three of the Tour favorites, Boogerd, Gotti, and Zülle, were caught up in the pileup at the causeway, and despite the help of their teammates, they couldn't close the thirty-five-second gap to Lance's lead group. With forceful efforts made by Lance's and Olano's teams, that gap grew to six minutes by the end of the stage—a great bonus for Lance so early in the Tour.

All of the following stages across west and northern France ended in mass sprint finishes; and because time bonuses were awarded to the top three each day, four of the sprinters moved ahead of Lance on overall time. That would change in the next, crucial stage, a hilly thirty-five-mile time trial at Metz. Once again, Postal's planning paid off. Lance had visited Metz in the springtime to ride two laps of the course. At that time, he did many of the sections at race speed, including the three long downhills, to learn the nuances of every critical turn. Then, on the morning of the stage, he rode the course alone to lock the final details into his mind.

Perhaps inspired by wife Kristin, who'd just arrived at the race, Lance started his time trial extremely fast—so fast that after only ten miles he was already leading chief rival Olano by eighteen seconds and thinking, "I'm already feeling tired . . . I'm in trouble." But his rivals were in more trouble. Top-ranked Julich swerved off the road on a fast curving descent, tumbled onto the shoulder, and had to quit the Tour, while Olano misjudged a turn and smashed into a hay bale before continuing. Lance kept on cranking; he caught Olano for two minutes and pushed himself harder than he'd ever done in a race against the clock to produce the winning time. At the finish he collapsed from exhaustion before standing up to hug a delighted Kristin. Astonished by his victory, Lance said, "I'm so tired it hasn't sunk in yet . . . I'm blown away more than I've ever been." All the other favorites, except for Zülle, lost five minutes or more. Lance was back in first place. He would wear the yellow jersey into the Alps.

What Lance was achieving in his comeback Tour was not surprising, considering his months of strenuous training, meticulous preparation, superb form coming into the race, and strong desire to pull cycling out of the doping morass it sank into in 1998. After he won the prologue, Lance said, "Remarks are made assuming we're all doped. That's bullshit. I'm here, and I hope the other 179 riders are here, to see cycling reassert itself and to reassure people that we are champions."

But his words did not impress all sections of the media, particularly the French press. Several journalists traveling with the race were there for a specific purpose: to look for and report on any signs of doping. They were influenced by the previous year's scandal-ravaged Tour, when police raids, rider strikes, and, ultimately, jail sentences for staff members of the Festina-Lotus team proved bad for cycling but not so bad for newspaper sales.

On the morning of the fifth stage of this 1999 Tour, the "scandal" reporters jumped on a short item in the French sports paper *L'Équipe:* An anonymous source said that one of four urine samples taken after the prologue had come up positive in a newly instituted test for detecting corticosteroids, a synthetic cortisone. A rumor quickly circulated through the thousand-strong press corps that the positive sample belonged to prologue winner Lance. To stop the story, the International Cycling Union (UCI) issued a statement later that day saying all the prologue tests were negative and that many riders were authorized to use small quantities of banned substances for therapeutic purposes.

That statement staunched the rumors, but when Lance held a press conference on the rest day following the Metz time trial, he surprised everyone by boldly addressing the ongoing debate between those who believed doping had destroyed cycling and those who saw it as a scar that could be healed. "I think we all have a responsibility to change the image of the sport," he said, "because I think we all love the sport, and we're all here for that reason. Either it's our job, or our passion, or both. Now, we can choose to do one of two things. We can try and break down a Tour de France that's been around forever, or we can try and repair it. I want to be part of the renovation."

Some journalists thought Lance's words hypocritical; others believed he was being totally honest; and the majority felt that he was giving a valedictory speech before he lost the race lead in the upcoming stages. In fact, they anticipated him losing it the next day on the Tour's toughest mountain stage.

The ninth stage stretched from Le Grand Bornand over six mountain passes and ended in Italy at the ski resort of Sestriere. The day's major climb was the giant Galibier, where Postal's Andreu and Hincapie set the tempo on the early slopes before Hamilton and Livingston paced Lance the rest of the way to the mountaintop. The six-hour stage was made even more grueling by torrential downpours, which caused Hamilton and Livingston to barely survive frightening high-speed crashes on the final downhill.

All that remained was the climb to the finish.

The fans were huddled together in groups, sharing their umbrellas and excitement as they waited to see who would first reach the foot of that final seven-mile climb. Suddenly, Spanish climber Escartin and Italy's Gotti appeared, evoking screams from the ecstatic Italians. The two men were quickly pursued by a small group of riders, and one of those riders was Lance. The fans were astonished to see *il americano* among the chasers; they were dumbfounded when Lance shot across the gap to join Escartin and Gotti; and they gasped in disbelief when he left them and surged ahead. Zülle made a belated pursuit, but he was still a half-minute back when Lance sped past the thousands of spectators lining the road to Sestriere to score a stunning victory.

Standing next to me in the sloshing rain at the finish line, an old-time Italian race fan shook his head vigorously and muttered,

"Doping . . . doping . . . doping. . . ." I was told that in the pressroom, there was bewilderment at the speed with which Lance made the climb at the end of a six-hour race. And when I got there, a French national radio commentator interviewed me about the American phenomenon. How was it possible, he asked, for a classics rider like Lance to not only beat cancer but also return to the sport and suddenly become the best climber in the Tour de France? I explained how Lance was always a good climber on shorter hills, and now he was just as strong in the high mountains because he was six kilos (13 pounds) lighter than before; I mentioned that he had matched the best climbers and placed fourth in the 1998 Tour of Spain; I noted that in his last race before this Tour, the Route du Sud, he won a stage on a Pyrenean mountaintop; and I described how he had perfected a high-cadence pedaling style and broken Tony Rominger's climbing record on the Col de la Madone. Then I pointed out that Lance had never tested positive in eight years of pro racing and that his hematocrit was well below the permitted level; and finally I added that he was the first man to ride all of the Tour's climbing stages as training for the race.

But for some, that wasn't enough. After Lance gave a brief news conference in which he thanked his "superb" team and praised his "scrappy" opponents, a British reporter came up to me and said, "Now we know Armstrong is a cheat. He couldn't have won like that without using EPO." When I disagreed, he stepped forward, placed his face inches from mine, and proclaimed, "You're just naïve or stupid—or both!"

But I wasn't the only one to ascribe Lance's success to superior genetics and better preparation. Sean Yates, the former Tour yellow jersey who was recognized as one of the sport's cleanest riders, said, "Why can't they accept that he's a better athlete, the same as Merckx was, the same as Induráin was, or Hinault? For me, Lance is this supreme athlete physically, with the mental aspect on top that makes him like Formula 1 world champion Michael Schumacher; he's the whole package."

The highly respected sports doctor Massimo Testa agrees: "If someone can win the Tour without cheating, the first person I can think of is Lance. That's because he's got all these qualities: the physiology, the brain, the business vision, the ability to manage a group and push everybody to their limit to get the most out of his teammates."

Because of the radical reactions to Lance's winning the 1999 Tour's most challenging mountain stage—extending his overall lead on Olano to seven minutes—Bruyneel decided to revise the team's strategy for the next day, which finished at L'Alpe d'Huez on the Tour's most celebrated climb. "I made certain decisions based on the press and the accusations and suspicions," Bruyneel says. "After Lance won on Sestriere, he wanted to win again on Alpe d'Huez, and I just told him, 'There's no way you can win today.' He wasn't happy about that, but I think it was the best thing to do. All of a sudden, we were in a position of having to brake and not win races, because of what would they say, what would they write, or what would they think."

The suspicions and polemic surrounding Lance escalated in the following days. *L'Équipe* devoted more pages to a possible doping scandal than to the actual racing. One of its lead stories said: "There is no evidence against him, so he is innocent; but he is a strange case . . . he's on another planet." And its sister newspaper, *Le Parisien*, continued to publish a daily diary column by Christophe Bassons, a young French team rider in his first Tour de France who was known as *Monsieur Propre* ("Mr. Clean"). Bassons had previously raced for Festina-Lotus, whose team officials said he was one of three men who refused to participate in the team's organized doping program. He openly condemned drugs in the hope that other riders would join him. But Bassons was ostracized in the peloton and, he says, some riders even tried to run him off the road.

In one of his columns, Bassons cast aspersions on Lance's performance at Sestriere, and the next day he claimed that the Texan came up to him during the race and told him to stop writing about doping all the time or get out of the Tour. There was also pressure from Bassons's French team to desist because the rest of the field was ganging up to stop his teammates from winning a stage.

In the end, Bassons didn't show up for the start of the thirteenth stage in St. Flour, where Lance called me into one of his team's camper vans to explain what happened in his conversation with Bassons. "I went to him because he puts down all the racers when he declares he's the only clean rider in the peloton. That's completely false," an irritated Lance said. "Then he says that no one can win a stage without EPO. That's bullshit! So I said to him, 'Christophe, I support what you're saying against doping but there are right ways and wrong ways of going about it. You're doing it the wrong way. You're just going to isolate yourself. The best thing you can do is be quiet.' And he replied, 'I don't have to be a cyclist. I can be a doctor . . . a lawyer . . . whatever.' So I said, 'Go and do it then.' That's all I said. I didn't tell him to go home."

"Bassons just pissed him off and made him go harder," Hincapie says. "If people ask me if Lance doped, I tell them they don't see behind the scenes. They don't see how hard he trains. They don't see the sacrifices he makes, like not eating a donut, not eating a chocolate chip cookie—the normal luxuries of life that he just sacrifices when he's in training. I trained with Lance and knew how much he suffered and how hard he worked."

Emotions were still high on the second rest day, just before the Tour entered the Pyrenees. Lance attended a short memorial service for his late teammate Fabio Casartelli at the site of his fatal accident;

he spoke at a press conference in St. Gaudens; and he had a lengthy interview with *L'Équipe*. Most of reporter Pierre Ballester's questions concerned doping allegations. To one of them, Lance answered: "If you discover a bag full of dope in my room, okay, you would have proof. But that's not the case. It never will be. These insinuations are an insult to me, to my family, and to the cancer community. Believe me, my proof is my performance."

Despite denying that he had ever taken performance-enhancing drugs, Lance continued to be pursued by the rumors. A pivotal moment came in Piau-Engaly, the same remote Pyrenean ski station where Lance had ended a seven-hour solo training ride on a cold, wet day in May. That was the day when Bruyneel declared, "This guy's gonna win the Tour!" Now, two months later, as he pedaled up the final slope of this fifteenth stage, Lance *was* winning the Tour—and by a wide margin.

The weather was hot and dry and Lance struggled at the end of the stage after being forced to make a fierce chase behind Escartin, the stage winner. Then, with his overall lead still intact, Lance accepted a new yellow jersey, completed the daily anti-doping test, and strode up a grassy hillside to an awaiting helicopter that would take him to his hotel. Just then a French TV journalist shoved a piece of paper in front of his face. The reporter said it was an article from that evening's edition of *Le Monde* stating that one of Lance's early-race urine tests had come up positive for corticosteroids.

"I was so tired I had no idea what he was talking about," Lance told me a few days later. "And he called me a liar. What can I do? It's desperate, sensational, vulture journalism."

Sounding tired and drained, Lance added that the ensuing twenty-four hours marked his psychological low point of the Tour. His stress subsided only after a press conference he gave the next day in Pau, where the UCI issued a communiqué that exonerated him.

It stated that the trace of corticosteroids in his sample was not enough to register a positive test and that it came from a topical skin cream to treat saddle sores, for which he had been issued a UCI therapeutic use permit. When I asked Lance about it later, he said, "It wasn't a saddle sore, but scar tissue. It was large and was killing me, so I used the cream sporadically."

Reflecting on that troubling period, Paul Sherwen, the television commentator who translated for Lance at the Pau press conference, says, "Imagine the pressure of that constant battering when you're looking at winning the Tour de France and you've got to worry about all that stuff. That's why he's such a powerful guy. As for people who say he must have used drugs, I say he's been so close to death in his life he's not gonna muck about with anything that could take him back to death's door."

While the critics and cynics chattered on about drugs, a wave of sheer excitement was spreading through Europe and across the ocean, waking up America to Europe's favorite summer sport and instilling pride and hope in millions of cancer survivors worldwide. With only four flat stages to go, Lance now had a lead of seven minutes, and few doubted that he'd win this Tour.

People made last-minute trips to Paris for the hoped-for celebrations. Jim and Rhonda Hoyt got the last two seats on a Friday night flight ("our first time overseas"). A bunch of Austin friends, including Bart Knaggs and Jeff Garvey, flew over to be there too. Och, Carmichael, and Stapleton were already on the race, Kristin was on her way from Nice, and Lance's mom arrived for the final two days. "Linda was at an all-time low that summer," her sister, Debbie, says. "She was divorced for the third time, and she was living in a little duplex. Then Lance is winning the Tour . . . and she did not have the finances to go." But nothing was going to stop the "barracuda mom" from seeing her son's coronation; Lance managed to get a ticket to her and she was on her way. Their good friend J. T. Neal wanted to be there as well, but his cancer had worsened and kept him in Austin, where he watched the finale on television.

Before being crowned the winner of the Tour, Lance won the last of the race's three time trials—with his mother screaming with excitement from the follow car—as if to emphasize that he was the best and needed no drugs to win the greatest race on Earth.

On July 25, 1999, half-a-million cheering spectators lined the Champs-Élysées. The American fans waved the Stars and Stripes; those from Texas brandished the flag of the lone-star state; and reporters from the major U.S. media all showed up to cover a cancer survivor's historic feat. For the winner's lap around the world's most magnificent boulevard, Lance and his Postal teammates were joined on bicycles by an excited Bruyneel and team owner Thom Weisel. And when Lance mounted the stage, the cheers from the crowd reached a crescendo.

Thirty months after ending chemotherapy, Lance was standing on the highest step of the Tour de France podium, the yellow jersey on his back, his right hand holding a U.S. Postal team cap to his heart, as a French army band played "The Star-Spangled Banner."

"I want to be remembered as the first cancer survivor to win the Tour," he said, and his gaunt face reflected the pride of arriving at this moment as well as the pain he had survived simply to get here. He stepped down to hug Linda and Kristin and posed for photos with one in each arm. "I was elated, ecstatic, grateful," Kristin recalls. "I was just so proud. And it was such a neat time. I was pregnant with Luke . . . so many happy things going on. It was hard to tell what was more exciting or more beautiful . . . one thing after the other."

She couldn't believe that her young husband had achieved the ultimate victory in his rugged sport. Even Stapleton would agree that *this* was a comeback, perhaps the greatest of all time.

On the train coming into Paris early that morning, I had sat next to Lance for part of the journey and asked him how it felt to be winning the Tour.

"It's beyond belief," he said. "I really didn't do that much. I trained hard, but . . . you can't win the Tour without a team, and I couldn't win the Tour without Kristin always being supportive, and Johan having the belief, and the sponsors being supportive, and the doctors saving my life. This win's for all of them. It's special for us . . . the Champs-Élysées . . . and to have my family there, and all my friends, Kristin's family, my mom. Crazy."

"Can you win the Tour again?" I asked.

"I don't know," he said. "Every year's different . . . but I'm not old. Is it true that Induráin when he won his first Tour was my age, twenty-seven?"

"Yes," I answered, ticking the years off my fingers, "twenty-seven, twenty-eight, twenty-nine, thirty, thirty-one—five years, five wins."

"Hmmm," Lance said. "Well, we'll see. . . ."

CHAPTER 18

KNOCKOUT

> That was my big motivation: Ullrich and Pantani back in the race. People said that in '99 without them it was a kind of TdF light.
>
> —LANCE ARMSTRONG

LANCE'S AMAZING COMEBACK from cancer to conquer the toughest sports event in the world resonated with the American public even more than Bill Stapleton had imagined. The Austin agent was no longer making fifteen calls to Nike just to get through. Instead, they were now loaning Lance their corporate jet so he could fly back and forth from Europe for one event after another: appearing on all the key talk shows ("Letterman was a little nerve-wracking"); visiting the White House ("Bill Clinton was into it; we gave him a bike, a helmet, and a yellow jersey"); and ringing the closing bell at the New York

Stock Exchange. His picture appeared on the Wheaties "Breakfast of Champions" cereal boxes, and he was now being recognized just standing in the street ("A big fire truck drives by, and the next thing you know five New York City firefighters are hanging outside the truck going crazy, shouting, 'Lance, you're the man!'").

Across the Atlantic, his winning the Tour de France against all odds turned Lance into a lightning rod for everything good and bad in the sport of cycling. The good was a fabled story of a poor boy from Texas winning the Tour after a near-fatal battle with cancer: "Comeback of the Century" claimed the influential *L'Équipe.* The bad was a skeptical public's perception that his metamorphosis could be explained by only one thing: doping.

No cyclist had ever generated such widely disparate reactions. The European media's feelings were best summed up in the Italian newspaper *Corriere dello Sport*, which said this about Lance's victory: "From a human angle, he is a symbol of hope, a symbol of joy in life. From a sports angle, he is just another athlete who has to comply with the rules. If that is what he did, then he deserves the success he has enjoyed. If not, he deserves understanding but certainly not approval. The doubts and suspicions are large, though there is no proof of wrongdoing."

Others voiced the opinion that Lance had won the Tour because its two previous champions had been absent—Ullrich recovering from a crash injury; Pantani caught up in drug accusations. "Wait until he has to race against Jan Ullrich and Marco Pantani," they said. "Only then can we really judge this new Armstrong."

"That was my big motivation," Lance says, "Ullrich and Pantani back in the race. People said that in '99 without them it was a kind of TdF light."

In a sense, they were right: Ullrich and Pantani would prove to be Lance's toughest future opponents. And while they, too, had their flaws and doubters, both men were immensely popular with Europe's millions of cycling fans. The burly, freckle-faced Ullrich, though two years younger than Lance, was called "the Kaiser" for his imperial air, the way he powered his bike rather than pedaled it, and how at his best he appeared invincible. The slight, shaven-headed Pantani was *Il Pirata* ("the Pirate"), whose hoop earring, goatee, and propensity for wearing bandannas emphasized his swashbuckling climbing style.

Ullrich, born in communist East Germany, was identified in his early teens as a future champion. He attended a state-controlled sports school and confirmed his promise by winning the world amateur road title at age nineteen. After joining Germany's dominant pro cycling team, Deutsche Telekom, he was thrust into the 1996 Tour at the last minute to help team leader Bjarne Riis. Only twenty-two and with no specific preparation, Ullrich raced with a natural ease. He was outstanding in the mountain stages, the strongest of all Riis's teammates, and he won the final time trial so easily he almost stole the overall victory from his leader. In 1997, the year Lance was recovering from cancer, Ullrich moved up from second to win the Tour by almost ten minutes. It was such a wide margin that many predicted the German prodigy would become the first man to win the Tour more than five times. He looked the part: Strong and proud, he had brown eyes, reddish-blond hair, and a big perfect smile. European girls hung his poster on their walls.

In contrast to the six-foot, turbo-powered Ullrich, who had a remorseless, bulldozer-like style, the five-foot-seven Pantani relied on his ultralight weight to make darting uphill attacks. His hero was Fausto Coppi, Italy's most famed cyclist, whose career spanned World War II. Like Coppi, Pantani became infamous for solo breakaways in the mountains that earned him multiple stage wins at the Tour and Giro d'Italia. After placing third overall at the 1997 Tour, Pantani raised his sights in '98: A spectacular victory in the Giro inspired him to challenge Ullrich for the Tour title. Two weeks into the race, the German had a comfortable three-minute lead and looked set to win again. But on a day of bitter cold, wet weather on a stage through the Alps, Ullrich faltered badly and lost the yellow jersey to Pantani, who went on to become that year's champion.

Commenting on his victory, Pantani said, "I don't want to boast, but if there hadn't have been Pantani, perhaps no one would have put Ullrich in crisis, and perhaps it would have been the same result as last year. And everyone would have said, Jan Ullrich is the strongest!"

In the buildup to the 2000 Tour, Ullrich *was* expected to be the strongest; Pantani was fighting court cases in Italy accusing him of "sporting fraud" because of a suspiciously high blood hematocrit reading at the '99 Giro; and Lance was preparing to defend his title in the forceful manner he established the year before. The Texan was energized by his desire to beat down rumors that he had won in '99 by doping or because the two big guys weren't there.

Lance also now realized how much his winning meant to cancer patients and survivors worldwide, and how whatever he did could affect and inspire them. "I don't consider this year a comeback," he said. "I think of this year as a confirmation—and that's important in the fight against cancer—a confirmation of what I did last year as a cancer survivor, especially as everybody is on the start line this year."

And on the home front, there was someone new: Lance and Kristin's eight-month-old son, Luke David. They were a family now, and that had a powerful effect on Lance, his values, and his life view. "Before cancer, it was me, myself, and I," Lance says. "Kristin wasn't there, Luke wasn't there, and I didn't really have a sense of community. Nothing resonated, nothing was personal, but now it was very personal to me.

"I've said that if I was good to my family, true to my friends, if I gave back to my community or to some cause, if I wasn't a liar, a cheat, or a thief, then I believed that should be enough. I think that's a very spiritual approach because that's why people often go to church, to learn all those things. Whether there's a God or other higher beings, it's instilling those values, a sense of community, a sense of self, a sense of family."

These were the values that now sustained Lance.

Heading into their second Tour together, Lance and Johan Bruyneel again held their cards close to the chest. They secretly previewed the courses for the forthcoming Tour, and mention of their early-May scouting mission to the Pyrenees only came out when Lance was rushed to the hospital in Lourdes after a dramatic high-speed fall. "It was a bad day, cold and rain," Bruyneel says. "Lance stopped at the top of the Soulor to fix a mechanical problem, and we were trying to get back to him in the car when he crashed on the downhill and smashed his face against a rock. He was lying in the road; he was in bad shape. We had serious concerns about him getting ready for the Tour." Fortunately, the main problem was a mild concussion. Lance recovered within a week, resumed training, and went back to previewing the courses.

Discussing Lance's closed-door Tour preparations, Bruyneel explains, "We always tried to be very, very separated from everyone else because that's the style we wanted. Strategy in cycling is rather complicated, and it depends on how mysterious you want to make it. One of my strategies was always, you know, let everybody think that Lance is a special guy, and we have a special way of working, and we do special stuff. We've not been open about our methods." The downside, Bruyneel admits, was how their secrecy backfired with the media.

"Lance was the guy who trained the most," his director says, "but I think that one of the things we should have done from 2000 on was to have invited some of the critical press to our training camps in May and June to really show everybody how Lance prepared for the Tour de France. I think that would have solved a lot of problems. We didn't do it because I thought that would give something away to our opponents."

If any reporters had been present when Lance returned to the Pyrenees ten days after his downhill crash to finish riding that stage, they would have seen just how exacting he was on these scouting trips. In cold rain, he completed the long descent of the Soulor down to a deep valley and then headed to a narrow road that went uphill for eight miles and ended at a desolate plateau named Hautacam. This was where Bjarne Riis sealed his 1996 Tour victory, and Lance wanted to etch this vital climb into his mind. The first part has erratic slopes and some tight turns leading to rustic villages, while the top section is a steep, steady slog. It's a difficult climb to memorize.

Hautacam would take just over half an hour to climb in the Tour, but Lance believed that a half-hour could determine the outcome of the whole race. And so, when he reached the windblown summit with the rain still lashing down, he told an astonished Bruyneel in the follow car that he needed to do it again. They returned to the valley and Lance made a second ascent, testing the turns to find the best ones from which to attack.

In contrast to Lance's painstaking preparations, Ullrich never reconnoitered the Tour's climbs. When asked why not, he said, "Sometimes it's best not to see where the end is." As for Pantani, he studied maps and profiles, but he didn't like to get the feel for a climb until race day, reflecting his instinctive approach to life.

The next step in Lance's preparation, which was also kept quiet, was a ten-day high-altitude training camp at the Swiss ski resort of St. Moritz. He was there with teammate Kevin Livingston, and they followed a schedule from their controversial Italian trainer, Dr. Ferrari. "The most important training sessions were six to seven hours," Ferrari says, "with up to five thousand meters [sixteen thousand feet] of total climbing." That was as difficult as the longest, toughest stage in the Tour itself, which explains why Lance was never fazed by what he'd face in July.

Anyone who has raced the Tour de France will tell you how brutal it is and how it batters your body and mind. In one sense, the event's extreme demands explain its attraction to both spectators and athletes; but few people choose to do it. "No normal person would want to ride the Tour de France," Tour veteran Allan Peiper says. "You don't do it for fun because you're balanced; you only do it because you're imbalanced. There's something that drives you to prove your worthiness or acceptance, or whatever it is that's buried deep down in your psyche."

Lance, Ullrich, and Pantani all had inner demons that pushed them to win the Tour and want to win it again. Both Lance and Ullrich had abusive fathers who left home when they were young, while Pantani was still the little kid who wanted to prove himself, a persona he adopted ever since he was big enough to get on a bike and race the bigger kids around the block.

At the 2000 Tour, the bigger kids were the Texan and the Kaiser, and the Pirate would get his first chance to demolish them on the climb to Hautacam, the first stage finish in the Pyrenees. All year long, people had been talking about these three champions doing battle at the Tour. The day of reckoning was finally here.

When Lance woke up the morning of the tenth stage and heard heavy rain beating down on his hotel window, he "was downright giddy," according to Postal teammate Tyler Hamilton. "Lance is the ultimate tough guy. He likes his challenges big." In contrast, while waiting for the actual start, Pantani briefly opened the door of his team's camper and nervously peeked up at the dark clouds, while Ullrich stayed sheltered in his team bus until the very last minute.

The German hoped the weather would clear before they reached the Hautacam, but five hours into the six-hour stage, as he made the last long descent in a twenty-strong group with Pantani and Lance, the wet, chilling conditions persisted. Across the valley on the cloud-covered Hautacam, the press corps was huddled inside a frigid military-size marquee, watching the race on television monitors. There was a palpable buzz among the reporters when the Tour's past three champions reached the base of the mountain for their much-awaited showdown. Small breakaway groups preceded them by two minutes and ten minutes, but all of the journalists' eyes were on the big three—the main contenders for the overall win. Pantani believed that this was the moment when he could put behind him a year of fighting charges that he was a drug cheat; Ullrich was cheered by a temporary halt in the rainfall, though the roads remained wet; and Lance had his game face on, hoping his body could respond to the expected attacks.

A wave of anticipation rippled through the pressroom when Pantani burst out of the pack with one of his familiar surges. Ullrich didn't chase; he just stared ahead, hoping that his steady, power-based climbing style would keep him in contention. But Lance, seeing the German's grim face, rose from his saddle and sped across the growing gap to Pantani. Once there, he went into his high-cadence training mode, firmly seated and gripping the tops of the handlebars, his blue eyes focused on the steep road ahead. Pantani, astounded by Lance's climbing speed, simply couldn't keep pace; he fell back and would lose more than five minutes to the American in the last six miles.

With Lance showing no signs of fatigue and quickly closed a two-minute gap on climbers like Fernando Escartin, many in the pressroom began shaking their heads. The veteran cycling writers couldn't remember anyone who pedaled this fast uphill without looking distressed—not even Miguel Induráin, the Tour champ who advised Lance to use a high-cadence style back in May '98 at the Ride for the

Roses. And when the reporters ventured out into the damp forty-degree air to see the stage finish, they saw Lance sprinting to the line in second place, only forty-two seconds behind Basque rider Javier Otxoa, who'd been ten minutes ahead of him at the foot of the climb.

Lance had caught and dropped everyone else, using his knowledge of the climb from his two pre-Tour scouting trips to accelerate on the steepest pitches, where he *did* get out of the saddle and pull up on the handlebars like Pantani. It was hailed as the greatest display of climbing since the most dominant days of Eddy Merckx in the Tour of '69. Lance pulled on the yellow jersey with an overall lead of more than four minutes on second-placed Ullrich. Barring surprises, this Tour was as good as done.

By climbing the Hautacam almost thirty seconds per mile faster than anyone else, Lance again engendered suspicions of EPO use. Nothing else could explain his supremacy, the skeptics said, even though all the riders knew that their urine samples were being frozen for later analysis with an EPO test that would be introduced at the end of that year. The now-standard pre-Tour blood tests had caught out three lesser riders with hematocrit levels above the 50 percent limit, but the scandal-hungry media wanted a bigger fish to fry.

With that goal in mind, and stunned by Lance's incredible climb to Hautacam, the state-owned France 3 television network detailed a film crew to discreetly trail Lance's U.S. Postal Service team, looking for any suspicious behavior, any evidence of doping. A week later, the reporters thought they were onto something. Outside the American team's hotel in Morzine, they saw two men loading bulging plastic bags into a Postal team car, which they followed. After filming the trash being dropped off at a roadside dumpster, the French crew retrieved the bags, which were later said to contain medical waste, including compresses and packaging, but no doping products. Three months later, following an anonymous tip-off, a Paris prosecutor opened an official investigation into the team's practices. An article in the French weekly *Le Canard Enchainé* then revealed that the only suspicious content of the trash bags was an empty carton of a product called Actovegin, a deproteinized derivative of calf's blood, which a Postal team spokesman later said was used for treating riders' abrasions and a staff member's diabetes, both of which were legitimate uses of this product.

The UCI added Actovegin to its prohibited list the following winter, describing it as a product that could potentially increase the blood's oxygen uptake—though there were no firm data to confirm this. Lance says he had never heard of the product. And when the French investigators eventually analyzed the Postal team's urine and blood samples from the 2000 Tour, they all proved negative for banned products, including EPO.

"We agreed to release all the samples from the UCI," Bruyneel says. "I was questioned for three hours by the police in Paris, and I asked them, 'Why is this investigation still going on?' They told me, 'We gave all the samples to a lab in Paris, a private lab, and they didn't find anything. And Lance's samples especially are so clean that the lab must have forgotten to test for something.' That's when I realized this is a battle we can never win." After eighteen months, the case was finally dropped.

That judicial case and the state television snooping were the only visible evidence of an official witch hunt, but the highly respected British TV commentator Paul Sherwen, himself a former Tour racer and team official, is among those who believe that other attempts were made to disgrace Lance. "I'm convinced that the French government at the highest level was having his urine tested and having his blood tested, and they couldn't prove a thing," Sherwen says. "If there was anything there, they would have found it. Those people would have found out because they *wanted* to find out. The Tour de France is a big powerful organization. If it can get the Champs-Elysées closed down, it can get anybody to test his hair follicles, his DNA, the whole bloody lot. So it's my belief that they tried hard to nail him, and they couldn't."

Sherwen's suspicions of anti-Lance sentiments within the French establishment were strengthened by a series of events that unfolded five years later. It began with evidence that someone at the state-run Paris laboratory (LNDD), which conducts drug testing for the Tour de France, deliberately leaked results of a secret research project to the newspaper *L'Équipe*, which is owned by the same corporation that owns the Tour de France. The project, authorized by the World Anti-Doping Agency (WADA), involved testing urine samples, including Lance's, which had been kept in cold storage since the 1999 Tour, where Lance scored his first win. The results were said to be helping WADA refine its analytical test for detecting EPO. However, the leaked summary of the research findings, which claimed that several of the old samples appeared to have tested positive for EPO, listed, against protocol, rider code numbers.

An investigative journalist at *L'Équipe* then worked to identify the rider code numbers that were held by the UCI in Switzerland. A staff member there was later reprimanded for releasing the information, which enabled the journalist to link Lance's name to the samples and for a damning article to be published by *L'Équipe* on August 23, 2005.

When a urine sample is taken at the Tour, it is immediately divided into two separate bottles, marked A and B. If the A sample tests positive for anything, the B sample is used to confirm the result; both are needed for conclusive evidence. Therefore, the only samples left over from the '99 Tour—and the only samples involved in this study—were the B versions of samples that had already tested negative. Because of this, none of the samples could later be used as evidence of doping. Yet that didn't stop *L'Équipe* declaring it as such.

In its front-page story, under the headline *Le Mensonge Armstrong* ("Armstrong's Lie"), *L'Équipe* said that six of Lance's fifteen urine samples taken during the '99 Tour tested positive for EPO. It further claimed that the alleged results were consistent with injections of EPO prior to the prologue and the Sestriere mountain stage. What it failed to mention was that Lance's performances throughout the 1999 Tour were not consistent with someone getting EPO boosts. He overreached on most of the Tour's key stages: At the Metz time trial, where he is alleged to have tested positive for EPO, he faded in the final three miles, losing sixteen seconds to Alex Zülle and flopping over with exhaustion after crossing the line; in his stunning mountaintop win at Sestriere, Lance actually lost twelve seconds to Zülle in the last two miles; and on the giant Pyrenean stage to Piau-Engaly, he was dropped by Richard Virenque and Zülle for nine seconds on the final mile of the climb to the finish. Someone juiced up with EPO is unlikely to fade like that three separate times in a ten-day period.

Furthermore, scientists were divided on whether urine frozen that long is still viable for testing. Christiane Ayotte, who runs the WADA lab at Montreal's Institut National de la Recherche Scientifique and received the Canadian Medical Association Medal of Honor in 2006, said at that time: "We are extremely surprised that urine samples could have been tested in 2004 and revealed the presence of EPO. In its natural state or the synthesized version, it's not stable in urine, even if stored at minus 20 degrees."

Scientists also questioned the test's validity because it's hard to distinguish between a person's natural EPO and an artificially enhanced EPO. The analytical test for EPO is not a simple one. It involves an electrical field pulling the proteins from a urine sample across a blotter to produce a series of stripes. There is considerable overlap between stripes created by the body's natural EPO and the chemical form of EPO, and a judgment call by the technician determines whether there is a positive or negative result. The stripe patterns can be easily distorted if the urine is not properly stored. And some chemists say that a false EPO positive can arise in a urine sample taken immediately after strenuous exercise.

L'Équipe's story was condemned by the UCI, which later commissioned an independent investigation by the former head of the Netherlands' anti-doping agency, lawyer Emile Vrijman. The resulting Vrijman Report exonerated Lance. It listed a number of conclusions, including these: "Had the LNDD conducted its testing in accordance with the applicable rules and regulations and reported its findings accordingly, any discussion about the alleged use of a prohibited substance by Lance Armstrong would not have taken place; it is completely irresponsible for anyone involved in doping-control testing to even suggest that the analyses results that were reported constitute evidence of anything; and representatives of the LNDD concluded on their own that the right answer to the question whether the alleged 'positive' urine samples constituted 'Adverse Analytical Findings' was an unqualified 'no.'"

These conclusions were rejected, however, and even ridiculed by WADA president Dick Pound, who said, "The Vrijman Report is so lacking in professionalism and objectivity that it borders on farcical." The Canadian official's response followed one of his earlier statements in which he unequivocally said, "The public knows that the riders in the Tour de France are doping."

Pound's fiery statements and *L'Équipe*'s incendiary article both angered Postal team boss Bruyneel, who says, "I think Lance became bigger than the Tour, and that's a feeling the French didn't like. . . . We were living with the feeling constantly present that they would do whatever to destroy our credibility. It all goes back to Dick Pound's accusation, and there's no way to defend yourself."

The French hadn't won a Tour in fifteen years, and they resented a young, brash American grabbing the plum of the sport, an event they once had dominated. Nonetheless, they had acquired a grudging respect for Lance, though they didn't like the apparent ease with which he shed his opponents on the steepest climbs. They wanted their champions to show the effort on their faces, and Lance didn't. So when he *did* falter, his critics often cheered. That was the case on the sixteenth stage of the 2000 Tour when he experienced what cyclists call a "bonk," a sudden drop in blood sugar that forces you to slow down or even stop pedaling, and makes you feel light-headed. It's caused by not eating enough food during a race and literally running out of calories to fuel your effort.

Lance's bonk occurred on the last stage in the Alps, after a daring attack from Pantani, who'd gotten bolder as the race went on. The Italian first showed his flair on the twelfth stage, two days after the Hautacam. On the barren slopes of Mont Ventoux, Pantani sped clear and Lance had to dig deep to catch him. The two men then rode side-by-side, fighting fierce crosswinds as they headed toward the steep ramp to the finish line. Lance knew that Pantani's life had been in crisis for a year, and he remembered that he had offered the post-cancer Lance a place on his team. So, planning to let the Italian win the stage, the American gestured to Pantani and said, "*Tu vince*," Italian for "you win." Pantani misunderstood and thought Lance said, "*piu veloce*," telling him to go faster—a sign of disrespect. So after Lance let his rival win the stage, an angry Pantani told the Italian press he'd been dissed.

Three days later, on the fifteenth stage, Pantani made another sudden attack on the mountaintop finish at Courchevel. This time, Lance couldn't respond. Concerned, he radioed Bruyneel to call Dr. Ferrari, who was at home in Italy watching the race on television, and ask him to calculate how much time Pantani might gain on him by the finish. Ferrari's answer reassured Lance, but Pantani did win the stage and moved up to sixth overall to remain in contention.

So when Pantani made a solo break on the first climb of the next stage, Lance took the move seriously. The Postal team chased Pantani so hard over rough mountain terrain that all of Lance's teammates, except for climbers Hamilton and Livingston, fell back. And when, after two hours of effort, Pantani had gained enough time to put himself in second place overall, the two Postal riders were forced to chase even harder, with Lance on their wheel. The speed was too great for Lance to grab a food bag at the day's feed zone, and because his other teammates were now minutes behind, he had no other way of getting something to eat.

Even though an exhausted Pantani was finally caught by the group led by Livingston and Hamilton, the two Postal men were hammered as well, and they dropped back once they hit the slopes of the gnarly Col de Joux-Plane. It was here, on the last climb of the stage, that Lance bonked. Less than four miles from the summit, after looking as strong as he'd been throughout the Tour, he suddenly ran out of gas. Lance began riding slower and slower. Ullrich turned his head in disbelief and pushed on. Over the team radio, Bruyneel told Lance to stay calm and ride within himself. But Lance was suffering as never before in a bike race, and he could barely keep the pedals turning. He pushed through the pain, and it was only his willpower and the encouraging shouts of some American fans that kept him going. One of those fans was his Austin buddy Bart Knaggs. When Knaggs saw Lance failing, he burst from the crowd and ran alongside him, urging him on.

With blind instinct, Lance managed to stay on the wheels of two Italian riders who caught him on the climb; and once over the top, he breathed with relief: It was all downhill to the finish. He still lost 1:37 to Ullrich, but it could have been worse—on the day Ullrich bonked at the '98 Tour, he lost nine minutes to Pantani.

Lance recovered well in the following days and won the final thirty-seven-mile time trial with the fastest speed ever recorded on a course that long—33.545 miles per hour—to clinch his second Tour victory by a six-minute margin over Ullrich.

On the last day of that Tour, the strong and proven Postal team traveled into Paris on *Le Train Bleu*, the Orient Express, before leading the pack onto the Champs-Élysées for the final stage sprint and traditional festivities. This year thousands more Americans were present among the massive crowds celebrating Lance's triumph. They exploded with delight as he hoisted nine-month-old son Luke, dressed in his own little yellow jersey, onto his shoulders and looked across to the other two loves of his life, Kristin and Linda.

Lance appeared more relaxed and confident and less surprised by his victory than he had the year before. It had been a far less stressful Tour than in '99 when, he said, "I needed the entire off-season to recover mentally." He also felt vindicated: He had beaten down the doping accusations and the two former champions, Ullrich and Pantani. When I asked him about future Tours and if he was still thinking about matching Induráin, he simply said, "I'll be here next year; I can promise you that."

Ullrich, too, would be back to challenge Lance in 2001, but not Pantani. The Italian never won another race, sank into depression, and became addicted to cocaine. He died of an overdose on St. Valentine's Day, 2004.

Twenty-five thousand people came to honor Pantani at his funeral in his hometown of Cesenatico, a small fishing port on the Adriatic. They came because of his popularity as an athlete, and also because they saw him as a sacrificial lamb in the ongoing fight against doping. The people felt that Pantani had been victimized by the media and the courts and that it was the system itself that needed to be purged. Lance sent a note of sympathy to Pantani's family. He felt empathy for a man who had suffered so much under the barrage of doping accusations. That was something he could understand.

Lance tells me it hasn't been easy to constantly be questioned about his integrity.

"I gotta admit, man, it's hard. There's so much stuff, and it's such a pain in the ass," he says. "It's too bad, it's too bad. It's just a damn hard sport. That was my very first impression as a fourteen-year-old kid on a bike—damn, this is hard! But that doesn't change when you get to be twenty-five or thirty-five at the Tour or the classics. You can't compare the pain of any sport with the Tour of Flanders or the Tour de France, or a day with three passes in the Tour over 240 kilometers. It's the hardest sport in the world, *and* it's high profile. There's a lot on the line: There's money, there's fame, there's attention . . . and, in Europe, there's the pride of your community—forever!"

While Europeans understand cycling because every community, like Pantani's, has a bike-racing hero, the American public has little comprehension of the sport's toughness. People have heard of the Tour de France but tend to think of it as merely a test of endurance, riding a bike around France for three weeks. In truth, the Tour challenges an athlete on multiple levels, and messing up just one of them can lead to ultimate defeat. What set Lance apart from his competitors was his ever-increasing attention to detail and his desire to always be on the cutting edge of any important element, whether it was bike technology, scientific training, logistical planning, physical and mental health, or just a balanced diet. Those who argued that he couldn't have achieved success at the Tour without performance-enhancing drugs did not look beyond what they saw in the race.

When Lance states that he has never tested positive in anti-doping tests—and he has been tested hundreds of times, routinely and randomly—skeptics say that's because his doctors found a way of avoiding detection. They claim that the use of EPO in micro doses wouldn't show up in drug tests yet could still help an athlete recover more quickly from the daily grind of the Tour. But Lance had his own special methods for recovery, starting with the healing services of Jeff Spencer, a leading chiropractic doctor. From 1999 onward, Lance depended on Spencer, who also tended to the needs of Tiger Woods at golf's major tournaments.

Every athlete in the Tour has a dedicated masseuse, who works on them after each day of racing. But Spencer was in a whole different league. Like Lance, he capitalized on every scientific or technological advancement and used each new piece of knowledge to raise what he did to an art.

The French authorities were so curious about Spencer that when they investigated the Postal team after the 2000 Tour, he was one of their prime suspects, according to Bruyneel. "The police showed me a picture of Jeff Spencer and asked me why he wasn't accredited for the Tour. 'Because he doesn't need to have a pass for the race,' I said. 'He just goes from hotel to hotel.' They told me, 'We think he could be one of the key persons in doping practices through genetic manipulation because that's very advanced in America.' They had some crazy theories."

A small, bald man in his fifties who wears narrow rimless glasses, Spencer likes to work behind the scenes and rarely gives interviews. Prior to being a chiropractor, he was an Olympic track cyclist and a close advisor to Mark Gorski when he won the sprint cycling gold medal at the 1984 Olympics. When Gorski became the Postal team manager, he brought Spencer on board as soon as he could.

"Lance and I hit it off instantly," Spencer tells me. "I immediately embraced his personality, his intelligence, and his wanting to be the best that he could be." Lance felt the same. In his book *Every Second Counts*, he writes: "Jeff is part doctor, part guru, part medicine man . . . without him, we knew we'd never make it to Paris."

Spencer's official title was team chiropractor, but Lance says he's "really more of a physical therapist. The first year, he had a lot of work. My left hip kind of got flopped, and he always fixed it. He pulled it, so I'd always say, 'I need a little leg pull.'"

In a typical day at the Tour, Lance would spend part of the morning with Spencer, mainly for stretching; and in the evenings, the last thing Lance would do is have Spencer come to his room for thirty minutes or more "to look over everything." Spencer, who talks fast and precisely and tends to speak in paragraphs, says, "We would look for tight areas in the body, muscles that were tight, muscles that were overactive, joints that were blocked, muscles that weren't firing correctly. We would up-regulate those muscles and try to take as much tension out of the body as quickly as possible, so the body could have a normal recovery, and he could get up the next day at his best possible physical baseline."

Spencer says it was Lance who prompted him to go beyond traditional chiropractic methods. "We always looked for and embraced new technologies that were not yet mainstream," he says. "It was my job to find things that weren't on the radar that would give him a competitive advantage. What I do, because of its nature, isn't transparent, and it's not meant to be.

"In 2000, we got into more advanced technologies, using such things as cold laser frequencies and neutron technology to create change in the body in a fraction of the time that other systems would do. That allowed us to accelerate recovery day to day so he wouldn't accumulate stress and strain in the body that could eventually lead to illness or injury. These new methods gave us the ability to look into the human body and see what's there and get rid of it before it even shows up."

Another vital ingredient for Lance's daily recovery was the altitude tent, which simulates a high-elevation, low-oxygen environment and promotes an increase in blood hematocrit while you are sleeping in it.

It's a safe, legal method for doing what EPO does illegally. "I think the secret to being a great Tour rider," Spencer says, "is to match your recovery to your effort. Altitude tents play a role, and Lance was comfortable using it."

Spencer is used to working with exceptional athletes, so he has the perspective to understand what makes Lance stand out. "There are many characteristics that distinguish him as one of the greatest athletes of all time," he says, first noting his unique physiology: "When you feel his body, it's supple but it's rugged; it doesn't feel the way other riders do at the end of a stage. It doesn't take the impact like other riders do, plus it's able to respond much quicker."

Finally, Spencer describes what made Lance a great team leader: "He never asks anybody to do anything that he wouldn't do ten times over. He always does everything thoroughly, and he shows great gratitude and immense respect for his teammates. He always makes decisions on what he stands to gain, not what he stands to lose. He's really the epitome of what it takes to get good and stay good."

Lance still felt a need to prove he was a true champion, and his appetite for winning wasn't sated by two Tours. But by shooting for a third consecutive victory in 2001, he was heading into rarefied territory. Only four riders had ever won three or more Tours in a row: Frenchmen Louison Bobet (1953–1955) and Jacques Anquetil (1961–1964), Belgian Eddy Merckx (1969–1972), and Spaniard Miguel Induráin (1991–1995). Lance wanted to be the fifth. But even before the start of the next Tour, things seemed to be conspiring against him.

Above all, the doping accusations were spreading, even in his own home state. "*Texas Monthly* did this big story about Lance and doping in cycling, just before the 2001 Tour," says Austin sportswriter

Suzanne Halliburton. "At the same time, my newspaper had arranged to have a freelance photographer take pictures of Lance, Kristin, and Luke to illustrate a Tour preview story I'd written and which was about to run. And then the *Texas Monthly* story came out and it had the same pictures. Kristin blew a gasket, so Lance was mad at us because of Kristin, and he said he'd never talk to me again. This was two days before I was due to leave for the Tour."

The lengthy magazine story was peppered with quotes about doping from mostly skeptical journalists and cycling insiders. There was one from a doctor on an American team who requested anonymity and whom the writer called a "Lance basher." He was certain that Lance was "doing all the major banned substances." Asked for proof, the doctor said, "I have none. It's impossible to penetrate the system—the code of silence perpetuates itself."

One of the journalists quoted in the piece was David Walsh, the chief sportswriter of *The Sunday Times* of London, which on the first day of the Tour published a long article by Walsh intimating that Lance was using performance-enhancing drugs. Walsh cited "evidence" from former Motorola teammates and revealed Lance's association with the "notorious" Dr. Ferrari. International journalists hungry for details assembled at the Postal team's hotel, but Lance didn't appear, and their questions were left hanging. Walsh would later use the article as the basis for his infamous book *L. A. Confidentiel: Les Secrets de Lance Armstrong.*

Circumstances were also lining up against Lance on the cycling front. He felt betrayed and dismayed when his Austin friend Kevin Livingston left the Postal team to join the enemy, Ullrich's Deutsche Telekom squad. To replace him, Bruyneel recruited two Spaniards, Roberto Heras and José Luis "Chechu" Rubiera, who were among the best European climbers. But it was tough to lose a trusted teammate.

Even so, after an impressive win at the ten-day Tour of Switzerland, Lance was the hot favorite for the 2001 Tour. And Ullrich was again his top challenger: He had just won Germany's one-day national road title, showing his best form after shedding most of his extra pounds at the three-week Giro d'Italia.

Once the Tour started, Lance had other problems to face besides the drug accusations. His top climber Heras banged up his knee after colliding with teammate Christian Vande Velde in the team time trial; a few days later, Vande Velde crashed again and had to quit the race; Lance and Bruyneel miscalculated the danger of a big breakaway group, which propelled Andrei Kivilev of Kazakhstan fifteen minutes ahead of Lance on overall time; and then another Postal climber, Tyler Hamilton, crashed the day before the race entered the Alps.

With injured teammates and determined opponents, Lance knew he'd have to be aggressive to make up time on Kivilev, a better-than-average climber, and to gain time on Ullrich, who after ten days of racing was only thirty seconds behind.

Lance's first chance came at L'Alpe d'Huez, the mythic climb where he held back in 1999, not wanting to engender more doping allegations after his Sestriere stage win. This time, everyone was expecting one of his bells-and-whistles climbing displays in the style he had shown the year before at Hautacam. Knowing that, and knowing that Heras and Hamilton were both injured, Lance devised a strategy to take the pressure off his teammates—and trick Ullrich with some false hope.

"I went back to the car and told Johan, 'We'll just let 'em listen in [to us]. Don't believe anything I say,'" Lance says. He stayed at the back of the leading group, feigned fatigue, and talked on the radio to Bruyneel. Ullrich's team manager, Walter Godefroot, fell for the ploy and, believing that Lance was truly suffering, ordered his men, including Livingston, to increase the pace. That effort was exactly what Lance had hoped for: It prematurely tired Ullrich's men and allowed the ailing Postal riders to conserve their energy for the final climb up L'Alpe d'Huez.

Lance's acting was so persuasive that even television commentators told their viewers that the American was hurting. One man watching with the crowds *was* an actor: Lance's friend and Hollywood star Robin Williams. "My favorite moment of all the Tours was that one moment when he pretended he was losing it; he acted in a way that deserved an Academy Award," Williams says. "Even Phil Liggett [the British commentator] was going, 'I don't know what's going on. It doesn't look like he has it today. Aagh, and there's Jan Ullrich. . . .'"

The flag-waving army of Ullrich fans screamed in expectation as their man moved up behind his teammates Livingston and Andreas Klöden on the first steep pitch of the climb to the finish. It looked like the Kaiser was finally in command—until Lance's new *compadre* Chechu Rubiera roared past Ullrich and his men so fast that only Lance could stay on his wheel. The quarter-million people lining the Alpe's twenty-one switchbacks watched in awe as Lance and Rubiera soared up the climb, followed by the brave Kivilev and Ullrich, who slowly clawed back to the two Postal riders. They caught them just as Rubiera eased off. Lance was now at the front, with Ullrich and Kivilev just behind. It was then that Lance turned around, stared straight at Ullrich, and seemed to be baiting him before speeding away.

"When he looked around they all realized the fucker had been faking it," Williams goes on. "They had wasted a lot of energy trying to put distance on him . . . and all of a sudden he had the fuel to burn them all out, and even Liggett was going, 'He really does have it. I was wrong. I don't know what's going on. Oh my God.'"

The look that Lance flashed back at Ullrich before his fierce attack has been famously labeled "the Look." Commentating on German television, Swiss star Tony Rominger called it "*ein provokation.*" But that wasn't what Lance intended.

"Everybody thought it was a taunt, but I was looking for Chechu Rubiera," Lance says. "I was thinking what you always think when you're gonna attack: 'I'm on my limit. I'm not sure this is gonna work. I might be able to get a little gap or they might come back on me. Where will I go if I'm suddenly pedaling squares and he rides away? Then I'm on the defense and I'm looking for my teammates.' So I was just checking to see where they were if I needed to get bailed out. I was literally looking through and beyond Jan Ullrich to see where Chechu was. I wasn't looking at Ullrich."

But a startled Ullrich *was* looking at Lance. At that moment, just before Lance sped away from him, the big German was like boxer George Foreman after he'd been hit by a rope-a-dope Muhammad Ali in their mythic world heavyweight contest in October 1974, best described by Norman Mailer in his book *The Fight:* "All the while Foreman's eyes were on Ali and he looked up with no anger as if Ali, indeed, was the man he knew best in the world and would see him on his dying day. He started to tumble and topple and fall even as he did not wish to go down."

Ullrich had just as effectively been knocked out by Lance, who on the remaining six miles of climbing through the throngs of fervent fans gained two minutes on the German, won the stage . . . and pretty much wrapped up his third Tour.

"You fucking did it, you fool!" Williams was thinking as he watched the dramatic way Lance emerged from faking fatigue to delivering the killer blow. He compares the tactic to "one of those great strategies in the movies where the Spartans are hiding under sheep crap—'Baa, baa'—and then all of a sudden they appear and you see two hundred thousand Persians go, 'Oh, this is crazy bullshit.' That was one of those moments. That was very powerful!"

Lance's victory on the Alpe was the defining moment of that Tour, but he didn't finish off Kivilev until he won another stage a week later in the Pyrenees and finally pulled on the yellow jersey for the first time in that race. Two days later, on the final day in the mountains, Ullrich also surpassed Kivilev to move into second overall. As he and

Lance crossed that finish line together at Luz-Ardiden, Lance reached over to Ullrich and shook his hand, just as Ali did after his historic bout with Foreman so many years before. Ullrich was Lance's greatest adversary, and he'd been beaten one more time. "I'm not ashamed of finishing behind Lance again, because I went to the limit," Ullrich said. "I fought like a lion. And this second place motivates me for next year."

On the podium in Paris, Lance again celebrated with his son, Luke, and wife, Kristin, who was now pregnant with twins. A relaxed and delighted Lance was glowing with a sense of abundance. "I have health, money, a family which will grow, friends who like me, a sponsor who supports me, fantastic teammates . . . and I always have this passion," Lance said. "I live a life of an honest man, a happy man. I wouldn't change a thing."

CHAPTER 19

THE BLUE TRAIN

He was not the same Lance. Everyone was concerned.

GEORGE HINCAPIE

"LANCE'S MINDSET IS such that he never believes he has arrived," says his chiropractor, Jeff Spencer. "While many athletes measure their success by what they have already done, Lance looks at every moment as another potential victory in front of him." It was this attitude that pushed Lance to win Tour after Tour, each one presenting him with a distinct overall challenge. In 2002, that challenge was finding new talent and personalities to assemble the athletic and emotional support he needed to claim his fourth title.

The dynamics of the Postal team had radically changed. While Lance attracted a growing army of American journalists to the Tour, some of his strongest teammates had gained their share of glory, too, and headed off for more. Kevin Livingston had already left for a bigger salary at Deutsche Telekom; Levi Leipheimer was similarly tempted and transferred to a Dutch team, Rabobank; and Tyler Hamilton moved to the Danish-based CSC to become its team leader. To replace them, the Postal team had hired more Europeans and become more efficient and, in the process, had lost some of its down-home Yankee spirit.

Lance's closest friends on the team remained American George Hincapie and Russian Viatcheslav Ekimov. But the always genial Hincapie focused his season on the spring classics and wasn't around for Lance's pre-Tour training camps, while Ekimov, at thirty-seven, was nearing the end of his career. And although Spanish arrivals Manuel Beltran, Roberto Heras, and Chechu Rubiera were very effective climbers, they weren't men that Lance confided in, trained with, or hung out with.

Enter Floyd Landis, a physically powerful, unsophisticated, twenty-six-year-old American, who'd had some great results in U.S. racing and seemed to share many of the qualities that made Lance so prominent in Europe. "Lance was a hero of mine to start with because he'd won the Tour three times before I even met him," says Landis, who grew up in rural Pennsylvania in a Mennonite family. "So just being able to be there and train with him was motivation enough for me."

Lance was impressed with his new teammate. He liked that Landis was also a family man, with a five-year-old daughter, and he admired his humility and sense of purpose. Landis told him early on that he was buried in credit-card debt. "I didn't get paid for much of the last year on my old team," Landis explains, "but I believed I could make it in cycling. So the only way for me to get through the rest of the year to where I was on Lance's team and actually getting paid was to get myself into a lot of debt." To enable Landis to earn bigger bonuses and eventually a bigger salary, Lance helped him develop as a racer, something he rarely did for other riders. The young American inspired Lance to become a mentor, the way Sean Yates, Steve Bauer, and Phil Anderson had been for him.

To prepare Landis to be his go-to guy at the Tour, Lance frequently trained with him when they were both in Girona, Spain, at their European homes—Landis shared a small modern rental with another racer; Lance and his family had moved here from Nice and now owned a spacious condo in a historic building. Lance also had his prodigy go with him to his intensive pre-Tour training camps. "He took me to St. Moritz," Landis says, "where we just trained and trained and slept. That's it. There was nothing else, no other entertainment. At the end of the day we were so tired, we just ate and went to bed. That's what you do if you want to win the Tour."

Landis says that Lance's Italian trainer Dr. Ferrari "would come to St. Moritz to do tests, mostly on a one-kilometer climb. I had a good experience with him. He's really straightforward, the nicest guy. We would do different intensities of riding, starting with a certain amount of watts. He would take a blood sample from your finger, do a lactate test, and then make a chart to see where this level was. That was our baseline for training."

The precise, targeted training, along with a week of tough racing at France's Dauphiné Libéré—which Lance won easily, with Landis taking a phenomenal second—gave Lance the best form he'd ever had for the Tour. What he didn't have was inspiring competition. Jan Ullrich, who had placed second to Lance for the previous two years, wouldn't be racing this time; he'd been out the entire season with an injured knee. In his absence, the third-place finisher at the previous two Tours, Joseba Beloki, became Lance's main challenger. A shy, easygoing Basque, Beloki was a solid time-trialist and a strong climber but an unassertive cyclist. His biggest strength was his powerful O.N.C.E. team, whose sport director was a fiery Spaniard named Manolo Saiz. "Ullrich was easier to get motivated for than Beloki," Lance says. "For us, the only fun thing about Beloki was Manolo Saiz. We liked to punish him!"

Bruyneel had raced for Saiz before becoming the Postal team director, and he had a competitive relationship with the O.N.C.E. team boss. Saiz had never produced a Tour winner and he resented Bruyneel's immediate success. "In 1999, Saiz was one of those directors who was desperate to win the Tour," Bruyneel says, "and I came along—thirty-four years old with a team nobody believed in—and we won the Tour."

The Postal team also riled Saiz, as well as other team directors, with their secrecy. "You can say, okay, it was a mistake to have this strategy like, 'We're training in a special way.' And it could have been a mistake PR-wise, but it was definitely not a mistake sports-wise," he says, noting that it gave Lance an aura of invincibility and weakened the confidence of his rivals.

That strategy proved effective when Lance came into the 2002 Tour as the overwhelming favorite, a man who could not be beaten. He started in signature style: On a festive evening in the city of Luxembourg, he won the prologue time trial comfortably on a difficult course. But lacking a rival like Ullrich to push him, he seemed less focused through the first half of the race. Even so, second places in the team time trial (behind Saiz's O.N.C.E. squad!) and in a long flat time trial in Brittany saw him reach the Pyrenees in second place, only twenty-six seconds behind race leader Igor Gonzales de Galdeano, another member of O.N.C.E. The thought of Saiz's man winning was incentive enough for Lance, whose motivated Postal riders launched him to consecutive stage wins in the Pyrenees. Each time, teammates Hincapie, Beltran, and Heras destroyed the opposition before Lance rode ahead in the final few miles to easy victories. These wins allowed him to don the yellow jersey and put him two minutes ahead of runner-up Beloki, a comfortable lead that he was ready to expand.

But to keep Lance in the yellow jersey, his team had to race at the front—all day, every day. They performed this task so artfully that the French media dubbed the navy-blue-clad Postal team *Le train bleu*, the Blue Train, comparing their speed and style to those of the luxury express trains that ply the rails of Europe. The team dynamics were back, right where Lance wanted them. And an unstoppable Lance would win his fourth Tour.

Newcomer Landis, making his Tour debut, quickly proved his value. He rode to his limit every day and took a respectable 61st place out of 153 finishers. He also managed to keep spirits high with his quirky sense of humor and the wild rock CDs he played on the team bus.

By working hard on every stage of the 2,036-mile race, Landis learned just how tough the Tour can be for a team worker like himself. "The Tour just consumed me," he says. "That's the most stress I've ever had, having to go there as Lance's helper and knowing this guy's won the race three times already. I believed I could do it, but then I put a lot of pressure on myself, and for that reason I had a few bad days in the mountains, but I got through. At first I was just going, 'Finish, finish!' I couldn't think. But, man, I was happy when it was over."

In contrast, Lance claimed this was by far the easiest of his four Tour wins and the most thought-out. His professionalism was growing, and so was his fame. He was fast becoming his own dynasty, with a following of ardent supporters, especially in the cancer community, from all over the world. Even a growing number of the French were now shouting from the roadside, "Allez, Lance!" instead of chanting, "Dopé, dopé." They realized he was developing into a true champion, and they gave him a raucous welcome when he once again stepped onto the podium on the Champs-Élysées. Women, who make up the majority of European viewers for the Tour, were warmed by the appearance of Lance's wife, son, and twin baby daughters at the finish; it helped enhance Lance's image as a genuine guy, not a cold-hearted robot. They would have liked him even more had they known the other qualities that attracted Kristin to her husband. "The moments that I've respected and loved him the most are the ones where, even in the face of all he has been accused of, he has a certain sweetness and softness to him that he shows very rarely," she says, "and to very few people."

While the Europeans were warming up to Lance, an exponentially growing number of Americans were now watching the Tour, either at home or from the roadsides of France. Austin reporter Suzanne Halliburton explains, "There was a whole new audience out there because of him. After we started measuring Internet hits on our Web site and he got the yellow jersey in 2002, he got the same number of hits as the top football story. He was as popular as the Texas Longhorns, and that's huge!"

The Postal team celebrated its victory in Paris at a flashy corporate banquet attended by hundreds. But before the big dinner, Landis says, "Lance had a little party for the team, just us and our wives, only twenty-five people" at the luxurious Hotel de Crillon. Traditionally, the Tour winner divides his prize money among the team members, but that night, Lance also gave each of his eight colleagues an envelope that just about doubled their bonuses. "He didn't have to do that," Landis says, adding that the six-figure payout cleared him of his debt. "That was probably the high point of my career up till then. I don't know what I was more happy about—the fact that it was all over or the paycheck. I was just relieved, and so tired.

"My wife was there and we stayed in Paris for a few days. I couldn't get up out of bed. I got room service and slept for *at least* forty hours. I was just so happy that everything was finally over, and it was actually worth it. I didn't want to move. My wife was the same. She had jet lag from just getting there. So we slept two days straight in the hotel room and then went to McDonald's. That was our Paris experience. I'll never forget that: the Tour, the whole thing."

While Lance was cruising to his fourth consecutive Tour win, a prescient essay was being handwritten for a British cycling magazine by America's only Olympic men's road cycling gold medalist, Alexi Grewal. The son of a Sikh father, the Indian-American Grewal had raced the Tour in 1986; he then went on to become a Christian minister, a master woodworker, and a champion of the homeless. He wrote these words about Lance's 2002 victory ride: "In this Tour we have seen something not yet seen in Tour history: a rider winning the greatest race in the world without this being his primary objective. What you really saw was Lance winning the Tour while preparing to win it a fifth, sixth and seventh time. The number '7' is a number which represents perfection beyond what can be perceived with the five senses. To me, the prospect is life-giving."

In the Tour's one-hundred-year history, five was the all-time record number of wins, a record that Lance had yet to meet. To contemplate matching Jacques Anquetil, Eddy Merckx, Bernard Hinault, and Miguel Induráin was audacious enough; but to envision adding a sixth and seventh to that total seemed as remote a prospect as a golfer, even a Tiger Woods, winning The Masters seven years in a row. And yet the ease with which Lance won his fourth Tour—albeit with teammates like Landis who worked their butts off—leant credence to Grewal's prediction. Nonetheless, the very idea of an American winning the Tour de France seven times was too outlandish for the British magazine, which decided not to publish the essay.

Skeptical Europeans still didn't recognize the effectiveness of Lance's training methods, nor the strength of the Blue Train that he and Bruyneel had worked so hard to put together. But before defending his title in 2003, the captain of the train would be tested by an unexpected onslaught of physical and emotional distress. Maintaining his confidence and focus in the midst of that would be the predominant challenge awaiting him that year.

From the outside, everything about Lance's life appeared magical. He had a job he loved, an income in the millions, beautiful homes in Austin and Girona, a cancer community he inspired and felt inspired by, thousands of adoring fans, a beautiful wife, and three loving children. But his almost fanatical focus on winning the Tour came with a heavy price. Most importantly, he and Kristin were having problems in their marriage; he had let things slip with his ailing friend J. T. Neal; and his relationship with his mom had been faltering for some years, in a time that was hard for Linda on many fronts.

Some friends, including J. T., had reached out. "He would tell Lance, 'You've got to call your mom.' And those were lonely times for me," Linda says. Another friend, Plano swim coach Chris MacCurdy, also tried to help. "When Lance and Kristin were having a hard time, there was a point when he wasn't giving much attention to his mom," MacCurdy says. "She was real upset. I left a message on his cell phone: 'You need to talk to your mom. Real important. She misses you.' And I sent him an e-mail; he sent me one back: 'You don't understand.' I said, 'Yes, I think I do, but you still need to talk to your mom.'"

The problems were accentuated by a coolness between Kristin and Lance's mother that had started soon after the marriage. According to Linda's sister, Debbie: "Kristin kind of cut her out." Kristin acknowledges that things were difficult. "The relationship between a daughter-in-law and mother-in-law is really complicated, and it's even more complicated when a mother and son are really close," she says. "I think I was too young and too immature to know how to navigate that well, and I think she also was at a time in her life where she wasn't too happy. The combination of those two things wasn't really in our favor."

Linda's unhappiness began to lift the summer of 2002 when she married Ed Kelly, a friend of MacCurdy's; but J. T., her close Austin friend, couldn't attend the wedding because of his leukemia. "He didn't want me to see him," Linda says. "That's when he was getting very sick. But J. T. sure gave it a good old fight. He bragged about the fact that he maxed out his insurance . . . he just thought that was the coolest thing. He'd be having a bone marrow transplant, talking on his cell phone. He was just the best friend."

On October 1, Linda had a call from J. T. His battle with cancer had worsened. "He just wanted to tell me he loved me, and he was so glad that I had found happiness," she says, starting to cry. "He said, 'Linda, I have hospice coming in.' 'J. T., you didn't tell me. I can come down right now.' 'No, I'll be fine. My son Scottie is on his way over.' When I called back the next day, Scott answered the phone and said, 'Well, he's asleep.'"

That day, the sixth anniversary of Lance's cancer diagnosis, Linda called her son's Austin house where his annual October 2 "*carpe diem*" party was in progress. "I don't know who answered the phone. I said, 'This is Lance's mom. Get Lance on the phone.' But he didn't come. They were celebrating his six-year. And I wasn't even there . . . and no one could get him on the phone.

"I couldn't sleep that night, as I knew Lance needed to be there, to say good-bye to J. T. I couldn't get it off my mind . . . and all of a sudden everything in the house went silent, and peace just came over me. And I know that was the spirit of J. T. And I'm still so mad that that person, whoever it was, didn't give Lance the phone, because if it hadn't have been for J. T., I don't think Lance could have made it in Austin. . . . And he couldn't be at J. T.'s side when he died."

Losing a friend to cancer, a friend who'd meant so much to him in both his personal life and his early cycling career, was difficult for

Lance. He remembered the time they were each battling cancer and had their photo taken when they were both bald. "He was a good man," Lance said, "a little eccentric, but that's what made him great. He could tell stories for hours. . . ."

J. T.'s funeral was the first one Lance ever attended, and he dedicated his autobiography to "J. T. Neal, the toughest patient cancer has seen." I once asked Lance if J. T. was a father figure for him. "Well, J. T. did everything for me, so yes, he was," Lance said. "He was great at trying to remove some of the junk you get bogged with at that age, and just helped me manage my life." J. T. seemed to still be guiding his young friend, as his death helped Lance and Linda begin to mend their relationship.

That winter grew even harder for Lance when his marriage began falling apart, culminating in his and Kristin's announcement of their separation in February 2003. "It was hard," Lance says. "There was a lot of emotion there, a lot of ill feeling, and fights over little things, you know . . . tugging on the kids, getting our parents involved. I mean, I liked the time when I loved her . . . and I still love her. I would do anything for Kristin Armstrong."

While Lance's personal life grew increasingly painful, there was little redemption for him in the public arena. Shortly after J. T. died, Lance was in Paris for the annual Tour de France presentation, where the following year's course was announced. To commemorate the Tour's upcoming one hundredth anniversary in 2003, the organizers invited all twenty-two living Tour champions to a reunion dinner. But Lance was grim-faced when he was put next to the other American winner, Greg LeMond, for an official photograph. The Texan was still smarting from LeMond's remarks the previous year. "When Lance won the prologue at the 1999 Tour I was close to tears, but when I heard he was working with Michele Ferrari, I was devastated," LeMond had told *The Sunday Times*. "If Lance is clean, it is the greatest comeback in the history of sports. If he isn't, it would be the greatest fraud."

That was the start of an ongoing feud between America's first two Tour champions. LeMond claimed that when Lance called to question him about his remarks, the Texan said, "You're telling me you never did EPO? Everybody does EPO." Lance vehemently denied saying that and his relationship with LeMond grew increasingly bitter over the years. (LeMond's disparaging remarks would eventually lead to a suit by Trek Bicycle Corporation to end its longstanding relationship with LeMond since Lance was Trek's official endorser and spokesperson. This provoked a civil action by LeMond Cycling, Inc. against Trek, which was settled out of court in February 2010.)

When Lance returned to Paris in July 2003 for the start of the centennial Tour, his feud with LeMond was just one of many issues sticking in his craw. His top priority was to get healthy, physically and emotionally, and be in top form for his bid to win the Tour and join the five-time record-holders.

"With his marriage breaking up, he was not the same Lance," Hincapie says. "He missed his kids, and he was lonely in his newly finished apartment. He was even coming over to my place to borrow movies and books, which he never ever did; he never had time for that before. I was thinking, 'Man, that's totally not Lance.' Everyone was a bit concerned."

Things weren't going well for Lance on the bike, either, and he hadn't won a single race when he lined up for the Dauphiné Libéré in June. It was Europe's hottest summer in living memory. The heat was especially oppressive at the weeklong Dauphiné, where Lance finally scored a win by taking the main time trial and wearing the leader's jersey into the Alps. But then, on the race's fifth stage, he had the worst race crash of his life on a zigzag mountain descent. In trying to avoid a loose water bottle bouncing on the road, Lance says, his right brake lever slipped, jerked the brake cable, and locked up the back wheel, causing his bike to fishtail at forty-five miles an hour. "I just ate shit, and my left arm was stuck out and got ground down." Despite a gashed arm and banged-up hip, Lance continued in the race and even chased down a violent attack by upstart Spanish climber Iban Mayo to defend his overall lead.

"After Lance crashed, he should have let Mayo go, instead of killing himself to win that race," Chris Carmichael says. "I had a hard time recuperating," Lance admits, "and I had to take antibiotics. That's never a good thing." Then, at his pre-Tour training camp with Landis in St. Moritz, Lance needed an osteopath to treat an aching back. And his tribulations continued when he returned to his Girona home. Kristin had brought the kids to Spain in an attempt to lift Lance's pre-Tour spirits and revive their shaky marriage; but the only tangible result was that Lance picked up a stomach virus from his son. "I had very bad diarrhea and stomach problems that almost prevented me making the trip to Paris on time," he said. He also developed tendinitis in his hip, caused by either new shoes and cleats or the different types of chainrings on his racing and training bikes.

Compounding his health problems, two days before the Tour's prologue time trial in Paris, Lance dined at a fancy restaurant, sharing a bottle of wine with his agent Bill Stapleton. "Bill thought I was crazy drinking, and I don't know what I was thinking," Lance says. "I had a really tight stomach; it had been bad all year. So I started the Tour all banged up from the Dauphiné crash, hip out, stomach bad . . . '03 was a bad year."

Lance's troubles showed on his strained face at a pre-race press conference. In contrast, his rival Ullrich looked loose and tan, and he flashed frequent smiles at the press in a short Q&A session. In the two years since the big German's last Tour appearance, he had undergone two knee operations; been convicted of drunk driving; been sacked by his Deutsche Telekom team after testing positive for amphetamines (he'd used Ecstasy at a party); joined a new team (Bianchi); moved to Switzerland with his companion; and become the father of a baby girl a week before the Tour. A finally happy and healthy Ullrich was more ready than ever to battle Lance for the yellow jersey.

After winning four Tours, Lance was regarded as a shoo-in to win a fifth, and pundits were predicting his usual six- or seven-minute margin—Ullrich or not. Instead, in the most drama-filled Tour in years, Lance struggled for the first two weeks and went into the critical fifteenth stage only fifteen seconds ahead of Ullrich, after surviving a series of calamities that would have seen any other racer quitting or lying in the dust. Two things saved him: his own gritty determination and the ever-growing Lance mystique, the belief that he could not be beaten.

The Texan's calamities would include falls, injuries, mechanical breakdowns, health problems, and a narrow escape from a horrific crash. It all started with his bad hip and upset stomach at the prologue time trial, where Lance finished a poor seventh; and it continued the next day when he was brought down in a huge pileup that put former teammate Leipheimer out of the Tour with a broken tailbone. Then, at the team time trial, Hincapie was surprised that Lance "was not the strongest guy. I remember him yelling at me to slow down. That never happened." Saved by the Blue Train's collective strength, Postal still won the stage, and Lance moved a half-minute ahead of Ullrich going into his favorite climbing stage to L'Alpe d'Huez. But Lance was in no shape to repeat his dramatic stage win of 2001, and his Dauphiné rival Mayo spurted clear to win the stage. Luckily for Lance, Ullrich was riding through a virus and dropped 1:32—a loss that would prove significant by the end of the race.

On the next stage, Lance's Tour almost ended. Speeding down the day's final descent, he was following Beloki, who was then sitting in second place overall. Suddenly, the Basque skidded on the melting tar, braked hard before a sharp right turn, and, according to Lance, "Beloki's tire exploded. It was my scariest moment on a bike." Instinctively, Lance steered his bike around the fallen Beloki, just missed crashing into a deep ditch, hurtled downhill across a bumpy field, and jumped with his bike across a six-foot-wide ditch to regain the road—in an escape he attributed to good luck. Beloki had no such luck. After slamming into the pavement at fifty miles an hour, he broke a leg, elbow, and wrist, and never raced at a high level again.

Lance's miraculous escape enabled him to fight another day, but his teammates were concerned. "This was a totally different Lance than we'd seen in other Tours," Hincapie says. "His mind was elsewhere; he wasn't saying, 'I'm gonna kill everybody,' and he wasn't as confident. He made us worry, and we were thinking, 'Maybe he's not gonna win this year.'"

That looked like a distinct possibility on the twelfth stage, a thirty-mile time trial on a burning hot afternoon, when Lance had what he calls his "worst day ever on the bike." Ullrich had one of his best days. The German powered over the hilly, back road course more smoothly than ever to set the fastest time. Lance tried to match Ullrich's speed, and he did for the first ten miles, but then all the missteps of that heat wave summer caught up with him. He ran out of water halfway through the stage and then ran out of steam. "I was the thirstiest I've ever been, and I had an incredible crisis," Lance said. "I felt like I was going backward."

His lips rimmed in salt and his legs flailing, Lance staggered up the hill to the finish and, incredibly, still placed second on the stage and held onto the yellow jersey. "He was so dehydrated I think he lost eleven pounds of fluids in an hour's effort," Hincapie says. "Anybody else doing a time trial like that would have lost six or seven minutes—you'd be done. And he only lost 1:36 to Ullrich."

"I was worried," team boss Bruyneel admits. "We spent a lot of time together after that stage analyzing, thinking, talking. I couldn't say to him, 'You're not so good.' So I just tried to find something to boost his morale. For the first third of the time trial, his time and Ullrich's time were exactly equal. He looked at it and said, 'Yeah, that's true.' So it was a good starting point for him to say, 'I'm not that bad.'"

Riding in the team bus to the next day's start, Hincapie was determined to lift Lance's morale. "I saw what he'd done in that time trial, lost only a minute and a half, and I told him, 'That was probably the most impressed I've been with you in your entire career.' And he looked at me as if I was crazy. So I told him, 'I was impressed that was all you lost after being so sick.'"

Ullrich planned to put away Lance on the next day's thirteenth stage. He knew Lance was weakened by battling dehydration and would be vulnerable on another one-hundred-degree day that ended with two difficult climbs—where Tour fans had been gathering for days, many hoping to see Lance crack. Ullrich was expected to attack on one of these climbs to make up the half-minute he needed to take the yellow jersey. But Bruyneel came up with his own plan: He put two Postal riders in an early breakaway, which forced Ullrich's Bianchi team to pull the chasing peloton, rather than Lance's.

On reaching the mountains after ninety miles of racing, the weary Bianchi riders fell back, and halfway up the first climb, the grueling Port de Pailhères, Ullrich was bereft of teammates. Lance, though, had two teammates to count on: He was bravely riding on Beltran's wheel and knew that Rubiera was still up ahead, the only survivor of the early break.

The ten-mile-long Pailhères climb put everyone at their limit; some Italian riders in the back group were crying with pain on the steep and narrow ascent. And an outnumbered Ullrich never attacked.

Even on the final climb, the German didn't budge until his former teammate Alexander Vinokourov dashed clear with a mile and a half to go. Only then did Ullrich take action. He hammered past Vinokourov and raced to the finish. Lance couldn't follow his surge, but he kept calm, and, using his knowledge from pre-riding the stage, he punched it on a flat section near the top to just barely save his yellow jersey. His overall lead was now merely fifteen seconds. But the fighter in him was pleased. He was still the leader, still in yellow.

Recalling that critical day, Bruyneel says, "I'm convinced that there were maybe three or four guys who were stronger than Lance at that Tour. But none of them believed they could beat him—especially Ullrich. I'm also convinced that if *I* had been Ullrich's *directeur sportif,* he would have beaten Lance."

Maybe, but maybe not. Even at 70 percent, Lance retained his external bravado, just like the great champions of the past. It's when things are going badly that a true champion emerges; and this Tour was revealing Lance in that light, so long as he could fend off Ullrich in the last seven stages. The toughest hurdle was the crucial fifteenth stage in the Pyrenees that looped around the so-called Circle of Death, crossed over the monstrous Col du Tourmalet, and swooped down a long descent before the final, arduous climb up Luz-Ardiden. Lance began the day with his fifteen-second lead intact.

"That morning I was sitting across from Lance on the bus going to the start," Hincapie says. "I talked to him a lot through that Tour. I was trying to be there for him, trying to make him believe that we all still had faith in him and knew he could do it. And on that ride I gave him my iPod. I was listening to a song called "Alive," by P.O.D., and he put it on. The lyrics definitely pump you up." The first words of that Christian rock band's song are: "Every day is a new day . . . I'm thankful for every breath I take." That's been Lance's mantra, he says, ever since his mom said it to him as a kid; and having cancer had reinforced that message.

When the two men stepped out of the bus before the stage start, Hincapie looked across at Lance and said, "I have a good feeling about today."

It didn't look that good halfway up the Tourmalet climb. Beltran and Rubiera had paced Lance to that point, but they fell back when Ullrich made the move he should have made two days' earlier: He attacked with twenty-five miles to go. Lance covered Ullrich's move with Mayo, the Basque climber, only to see the German accelerate again—at a speed Lance couldn't match. "Okay," Lance was thinking, "if you're gonna ride like that all day you can win the Tour de France because I can't continue at that pace."

Still, Lance remained calm and centered as he watched Ullrich gain twenty-five meters and hold that gap, minute after minute. When Ullrich saw he couldn't extend his lead or shake off Lance, he realized that his rival was stronger than he thought and eased off the gas. He would try again on the final climb, Luz-Ardiden.

Fifteen others managed to reach the two protagonists on the Tourmalet's long descent, but when Mayo accelerated at the foot of Luz-Ardiden, only Lance and then Ullrich chased after him. Lance had revived, almost miraculously. He surged clear, looking as strong as he did when he set out at Sestriere in 1999, Hautacam in 2000, and L'Alpe d'Huez in 2001. The throbbing chorus of that P.O.D. track was still in his mind: "I feel so alive / For the very first time / I feel so alive / And I think I can fly."

Back home in Austin, as the stage unfolded on television, Lance's friends Bart Knaggs and John "College" Korioth were watching and desperately hoping that Lance could fly up Luz-Ardiden. "We were worried every day, wondering what was going on with Lance," College says. "That morning, I walked into Bart's office and the race is getting close to Luz-Ardiden. I had a theory that Lance would somehow pull through, and I said to Bart, 'Has he ever done anything, and not by design, that wasn't dramatic? There was his world championship win, his fight back from cancer, that downtown crit. . . .' Bart goes, 'I like your theory. I like it, I like it.'

"Right then, Lance makes the move, he starts the attack, and Bart and I are standing up in front of the TV screaming at him. Then this kid's bag gets caught in his bars and Lance crashes to the ground, and Bart and I both drop to our knees, the air just sucked out of our lungs: 'Aagh!' And Bart goes, 'Get up, get up, get up!'

"Lance gets back up, he gets going, and then he almost drops the chain: 'Aaagh!' Then he goes away again, and we're up on our feet again screaming at the TV. And he gets away from Ullrich, he wins the stage, and Bart looks over at me and goes, 'He never does anything that isn't dramatic.'"

College and Knaggs weren't the only ones shaking their heads at Lance's amazing forty-second stage victory over Mayo and Ullrich. Bruyneel, driving the Postal team car in the center of the action, says, "I'm still convinced that what he did on Luz-Ardiden, he shouldn't have been able to do physically. He'd made up his mind he was gonna win, and nothing could stop him, not even that crash. And after the stage we even found out he was racing with a broken frame." The carbon-fiber tube next to his chain was cracked in the crash. "And when we took the back wheel out of the bike the frame fell apart."

That last bizarre twist on a drama-filled day just added to the excitement of Lance's Postal teammates as they clambered onto the bus for the journey back to their hotel. Lance would be following in the team car after fulfilling the winner's post-stage obligations.

"As we were going down the mountain, the bus suddenly pulled over," recalls team chiropractor Spencer. "The door flew open, and Lance jumps on the bus and shouts, 'What do you think of me now, guys?' And the whole team erupts into applause and laughter, just holding each other and rolling around on the floor. Lance really appreciates his colleagues . . . and I don't know how anyone's gonna beat him. He's always going to find a way. He has the persistence, the intelligence, the planning skills, and the courage to execute his plans. And he's never gonna crack. Never. You can't look at the parts and say why and who he is. He defies statistics. He's simply Lance."

But this Tour wasn't over. The penultimate day's thirty-mile time trial was the same length as the one where Lance dehydrated and lost 1:36 to Ullrich, so Lance's overall lead of 1:05 was far from secure—especially since the race was held in wet, windy weather that had spectators huddled under umbrellas. The slick roads caused several riders to crash before the last two men, the leader and his challenger, set out on their time trials, with Lance starting three minutes after Ullrich. The German began like a tornado to gain six seconds on the Texan in just one mile. Lance fought back in this gloves-off contest of flat-out speed and bike-handling skills. They were flying through the rain, blown by the gale, their intense efforts showing on their pain-contorted faces. "There were moments when both wheels were sliding out," Lance said.

After ten miles, raced at a record-shattering thirty-five miles an hour, their times were dead even. Ullrich continued racing as fast as he'd ever raced in his life, hoping that Lance would crack or maybe crash. But the thin line between dream and disaster was broken when

Ullrich hit a patch of oil as he slalomed through a roundabout. He lost traction, skidded sideways, and slammed into plastic-covered hay bales. Ullrich picked himself up but his challenge had ended. Lance smoothly coasted into the stage finish at Nantes to virtually seize his fifth consecutive Tour. The next day's finale, a largely ceremonial ride into Paris, would be uncontested by the protagonists.

When Lance stepped up to the victory podium in Nantes, five-time Tour winner Bernard Hinault smiled, warmly shook his hand, and said, "Welcome to the club!" The exclusive club of five-time Tour champions. Lance had already proven he was one of the sport's greatest athletes. Now, by winning when all odds were against him, he proved he was one of its greatest champions.

CHAPTER 20

AN IMPOSSIBLE DREAM

Everything revolved around Lance winning the Tour de France again, and he was the CEO.

CHRIS CARMICHAEL

LESS THAN A MONTH after his greatest triumph, Lance experienced what he calls his greatest failure. "In August, he told me he wanted to be divorced," Kristin says. The couple's attempt to get back together, four months after their separation, hadn't worked out. With their children, they had celebrated Lance's fifth Tour win on the Champs-Élysées, each raising five fingers as they posed for the media, and they had a family vacation right after. But on their return to Austin, Lance and Kristin began divorce proceedings.

Mistakes were made on both sides, Lance says, and having three young children made the decision that much harder. "The divorce is one thing when there are no children, but when there are children involved, it's a huge issue. Now, I don't think that people ought to stay together, even with kids, when they're not happy, because I think that immediately trickles down."

In her only public statement on the breakup, Kristin told Oprah Winfrey on her show in 2006: "If you give up certain things of what you are, it takes something from the relationship. It wasn't Lance . . . making a mandate and me being a mouse. It was me trying to emulate whatever I thought would be the perfect wife or the perfect mother. . . . And I think he would probably say, 'Well, that wasn't the woman that I fell in love with.'"

Lance has his own reflections: "We dated quickly, got engaged and married quickly, and had kids quickly. I mean, we were engaged in October of '97, and within a year and a half you had engagement, marriage, children, Tour. It was just. . . ."

He leaves the thought unfinished, but his longtime coach and confidant Chris Carmichael, who was closely involved with the couple during their six years together, says more: "I think what ended his relationship with Kristin was it happened too soon after cancer. They had a healthy relationship—as healthy as any marriage is—but when they met, he was still struggling with post-traumatic stress from cancer; and if they had met a little later on, it might have taken a different twist. But what I think also happened was Lance tends to be all or nothing. A relationship starts and it's frigging quick, and it's hot, and it goes; and you better put on your seatbelt for that ride. But as time wears on, I think that with his relationships, the normality of it gets more tedious, and that's perhaps been a challenge for him."

But, Carmichael adds, "It's always so easy to point the finger and say this or that, and I've never known anybody in a marriage that doesn't say it's a challenge. And I think all the changes in his life were tough for Kristin: him going from winning the Tour to the celebrity-ism to all the attention from the cancer community."

Kristin alludes to Tour-related problems when she says, "I wish that Lance had been able to show the same kind of commitment and determination [in his personal life] that he showed in athletics . . ."

Floyd Landis saw from the other side how his teammate's ambition affected his marriage. "There's a thousand qualities that you need to do what he did," he says. "You have to be obsessive about things, you have to be a perfectionist, you have to care more than the other guys, you have to work harder than the other guys, and you have to . . . I mean, his whole life revolved around winning the Tour."

There are some widely held misconceptions about Lance and Kristin's divorce, one of which disturbs his mom. "People say: How dare he divorce his wife when she went through cancer with him. Kristin didn't go through cancer with him," Linda says. "He didn't even know her then. So people need to get their facts right."

Perhaps what's most certain is the sadness and regret both Lance and Kristin still feel. Lance says, "When I'm asked what's the biggest regret in my life, I say, 'Being divorced.' By far. . . . It's a monumental failure, and I don't ever want to do it again."

Kristin concurs. "I will say it is a big regret."

But they both were committed to making the divorce as amicable and livable as possible. Lance remained in the same Austin neighborhood as Kristin so the kids could move easily back and forth with their nanny and feel comfortable living in both homes. And Lance worked hard at being a good dad and not letting down his children as he felt his fathers did with him. "I think he has tried to transcend that experience in childhood," Kristin says, "to be a different kind of man. It's probably hard for him sometimes because he didn't really have the role model that would be so helpful today. But the kids and I have always been a priority to him, which is nice."

In their difficult time of transition, Lance was getting support from his friends, teammates, and business partners. And when he was in Austin between travels, his mom usually came to help out with the kids and the cooking. "But he's a guy who always likes to have a relationship," Carmichael says. "You don't see him often without a girlfriend."

The new girlfriend this time would be a star like himself. Lance was always meeting people in his work for his cancer foundation, generally at fundraisers, and that's how he connected with singer-songwriter and musician Sheryl Crow—at a charity event in Las Vegas a few months after he and Kristin filed for divorce. It wasn't the first time the two had met. That happened in early '97 when Lance was still bald from chemotherapy. He was invited to a concert by the lead guitarist of The Wallflowers, Michael Ward. "We were the warm-up for Sheryl," Ward says. "I didn't know Lance then, just knew he was recovering from cancer, and I'd heard he liked music so we tossed him an invite. He and College came to the gig. They had a great night, and I introduced Lance to Sheryl."

Seven years later, Lance and Sheryl were dating.

They admired each other's talents, achievements, and activism to make a better world; they had similar outlooks, backgrounds, and humor; and they were soon living together—when their schedules allowed. The fact that they *both* had demanding schedules and a deep commitment to their profession made it easier for them to understand their partner's life and needs.

Along with loving each other, they loved entering each other's worlds. Lance also loved Sheryl's music and watching her perform at concerts in Paris, Brussels, and London. He went training while she rehearsed.

Sheryl was just as enthused about Lance's passion. "She threw herself into cycling," Lance says. "She learned tactics, the names, the team . . . Her support was so great because she had a big life, yet she traveled with me and was always encouraging." That support and their love gave Lance something he greatly needed in his then tumultuous life; and it was a base from which he could tackle his next major goal: a sixth victory in the Tour.

After winning the Tour for five consecutive years, Lance had gained enormous renown in Europe, where he was now regarded as one of cycling's greatest champions—despite some commentators continuing to express doubts about his being a drug-free athlete. In the States, his celebrity was of a different and far greater magnitude. His return from cancer to become the Tour de France champion remained the core of his fame, while his high-profile mission to promote cancer awareness and his new romance with a country-rock star elevated him to high celebrity status. Winning a sixth Tour couldn't take him any higher. But Lance had other reasons pushing him on.

As an athlete, he was still the young boy who always wanted to reach the top of every hill first. Now, he wanted to be the first man on the planet to win the Tour de France six times. He also felt an obligation to the cancer community to keep on racing and inspiring those who were fighting or surviving the disease.

"Lance is this go-between vehicle," his friend Bart Knaggs says, "between his mother Linda's willpower and life force as the push, and the pull of all these people that are suffering and inspired and connected around cancer. Lance is just the mechanism to connect them with his charisma, his looks, and his talent."

Those qualities were also attractive to the growing number of companies that were paying him millions to be their pitchman—companies as varied as Subaru, Nike, and Bristol Meyers Squibb, which makes many of the drugs he used to combat cancer. And those same qualities helped maintain the U.S. Postal Service as his team sponsor.

But in the world of sports sponsorships, once brand awareness has been established, most companies switch their marketing budgets to other areas. The Postal Service was no different. That year it told the team owners, Thom Weisel's Tailwind Sports and Bill Stapleton's Capital Sports & Entertainment, that it would be pulling out at the end of 2004. This was one more reason Lance felt compelled to keep racing. Without Lance as their captain, it would be tough for the team to find a new title sponsor as good as Postal; but Lance shooting for an unprecedented sixth Tour victory would bring the publicity that any sponsor craved. He did not want to let down the retinue of people—racers, staff, management—that relied on him for their livelihood.

The European media was full of stories that winter about Lance going for a sixth Tour win: cycling's impossible dream. Most of the stories pointed out relentlessly that all four of the previous five-win champs had come up short trying to win a sixth. In the 1966 Tour, Jacques Anquetil lacked the drive needed to win another Tour and, before dropping out of the race with bronchitis, he helped a teammate take his place as team leader. In 1975, Eddy Merckx was leading the Tour when a crazed spectator lashed out at the Belgian and punched him in the kidneys as he was riding slowly up an ultrasteep climb. Merckx carried on and two days later made a bold attack in the Alps, but he was passed on the final climb, lost the yellow jersey, and never regained dominance in the sport. In 1986, Bernard Hinault led the race until teammate Greg LeMond proved stronger in the Alps and beat him into second place; the Frenchman retired from racing that year. And in 1996, Miguel Induráin suddenly bonked on an uphill finish, didn't recover from the setback, and finished the Tour in eleventh. He quit cycling the following winter.

Now, it was Lance's turn to fail. At least, that's what most Europeans thought. His supporters, though, were thrilled that he was attempting something no man had pulled off. Thousands from around the globe, including Americans, Australians, Britons, and Canadians, booked trips to France for the 2004 Tour just to watch Lance do the impossible—or so they hoped.

As the excitement grew around his improbable goal, Lance's excitement grew as well. He wanted to defy history, prove the skeptics wrong, and establish himself as the supreme champion. He knew that a lot of things were working against him, most notably the emotional stress from his divorce and being separated from his children while he was training and racing in Europe. And after the myriad problems he had suffered in taking a fifth Tour, questions lingered about his form. Some even questioned if he had it in him to win another time. After all, they argued, look at how he struggled in 2003.

"That 2003 Tour de France was a wake-up call for Lance," Carmichael says. "After 2002 was a piece of cake, he kind of took 2003 for granted—and it was anything but. So we spent a lot of the spring together in 2004, mostly in Los Angeles when he was dating Sheryl. It was two weeks, three weeks at camps, me coming to stay at Sheryl's house, and Lance riding his bike. There were always the same questions: 'What are we doing for training? What are we analyzing on the power files?' I'd get back an e-mail from Michele Ferrari, who would make comments on his power files. And we'd talk about it and go forward. But Lance was always the decision maker."

This year was different, Carmichael says, from all the others. "Everything revolved around Lance winning the Tour de France again, and he was the CEO. Johan, Michele, myself, and the various people that were involved in his being prepared for the race, were all VPs reporting to Lance, and Lance made the decisions. Now this was not disrespectful of anybody's position or experience and what they accomplished, but it was very different than Lance in '94 or '95, before cancer, where it was more subordinate. Now it was like, 'We need to change this, or we need to change that.' It was clear that everybody reported to Lance. And we had some great leadership."

One member of the Postal team who immediately saw Lance's leadership qualities was Canadian racer Michael Barry. "The first time I met Lance, he walked in the room when we were all eating dinner, and immediately all the guys stopped what they were doing. I think a big reason why he was able to win all the Tours and so many other races was the combination of fear, respect, and confidence he always emoted. You could feel that the guys were a little more tense or cautious when he was around. It was like having your boss next to you all the time. When he was at a race, everybody did their job amazingly well. Lance could command that respect because 90 percent of the time you knew *he* would perform well."

Barry has seen the harder side of Lance as well, particularly when teammates fell out of line. "When riders didn't do their job properly, if they were not in good condition at the races, or if they were racing for themselves, you could tell they weren't going to be on the team much longer," Barry says. "It wasn't exactly a culture of fear, but he has such a strong character that he does invoke that fear that if you screw up you're gonna be in trouble. . . ."

Choosing his very best teammates for the Tour was only part of Lance's grand plan for his 2004 effort. He also knew he needed to review and correct his mistakes that nearly cost him the title in 2003. And to upgrade his performance by using the most current technology, he initiated the F-One project, a collaborative effort between his equipment sponsors to replace his "old technology" time-trial bike with a much faster machine. This was the first time that different manufacturers came together to produce a new bike that would be designed with the complete bike-rider combination in mind. The project, coordinated by Bart Knaggs, involved components, wheels, aerobars, helmet, skinsuit, and racing shoes that were totally compatible. "Bart made it his personal mission to create the whole aero plan," Lance said. "We brought everybody together, all the people that are working on the bike and on me."

A key change that emerged from this project was to bring Lance's legs closer together on the bike by making the distance between the pedals slightly smaller. Tests in the wind tunnel showed that this made Lance's riding position even more aerodynamic than before; but it still had to be proven in an actual race. That test came in Spain's Tour of Murcia in March. There were potential problems, partly because the narrower position restricted Lance's leg movement and stopped him from producing a steady output of power. Fewer watts translates to a slower speed, however aerodynamic the bike.

"I remember that Tour of Murcia," teammate Barry says. "We were the team's last two guys to go off in the time trial. Lance was trying the new bike with its narrow bottom bracket, and he finished only fifth. He was annoyed with his performance.

"We were on the team bus afterward when he started quizzing me about how the watts should be in the time trial. Suddenly he was questioning his training and questioning everything because his watts had been slowly going down during the time trial instead of staying steady.

"It was strange for me because he usually came across as being so confident; and then you see this other side of him where inside there was a lack of confidence a lot of the time, and he would defer to other people to try to boost his confidence."

The problems were solved by the time Lance entered—and won—his next time trial. And another problem he had faced in 2003 was corrected when his schedule was modified so he'd spend more time training and racing in America. This allowed him to be with his kids more often. It also allowed him to enter the Tour de Georgia, which he easily won.

The American race saw the launch of the LiveStrong yellow wristband. Inspired by the Tour leader's yellow jersey, the wristband was designed by Nike's ad agency as a fundraiser for Lance's cancer foundation. Lance, who sees the band as a constant reminder of his life's mission, has worn one from the start of 2004. It soon became a sought-after item around the globe and reached its initial target of $70 million in sales within six months. This gave the foundation and its LiveStrong brand the biggest boost in its seven-year history.

That spring, Postal looked more impressive than ever: Floyd Landis was getting stronger and more used to European racing; George Hincapie had modified his schedule and training to be better on the climbing stages; and the powerful Portuguese José Azevedo had replaced Roberto Heras as its top climber. Their combined strength helped the team secure Discovery Channel as its future title sponsor.

But while Postal grew stronger, there was a more powerful field of Tour rivals getting ready and just aching to bring Lance down. Ullrich was expected to again be his chief opponent, although the German, who had a weakness for pastries and the soft life, began the racing season more overweight than usual and struggled to find his form. Part of the problem was his Lance complex, aptly described by Lance's former teammate Andy Hampsten.

"Lance was very good at being a favorite and intimidating guys," Hampsten says. "He made sure that anyone who wanted to win the Tour was thinking about Lance before they were thinking about themselves. He raced with Ullrich, who is physically very strong but psychologically a piece of cake. Lance probably gave Ullrich an eating disorder all year long."

Lance also had to watch out for Ullrich's German teammate and friend Andreas Klöden, a talented all-around rider whose career was now on an upswing; the fast improving Ivan Basso, a handsome young Italian who'd taken over as leader of the CSC team from Tyler Hamilton; and Hamilton himself, who had helped build his own team, Phonak. But in the weeks before the Tour, it was Iban Mayo, the Basque climber, who rose to the top of the challenger list. Mayo dominated the Dauphiné, the June race where Lance had overextended himself to beat Mayo the year before. This time, Lance was well off Mayo's climbing pace, losing two minutes to the Basque in the long time trial up Mont Ventoux—a performance that had many worried or cheerful, depending on how they felt about Lance.

A few hours after that time trial, the Postal team held a press conference in the walled medieval town of St. Paul-Trois-Châteaux. It attracted a packed house of reporters, who hounded Lance about his poor time-trial showing. Several questions centered on his form and whether he'd be ready to defend his Tour title the following month. The media was skeptical that he could turn things around in time, though Lance displayed his usual assurance. In reply to a question about his losing so much time to Mayo, Lance replied, "Two minutes is a lot, but it's a long way to the Tour de France." But wasn't he worried? "I'm worried every year before the Tour," he said. "For me, it's a constant struggle to find the best condition, and you learn a lot more from poor performances than from successful ones."

While Lance exuded the air of a winner and did everything he could to improve his performance by small percentages—whether it was with the F-One project, altitude tents, or other legal means—investigative journalists were still trying to nail him with their accusations and suspicions. The most persistent of his accusers were Frenchman Pierre Ballester, formerly with *L'Équipe*, and Irishman David Walsh, the chief sportswriter of the British newspaper *The Sunday Times*. They co-wrote a book that was published in France right before the

2004 Tour. Titled *L. A. Confidentiel: Les Secrets de Lance Armstrong*, the book was instigated by the work Walsh did for his 2001 newspaper article that had labeled Lance a drug cheat and detailed his association with Dr. Ferrari. *L. A. Confidentiel* greatly expanded that article and was the result of years of near-fanatical research with one intention: exposing Lance. Yet despite its endless details, the book's evidence remained hearsay, circumstantial, guilt by association, or a case of he said, she said. Still, it caused a sensation in France, where it became a bestseller. But when its incendiary claims were summarized in an article published by *The Sunday Times*, Lance sued for libel.

At the start of the Tour de France in Liège, Belgium, the Texan was confronted with more questions about doping at the pre-race press conference, where David Walsh sat front and center. "Extraordinary accusations must be followed up with extraordinary proof," Lance famously responded. "Mr. Walsh and Mr. Ballester worked four or five years and they have not come up with extraordinary proof. I will spend whatever it takes, and do whatever it takes, to bring justice to the case."

While Lance addressed the journalists, who mostly quizzed him about his form two days before the Tour, Sheryl Crow stood anonymously at the back of the dimly lit hall. She was wearing jeans, sunglasses, and no makeup and seemed happy to answer my questions about her relationship with Lance. Excited to be watching him for the first time at the Tour, she said they shared not only demanding careers but also many traits: "We both have a wacky sense of humor, we both take what we do seriously, and we're both *extremely* competitive and ambitious." What she found amazing was "how similar he is to my family. He grew up in a really small town, a kind of rural town. We're all Southerners and both have a tight-knit family. So everybody's happy."

While many were betting against the Texan's chances to take a sixth Tour, Lance was gambling—literally—that he'd win. Along with his desire to make Tour history, Lance had another little-known incentive. He puts it tersely: "Ten million dollars." That was the total payout he'd be getting from three risk-coverage insurers should he become the six-time champion. Half that amount would come from SCA Promotions. Prior to the 2001 Tour, Lance and team owner Tailwind Sports had paid SCA a $420,000 premium wagering that he could win every Tour for the next four years . . . and make it six in a row! SCA gambled that Lance wouldn't even win a third consecutive Tour. And now, on the eve of their showdown, the SCA people were worried—with good reason.

If the Tour were contested by individuals, like the hole-in-one golf events that SCA normally insures, a bet against one man winning the race four more times in a row might have been safe. But cycling is a team sport, and Postal had become the strongest, most cohesive team in Tour history. It had been carefully created and groomed for success by Bruyneel and by Lance—who, as Carmichael noted, now led his team like a CEO, a hands-on CEO. That was one of Lance's greatest strengths in 2004, and it was how he planned to win that Tour. His ability to lead and unite his team, to inspire their confidence—in him and in themselves—and to earn their dedicated support was yet another aspect of what made him a great champion.

"We went to the Tour with a single-minded focus," Landis says. "Most teams go there hoping they can win; we went there just assuming we can win—if we do things right. Most guys in the Tour have never been on a team that thought like that."

Landis says their winning attitude flowed directly from Lance. "What made him the best was his focus," Landis says. "Whatever he did, it revolved around his goals. Most people couldn't do it. If they got that obsessed with one thing, their whole life would fall apart; they couldn't manage everything. And that was what impressed me about Lance, that he could manage all these things and still make decisions on the team. He managed more stress than I've ever seen anybody handle and still stay focused on what they're doing."

A year after a Tour in which Lance had only just weathered all the challenges thrown at him, physical and emotional, he was now delegating more of his duties while retaining overall control. That was the case with the F-One project, and it was the way he tackled the Tour itself, where he, Bruyneel, Carmichael, and their team made his winning the race an absolute priority.

But in 2004 the race organizers designed a course that on paper worked against Lance's strengths as a time-trialist and climber. There were almost two weeks of racing before the first mountain stage, no long time trials until the third week, and just small-time bonuses awarded in the team time trial—the event that netted Lance important time gains in the past and the event where Postal's teamwork was again expected to shine.

That forty-mile team time trial proved to be the most decisive and dramatic stage of the Tour's first half. Raced through thunderstorms, with high winds and heavy rains, it rewarded the best-organized teams, the ones that used the right equipment for the punishing conditions and rode carefully on the slick roads. Ullrich and his T-Mobile squad lost speed by not using disc wheels; Hamilton's Phonak formation suffered multiple flats by choosing lighter tires; and Basso's CSC squad were slowed by a slew of crashes after taking too many risks.

The Postal riders suffered no such problems, and Lance inspired them to fight back from a slow start to beat all their rivals by a minute or more. "When for the first time we were up in the time splits, Lance just started screaming encouragement at everybody," Hincapie said. "He was just a ball of energy, almost like it was his first Tour de France. He was totally consumed by the fact that we were going to win . . . and it was going to be an amazing team effort, not just a Lance Armstrong effort."

Lance was charged up by the team's performance and relieved to get through the day, which had included racing over wet, centuries-old cobblestones. He'd been wary about riding the cobblestones in the Tour. "In this race, I'm always scared," Lance said. "And when you factor in the rain, the wind . . . the last few days for me have been totally traumatic." Despite his fears, Lance emerged from the team time trial with the yellow jersey and a small lead over his main rivals—Ullrich, Hamilton, and Basso. Mayo was out of contention, having crashed the day before, and Hamilton was seriously injured in one of the Tour's twenty-five crashes that opening week.

The next display of Postal power came a week later, when the Tour finally reached the mountains. After days of heat-wave conditions, the peloton entered the Pyrenees in a full-out rainstorm that turned the roads into rivers and dropped the temperature by thirty degrees. Hincapie and Landis, the ultimate team riders, set a pace so fast on the opening climb that they shed most of the field, stopped rivals from attacking, and set up Lance for his own acceleration to the summit finish at La Mongie. Basso, who was strong enough to go with him, took the stage. "I think Lance gave me the win because my mother is in the hospital with cancer," the twenty-six-year-old Italian said. The two men had developed a friendship, and Lance's foundation was helping Basso's mom fight her disease.

Hamilton, still hurting from his crash, couldn't follow the pace Lance and Basso set on the climb to La Mongie, and Ullrich also fell back, losing two-and-a-half minutes. The German would need to fight harder than ever to have any hopes of challenging Lance, and he told teammate Klöden to stay with Lance as long as he could. Despite their efforts, at the end of that stage, Lance had a strong lead, with Basso and Klöden more than a minute back and Ullrich close to four minutes in arrears.

But it was on the following stage, a marathon of almost 130 miles over seven mountain passes and ending at Plateau de Beille, that

Postal gave its greatest show of collective power. By the fifth climb, only twenty-two riders were left in the front group, and seven of them were Postal men. Hincapie and Landis then pulled the group all the way to the base of the 10-mile climb to the finish, where they gave way to a long effort by Rubiera before newcomer Azevedo launched Lance three miles from the summit.

"All these guys are like hard-core soldiers working for him," says actor Robin Williams, who followed several Tours with Postal. "They're protecting him, literally feeding him, and warding off the rest. It's a team . . . and Lance is the final stage of the rocket."

Once the rocket took off, there was no stopping its explosions. Lance dashed to a sprint win at the Plateau finish—where Sheryl was waiting "to see Lance win" and already sipping champagne. Then he sparked three more champagne celebrations in the Alps by stamping out his rivals: He outkicked Basso and Ullrich to take the stage win at Villard-de-Lans; crushed Ullrich by a minute and Klöden and Basso by two in the uphill time trial at L'Alpe d'Huez; and angrily outsprinted Klöden and Ullrich for the victory at Le Grand Bornand after the two Germans scuttled his plan to set up teammate Landis for the win.

No previous champion had won four mountain stages in a row—and it would have been five had Lance not gifted one to Basso. But his overwhelming dominance did not upset the fans; they were more enthusiastic than ever. An estimated half-million lined the twenty-one switchbacks of the legendary Alpe d'Huez climb, where the fervor surrounding Lance's attempt to win a sixth Tour was so great that police took seriously a death threat against him. They were concerned about beer-drinking fans wielding flags or throwing punches as he raced past, just inches away and with no barriers between them. Undercover officers were placed in vehicles ahead of and behind Lance during his ride, and he emerged unscathed.

His stage wins in the mountains, followed by a victory in the last time trial at Besançon, pushed Lance's winning margin to more than six minutes over runners-up Klöden and Basso. A strong-finishing Ullrich came in fourth and missed the podium for the first time in his Tour career. "I just missed out this year, and that's a pity," said Germany's top cyclist and the 1997 Tour champion. "I must confess I felt a little sad watching the ceremonies on the Champs-Élysées. But my goal hasn't changed. I still want to ride into Paris again with the yellow jersey on my back."

Lance's record-breaking sixth victory garnered praise around Europe. The newspaper headlines screamed: "Champion of Champions" . . . "Greatest of the Greats" . . . "Lord of the Tours." But some of the stories below the headlines contained negative or cynical remarks. Lance was called "a unique but disturbing champion" by one publication and "cold and arrogant" by another. A third said it was holding him "between doubt and admiration." Perhaps such skepticism was inevitable when a book implying that Lance was a drug cheat was still riding high as a French bestseller.

The insinuations in that book reached across the Atlantic: SCA Promotions refused to pay Lance the final $5 million bonus he earned for winning the 2004 Tour until their lawyers had investigated the book's claims about doping. In mid-September, six weeks after the Tour, Lance's legal team filed a lawsuit to seek arbitration on SCA's nonpayment of the bonus. The suit noted that the other insurers had made prompt payment of their $5 million and that all of Lance's drug tests at the Tour were negative.

But the SCA problem was only one of many that Lance faced that fall and through the winter. Another was a judgment in the long-running Italian court case against his trainer Dr. Michele Ferrari. The Italian sports doctor was acquitted on the most serious charge of distributing doping products, but was convicted of acting illegally as a pharmacist and of "sporting fraud"—a legal term that covers everything from doping racehorses to soccer teams fixing games for profit.

After that judgment was reached, Lance released a statement saying: "I was disappointed to learn of the Italian court's judgment against Dr. Ferrari [who] has been a longtime friend and trusted adviser to me and the USPS team, during which time he never suggested, prescribed, or provided me with any performance-enhancing drugs. I have always said that I have zero tolerance for anyone convicted of facilitating the use of performance-enhancing drugs. As a result of today's developments, the USPS team and I have suspended our professional affiliation with Dr. Ferrari as we await the release of the full verdict."

This decision ended nine years of working together. "Lance always had and still has a tremendous amount of respect for Michele," says Lance's other coach, Chris Carmichael, "and he obviously helped Lance tremendously." Hincapie, who, like Landis, worked with the controversial trainer over several years, agrees: "Ferrari was a good guy, very smart trainer, very knowledgeable."

Another matter confronting Lance was a falling-out he had with his personal bike mechanic and general assistant, Mike Anderson, whom he fired that winter. Anderson then sued for promises broken and claimed that while cleaning out Lance's apartment in Spain in 2004 he found a box of what he called "androstenin" that he believed was a steroid-like product. Bodybuilders and baseball players are known to use "andro" drugs to enhance muscle development, but its weight-gaining properties wouldn't help a cyclist. However, it again raised suspicions about Lance's integrity.

All these issues, combined with ongoing libel suits against British and French publishers and his many, varied responsibilities, weighed on Lance that winter. The man who could handle multiple problems while maintaining his focus had reached his limit. One morning, while training in the hills near Los Angeles, Lance says he received "a bunch of distracting e-mails regarding our cases against *The Sunday Times* and SCA." It was then that the confluence of accusations, emotions, and obligations became so overwhelming that Lance hurled his BlackBerry into a canyon, symbolically throwing away his life. But he couldn't throw away his problems.

CHAPTER 21

ONE MORE FOR THE ROAD

It works better for me to be nervous and hungry.

—LANCE ARMSTRONG

LANCE HAD NO MORE RECORDS TO BREAK, except his own. And he was now thirty-three, the age by which most pro cyclists have retired. What prevented him from joining them was a clause in his contract with the team's new title sponsor, the Discovery Channel network. The clause stated that Lance had to ride one more Tour, in either 2005 or 2006. He could have broken the contract, but once Lance makes a promise—to a friend, the cancer community, or a sponsor—he always keeps it.

In late January, while staying with Sheryl Crow in Los Angeles, Lance went for a training ride with his musician friend Michael Ward, who says, "It was on that ride he said to me, 'Know what? I'm gonna ride the Tour one more time. I don't want to do it; the Discovery guys want me to do it.' And he said, 'I'm either gonna call a press conference and let everyone know that's my plan, or I'm gonna do it spontaneously on the spot. What do you think?' I told him to announce it so that everybody from around the world, all his fans, could make their plans and come and see him one more time."

On February 16, 2005, Lance announced that he would ride that year's Tour; and, he made clear, it would be his very last one. He knew he was getting a late start preparing, and his challenge would be getting into shape fast while searching for a meaningful incentive.

His heart just wasn't into bike racing that year, and he certainly wasn't into facing more accusations about doping. Another investigation had just opened in France based on interviews in David Walsh's book *L. A. Confidentiel.* In response, Lance released a statement saying, "I do not use, and have never used, performance-enhancing drugs. The investigators . . . are welcome to review my long history of tests for performance-enhancing drugs, which I have never failed. Last year [2004] alone I was tested twenty-two times by the UCI, WADA and USADA."

Walsh himself acknowledged about his book, "We don't actually prove anything. We just set out the facts and let the reader decide for himself who's telling the truth." The French case was ultimately dropped.

While his other legal entanglements continued, Lance stayed at home to be with his children or spent time with Sheryl. The two-star couple gained the tabloids' attention at the Grammy Awards, and Lance enjoyed going backstage at her concerts, where he'd mix with the musicians she played with, whether it was The Wallflowers or the Rolling Stones. He delayed his return to Europe and racing until March.

Still jet-lagged two days after arriving, Lance started the weeklong Paris-Nice stage race. It began badly for him with the worst time trial performance of his career: He placed a lowly 140th out of 168 riders. On the fourth stage, when the weather turned brutal, Lance quit the race and returned to his home in Spain.

There wasn't time, though, to dwell on his poor form. Besides the vortex of unresolved legal suits, he had constant obligations to his Lance Armstrong Foundation, the President's Council on Cancer, and his various sponsors, which took up more and more of his time. Even when he was in Girona solely for training, he rarely had a moment to kick back. "He was always on the phone doing meetings with the Foundation, or Nike, or whoever," his friend and teammate Hincapie says. "One time, when he was staying with me while his apartment was being worked on, I caught Lance lying on the couch for the first time in weeks. It was so unusual that I took a photo. But it *was* after a seven-hour training ride."

Lance's spirits improved when Sheryl arrived in Girona after completing work on her new album, *Wildflower.* It contained several love songs that many attributed to her romance with Armstrong. On the first track, Sheryl sings: "They say love keeps on growing/It's the one thing that I've felt I've always known/Cause it wouldn't matter where you're going/Cause where you are is where I wanna go."

In early April, Lance's teammate Barry joined the couple in a private jet to fly to Belgium's Tour of Flanders race. "It was just the three of us. I had a conversation with Sheryl the whole flight, but Lance didn't say much at all," Barry says. "She was very personable and I think genuine as well. She obviously thought he was fantastic. She embraced the sport and everything he did and was super-interested in his life. She also had a real interest in what everybody was doing in their 'other' lives. That's one thing with Lance: He never really was someone to be like, 'Hey, how's your family doing?' whereas Sheryl would sit at the table and be chatting with the guys."

At the races, Lance was all business, still acting as the CEO, and he wasn't pleased with his team's results that spring. "Lance was very structured and hated being beaten," Barry says. "After Flanders, I was in the bus when the race finished. None of the guys made it to the front in the finale. Lance was furious. He came into the bus, cleans up, shakes your hand, and is gone. Not chatty or anything. The message was clear: The team hadn't performed. He doesn't joke around."

Two weeks later, Barry was with Lance at America's Tour de Georgia, where among their competitors were Floyd Landis and Dave Zabriskie—two more of Lance's teammates who had left the fold and joined rival squads.

"Our team had just done pretty poorly in the time trial," Barry recalls. "Floyd and Zabriskie had finished first and second . . . and the first guy on our team was seventh. At dinner, Lance was really quiet and had his baseball hat pretty low on his head. He left the table before everybody else was finished and just went to his room. He didn't say anything that night, and the next day on the bus Johan did his little team meeting, and everybody understood what we had to do.

"Then Lance just started speaking and said, 'We got our asses kicked yesterday and this was an embarrassment, especially because these two guys [Landis and Zabriskie] left the team. So today we've got to kill 'em.' He said very few words, but they were potent. That day, everybody was up front the whole time."

Lance's booster talk had the desired effect when Discovery's Tom Danielson won the next day to displace Landis from the overall lead, and he went on to win the Tour de Georgia, with Lance in fifth.

With his climbing and time-trialing form still lacking and with no real incentive yet in sight, Lance was racing against time to be ready for his final Tour. He would have to turn things around at his May and June training camps, where he again wanted Sheryl around. This led to a rare confrontation between Lance and his coach.

"I told him he shouldn't have Sheryl come to the next set of training camps in the Alps and Pyrenees," Carmichael says. "I felt it was a distraction. That was a difficult discussion. I think Sheryl's a great gal, a wonderful person, and he clearly had a great deal of affection for her; but it was also clear there was something not right in that relationship. I don't know what, but it was a distraction for him, and it was going to impact his performance in his last Tour de France. I'd had discussions with him before, but. . . ."

It wasn't easy at this point for the coach to give directions to his longtime friend. As Carmichael puts it: "You're talking now to a guy who's done something that no human's done. He's won the Tour de France six times. He's made millions of dollars. He's an international celebrity. . . . But I said to him, 'Lance, I'm gonna tell you this, and you can tell me to drop dead, but I've said I'm always gonna tell you what isn't going to work for your performance, and I'm gonna tell you something that you may not want to hear. And that is, I don't think Sheryl Crow should come to these next series of training camps, because I think your relationship is volatile, and it's a distraction, and it's gonna impact your performance.'

"He was like, 'You know what? I've been thinking the same damn thing.' And he says, 'Let me figure it out.' And she didn't come to the next camp, but she came to the following one. And this was 2005. If it had been 1995, I could've said, 'Look, she can't come.' But I can't do that now."

The training camps did improve Lance's form, but it was still below where his coach wanted it to be. That was clear in his last pre-Tour race, the Dauphiné, where his best placings were third in a time trial and fourth on a mountain stage. So, for the first time in his thirteen years of professional cycling, Lance went into the Tour de France without having won a single race that year. Still, he was more relaxed than in 2004, when he was bidding for a record-breaking sixth victory. "I'm not chasing a legacy this year," he said. "I'm just here to have a good time, enjoy my last Tour, and enjoy the good form I *think* I have."

The Texan's likely contenders at the Tour, Ullrich and Basso, were looking far stronger than they did the previous year, and each of them was backed by a powerful team. Because Tour podium finishers Klöden and Alexander Vinokourov were now both on Ullrich's T-Mobile team, their boss, Walter Godefroot, said on the eve of the race, "I've been trying for a long time to prove there's strength in numbers, but I've never been able to get everything to come together."

Godefroot and Ullrich were both eager to prove the theory, though Godefroot's conclusion, "I believe he can beat Armstrong," didn't sound all that convincing.

Considering Lance's state of mind earlier that year, it was surprising to see how confident he looked going into this Tour. It was as if he knew that winning a seventh time *was* his destiny—as Alexi Grewal had predicted back in 2001.

Ullrich had a different destiny: He seemed fated to continue as the Texan's runner-up. How else to explain a freak accident that almost put him out of the Tour twenty-four hours before the start? In wanting to be totally prepared for the opening time trial, the German had taken a page out of Lance's playbook by pre-riding the course—and he did it at race speed, motor-paced at thirty-five miles per hour by his team's station wagon. He was halfway through, riding inches from the fender, when a truck turning across their path forced the team car's driver to slam on the brakes. Ullrich had no time to react. He smashed into the wagon's rear window and cut his neck on the broken glass. Although he escaped with minor injuries, he was in a state of shock.

Like two gladiators, Ullrich and Lance circled on their bikes as they readied themselves for the opening time trial, a contest of raw speed. They were the last two starters, the ones the crowds had been waiting for. Ullrich was the first to go and soon hit his stride, racing up and over a high bridge in the first mile before reaching the flat, straight roads he loved. Starting a minute later, Lance had a scare when his right foot shot from the pedal as he raced down the start ramp. He quickly recovered and was riding smoothly when he topped the bridge to get his first glimpse of Ullrich's pink jersey. That distant speck was all the incentive Lance needed. The target kept getting closer as he kept cranking faster. And the closer he got to Ullrich, the greater his focus. If he caught his biggest rival now, he could break Ullrich's spirit and lift his own for this Tour.

The world was watching as a helicopter shot showed Lance hurtling toward Ullrich, and then, incredulously, bolting past him with two miles still to race. In a moment strong in symbolism, Lance left his fiercest foe in the dust. He was a win-hungry beast once more.

It was a spectacular turnaround for "Mr. July," who had struggled to find form from March though June. "It works better for me to be nervous and hungry," he said. "Paris-Nice was not a pleasant experience, nor was Georgia, nor was the Dauphiné. All of those things led me to ask myself, 'How bad do you want it?' And every time I've answered and stepped it up, and maybe a good three weeks [at the Tour] is the end result."

Lance planned to deliver the killer blow on the tenth stage, which ended with twelve miles of climbing to the Courchevel ski resort in the Alps. It was a stage that showed off the depth of the Discovery team. Hincapie's long, hard pull caused Ullrich to fall off the pace seven miles from the summit. "It was too much for my legs. My ribs were hurting," said Ullrich, who had a heavy fall on the previous stage. Two miles later, Basso fell back. "My legs didn't feel as good as I'd hoped," he said, "but I was able to limit the damage."

The time his two rivals lost there—Basso, a minute and Ullrich, two minutes—buried their hopes of challenging Lance, who underlined his supremacy in the Pyrenees. American challenger Leipheimer recalls how he, Ullrich, Basso, and Landis were the only ones able to keep pace with Lance on the steepest pitches of the Tour's toughest climb, the Port de Pailhères. "He was frustrated we couldn't—or maybe wouldn't, in his mind—ride as fast as he wanted to," Leipheimer says. "I was on the limit and I'm sure I wasn't the only one. We couldn't pull through at his pace, when he said, 'What are you guys doing? This is ridiculous.' Perhaps it was normal sports trash talk, but it was clear he was barely breaking a sweat."

Lance capped his seventh Tour victory by winning the final time trial, at St. Etienne, a day before the finish in Paris. Fittingly, the day's runner-up, a half-minute back, was eternal rival Ullrich, who never really had a chance. For Lance had prepared for this time trial just as painstakingly as he had for the one that earned him his first yellow jersey, at Puy du Fou in 1999. Before the start of this Tour, Lance stopped off in St. Etienne to ride the complete thirty-five-mile time-trial course—not once, but twice. He made a third reconnaissance the morning of the stage, memorizing every foot of the 2,242 feet of climbing (and descending) on what was by far the hardest time trial at the Tour since he made his debut twelve years earlier.

After clinching the twenty-second Tour stage win of his career, Lance revealed what had given him the fire and motivation to claim this last Tour. "For me, there was no pressure for the victory," he said.

"It was just something I had within myself. As a sportsman, I wanted to go out on top. And so that was the only incentive and the only pressure." Lance then praised his "close friend" Bruyneel, saying that without his Belgian team director he wouldn't have won any Tours, let alone seven.

Twenty-four hours later, on the Champs-Élysées, Lance was crowned Tour champion for the seventh consecutive time. He was quick to congratulate runner-up Basso and Ullrich, who finished third. Standing on the top rung of the podium, as sunlight angled on the Arc de Triomphe behind him, Lance leaned over and gave his longtime German rival an awkward hug. "Jan's a special rider and a special person," he said, before turning to Basso. "Ivan's a good friend . . . the future of the sport."

That night in Paris, unlike the twenty-one-year-old kid standing outside a bar "with a chick on each arm and two bottles of beer in each hand," an accomplished thirty-three-year-old champion attended the Discovery team's victory banquet in a plush ballroom to celebrate his new record. "He was the last rider to be interviewed by the emcee," chiropractor Jeff Spencer recalls. "So Lance took the mic and said there's still another rider to introduce, and he introduced Jan Ullrich. There were 750 people there and they went crazy, giving Ullrich a standing ovation. Ullrich was beside himself; he didn't know what to do. They were two competitors who were equally important to each other because they brought out the best in each other. It was a moment of reconciliation—and true respect."

As if realizing for the first time that he had just completed what he believed to be the final bike race of his life, Lance said, "There's no reason to continue. I don't need more." He then concluded, "My children are here, thank goodness. Come Monday morning, we're going to wake up in Paris, and the kids and Sheryl and I, and a group of close friends and family, we're going to fly to the South of France and enjoy ourselves for a week, and lie on the beach and drink wine and not ride a bike, and eat food and swim in the pool, splash around with my kids and not worry. This job is stressful, and this event is stressful, so it will be a week's preview of what my life will be like for the next fifty years. No stress."

CHAPTER 22

WORLD'S GREATEST CHAMPION

We each try to get over our own little anthills of problems,
and this man just goes searching for mountains.
—ELIZABETH EDWARDS

As THE SEVEN-TIME CHAMPION of the Tour de France, a cancer survivor, and the leader of a worldwide cancer-awareness movement, Lance had every right to hope for some time without stress. And he did enjoy, as planned, a week's vacation on the French Riviera. He went there with his three kids and Sheryl in early August of 2005. But before the month was out, the Paris newspaper *L'Équipe* went to press with its inflammatory report, "Armstrong's Lie." Based on results from new tests done on frozen urine samples, the article claimed that Lance used EPO to win the Tour in 1999. The paper's allegations struck at his very integrity, and without that, his Tour feats meant little and his heroic standing in the cancer community would be ruined.

Later, both the article and the tests it was based on were strongly denounced by an independent investigation commissioned by the UCI. But despite that denouncement and the concerns raised by the scientific community about the test's validity, the damage had been done. To diminish the doubts reignited by the *L'Équipe* story, Lance and his surrogates immediately issued statements, went on television, and circulated e-mails to defend his reputation. It's a subject still discussed by those who know him best.

Lance's former swim coach, Chris MacCurdy, speaks from his decades of training athletes at the highest level. "What's happening in cycling leads people to believe that to be as good as Lance you have to be doing something outside the norm, and it's probably gonna be illegal," he says. "But he is so meticulous about everything he does, and he's such a rare human being, physically, that he doesn't have to *do* that. Not a chance, not a chance."

Sports agent and coach Scott Eder, who mentored the teenage Lance in triathlon, has a different take. "I know a couple of guys that raced on pro teams in Europe, and they came back because they didn't want to take drugs," Eder says. "Was that because you have to take drugs to keep up? I have an open mind. I know how many masking agents there are, but it seems unlikely that he would be tested as much as he was and pass every test. I want to believe that he didn't take drugs, and I think at this point he has proved that he didn't."

Cycling expert Len Pettyjohn, who directed rival teams in the early years of Lance's career, believes that Lance proved himself from the start. "I've watched both Lance and Greg LeMond grow from the time they were junior athletes to Tour de France and world championship winners," Pettyjohn says. "They both demonstrated singular focus and ability. They were nineteen years old, and they were not doing drugs. They were just better. So if somehow they ended up in a drug culture, with other people, they were still better. It doesn't take away from their accomplishments at all."

And Olympic gold medalist Alexi Grewal, who often raced against Lance, finds the drug question irrelevant. "All the drugs in the world aren't going to make you win the Tour de France," he says. "You either have the capabilities or you don't. Lance was the best Tour rider that ever lived, and in an era where people specialized to try to beat him, in an era where there were some very good riders—Pantani and Ullrich especially—he kicked their butt, every time."

Besides reviving old doubts about Lance, the article in *L'Équipe* potentially strengthened SCA Promotions in its arbitration hearing seeking not to pay the $5 million bonus to Lance for winning the '04 Tour. "SCA was willing to do anything," Lance claims. "They were making stuff up, obviously, and bringing out maybe a dozen people [to testify]. And when we cross-examined, it was pure theatre watching them get discredited."

One of the people SCA approached as a potential witness was '92 Olympian Bob Mionske, now a lawyer. "People were calling me from SCA thinking they were getting information that would help them sink Lance," Mionske says. "They tried to induce me and get me hired as a lawyer on the case. Basically, there would be money involved. That stunk."

Perhaps the most damning witness SCA managed to find was Betsy Andreu, the wife of Frankie Andreu, one of Lance's former teammates. She testified that when she and Frankie visited Lance in the hospital after his brain surgery—more than two years before he won his first Tour—she overheard him tell a doctor that EPO was one of several performance-enhancing drugs he had taken in the past. However, Chris Carmichael, his wife, and others who were then present in the hospital room can recall no such conversation; and an affidavit from oncologist Dr. Craig Nicholls, who treated Lance at the Indianapolis hospital, said there was no record of the alleged conversation. This led most to conclude that the Andreus had either misheard or misunderstood the exchange.

"I could have gone four-hundred-deep with witnesses," Lance says, "and we'd be [at the SCA hearing] for a year, so we decided that we wouldn't be bringing all these people in. We could have brought in people like Mark Allen, all the way back. That's what I am most proud of, that I was good forever."

Had triathlon legend Allen been called to testify, he could have told the arbitrators how Lance was already a phenomenal athlete at age fifteen, and how he made the most of his natural assets to continue winning the biggest races for the best part of two decades. Allen, who was the Ironman World Champion a record six times, could also have told them how tough it is to win your sport's supreme title, and what it takes to then repeat, year after year, as he did in Hawaii and as Lance did in France.

Almost a year went by before there was closure in the SCA case. Before the arbitration panel made a ruling, SCA agreed to pay Lance his $5 million bonus, plus $2.5 million in interest, costs, and attorney fees after, Lance's lawyers claimed, SCA failed to prove he had used illegal methods to win the Tour.

Further vindication came in June 2006 when the London newspaper *The Sunday Times*, which Lance had sued for libel, settled out of court once it looked certain it would lose the case due to a lack of any concrete evidence. Referring to its article that summarized the exhaustively researched book *L. A. Confidentiel* that set out to expose

Lance, the newspaper issued this statement: "*The Sunday Times* has confirmed to Mr. Armstrong that it never intended to accuse him of being guilty of taking any performance-enhancing drugs and sincerely apologized for any such impression." Its insinuating article had detailed Lance's association with the controversial Italian sports trainer Dr. Michele Ferrari, who was now finding his own vindication: He won his appeal against a conviction of sporting fraud and abuse of his medical license in May 2006.

But in the summer of '05, the *L'Équipe* story and its accusations were very much on Lance's mind. And the "Did Lance cheat?" debates were still filling the airwaves in late August when he and Sheryl escaped to Sun Valley, Idaho, for a mountain bike trip. It was there, adrift on a mountain lake in a boat that ran out of gas, that Lance proposed to Sheryl, and she accepted. They said they'd get married in the spring.

Throughout the fall, Sheryl proudly wore her six-carat diamond engagement ring and spoke to women's magazines about the upcoming wedding; and Lance shared their story on the Oprah Winfrey show. Their friendship and romance seemed stronger than ever and was apparently enhanced by Sheryl's growing closeness with Lance's children. At the same time, Lance, at age thirty-four and suddenly retired, was struggling with confusion and concerns. "You're like, 'Are we compatible? Should we get married? Because if it doesn't work out, that's divorce number two," he says. "And I don't want number two."

In late January 2006, five months after they became engaged and two weeks before Sheryl's forty-fourth birthday, the couple announced they were calling it off. "The relationship was kind of a struggle for a while," Lance says. "I think Sheryl's a great lady, but she wanted marriage, she wanted children; and not that I *didn't* want that, but I didn't want that at the time because I had just gotten out of a marriage, I'd just had kids, so I was just trying to—whoosh—what's going on? Yet we're up against her biological clock—that pressure was what cracked it.

"We tried going to a counselor, but really there's no way to counsel that situation. Because if somebody wants a child—man, that's the greatest gift you can give a woman—so who are you to stand there and say I don't want one. So we were just at different points in our lives. We were not compatible on that issue, which is so incredibly important for a woman and also to a man, but I felt like I wasn't ready to do that at that time. . . . I would have been in the future, but not then."

Sheryl told *Vanity Fair*, "It would be easy to say this is all about my wanting to get married and have kids, but it was never that simple. It was much deeper than that." She has been reticent to say more about the relationship. Once again, though, she gave intimations of her feelings through the lyrics of her songs. In "Now That You're Gone," which she composed after they broke up, Sheryl wrote: "Your face is all around me / Your keys are in my hand / And everywhere I go / I'll try to remember / Exactly who I am."

Lance was feeling deeply lost as well. "He was devastated when he and Sheryl broke up," says Austin journalist Suzanne Halliburton, who spoke with him at that time. "Any man would be crushed breaking up with your best friend."

It was in that mood that Lance decided to get away on his own, and he immediately cleared his calendar for a road trip. "I'd never done one," he says. "I'd never been alone. I'm always with people, especially now; and on the business side and the foundation side, it's really an entourage." He mapped out his route: Take U.S. Highway 1 along the Pacific coast up through Northern California and Oregon. But right after he began his trip, Lance received a text message from Sheryl on his BlackBerry: She had just been diagnosed with stage 1 breast cancer.

"I actually turned around to make the drive to L.A.," Lance told *Vanity Fair*. "We talked along the way, and she said, 'You know, I just don't think that's a great idea.'" Crow felt it would be "hard on her trying to manage a breakup and the diagnosis." She needed a core of support that would be unconditionally there and not have other layers of emotion involved; and for that she turned to her family.

"It was difficult. I know he wanted to be there," Sheryl later said. "I would have loved for him to have swept in and carried me through." Lance would have wanted that too.

Ever since he won his own battle with cancer, Lance has quietly helped hundreds, maybe thousands, of people cope with cancer through his visits, phone calls, e-mails, letters, and signed photos. Most of these people are strangers to him, who have on their own or through friends reached out for his help. And no matter how demanding his schedule, he always finds time to talk at length to a patient with terminal cancer or write an inspirational message that will be read at a memorial service for someone he's never met. "He's a shy guy. He's not good at initiating conversations, and he's not great at small talk," his friend Knaggs says, "so he's probably ill equipped to cold talk to someone who's on their death bed." Still, he does it anyway.

Now Lance had to cope with a cancer that had stricken the person he'd been closest to for more than two years, the one he'd most want to be there for and help. He says that thoughts of Sheryl never left him on his five-day, thousand-mile solo road trip. "Most of the time I was trying to figure out her stuff," Lance says. "You're trying to break up and you're trying to be very close and talk about the situation, and she's trying to break up and manage her situation. It was awkward because I kept wanting to check on her, talk to her once in a while, talk to her doctors . . . that's why I ended up talking more to her mom. Her mom's real cool, Bernice, a very elegant, classy lady."

Feeling even more confused, Lance headed north in a rented SUV. "I didn't make any reservations," he says. "I just walked in, talked to the lady in reception, and I always wore a hat and glasses." When Lance put down his black AmEx card, the reception person "would do a triple take on me, but nobody bugged me. I'd eat in my room—got a massage a couple of times—other than that didn't talk to anybody."

He spent two days in Mendocino and "ran a lot. It was breathtaking up in the redwood forests, running on hard-packed but soft dirt trails."

Lance headed on past the Lost Coast, where surfers seek their biggest waves, and up through Arcadia to Eureka. "There's no radio up there," he says. "You push 'seek' and it just keeps scrolling. But I had books on tape. I listened to *The Four Agreements: A Toltec Wisdom Book*, by Don Miguel Ruiz."

Those four agreements are: Be impeccable with your word; don't take anything personally; don't make assumptions; and always do your best. Lance liked the book's message—it highlighted his own values—and he was interested in applying it to all aspects of his life, whether as a father, son, partner, or friend; as a cancer advocate; as an athlete; or even as a celebrity.

It's hard to know when Lance moved into the celebrity category, though it might have been as early as the fall of 1999, not long after his first Tour de France win. On returning to Austin he was greeted like a true hometown hero with an official parade starting at the floodlit state capitol. But his star status wasn't really evinced until soon after when he attended the premiere of a baseball movie, *For Love of the Game*, at Austin's Bass Theatre. He'd been invited to appear there along with the movie's lead actor, Kevin Costner, and another film star and part-time Austin resident, Matthew McConaughey. "Before the film, they introduced celebrities in the crowd," McConaughey recalls. "They introduced me. I got big applause. Then they introduced Lance, who was sitting behind me. And there was this roar from the crowd. I turned around, and he goes, 'That was louder than yours, wasn't it?' And I thought, 'I like this guy.'"

Lance's status moved up another notch a year later, says superstar triathlete Mark Allen. "Nike did this big congratulatory bash for him after the 2000 Tour, and at that point he'd become big time. There was definitely a shift in him since I saw him at the 1998 Ride for the Roses, where he was the most innocent and humble and grateful I've seen him," Allen says. "The Nike party was in Beverly Hills at a studio director's gigantic mansion overlooking everything, absolutely stunning view. Golf carts took us up this long driveway. And then Lance arrived. It was a dramatic entrance. For him, it was fly in, meet and greet, and fly out . . . back to Europe."

As much as Lance was born to be an athlete, he wasn't born to be a celebrity. He had to develop an ease and a public manner that didn't come naturally to him. Aside from being shy—which he shows only when "he's put in a situation where he doesn't feel in control," suggests ex-wife Kristin—he is not known for his humor. "He's not that funny," says Knaggs. "He tends to repeat the same jokes over and over again," adds former teammate Michael Barry, "and the jokes are usually kind of lame." Nor is Lance all that relaxed talking spontaneously or giving speeches. Five years before that Nike bash, Davis Phinney recalls, "we were at a black-tie dinner, USA Cycling's Night of Champions. I got a lifetime achievement award and gave a speech. Then Lance stood up to get U.S. Rider of the Year in the *VeloNews* Awards, and he just said, 'Thanks to everyone for coming. Have a good time.' That was it. We talked afterward, and he asked me how I made good speeches. I told him, 'I just have fun, enjoy telling stories.' And he listened. A couple of years later at one of his Austin fundraisers, he was much more comfortable with public speaking."

Lance draws people in with his persona, not with witty conversation or humor; and today, his agent Bill Stapleton says, Lance's fee as an inspirational speaker is $150,000. There are also appearances he does for free, such as the ones he made in Iraq and Afghanistan in December 2007 when he accompanied Robin Williams on a USO trip to entertain the troops. "Lance can be inspiring, but to see him inspired by meeting people that face life and death every day, it changed him in a good way," Williams says. "He came out just saying to them, and he meant it, 'You are my hero.'"

"He's never wanted to be regarded as a celebrity," says Jeff Garvey, the first president and now vice-chairman of the Lance Armstrong Foundation. "He just wanted to be a bud." But for Lance, being a celebrity is a powerful means to an end: to promote and advance his cancer foundation. And his success in that endeavor has nearly matched his athletic achievements. From its humble beginnings in College's disheveled condo, the organization has grown into a powerful nonprofit and raised more than a quarter of a billion dollars to fulfill its mission: "to inspire and empower people with cancer to live strong . . . through education, advocacy, public health and research programs." Some of its major contributions include a prominent Web site promoting health and fitness and an annual LiveStrong summit that has now become global.

"Go to a LiveStrong summit and you'll see how important he and his organization are to people across the country," Elizabeth Edwards, wife of former Senator John Edwards, tells me. "This is their lifeline, where they go for information, where they go for support; and if you're going for wide and deep impact, I think he's really found the perfect match with his skill set and his appeal."

Edwards, who describes herself as "a model for females best known for having cancer," first met Lance, "the male in the country best known for having cancer," at one of those LiveStrong summits, and they have since worked together on promoting cancer awareness. Despite having a cancer that has metastasized and given her a tough prognosis, Edwards feels hopeful, and her hope has been strengthened by Lance's example—especially when he announced his comeback at age thirty-seven in 2008.

"I think that the thing that really means a lot to people like me who have a cancer is what he's doing right now, training and racing again," Edwards says. "We each try to get over our own little anthills of problems, and this man just goes searching for mountains. It makes it a little harder for you to complain, whatever it is you're facing. And I know that when he does that it's for a lot of complicated reasons, personal reasons. But I don't know if he really appreciates what it means for other people. He keeps on doing these *impossible* things when we're faced with really possible tasks, tasks that are possible compared with what he's going through.

"You've seen other athletes who've tried to make comebacks, like Michael Jordan, but cycling is such an incredibly physically demanding sport, and the length of time he's been doing it is just mind-boggling. This is not kicking a football, not playing a certain number of games over a five-month period. It's a great physical challenge even for young men; and in cycling, he's now an 'old' man. He's taken his body apart and put it back together again, and even if you took the cancer story out, it's staggering; but if you put it in, it just takes your breath away."

While he spends a large part of his life giving support and inspiration to others, Lance gets much of his own support through his male buddies: old Austin friends like College and Knaggs, and new movie-star friends like Robin Williams and Matthew McConaughey. McConaughey says he didn't see Lance for eighteen months after their initial encounter at the '99 film premiere. He returned to Austin in his Airstream trailer, parked at a local campsite, and called Lance to suggest they get together sometime. "Typical Lance," McConaughey recalls. "He says, 'What are you doing tonight?' No one goes faster from A to B than Lance. 'I'll come and pick you up in a couple of hours. Where are you?' 'Well, I'm in Lot 12 at this RV park.' And he's like, 'What?! Okay, hang on a minute. You are *not.*' 'Yes I am.' So I give him directions and he pulls in. He's shaking his head. 'What are you doing here?' He didn't quite get the whole thing with my Airstream.

"So we went over to Eddie V's for a steak, grabbed a booth in the back corner, got a bottle of red, and sat down and had dinner. Sat there for four or five hours. Got to know each other, philosophizing, just talking as two young men with our big lives. From that night on we've been good friends and go back to that same booth."

"And that was eighteen months after 'My noise was louder than yours, wasn't it!'" McConaughey says, slapping his knee and laughing.

Friendships with men have always played a major part in Lance's life, particularly when the personal and business relationships merge, as they have with Knaggs, Stapleton, Bruyneel—and Carmichael, his longtime coach. "When he was trying to figure out who he could rely upon and who he couldn't, he tested me a few times, and I didn't betray him," Carmichael says. "I think he was very sensitive about being betrayed because it happened in his childhood, it happened with Eddie B, and it happened . . . in other sports . . . but it didn't happen with me. And I think he was always looking to see if that would happen. And when it didn't, he felt safe and comfortable.

"If you look at the way his career has gone, it's basically been the same people the whole time, a relatively small group of people that he's worked with: Bill Stapleton, Och or me, Ferrari or Johan. I think along the way each one of those people had stages, like the things I faced, until he thought they earned his trust.

"It's a cool thing to be able to live through somebody's lifespan like that. Someone asked me the other day, 'Aren't you looking for another Lance?' And I said, 'No, I can't take it. There's only one Lance Armstrong in somebody's life.' I was fortunate that we had this relationship, very fortunate. It's been good for Chris Carmichael, obviously, and good for Lance; but as involved as you get . . . you can't get as involved as that with a multitude of riders. I first met this guy when I was twenty-nine. So am I gonna meet another Lance when I'm fifty and work with him for another lifetime? No, that's all there is."

Carmichael coached Lance through each of his seven Tour victories, but his coaching didn't stop there. Lance likes to always have an athletic challenge and the fitness and preparation to do it well. So he turned to Carmichael for the training schedule that enabled him to beat three hours in his first marathon ever, in New York City in November 2006. And it was Carmichael who encouraged him to train for the Leadville 100 mountain bike race in Colorado. "Just for fun," Carmichael said, having done the race twice himself. So the two men did the race together in August 2008, and Chris was right: Lance had fun. He enjoyed the training, the competing, and the way it made him feel—fit and fully alive. "He had about three weeks of solid training for Leadville," Carmichael says. "Before that he was just screwing around."

It was during the last week of training that Lance's idea to return full-time to professional cycling germinated. "Initially, I thought he was joking," Carmichael tells me. "He wasn't really firm on it, just saying, 'It keeps me out there, keeps me fit . . . and it can allow me to drive some cancer initiatives.' Bono [the Irish singer and world activist] told him how he used his platform as a rock star to really drive some of his social initiatives. And Lance did that a little when he was racing before but not to the magnitude that he can do it now."

At Leadville, Lance surprised everyone when he placed second in the seven-hour race, and his idea for a comeback was bolstered. He would try for one more Tour, and he would clear his name for the sake of his kids, Luke, Grace, and Bella. But first he had to get Kristin, their mother, to approve.

"We had a great conversation," Kristin says; and she was so touched by his concern for her and the kids that it made her cry. "He told me what he was planning to do. Obviously, it was a huge commitment and a huge undertaking, and probably now more than ever it's having an impact on the kids. They're older, and it's hard for them when he's gone." Kristen stresses, though, that Lance is a wonderful father. "He is devoted, he's tender, he is involved," she says. "I feel like the children and I have complete access to him, regardless of where he is in the world."

Fatherhood has always been a top priority for Lance. That's why he included his kids in his relationship with Sheryl and with other women he's been involved with since, including Anna Hansen, who, he announced in September 2008, was pregnant with their child. "I met her in Denver in early 2007," Lance says about the blonde, athletic Coloradan, who has a degree in biology and was then working for a nonprofit that offers outdoor adventures to young adults with cancer. "I was there for a speech, a T-Mobile presentation, and we went out for a beer . . . and kept in touch. She was working for First Descent, a little-brother organization of ours."

They started "seeing each other more seriously" in July 2008, Lance says, when he was training for the Leadville race. "It's the most private relationship I've ever had, and she likes that. She doesn't want people in her stuff, which is good. And it's good for me."

Respecting that desire for privacy, he is reluctant to talk much about Anna or their plans. When I ask if he was surprised when Anna became pregnant, he gives one of his nervous laughs. "I think we were a little surprised," he says, knowing this would be his first child to be conceived naturally; he was no longer sterile from cancer. "Happier than we were surprised," he adds. "Anna and I are excited, and all the people that matter are excited. My mom's excited; Kristin's excited; and Luke, Grace, and Bella are excited."

Kristin confirmed her good feelings about Lance's relationship and the new baby who was about to join their extended family. In the winter of '08, she says, "it was December 18, and Lance, Anna, a couple of junior cyclists who were training with Lance, myself, and the kids, we all went off and had wine and pizza in Lance's Airstream," the aluminum trailer like McConaughey's that Lance now owns. "Then we went to look at the Christmas lights. We had a lot of laughs and a lot of fun, and the next day I realized that December 18 was five years since we were divorced, and it didn't even occur to me on the day.

"If someone had told me in 2003 that five years from now you'll be going around the Trail of Lights and you'll be with your kids, Lance, and his girlfriend, and she'll be pregnant, and [you'll be] having fun, I probably would have laughed: 'Oh yeah, sure.' That's just a beautiful example of healing, and it's a beautiful example for me personally; it was just the way that God can sustain and make different situations be okay."

With his private life seeming more settled than ever, Lance was set to return to his sport. He was training hard to compete with the best racers at the biggest races, including his favorite, the Tour de France; and he was ready to begin the most thorough and independent program of drug testing—once or twice weekly—so he could bring closure to any questions of doping. He would prove himself once more. He would promote the global fight against cancer. And the world would be watching for another flash of greatness.

Some say Lance was born with the qualities that allowed him to become a supreme athlete: the perfect physique, a rare cardiovascular makeup, and a high tolerance for pain. Others say his ascendancy was due to his obsessive but disciplined training, his innovative ideas, and his enormous drive, sheer ambition, and winning instinct. And many point out how brilliantly Lance assembled the best team of coaches, sport directors, physical therapists, technical experts, and riders. All of this is true, yet not enough to explain what he achieved.

Davis Phinney, the one man on the rival Coors Light squad who refused to participate in the deal that favored Lance winning the million-dollar Triple Crown in '93, goes further in capturing what makes Lance unique: "I think he's like the perfect storm, having this fantastic genetic capacity, the work ethic, and the attitude to pursue that level of a goal. Then, he went through the experience of being faced with death and came out the other side with this tremendous appreciation of life and the gifts that he had. Not everybody is going to make those realizations. Lance understands it's hard to be the exception, but the exception is what you want to be. To me, there is destiny in the Lance Armstrong story, and I'm just so grateful that I was around to witness it."

There does seem to be a destiny in Lance's story, starting when he was very young and his family moved to a home across the street from Jim Hoyt's bike shop. Hoyt was just one of many who would influence Lance and help him realize his dreams and potential. Even the people who left his life, his birth father and adoptive father, gave him gifts: an anger and a fire that would fuel him to win.

But it was the people who came into his life that enabled Lance to become the world's greatest champion: the friends who taught him alternative sports in his teenage years; his mentors, coaches, directors, and trainers; the doctors and nurses who helped save his life; his teammates, team bosses, and staff; the women who gave their love and support; and his male friends who were always there. Every step of the way, someone emerged to give Lance what he needed on his mythical journey.

It all started with Linda, his mother.

"I think I was raised with the mentality to be a champion, not born with it," Lance says. "You're not born with aggression or a killer instinct. But my mother taught me to be a fighter and to never quit. She would say every day, 'Go git 'em!'"

And he did.

AFTERWORD

July 20, 2009. It's a calm, sun-filled afternoon in the small Swiss city of Sion. Just one week remains in the 96th Tour de France, and Lance's comeback to the world's greatest bike race isn't going as well as he'd like. By this point in the twenty-three-day event he hoped to be challenging for final victory. But instead of discussing his chances of winning the yellow jersey with a global TV audience, he's lying on a king-size bed in a hotel room chatting with his team manager Johan Bruyneel.

The man who does have the yellow jersey, Lance's teammate Alberto Contador, is three stories below at a crowded press conference. The Spanish cyclist's narrow face is almost hidden from view by a black, pulled-down baseball cap and a forest of microphones as he speaks to the millions Lance was used to addressing. One reporter asks Contador whether he's realized he can become the first man "to beat Lance Armstrong at the Tour" in more than a decade. The slight Spaniard, who was only sixteen when Lance first won the Tour, hesitates and then says, "When I was younger, I was always watching Lance racing on television and wondered what it would be like to race against him. When he retired, I never thought we would race in the Tour together. I couldn't have ever imagined or dreamed that I would be in this position that I am in right now."

It's a position that Lance never really imagined either. But the hard truth was undeniable: In the three-and-a-half years he'd been away from competition, Contador had more or less taken his place, both as the leader of Bruyneel's team (now sponsored by companies from Kazakhstan under the title of its capital city, Astana) and as the world's top bike racer. At twenty-six, he had already won Europe's three grand tours—the Tour de France, Giro d'Italia, and Vuelta a España—in record time, only fifteen months, from July 2007 to September 2008. And he was now on his way to winning his fourth, following a blazing solo attack on the previous day's summit finish to the alpine resort of Verbier. On that climb, Lance lost steam in the final two miles and conceded a yawning one minute and thirty-five seconds to Contador; and though he has moved up to the runner-up spot, the Texan's chances of winning this Tour seem as good as over.

"I expected to feel better," the Texan admits, stretched out on the bed, a BlackBerry at his side. "But when somebody's that good and I go as hard as I can . . . I'm not gonna beat myself over the head with that. I am sitting in second." A somewhat frustrated Lance doesn't want to give excuses. Still, he's guessing that the stress he's been experiencing might have cost him something. "There's constant tension," he says. "Even the rest day, you go out to ride and there's people everywhere, motorcycles and guys trying to ride with you. There's no peace in the middle of this event unless I'm cooped up in my room, which I end up being most of the time."

During his seven-year reign as Tour champion, Lance never let stress get in his way; but this Tour is different. He's taken a big gamble on coming back to the race at age thirty-seven after a four-year absence. And even though he's doing far better than most fans or the media predicted, he knows that several factors have stopped him from reaching his best form. His age and the time away from top competition were expected obstacles, but there have also been other, more subtle reasons that have kept him from matching Contador.

Lance's return to professional cycling, and the publicity generated by his announcing the LiveStrong Global Cancer Campaign, emphasized just how big a celebrity he had become—and that was one of the factors that would work against him. In the years since his retirement, other than being hounded by the paparazzi or doing charity bike rides and occasional marathons, Lance had spent a purposefully quiet life. So the massive crowds he attracted on his comeback to racing were a real shock. Record numbers of European reporters showed up at the Astana team's pre-season training camp in distant Tenerife. A reported 138,000 Australians came to watch Lance make his actual return to competition at a short circuit race in an Adelaide park on January 18, 2009. The following month, his presence boosted the number of people lining the roads of the nine-day Tour of California to an estimated two million. And within a year of opening a Twitter account, he had almost two-and-a-half-million followers.

His fans weren't concerned that Lance was using the early-season events as training; they just wanted to see him, grab his autograph, get up close. At Australia's Tour Down Under, local racer Graeme Brown described how he chose to climb a steep hill right behind Lance because of the walls of frenzied spectators: "I thought it would be the safest place in the peloton," he said, "following the king of cycling! Seriously, it's the worst place in the world to be. Everyone's trying to touch the bloke and take photos—they don't care who's behind him. Then I started laughing because some girl was squealing, 'I touched him! I touched him!' Never again . . ."

At a time when Lance needed to focus on enhancing his form, this constant pressure of coping with huge crowds was an unneeded distraction. Then there was his self-inflicted distraction: fulfilling his commitment to the cause of cancer, a commitment he had announced upon his return. Lance took time out from his season to work for the Global Cancer Campaign. He visited such heads of state as Prime Minister Kevin Rudd of Australia and President Felipe Calderón of Mexico; and he helped plan LiveStrong's first international cancer summit in Dublin, Ireland, to take place after the Tour.

Another early problem Lance acknowledged was not committing

wholeheartedly to his training. He admits that between January 2009's Tour Down Under and February's Tour of California, he "goofed off a bit too much, and suffered bad" in the American race. But an even greater concern was reacquainting himself with the skills and dangers of racing inches away from spinning wheels and pedals in a tightly packed, two-hundred-strong peloton. Riding in the pack is instinctive when you're doing it every day, year after year; but Lance had been away from all of this for 1,273 days.

He paid for his rusty skills when he crashed on the first day of a Spanish stage race in late March. Two riders fell directly in front of him when they crossed wheels, and Lance landed heavily on a narrow, pot-holed back road. "Before it happened, I was scared like hell," he recalled. "In the past, I never hit my brakes, always rode first ten. At the beginning of 2009, I was always on the brakes, and when you're always on the brakes you just get pushed further and further back in the peloton. I crashed because I was in the back with guys I shouldn't have been with."

Lance had crashed before in races, but the only time he'd fractured anything—a vertebra—was when a car crashed into him and wrecked his bike during a training ride in Provence, prior to the 2000 Olympics. That time, his former wife, Kristin, drove to the remote location and took him to the hospital in Nice; this time, he sat in pain at the roadside until he was helped into a race ambulance. This crash—and the broken right clavicle that needed a stainless steel plate and twelve screws to repair it—caused Lance to have second thoughts about his comeback. "I've got three kids at home, I'm out here racing for free [he did not take a salary from Astana] and going to some random hospital in the middle of Spain, and I'm thinking, 'What the fuck am I doing here?' I kept thinking that for a couple of weeks," he told a Dutch TV journalist, almost repeating the thoughts he had during his aborted comeback from cancer in 1998.

Back then, bad weather and low spirits contributed to Lance quitting on the second day of the early-season Paris-Nice race, and then spending weeks back in Austin before unpacking his bike bag. His 2009 crash in Spain had a similar effect. "I could have said, 'Here's my out.' I thought about it, and thought about it. After the surgery . . . I was *not* excited about getting back on the bike," he said a week before the Tour de France, when I saw him at his new second home in Aspen, Colorado. "But I came here in early April and started riding again . . . just kind of getting my legs back. Johan kept calling me, sending text messages, and I never returned them. Finally he got me on the phone: 'What are you thinking? What's up?' And I said, 'I think maybe I should just bail on this whole thing.' And in typical Johan fashion he said, 'Dude, you can *not*. You're going to let down all the people, the millions of people that want you to do this. And, you're going to make the year for a handful of people who don't want you to do it. You can't. You have *got* to do this.' It was like, end of discussion. That was it. I never talked about it again."

Lance's multiple-fractured collarbone, the enforced layoff, and his tentative return to training all added to his problem of finding top form. By this point in a normal season he would have had twenty or so days of racing in Europe. But in the first four months of 2009, he raced for a week in Australia, another week in California, and just two days in Europe. Understandably, he hadn't come close to winning a race. In contrast, Contador, in his seventh season of pro cycling, had already notched seven victories in twenty-two days of competition. After his shoulder surgery, Lance said, "I wasn't in good shape, and it was hard training [at elevation] in Colorado." He knew he had to have a few days of racing in his legs before heading back to Europe, so he took in the low-key Tour of the Gila, a five-day event in Silver City, New Mexico, against purely domestic teams. He managed to finish second overall to U.S. teammate Levi Leipheimer, less than a week before they started May's Giro d'Italia. This would be Lance's first grand tour in four years: an absolute necessity before tackling the Tour de France, to get his body and mind accustomed to racing day in, day out for three weeks. Given the circumstances, he surprised many critics in Italy with his solid twelfth-place finish—while riding in support of Leipheimer, who ended up in sixth.

Lance knew he had to complete all twenty-one stages of the Giro, but in the final day's time trial on the wet cobbled streets of Rome, his thoughts were elsewhere. As soon as it was over, he dashed to the airport to catch a transatlantic flight. Back in Aspen, his partner Anna Hansen was about to give birth: Maxwell Edward Armstrong arrived four days later. Lance's family enthusiastically greeted his fourth child, as his three other kids and their grandma Linda took turns holding baby Max in their arms. Lance remained in Colorado for four weeks to spend as much time as he could with his young family before returning to Europe. And he emphasized his commitment to fatherhood by making his unpretentious Aspen home his virtual pre-Tour training camp—his U.S. teammates Leipheimer and Chris Horner even moved in next door and joined him on long training rides in the Rockies.

In the past, Lance had prepared for his seven straight Tour victories by spending the month of June in another high-altitude ski resort, Switzerland's St. Moritz. Aspen seemed to be just as perfect a location to recover from the Giro and hone his fitness for the Tour; but the fact that it is 2,000 feet higher than the Swiss town made it too high for ideal altitude training, especially on the surrounding mountain passes. "This house is at 8,000 feet," Lance said, sitting at the kitchen table while partner Anna tended to their new baby. "Independence Pass is 12,000, and Snowmass is 10,000. Pretty high. It's good for the blood, good for metabolism, good for leanness, but not good for power. At the top of the pass, if you see 300 watts [on your power meter at anaerobic threshold (AT)], you're moving. You just can't generate power."

Despite the overly high location, Lance's hill-climbing tests with his Austin trainer and former teammate Kevin Livingston revealed that his AT was 435 watts at an elevation of 2,000 meters (6,560 feet), which is equivalent to about 475 watts at sea level. Knowing his weight would be around 160 pounds (73 kilos) when he reached the Tour's climbing stages, a pumped-up Lance said, "That's 6.5 watts per kilo . . .good enough to win the Tour. If I race smart, recover well, avoid problems, we're gonna win. . . . People are gonna be *very* surprised." Then, remembering his higher motives and considering the challenges he'd face, he added, "Even if I'm top ten or top five or top three in the Tour, we'll have answered the doping question." Indeed, the anti-doping authorities had been testing him at a frequency of once a week since he began his comeback, so he hadn't needed the private testing program he initially announced. Generally, the testers would show up at his door before breakfast, obtain vials of urine and blood, and take them back to the lab for analysis. All the results, which Lance posted on the LiveStrong Web site as soon as they became available, were negative.

When his weeks of hard training gave rise to exceptional physical-testing numbers, Lance left Aspen believing that victory at the Tour was possible, but he was unsure how sharing team leadership with Contador would play out. It's not uncommon for two riders to start the Tour as co-leaders of one team. That's how Contador and Leipheimer began the race in 2007 for Bruyneel's Discovery Channel squad; and when Contador proved stronger in the mountains, Leipheimer sacrificed his own chances to help his teammate win, while the American ended up in third. Now, even though Contador had been the sole Astana leader before Lance made his unexpected comeback, the Texan was counting on equal support, based on his track record and ambitions. Team manager Bruyneel felt conflicted:

Lance was his friend, but Contador had earned the right to be team leader. The Belgian diplomatically stated before the start: "In this moment, Alberto is the leader. And with Lance, I honestly can say I don't know what to expect."

Lance didn't relish sharing team leadership with Contador, but his problems didn't end there. His weight may have been on target, but too much of it was in his upper body, the result of working out with weights during his time away from cycling. That, combined with his legs not yet having their former fitness, had reduced his power-to-weight ratio by a percentage point or two, which would make it difficult to match the Tour's top two climbers, Contador and Luxembourg's Andy Schleck. Another negative was the fact that Lance didn't pre-ride any of the stages except for day one's time trial in Monaco. And only in the final days before the start did he get time to look at the alpine stages and the team time trial course. Also, other than a two-hour circuit race in Nevada City, California, and a short local time trial near Aspen (both of which he won), Lance didn't compete in the five weeks before the Tour. All of these factors put him at a distinct disadvantage compared to his rivals and his Tour preparations in the past. So no one was betting on Lance to win the Tour. In a survey of team directors and in predictions by the French sports newspaper, *L'Équipe*, Contador was listed as the overwhelming favorite, with Lance picked at number six.

Without his best form, Lance knew he'd have to work his way into the 2009 Tour, try to keep a low profile and avoid stress. That's why he chose to race the first day's time trial in Monaco as one of the early starters, instead of three hours later in a favorite's usual starting slot. "You can't put too much pressure on yourself," he later said. "I wanted to get it over with, go back to the hotel, keep my recovery going." Lance took a respectable, if disappointing, tenth place, and conceded twenty-two seconds to Contador, who was second on the stage. At the end of the first week, when he was sitting in third place overall, Lance was asked whether he had deliberately tried to expend the least amount of energy. "Definitely, physically speaking," he replied, "but also mentally, trying to avoid all the . . . conflict. That would just wear you out."

Contador was *not* avoiding conflict. He was ready to step right into it—if it would help him win the Tour, the prize he had expected before Lance showed up. So on stage seven, at a critical point on the windswept climb to the Tour's mountaintop finish in Andorra—just when Lance was on the wheel of Astana's German workhorse Andreas Klöden chasing down a breakaway rider, and while Leipheimer was in recovery mode from a long chase after crashing at the foot of the mountain—Contador surged from the middle of the group and bolted past his teammates. Living up to his nickname of *el pistolero* by going freelance, he was shooting for the yellow jersey in front of his rowdy Spanish supporters—and disregarding the team orders Bruyneel was feeding him via his radio earpiece. The wily team boss didn't want the overall lead so early in the Tour because that would force his riders to defend it for a full two weeks. It was just as well for Contador that a strong headwind slowed his effort and he fell short of taking the jersey by six seconds.

"I expected that," Lance said about Contador's contrary move, "but the message was so clear from Johan on the radio that I started to think, 'Well, that's the team directive so maybe it won't happen.' But he ignored that and did his own thing. Which pissed me off, and more importantly pissed off everybody else. . . . The whole thing was just bad." Along with the negative vibes within the team, Lance also had to cope with losing loyal teammate Leipheimer, who crashed and broke a wrist a couple of days before the race reached the Alps. Yet despite these many factors, there were also encouraging signs that Lance still had the fire needed to be a Tour contender.

One sign was his leading the Astana riders to victory in the opening week's team time trial, a feat that took Lance within a split second of wearing the yellow jersey. Another, more important example, came on stage three in a move that showcased his winning mindset and tactical acumen. When a 25-strong breakaway group split from the peloton on a sharp turn in fierce crosswinds, Lance was the only race favorite who made it across. Contador, Andy Schleck, and the others would concede forty-one seconds to the Texan that day. The media was impressed and astonished, and began to see him as a true contender. A typical comment came from the next day's French newspaper *L'Humanité*: "At the very least, Lance Armstrong was an opportunist. Carried by the wind, he opened the psychological battle earlier than expected . . . catching out Contador. There had to be a great ambiance in the Astana team's hotel last night!"

Lance described the move with gusto. "I was stuck in the middle of the field before that turn, and something told me you've gotta get out of the group before we get up there," he said. "So I just started muscling my way out, moving guys with my hands and yelling, and then just sprinted up the side and went around about twenty guys right before the corner, just no brakes. That split in the wind made me happy—that was racing!"

The confident Texan wasn't so exuberant while lying on his hotel bed during the rest day in Sion, Switzerland, with six days of racing to go. But his champion's attitude remained strong. "I don't know how it's gonna end here," he said about teammate Contador keeping the race lead until the finish in Paris, "but if I ride in there on the podium with a win for my teammate, it's a win-win for me. I proved everything I wanted to prove. He proved he was the best . . . and we want the best man to win. No shame in that."

In the final days of the Tour, despite riding a lackluster time trial, Lance continued to surprise people—including Bruyneel. "To have him back on my team and at the front in the Tour is just so special," Bruyneel said. "And to see him back at such a high level is just amazing." By the end, Lance did lose second place to Andy Schleck. And yet on the final climb in each of the last three mountain stages, Lance wowed the fans and media alike with the kind of surges that lit up the Tour during his seven-year winning streak. The most impressive of his efforts came on the penultimate day's thirteen-mile-long, windswept trek up Mont Ventoux, considered the toughest mountain climb in France. Lance matched every acceleration made by the younger men trying to grab his overall third place—Britain's Brad Wiggins and Schleck's elder brother Fränk—and he even left them behind before the 6,273-foot peak, where he crossed the line on the wheels of Contador and the younger Schleck.

A measure of that Ventoux ride was the power generated by the leaders. On the ascent's steepest stretch, when all the attacks were happening, Lance's power-to-weight ratio was estimated at 6.27 watts per kilo—not quite the 6.5 he thought could win him the Tour, but not far off the astonishing 6.73 that Contador produced on the much shorter Verbier finish.

On the morning of the Tour's final day, the French daily *L'Équipe*, which persistently connected Lance with doping during his glory years, made the ultimate mea culpa by choosing him as the subject of its front-page headline: "*Chapeau, le Texan*." That "hats off" compliment echoed the changed feelings of French spectators, who now saw the American as a more likeable underdog rather than a cold, dominant robot. Later that day, in front of hundreds of thousands of fans lining the Champs-Élysées, Lance stepped up to the Tour podium for the eighth time. His mom Linda, Anna and his four children, dressed in yellow, were there to greet him. But this time, the *maillot jaune* went to the new champion, Contador. Two steps below him, in a typically defiant stance, Lance sent dark looks to the young Spaniard. The Texan didn't like losing. Still, the media was shocked and impressed to see him end the Tour in third place. They never expected him to get this far, and many asserted that this was the most amazing comeback in sports history.

Lance had reaped most of what he wanted from the 2009 Tour—including finishing ahead of all the previous year's top place-getters. But even before he knew how it would end, he was plotting another chapter in his seemingly never-ending story. Back in that Swiss hotel room, one week before the Tour finished, he picked up my tape recorder from the bed, snapped a photo of it with his BlackBerry, and texted it to someone special. "This is our new sponsor," he explained, "and I'm sending it to the CEO. He'll like this."

It had been rumored for weeks that Bruyneel was planning to leave Astana to start a new team. Lance was now confirming that he'd be on the team and racing the Tour again—against Contador—with the intent of winning it for an eighth time. And his new team's sponsor is the name on my tape recorder: RadioShack. A text came pinging back to Lance, who said, "He liked the image but says you need to update." Smiling again, Lance was thinking about his own update. "Got a new sponsor," he beamed. "It feels good to continue on with Johan. Alberto will go one way, we'll go the other. And we'll come back to the Tour next year with all our guys—Levi and Klodi, Jani, Zubeldia, Vaitkus, Rast, Horner. I would not like to fuck with that team!"

As the 2009 Tour ended, Lance was back to his belligerent best—or worst. But Contador didn't show his true emotions until he was back home in Pinto, a suburb of Madrid. "My relationship with

Lance Armstrong is zero," he stated to the Spanish media. "He is a great rider and has completed a great race, but it is another thing on a personal level, where I have never had great admiration for him and I never will." Lance was in the Bahamas with his family when he read Contador's words on the Web. He sent a message on Twitter: "Seeing these comments from AC. If I were him I'd drop his drivel and start thanking his team. w/o them, he doesn't win." And then, a few minutes later, came this: "Hey pistolero, there is no 'i' in 'team. What did I say in March? Lots to learn. Restated."

This war of words wouldn't be forgotten when the two men returned to the Tour to fight a new battle: Lance in total control of his own Team RadioShack, and Contador as the leader of a completely revamped Team Astana—new manager, new riders, new staff. The two men did see each other that fall in Paris at the glitzy presentation of the 2010 Tour; but they were seated, symbolically, on either side of their younger rival, Andy Schleck. The media was excited about their future clash.

It was "just an idea," Lance said in August 2008, but his comeback had developed into something bigger than even he expected. Not only had he proven himself as a clean athlete to the world and for his children, but he had also returned to the very top of his sport. And, as planned, he was combining his racing activities with his work for the cancer community. In a statement, Team RadioShack said that all its riders would "stand as ambassadors of the global message of LiveStrong—a message that represents hope, courage, and empowerment for the twenty-eight million individuals living with cancer today."

With his growing worldwide celebrity and continued athletic excellence, it was no surprise that Lance was one of the rare Americans considered for end-of-the-decade recognition in sports by organizations around the world. One of those, Britain's Press Association, named him its Sportsman of the Decade and wrote: "Courage, stamina, a will of iron. He possessed them all, and just for good measure he came out of a retirement at the age of thirty-seven, and no one could say he did not deserve to finish third in the Tour de France. That is the hallmark of greatness."

February 5, 2010: A new cycling season is under way. Lance has raced in Australia's Tour Down Under for a second time, and people said he looked slimmer and stronger than the year before. He's now training harder than ever, despite uncharacteristically cold, wet weather in the Texas Hill Country. The Tour de France begins in less than five months.

I've been trying for several days to set up a brief text chat. Just three questions, I assure him. Then, a message hits my in box. It's Lance, at home in Austin. "Send them when u can and I'll try to get after it although it's very hectic right now w/ all the kids, training my ass off, and shooting a RS commercial tomorrow." I send off my questions, and his answers fire back.

"How's your form compared with a year ago?"

"Form is better than 09—feel stronger and more comfortable on the bike. Also more at ease in the bunch when it gets hairy."

"And the yoga you've been doing—how has that helped?"

"I'm new to yoga but have found it very helpful. In the past I've had some pretty bad back pain in the early season but the yoga has really helped ease it."

"What do you see happening at this year's Tour? Any predictions?"

"I see an exciting Tour. Alberto is clearly the favorite with a variety of others just behind. This group includes myself, the schlecks, levi, klodi, vdv, wiggins, and a few others."

It's clear that Lance is revving up for another stab at the Tour. When it's over he'll be seven weeks short of his thirty-ninth birthday—if he wins, he'd be the oldest winner by thirty months. But the outcome doesn't really matter. Lance has already claimed and reclaimed the title: He's the world's greatest champion. Any takers?

ACKNOWLEDGMENTS

When my editor at Da Capo Press, Kevin Hanover, suggested I write a book about Lance Armstrong, I knew I'd accept his challenge. Not because I've known Lance for all his adult life and interviewed him dozens of times, and not because I've written hundreds of thousands of words about his deeds as a professional cyclist. No, I wanted to write this book to discover the things I didn't know about him—things that I could only learn by talking with the people who have most affected or influenced his life. I wanted their voices to tell the story of a remarkable individual who has achieved amazing things—both within and outside his sport—while rousing strongly opposed emotions among his supporters and his detractors.

I wouldn't have been able to write this book without the candor of the more than sixty individuals I interviewed, most of them face to face. I want to especially thank the ones I met with but whose names or words do not appear in the book—their time was not wasted because they brought insight to a certain aspect or period of Lance's life or provided details I later used in interviewing others. I also want to thank the family members and friends who loaned me photographs from their personal collections, as well as those who supplied or helped locate other hard-to-find images or assisted in obtaining permissions for using those photos in the book.

Lance helped me tremendously in this project, by making time for new interviews at his home and during his travels, and by giving me the opportunity to talk with people who otherwise might have been hesitant to speak openly about him. Perhaps more importantly, and impressively, Lance didn't ask to see anything I've written here.

Above all, I want to thank my wife, Rivvy Neshama, whose vision, wisdom, diligence, long hours, literary skills, love, and constant encouragement helped me make this book everything I hoped it would be.

John Wilcockson
April 2009

INDEX